# But Not in Anger

Roderick Grant
&
Christopher Cole

# But Not in Anger
## The RAF in the Transport Role

LONDON
IAN ALLAN LTD

First published 1979

ISBN 0 7110 0909 0

Published by Ian Allan Ltd, Shepperton, Surrey;
and printed in the United Kingdom by
Ian Allan Printing Ltd

# Contents

# Introduction

This book is not a history of Royal Air Force Transport Command, which existed from 1943 until 1967. Nor does it attempt to describe all the air transport work undertaken by the RAF from its formation in 1918 to the present day.

Its main purpose is to record the highlights of British military air transport in the early years, when flying itself was an adventure, and the RAF was pioneering air routes beyond the resources of civil aviation, finding out by trial and error how best the transport aeroplane could assist in supporting Britain's military obligations overseas. Much of this work has never been described in any detail, and faded files in the Public Record Office contain some remarkable, stranger then fiction, stories.

During World War II air transport may be said to have come of age. The old concept of a dual-purpose bomber-transport aircraft served admirably for the 'little wars' of the 1920s and 1930s, but thereafter combat aircraft developed rapidly to the extent where such compromises were no longer acceptable. Air transport became a normal — and reliable — method of travelling, and commercial aircraft — largely American — were readily adaptable for military use.

It has not been possible within the space of this book to deal with all the outstanding air transport activities of World War II, if for no other reason than that there were so many of them. Nor have the historic major airborne forces operations been included, since they are already well covered in specialist works. The emphasis has been directed towards the lesser-known flights of the second war, and on the air transport contribution to some of the actions better remembered for the work of the land forces.

Perhaps because transport flying lacked the 'glamour' attached to bomber or fighter operations it is sometimes considered to have been less demanding on the crews. This was far from the case. A crew battling through the monsoon to reach a tiny jungle dropping zone, then circling for 45 minutes while making up to 10 accurate drops, was required to display flying skills and determination of the highest order. Crews readily understood that the ground troops' very survival could depend upon air supply, and they would readily press on in conditions which would have

well justified abandoning the sortie. Consider, too, the courage required to fly an unarmed aircraft deep into enemy territory, then land by the most minimal makeshift flare-path on a small and unfamiliar strip to pick up an agent or secret information vital to the war effort.

Many crews found transport flying immensely satisfying, and their feelings were admirably expressed by a Canadian NCO in a Dakota squadron to a war correspondent in Burma: 'The thing I like about this job is that you're helping somebody to live, not bombing them off the face of the earth'.

Any study of the history of RAF transport flying inevitably brings to mind that oft-quoted cry from Ecclesiastes, 'there is no new thing under the sun'. Some techniques of World War II — for example the double-bagging of food grain for free-dropping — were identical to those first devised in World War I, re-invented between the wars and discovered yet again in the 1970s. Enormously valuable and varied air transport work was performed in the Middle East during the 1920s, and although some of the lessons learned may have languished in the files of that young and enthusiastic air force — perhaps less conscientious over paper work in those more carefree days — a basis of sound experience was available when World World II produced its insatiable demands for air lift.

### Acknowledgements
The authors wish to thank the following, mostly retired RAF officers, for providing information or photographs which have been of great value in supplementing the material available from official records: Air Marshals Sir Leslie Mavor and Sir John Whitley, Sir Malin Sorsbie, Air Commodore R. J. Davenport, Group Captains D. Groocock, R. Halley and W. E. Rankin, Wing Commander W. H. Burbury, Squadron Leaders J. W. Burley, R. A. Collis and M. Vlasto, Dr S. G. Culliford, Flight Lieutenant A. J. Blagden, T. C. Marvin, H. Dawson, W. H. Cox and the late Major J. Ronald McCrindle. Thanks are also extended to Chaz Bowyer, E. F. Cheesman, P. J. R. Moyes, Bruce Robertson and Gordon Swanborough for the loan of photographs.

# The Siege of Kut

## 1

In October 1913, before the start of World War I, a British civil aircraft, the Grahame-White Charabanc, had successfully lifted its pilot and nine passengers — a payload of 1,372lb. But this caused no great stir in military circles, where aviation was seen as essentially an aid to reconnaissance. The aeroplane had given commanders the immediate advantage of being able to see what lay on the other side of the hill — though some of the more conventional military minds were even sceptical about its value in this role. This did not deter enthusiasts in the Royal Flying Corps from experimenting with machine-gun mountings and with bombing, but the war had been in progress for some time before specialised fighters, bombers and other categories were developed. There was no foreseeable requirement for air transport on the Western Front, and any isolated calls for work of this sort could doubtless be met by improvisation.

When the need did arise, with desperate urgency, it was in a situation far from home, an incidental phase of one of the greatest British military disasters of all time. It was a classic case of too little and too late, and when the full tragic story emerged the valiant efforts of a few pilots to achieve the impossible were overshadowed by the human aspects of the catastrophe.

For the British soldier or airman of World War I, service in Mesopotamia, now Iraq, was about as popular as service in the jungles of Burma was to his World War II counterpart. The climate was an additional enemy, amenities were minimal and, in the early years of both wars, the priorities always seemed to be centred closer to home. The troops had the same feeling of belonging to a forgotten army.

When Turkey entered the war on Germany's side in October 1914 it was decided that operations on the Mesopotamia front should be conducted with a force provided by the Indian Government. All went well at the outset and the port of Basra was captured in November. Between May and October 1915 the 6th Division under Major-General Charles Townshend made steady progress, and the troops began to talk about reaching Baghdad by Christmas. Then, on 22/24 November, Townshend's forces failed to break through the heavily reinforced Turkish positions at Ctesiphon, covering Baghdad, and suffered severe losses which forced them to retreat. By 3 December they were back in Kut, which they had taken two months earlier, and where Townshend considered that he had sufficient food and ammunition to make a stand until

reinforced from Basra. With 24 hours Turkish forces had surrounded the town.

The distant prospect of Kut el Amara, dominated by its mosque, with date palms studding the mile long frontage on a wide bend of the river Tigris, was perhaps romantic — but very misleading. It was not an attractive place. It had a mixed, predominantly Arab population of about 6,000 and was a centre for the local grain trade. There were a few well-to-do houses set in gardens away from the sordid conglomeration of hovels and bazaars. Drains and sewers were non-existent and the Army medical authorities considered it the most insanitary place occupied in Mesopotamia. After its capture the British forces had constructed a temporary hospital for 500-600 patients, and there was dismay when it was learned that Townshend's force of 11,607 troops plus 3,500 non-combatants included several thousand wounded from Ctesiphon.

Skeletal air support for the 6th Division had been provided by a mixed unit from India, Australia, New Zealand and Britain, augmented during the summer by a Royal Naval Air Service detachment transferred from East Africa. Over an eight month period this 'force' was issued with about 14 aircraft of six assorted types, of which perhaps half had been shot down or crashed beyond repair. In August 1915 it was agreed that the British Government should assume responsibility for the Mesopotamian campaign (although the effective date was deferred until February 1916) and the Royal Flying Corps took over the original mixed flying unit. This became A Flight of No 30 Squadron and in October two BE2c aircraft and additional personnel were sent from England to become B Flight. For a time the squadron headquarters remained in Egypt.

Following the defeat at Ctesiphon the aircraft flew to Kut and on 2 December the RNAS machines were shipped down the Tigris to Basra for refit. Meanwhile, the commanding officer of No 30 Squadron, Major S. D. Massy, had arrived from Egypt, and was followed by his remaining personnel who became C Flight. Their aircraft had been left behind for the units taking over the Egyptian commitment. On 5 and 6 December the Turks began shelling Kut and it was apparent that the RFC aircraft stood a good chance of being destroyed. Two BE2cs and a Martinsyde were, in any case, hopelessly unserviceable and unlikely to fly again. At 0800 on the 7th, Massy and Captain H. A. Petre in a Maurice Farman and Captain E. M. Murray and Lieutenant G. A. R. Spain in BE2c No 4500 left for Ali Gharbi to join up with the relief force,

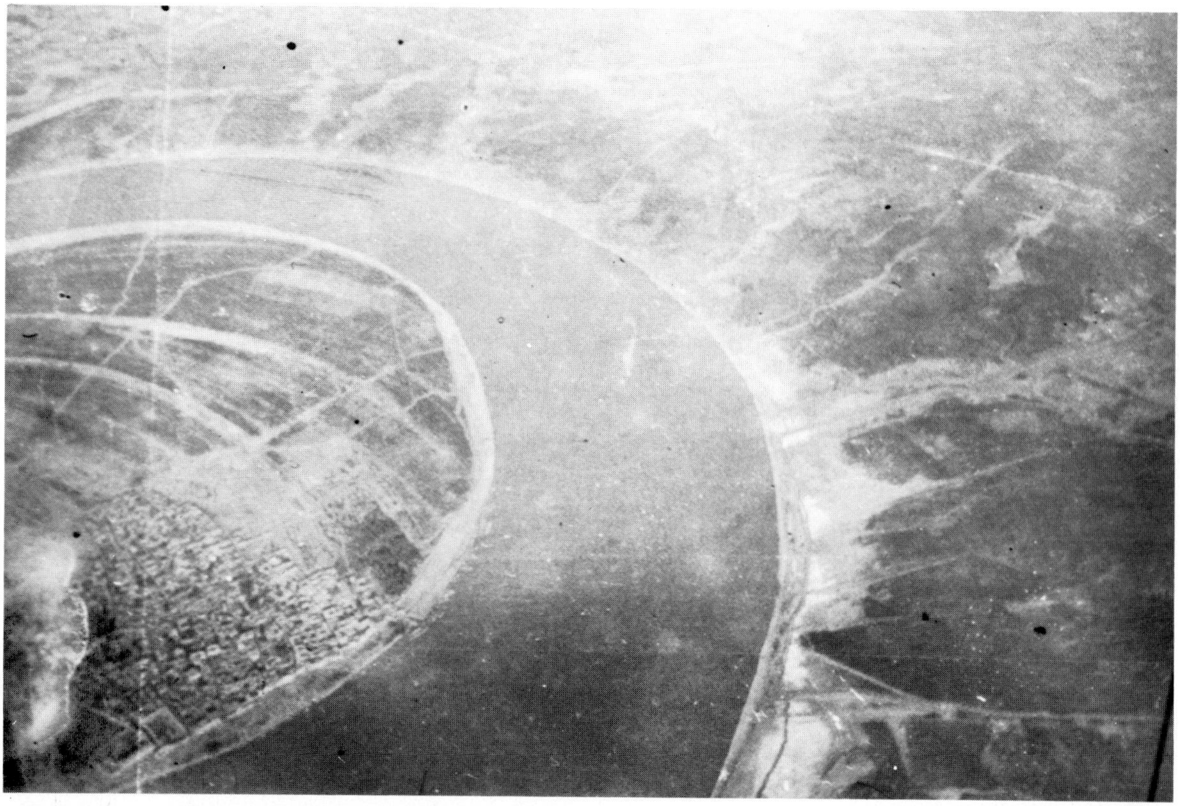

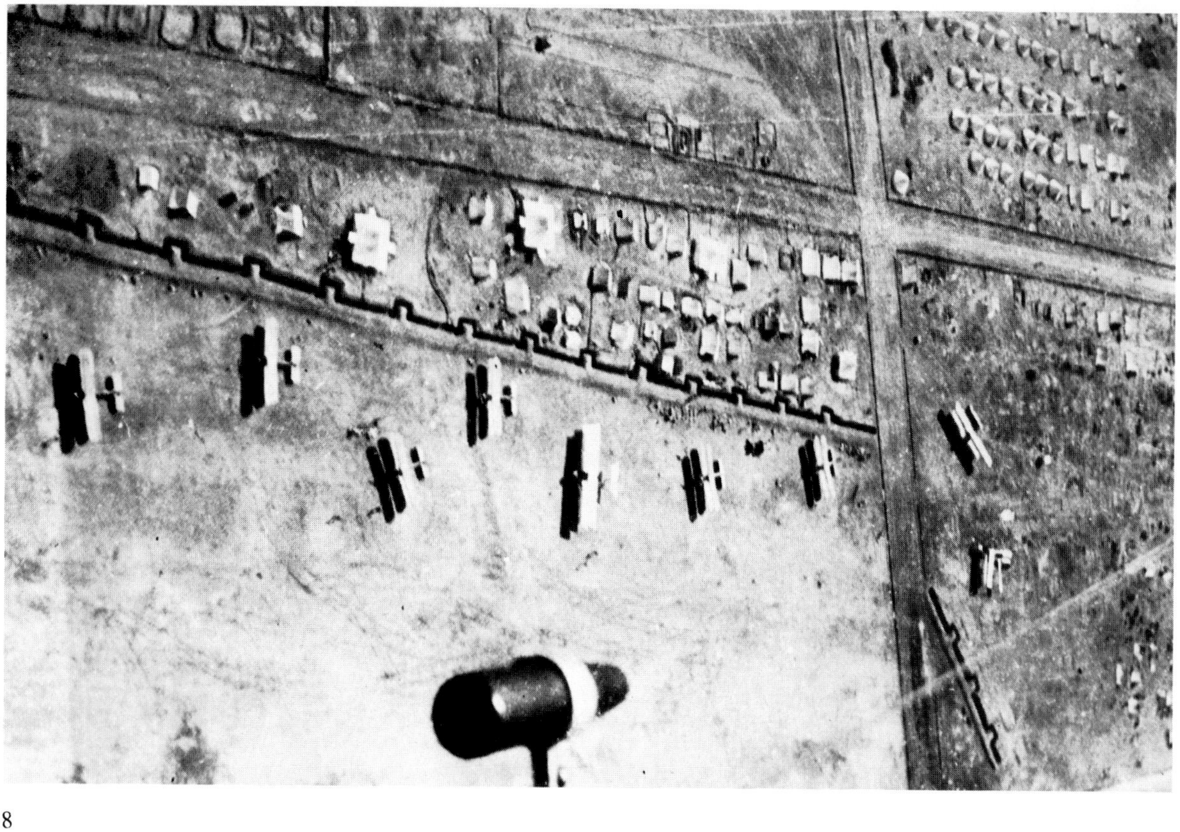

and for the next two months these were the only British aircraft still remaining serviceable in the entire Mesopotamian theatre. Another BE had tried to get away from Kut but its engine refused to start.

Several books have been written about the siege of Kut el Amara, and it is not the purpose of this account to recapitulate the terrible hardships suffered by the garrison, the almost unbelievable misfortunes of the relieving forces, the muddles and confusion or to apportion blame for the disaster. With five officers, 40 technicians and four aircraft non-effective in Kut, the tiny remaining operational element of 30 Squadron had plenty of problems in the early weeks of 1916, desperately trying to keep the ancient Farman and the BE in some sort of flying condition. They were exposed to extremes of weather and spares were almost non-existent, but somehow one was nearly always available when yet another reconnaissance was requested.

Seaton Massy, whose regiment was the 29th Punjabis, had learned to fly with the old Air Battalion of the Royal Engineers in 1911, before the formation of the RFC, and held Royal Aero Club flying certificate No 84. A reserved yet determined personality, he had gone to Egypt in November 1914 with the original RFC detachment which grew into No 30 Squadron. Writing up the squadron official War Diary on the last day of February 1916 he expressed his feelings with a frankness and vigour rarely encountered in such documents:

'I have throughout found great difficulty in persuading the staff to place a limit on the number of reconnaissances called for, having in view the paucity of machines, the lack of plant for keeping them in good flying trim and the adverse working conditions generally.

'Very few indeed of the staff possess even the most elementary knowledge of aircraft, their fragile nature and the difficulties connected with their maintenance, and are inclined to regard them as a machine as reliable as any well-established make of motor car, and have wished to use them as such and as frequently, and it has been necessary to protest that this is not the case.

'Observers and pilots in France but rarely are called upon to carry out more than one reconnaissance in every two days, and this in a country where the source of supply both in personnel and material is close at hand, whereas here it is the rule rather than the exception for them to be called upon to go out twice and sometimes three times in the day, and on machines which owing to force of circumstances it has been impossible to keep properly tuned up.'

By 16 January the two 30 Squadron aircraft had advanced with the relief force up the Tigris to Orah, about 23 miles from Kut, and during February they were re-joined by the RNAS whose aircraft were largely flown and serviced by RFC personnel. The RFC situation gradually improved and by 11 April No 30 Squadron had eight BE2cs. The entire air element was placed under Army GHQ control, and commanded in the field by Wing Commander Robert Gordon, RNAS.

Heavy floods on 6 April further delayed the relieving forces and the situation in Kut was becoming critical. The troops eked out their basic rations with horseflesh and assorted vegetation which sprang up after the rains, euphemistically known as 'spinach'. Townshend signalled GHQ, Basra, that all food supplies would be exhausted by 24 April except horseflesh — and that would last only until the 29th. His men were becoming weak from lack of food and sickness was rife. At one urgent GHQ conference held to consider means of enabling Townshend's men to exist just a little longer until the relief forces could regroup and try again, somebody remarked that if aeroplanes could drop bombs, surely they could drop food. Major P. W. L. Broke-Smith, aviation staff officer, calculated that Townshend's minimum requirement of 5,000lb to give each man a six ounce ration of essentials could be dropped if about 70% of the aircraft flew three sorties a day. The items mostly needed were flour, sugar, chocolate, salt and ghee (clarified butter used by the Indians for cooking). On 10 April the GOC, General Sir Percy Lake, ordered maximum effort on food dropping, subject to urgent reconnaissance and artillery observation needs.

Since 13 January, when a package of detonators intended for the forces in Kut had fallen in the enemy lines, about 30 successful supply drops had delivered official mail, occasional newspapers, medical supplies, cash and other urgently requested items. The cash dropped — equivalent to £10,366 — had included 1,000 lira in gold and 25,000 rupees in notes. Among other articles were spares for the garrison's wireless equipment, guns and motor launch and a one mile length of seine fishing net. All these had been free dropped, but the most impressive item, a 70lb millstone, required a special parachute. It was released at 0900 on 27 March from BE2c No 4361, crewed by Lieutenants R. E. Cuff and R. M. Dickinson.

Precisely when the order for the full scale food drop reached Gordon's unit is not known. Clearly it required considerable planning and organisation compared with the small ad hoc air lift which had operated for the last three months. Four 30 Squadron BE2cs, and three Short floatplanes, a Voisin and a Henry Farman of the RNAS were allotted to the task, leaving four BEs and one Short available for other essential operations. Work started on devising suitable packing and a method of dropping supplies, which had to be operated by the pilots since observers were being dispensed with on all except the Shorts to give maximum payload. Several ideas were tested without great success until Captain Eric Murray, now B Flight commander, came up with his 'see-saw' system. This was a metal bar attached to the BE2c fuselage bomb racks, from which the guides and other fittings were removed. It was pivoted at one end, and the other was secured by a quick release controlled from the pilot's cockpit. The tops of two sacks were sewn together so that when filled they hung down on either side of the bar. When the rear end of the bar was released by the pilot the sacks simply slid off.

Although the inherently stable BE2c was the most

9

advanced design among the landplanes available, it was by no means the most efficient supply carrier. Weight had to be distributed as evenly as possible around its centre of gravity and on the first trial with a 200lb pack the aircraft nosed over and crashed before getting airborne. The best loading arrangement was eventually found to be two 25lb sacks on the dropping bar and another two 50lb sacks tied above the lower wing, one on each side of the fuselage. These were fastened by a slip-knot which was loosened or cut by the pilot and the load pulled backwards over the trailing edge. The BE was never a sprightly performer, and the head resistance of the bulky sacks had an effect out of all proportion to their weight. Cruising speed was cut to something a little above the stalling speed and the aircraft had to be flown with great care. Experienced pilots were given discretion to increase the total load to 200lb in suitable conditions.

This release gear was also adapted for the Farman and Voisin, which carried 200lb and 150lb loads respectively in single packs. Metal containers made from four gallon petrol tins were used on their first sorties because it was thought that sacks might foul the pusher propellers, but food dropped in this way was so badly damaged that sacks were tried and found to cause no hazard. Standard issue sacks were used, an inner one tightly packed being enclosed in a loose outer one to retain the contents after the almost inevitable impact burst. The crude home-made dropping gear had the merit of simplicity, and there was not a single hang up throughout the operation.

It was not suitable for the Short floatplanes as the sacks trailed in the water, so their loads — in single packs weighing 200-250lb — were attached under the bomb racks by a broad canvas band, and also released from the pilot's cockpit. This was less foolproof and the Shorts suffered at least one hang up.

Airmen worked far into the night of 14 April to modify the supply dropping fleet for a maximum effort the following morning. Despite perfect weather on the 15th and a good start to the operation serviceability problems affected Gordon's slender force and at the end of the day deliveries were well below target. Only 3,350lb of food was dropped in about 20 sorties.

A dropping zone had been marked on the old aerodrome to the north of the town and there was dismay among the watching troops when one of the first sacks fell into the Turkish lines and another in the muddy brown waters of the Tigris to join a bag of gold coins inadvertently deposited there earlier by an RNAS aircraft. Accuracy remained a serious problem, and about 10% of the supplies dropped were not recovered. Because of enemy artillery, which was reinforced as the supply drop proceeded, and the intense volume of small arms fire, aircraft had to fly between 5,000 and 7,000 feet and the behaviour of the sacks after release was quite unpredictable. Some followed a forward trajectory but others immediately lost speed and were blown about by the wind. To fly lower down would have been to invite the rapid annihilation of the whole force by ground fire.

Perhaps for no better reason than that they belonged to the senior Service, the Naval aircraft were said by the

troops to be the worst offenders — and it is possible that the less reliable release gear on the Shorts and the more erratic behaviour of their larger food sacks did combine to reduce accuracy.

On the second day the air drop slipped even more behind target and the Army reported that only 1,333lb had been retrieved. Included in the day's deliveries were seven bags of rupees, which provoked a vigorous complaint from Townshend that food must have absolute priority. It was on this day that an unfortunately high percentage of the supplies fell into the river or enemy hands. Bad weather on the 17th limited operations to three BE sorties which dropped only 400lb of food, and on the 18th and 19th a serious bout of engine troubles restricted No 30 Squadron to five and two sorties respectively.

From this time Townshend seems to have decided that the air lift had failed. To his conventional military mind it was a simple question of mathematics. The air experts had said that they could deliver 5,000lb each day, and had significantly failed to do so. The somewhat acid tone of these passages from his account of the campaign, published in 1920, suggests that Townshend never did have much faith in the air lift:

'I had misgivings that the air service would break down, and in any case weather conditions would greatly affect it, to say nothing of enemy aircraft, which would quickly see what we were doing and obstruct our machines'.

and later:

'My anxiety now regarding food was intense, for it was patent to all of us that the air food-supply service was a hopeless failure. When the weather was at all stormy they could not operate, and when it was fine they were effectively attacked by the German monoplane, or else they had engine trouble'.

His scant understanding of the difficulties facing the pilots is shown by this comment after seeing two aircraft loads fall into the Tigris on 22 April:

'I had had to report the air service several times for dropping bags of parcels and letters into the river; but 400lb thrown into the river in a morning was a most serious loss to me!'

Townshend suggested a naval attempt to run the river blockade, and while arrangements were being made to despatch 270 tons of supplies in HMS *Julnar* he learned, on 22 April, of yet another failure by the relieving army to break through. Three days later, after a heroic dash under heavy enemy fire, *Julnar* was captured within sight of Kut after fouling a steel cable laid across the Tigris for that precise purpose, and with 20 of his men dying daily from starvation, Townshend was authorised by the British Government to start surrender negotiations.

Meanwhile, after reaching its lowest point of only one BE sortie on Easter Sunday, 23 April, the air lift started to improve, and over the three days 24-26 April No 30 Squadron managed to fly 32 sorties. No detailed record of

Above: Lieutenant J. Ronald McCrindle, of No 30 Squadron, RFC, who made 16 food-dropping, and several escort, sorties to Kut during the siege, seated in BE2c No 4362. Note grain sack on lower wing.

Left: Lieutenant D. A. L. Davidson in the Henry Farman which proved the most efficient load carrier during the siege. In the foreground is Captain L. W. O'Gowan.

the RNAS effort appears to exist, though a few isolated features are recorded — including the fact that the solitary Henry Farman, described as '... very satisfactory, attaining a speed of 65mph', flew more sorties than any other individual aircraft. Against this, the 250hp Sunbeam Short seaplanes proved highly unsatisfactory and made very few food flights. Their engines continually gave trouble, the aircraft were in dire need of re-rigging, and frequently failed to unstick from the surface of the Tigris for various reasons.

Enemy aircraft had been using an aerodrome six miles north of Kut since mid-February, and apart from the unhappy frequency with which their small bombs hit the hospital, were of little more than nuisance value. On 24 April, however, a single-seat Fokker monoplane fighter shadowed two of the food dropping BE2cs, doubtless noticing that they were unarmed, and flew off without making an attack. One of the British pilots hopefully sped it on its way with a few shots from his revolver. There was no interference next day, then on the 26th the Fokkers[*] pounced.

Up to three were reported, and the first victim was a Short seaplane shot down over the sand dunes on the

* Although contemporary reports describe these aircraft as Fokkers, they may have been of the very similar Pfalz type.

Turkish side of the line, the observer being killed and the pilot wounded. Later in the day Lieutenant D. A. L. Davidson in a BE2c suffered a prolonged and persistent attack when returning from Kut, and by skilled evasive action managed to escape destruction. The Fokker broke away when nearing the British base and, despite substantial damage to his aircraft and hits in his left shoulder and arm, Davidson nursed the BE home to Orah where he actually waited for the aircraft ahead of him to land instead of claiming priority, then insisted on making his report before being carried off on a stretcher. The aircraft was found to have 32 bullet holes, and its right aileron control cable had been shot through.

Although this was not an impressive performance by single-seat fighters against dismally slow and mostly unarmed biplanes it did represent an unacceptable loss rate which could rapidly eliminate the British supply dropping force. The BEs had no fixed forward gun for the pilot, as was fitted to later types of two-seaters, and since they could not carry a gunner plus any useful load of food, the only remedy was for a few to act as armed escorts, despite the reduction this imposed on the air lift capacity. Three Maurice Farmans from Basra were ordered to join the force, but they arrived too late to be of any help.

The provision of escorts caused a substantial slump in the number of food dropping sorties on 27-28 April, and after a few early morning flights on the 29th notification was received of the formal surrender and the air lift came to an end. Of the 12,000 prisoners who were marched 700 miles into captivity in Turkey, some 4,000 did not survive.

Any contemporary breakdown of sorties and deliveries kept by the supplies and operations officers has long since vanished, and to explain the discrepancies in some of the surviving figures is a matter for surmise. For example, the accepted total of 19,000lb dropped (of which 16,800 was acknowledged as being received in Kut) by the combined RNAS/RFC force in 140 flights is substantially less than the quantity which should have been lifted if all these aircraft carried their prescribed loads. The probable explanation is that the figure of 140 included abortive sorties. No 30 Squadron records show that its BE2cs flew 75 sorties between 15 and 29 April (less 16 April for which no figure is quoted) and carried 9,442lb. The BEs expended 179 hours 50 minutes flying time on food flights and another 19 hours 35 minutes on escort work.

The picture is further confused by an error in the Air Ministry's usually reliable *Short History of the Royal Air Force* (1936) which attributes the total weight dropped by the combined RNAS/RFC force — nearly nine tons — to the Naval aircraft alone.

Despite the feeling of stunned dismay which followed news of the surrender, GHQ found time to signal this message to Major General C. F. Gorringe, who had commanded the relief force since 12 March:

'The Army Commander desires you to convey to the combined air service — the Royal Naval Air Service and the Royal Flying Corps — his appreciation of their persistent and meritorious work during the last few weeks. They have been called upon for very arduous and trying efforts in keeping up the reconnaissance and observation services at the same time as the transport of supplies to the beleagued garrison of Kut. All this involved a very serious strain on all ranks, but every call for their services was at once responded to with readiness and resource'.

In his own report on the operations Gordon wrote: 'I consider that the absence of accidents was most praiseworthy and only very skilled pilots could have carried out these flights in all weathers so successfully'.

On the face of it the heroic efforts of a handful of pilots to achieve the impossible in their rickety old biplanes fell sadly short of expectations. In 15 days only 140 sorties were flown compared with the planned 400, and the daily food delivery averaged less than a third of the necessary 5,000lb. Such a large shortfall poses the question whether, in fact, any specific target was put to the air forces? In the squadron diary Massy merely wrote: 'Instructions issued [ie by HQ] for the dropping of as much food into Kut-el-Amara as possible, detailing machines withal for reconnaissance and co-operation with artillery'. This lack of precision is uncharacteristic in view of the considerable detail with which he described other aspects of the operations.

The commission appointed by the British Government to inquire into the full circumstances of the defeat virtually ignored the air lift, which rather suggests that the distinguished members did not consider it to be a significant part of the relief operations.

The simplest and the most probable explanation is that the three sorties per aircraft per day target was a paper target only, something which could theoretically be achieved with a full complement of pilots and 100% technical backing. It was quite unrealistic and manifestly beyond the reach of a small force in the field operating with such severely limited spares and servicing resources. On top of this, when the supply of BE2cs eventually improved just before the start of the air lift there was a shortage of pilots to fly them. Several of those newly posted to No 30 Squadron in early April had received the bare minimum of training and had never before flown the BE. They severely damaged two of them in crashes, and common sense then dictated that since no replacements were available, these aircraft should be flown only by the experienced squadron pilots.

Compared with the Kut garrison the men of the relief force lived like kings, but their general conditions and rations were not of a standard to provide much bodily resistance, and the number of available pilots from day to day was drastically reduced by sickness — dysentery, severe diarrhoea and that mysterious complaint which has afflicted thousands of servicemen overseas, PUO (Pyrexia of unknown origin). Pilots flew when they had every justification for taking to their sick beds, and in some cases required help to climb into their aircraft.

Massy's overall report on the campaign had this to say:

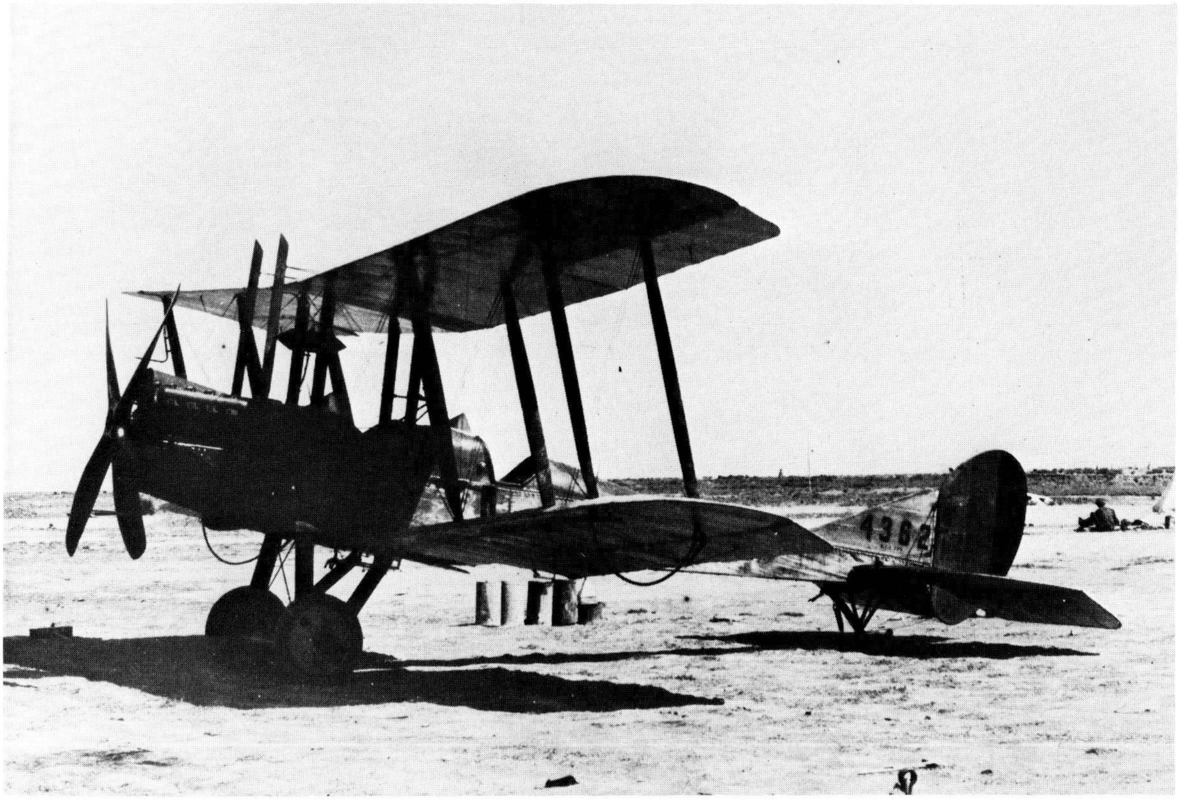
4362

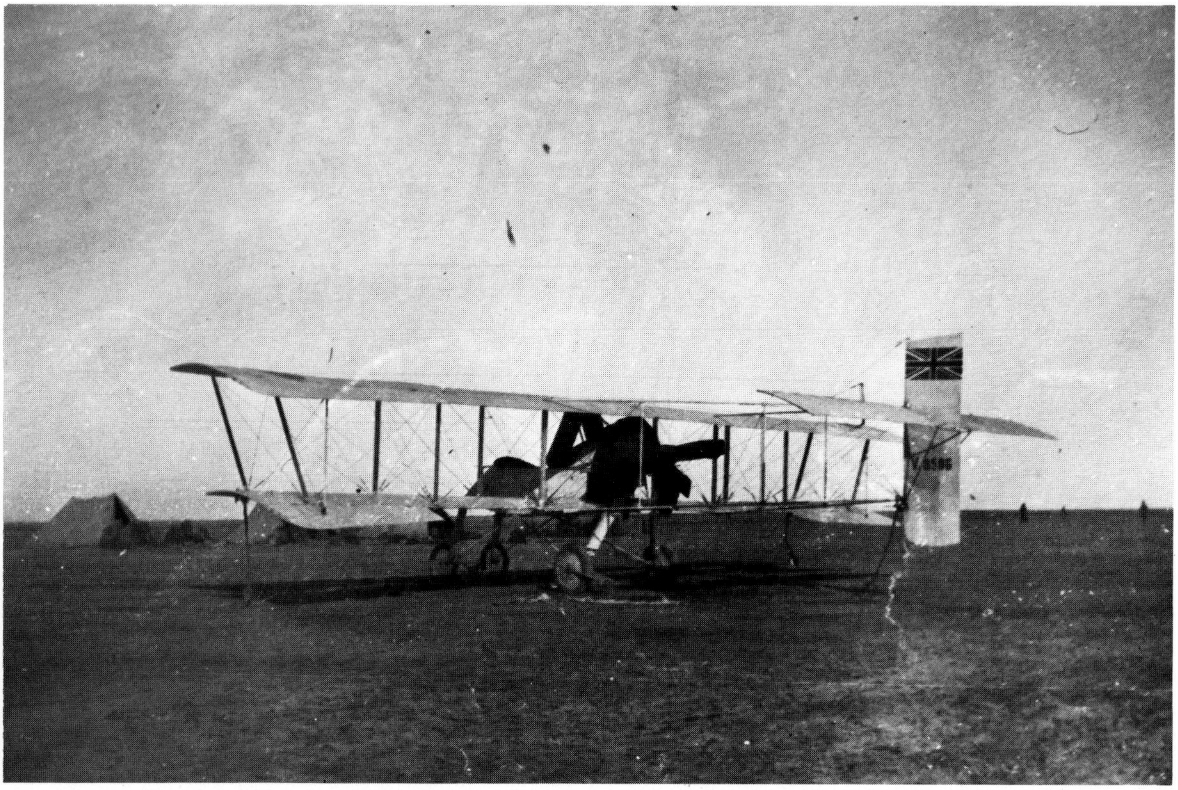

'For many weeks the weather was persistently bad and greatly hampered the work, producing a state of affairs that is better imagined than described. Suffice to say that never before in my experience have pilots been called upon to fly machines in less airworthy condition — a condition produced by being exposed day and night to prolonged spells of rain, mud and wind, with a minimum of spare parts for their upkeep'.

Equally strong words were used 20 years later by Lieutenant-General Sir Fenton Aylmer, who preceded Gorringe as relief force commander — though it should be remembered that he could speak only for the earlier weeks of 1916, when the air support was at its lowest ebb. In a letter to H. A. Jones, the RAF Historian, commenting on a draft chapter of *The War in the Air*, he wrote:

'I do think that you should bring out more strongly the miserable things that were sent to the Force and called aeroplanes. Major Massy did everything to my entire satisfaction, and I shall always be grateful to him and the splendid officers under his command for their devotion to duty under most trying conditions'.

Through no fault of the air services, Kut was not a reassuring advertisement for air supply, and two years passed before the next recorded operation in this category.

On the Western Front in June 1918 No 3 Squadron, Australian Flying Corps, made experimental parachute drops of ammunition from RE8s over their aerodrome which were sufficiently promising to warrant a full scale application of the technique at the first suitable opportunity. This arose on 4 July during a planned advance by the 4th Australian Division east of Nieppe, and No 9 Squadron RAF, commanded by Major J. R. Rodwell was detailed for the job. The bomb racks of 12 of their RE8s were fitted with clips to hold two boxes each containing 2,000 rounds of .303 ammunition, above which were metal cans for the packed parachutes. These were 14 feet in diameter, with a one foot hole in the top and made of aeroplane fabric. The observer released the boxes via a Bowden cable and their weight pulled the parachutes from their cans. Parachutes and boxes were prepared in advance, and a team of 16 men specially trained in packing and loading procedures to ensure speedy turn-rounds.

As the advance developed troops marked the main dropping points with a white 'N', while individual machine-gun posts requiring ammunition displayed the letter 'V'. Dropping began mid-morning and by 1500 when the objective had been gained the 12 aircraft had each averaged four 30-minute sorties to drop 93 boxes, a total of 111,600 rounds, on six aiming points. Refuelling and reloading had averaged 20 minutes. Eight of the RE8s had supplied main dumps and four 'rovers' had concentrated on the machine-gunners' requirements. To achieve the necessary accuracy aircraft had released their parachutes from an average height of 800ft. Two were shot down.

This technique was of immense benefit to the infantry and on 21 August Armstrong-Whitworth FK8s of No 35 Squadron dropped many thousands of rounds to advancing troops in the battle of Bapaume, and next day RE8s of No 53 made a smaller delivery which included signal flares and nine coils of barbed wire. In another area on 1 October RE8s and FK8s of Nos 7 and 82 Squadrons respectively flew 32 sorties to drop 63 boxes of ammunition and on the 2nd, squadrons of No 2 Wing delivered a further 58 boxes.

A supply drop which demonstrated even more clearly the great progress in aircraft performance and Allied air superiority achieved since the heroic attempt to feed Kut took place on 2 and 3 October. During a rapid advance along the Moorslede-Staden-Dixmude line, French and Belgian troops used up their food reserves and the situation imposed long delays in resupply by road. Nos 82 (FK8) and 218 (DH9) Squadrons, at Proven and St Pol respectively, were therefore detailed to join with Belgian squadrons in providing a total force of 80 aircraft for a large rations air lift. Overnight, lorries delivered 6,480 rations, packed in bags of earth to prevent damage in the free dropping from 300ft, and at 0600 on 2 October the aircraft started their shuttle services through low clouds and drizzling rain. Soon after 1300 No 218 Squadron had delivered its allocation of 242 sacks, but No 82, whose larger commitment to drop 980 sacks was interrupted by a

**Left:** BE2cs at Ora before take-off on the last sortie to Kut on 29 April 1916. Two armed escort aircraft are in the background.

**Below:** The Handley Page O/400 (C9681) which was used as a temporary freighter in the Middle East in 1918. This aircraft also made the first England-Egypt and Egypt-India flights.

midday call for a bombing strike, continued its grocery delivery the following day. The dropping zones at Oostnieuwkerk (for 82 Squadron) and Stadenburg (for 218 Squadron) were marked with white crosses and the ration packs survived the drops virtually undamaged. In the two days the entire force dropped 15,000 rations, weighing about 13 tons.

The last recorded supply drop of World War I took place on 13 October, a misty, rainy day which grounded a large proportion of the Allied and enemy aircraft. The retreating German forces had largely abandoned Le Cateau, and it was reported that the French civilian population was near starvation. Strong enemy machine-gun posts still held the town and the situation called for an aerial delivery. No 35 Squadron operating from an advanced aerodrome at Elincourt was instructed to arrange a food drop, and during the afternoon its FK8s flew 17 sorties to deliver two tons of bully beef and biscuits.

The closing months of the war produced one notable transport support operation overseas. The Allied advance on Damascus was being harassed by four enemy two-seater aircraft and it was proposed to position two Bristol Fighters of No 1 Squadron AFC to deal with this nuisance. The problem of how to supply the Bristols on their remote patch of desert was solved at the highest level — by the RAF C-in-C, Major-General Geoffrey Salmond. He suggested that the solitary Handley Page O/400 night bomber in the theatre might be used as a temporary freighter. The two Bristols went to Umm-es-Surab on 22 September 1918 and next day the Handley Page flew in

with a ton of petrol, oil, spares and other supplies. News of its arrival spread rapidly among the Arabs, who flocked to the scene, gazing in awe at the 100ft span twin-engined monster parked beside the Bristols. This was the setting for their often-quoted comment, recorded by T. E. Lawrence in *The Seven Pillars of Wisdom*: 'Indeed and at last they have sent us *the* aeroplane of which these things were foals'.

The most glamorous type of air transport operation developed in World War I was 'special duties' — the dropping of agents in enemy territory — and probably because it was highly secret at the time, few detailed records have survived.

One of the first such flights was by Captain J. W. M. Morgan, of No 6 Squadron, who took off early on 13 September 1915 to place a Belgian agent behind the lines near Courtrai. The selected landing site was a small field bordered by woods, and while making its final approach at 0445 the BE2c hit a tree and crashed, both occupants being injured. The agent in the front cockpit broke both his legs and was protected from even worse damage by the box of carrier pigeons in front of him. Friendly villagers were soon on the scene and took over the birds, miraculously unhurt, and other evidence showing the purpose of the mission. It was an hour before any German troops arrived and the casualties removed to hospital. On 28 September Captain G. L. Cruikshank of No 3 Squadron successfully completed a similar mission in a Morane Parasol.

On 3 October Lieutenant J. W. Woodhouse of No 4 Squadron suffered some acute anxieties while delivering a French agent named Le Marrier to a point a few miles south of Cambrai. With the idea of making a silent approach he switched off the engine of his BE2c on recognising the selected field in the last of the evening light, and although it failed to pick up on the final stage his judgement was good and the landing uneventful. When he tried to start up for take-off the engine refused to fire due to the mixture having become over-rich during the descent. Le Marrier's generous offer to stay and help was gracefully declined, and after pulling the propeller backwards a few turns to clear the surplus petrol Woodhouse got the engine to fire. He hastily climbed aboard as the BE started to move, but could remain airborne only for a few minutes before the badly missing engine forced him down again. Fortunately he was in another sizeable field, and after running up the engine for several short bursts took off once more. By this time he had lost his bearings, so turned due west and flew well beyond the trenches, then let down gradually in the darkness. His luck still held, and he touched down near Villers Brettoneaux with no more damage than a broken propeller.

During the summer of 1916 experimental night reconnaissance flights over the Somme front were made by a black-doped SS40 Naval airship. There were plans to use this and similar 'blimps' for parachuting agents, but tests indicated that better results could be achieved by aeroplanes.

Further afield, two notable daylight flights were made by Lieutenant Walter S. Scott, of No 17 Squadron, in BE2c No 4477 from Salonika to deliver Greek agents behind the lines. The first was on 16 December 1916, and when Scott

**Above: Lt J. W. Woodhouse, No 4 Squadron, with a French agent he dropped behind the enemy lines, 1915.**

reached his destination in the aptly named Drama Valley he found solid cloud from 200 feet down to ground level. Although fully justified in abandoning the sortie he continued his let down, and with considerable skill — and even more good luck — managed to land, and take off again in less than 10 yards visibility with only minor damage to the aircraft. His second flight to the same area was on 1 January 1917.

Early in 1917 the Western Front special duty operations were for a short time the responsibility of No 19 Squadron. This unit had been flying BE12s, makeshift single-seater adaptations of the BE2c, which, after proving useless in their intended fighter role, were switched to bombing, including experimental precision night attacks. When the squadron rearmed with the excellent French SPAD in December 1916 it was evidently decided to employ the recently acquired night flying expertise by retaining some of the BE12s, and adding a few BE2cs and 2es, for special duties. Several missions, including para-drops, were flown by Captain W. J. Cairns and, Lieutenants G. S. Buck and W. E. Reed, but no details have survived in the squadron records.

There were obvious difficulties in running a squadron with two such different roles, and in March the all black

BEs were handed over to the newly formed No 9 Wing Special Duty Flight, commanded by Woodhouse, now promoted to captain.

The rare type of courage required of special agents must have been strained almost to breaking point by the perilous manner in which they were flown to the dropping zones. On the BE12 the passenger occupied a small external seat fixed above the rear spar of the lower wing and facing the tail. He was secured to one of the struts by a belt and cord, with a quick release activated from the pilot's cockpit, and also attached to a Calthrop Guardian Angel parachute packed under the fuselage. The head resistance created by the passenger sitting exposed to the air-flow considerably reduced the BE12's modest speed and climb, so after a few trips a new method was devised. An open-topped plywood structure bearing a macabre resemblance to a coffin was fitted on the lower wing, parallel to the fuselage, in which the heroic agent lay face downwards. On arrival over the dropping zone he slid out of the open rear end, and his weight activated the parachute release.

On one flight the agent evidently began to think that there were better ways of serving the Allied cause. As he emerged into the slip-stream some superhuman feat of strength, born of desperation, enabled him to grab the edge of the cockpit and then the pilot's arm. Woodhouse was the pilot, and in the ensuing struggle he lost control of the aircraft, which dived from 1,600 feet down to 700. He loosened the agent's grip and regained a straight and level altitude. Since only some drastic action seemed likely to prevent a crash he struck the unfortunate agent over the knuckles with his revolver, causing him to let go of the cockpit side. Woodhouse peered down into the darkness but saw no sign of the opening parachute. He was relieved to learn some weeks later that the agent was safe — and had offered apologies to the pilot for causing so much trouble.

The RAF assisted with at least one agent dropping night flight on the Italian front. In August 1918, Major W. G. Barker and Captain W. Wedgwood Benn crewed an Italian SP4 twin-engined bomber which parachuted an agent, Allesandro Tandura, behind the Austrian lines near Vittorio. Despite the complicated parachute release gear devised for this aircraft, the drop was successful, and during the following days several supply drops were made.

Throughout the war carrier pigeons formed an important part of the agents' equipment, and these were parachuted behind the lines in special boxes from various aircraft types, including Sopwith Pups. The boxes always included a copy of the day's French newspaper, to reassure agents that they were not decoys planted by the enemy.

# A Dream Fulfilled

## 2

Long before the existence of practical flying machines, men had dreamed of fanciful contraptions to carry passengers and mail across the oceans and continents to remote parts of the world. The dream began to approach reality with the invention of the aeroplane, but its substance belonged to civil rather than military aviation, and the first experimental mail flights were made in 1911, before the formation of the Royal Flying Corps.

The temporary halt which World War I imposed on civil aviation saw the development of aircraft far beyond the 'stick and string' stage, and although the RAF did not possess any real transport machines, it had acquired a wealth of flying experience. Therefore, when the Government, only days after the Armistice, formulated requirements for passenger and mail services the RAF was the obvious candidate for the job. The new Service rose to the occasion supremely well, gaining experience which proved invaluable to commercial aviation when it got off the ground soon afterwards. But this first lesson in scheduled all-weather flying operations was learned the hard way, at some cost in aircrew lives.

On 22 November 1918, the Foreign Office formally asked the Air Ministry to organise a twice daily 'messenger service by aeroplane' between London and the Paris headquarters of the British peace delegation to start on 14 December, with additional twin-engined Handley Pages to carry senior delegates. At the same time, a separate scheme for air mail services to British military headquarters in France and Belgium, and the British Occupation Forces in Germany, was being discussed between the War Office and the Air Ministry.

For the London-Paris route, the RAF already had a suitable nucleus organisation — the outcome of an unhappy experience suffered by the Air Minister, Lord Weir, five months earlier. In the course of six flights on a visit to units in France his aircraft made four forced landings, culminating in an engine failure over the English Channel on the return trip. This escaped the biggest newspaper headlines thanks only to some good luck and a skilled pilot, who avoided ditching and just scraped into a coastal aerodrome.

On 15 July, after discussing the matter with Winston Churchill (then Minister of Munitions), Weir asked the Chief of the Air staff to consider forming a special unit for the exclusive use of Cabinet Ministers, Members of Air Council and other VIPs travelling on urgent business. He emphasised that an efficiently operated passenger and despatch service could provide valuable experience and prestige for the RAF — and further, suggested Captain Cyril Patteson who has so competently handled his recent forced landings as the right man to organise it.

Files sped through the corridors of the Hotel Cecil, and on 27 July the Communications Squadron under the command of Patteson was formed at Hendon. A Flight was charged by Air Ministry directive 'to maintain an efficient service for long-distance flights' with Rolls-Royce engined DH4s, to be used only by authority of the CAS. B Flight had two Avro 504s, two BE2cs and a few other types for use by Air Ministry staff officers.

The DH4 two-seater day bomber had entered service in the spring of 1917 and was one of the great aeroplanes of World War I. Despite a superb performance which made it difficult for enemy fighters to intercept, it nevertheless inspired a sort of love-hate relationship with pilots because of certain design shortcomings. The long gap — occupied by a large petrol tank — separating the two cockpits was said to create crew communication difficulties, and pilots did not relish the prospect of being sandwiched between this tank and the engine in a crash.

One of the squadron's most regular passengers was the CAS himself. Major-General Sir Frederick Sykes, who in his autobiography, *From Many Angles*, described the VIP flying, 1918 style:

'I used to enjoy the old open cockpits, with the wind whistling in the cowling, but they had their disadvantages; if oil or sleet got on to one's goggles or windscreen one was practically blind. Fog was then a terrible bugbear to flying, as there were no proper wireless installations and blind flying was in its infancy. In foggy weather the Channel had to be crossed at ten or twelve feet above the water, and once we came suddenly upon the cliffs of Dover right in front of us and were forced to land on the shore aerodrome at Hawkinge. On another occasion, while looking for Croydon, we saw the dome of St Pauls looming a few yards ahead. We turned abruptly, and after some rather anxious moments, managed to find a clear patch at Northolt.'

Top right: Officers of No 1 (Communication) Squadron in front of a DH4 at Hendon, December 1918. Left to right: Lts D. H. Owen Edmunds, H. 'Jerry' Shaw, A. C. Campbell Orde, Capt G. E. Chadwick, Lt Roberts (Adjutant), Maj Cyril Patteson (CO), — (not known), Lt E. M. Knott, Lt Hewer, Lt Cochrane, — (not known).

Right: DH4A prototype / *MOD*

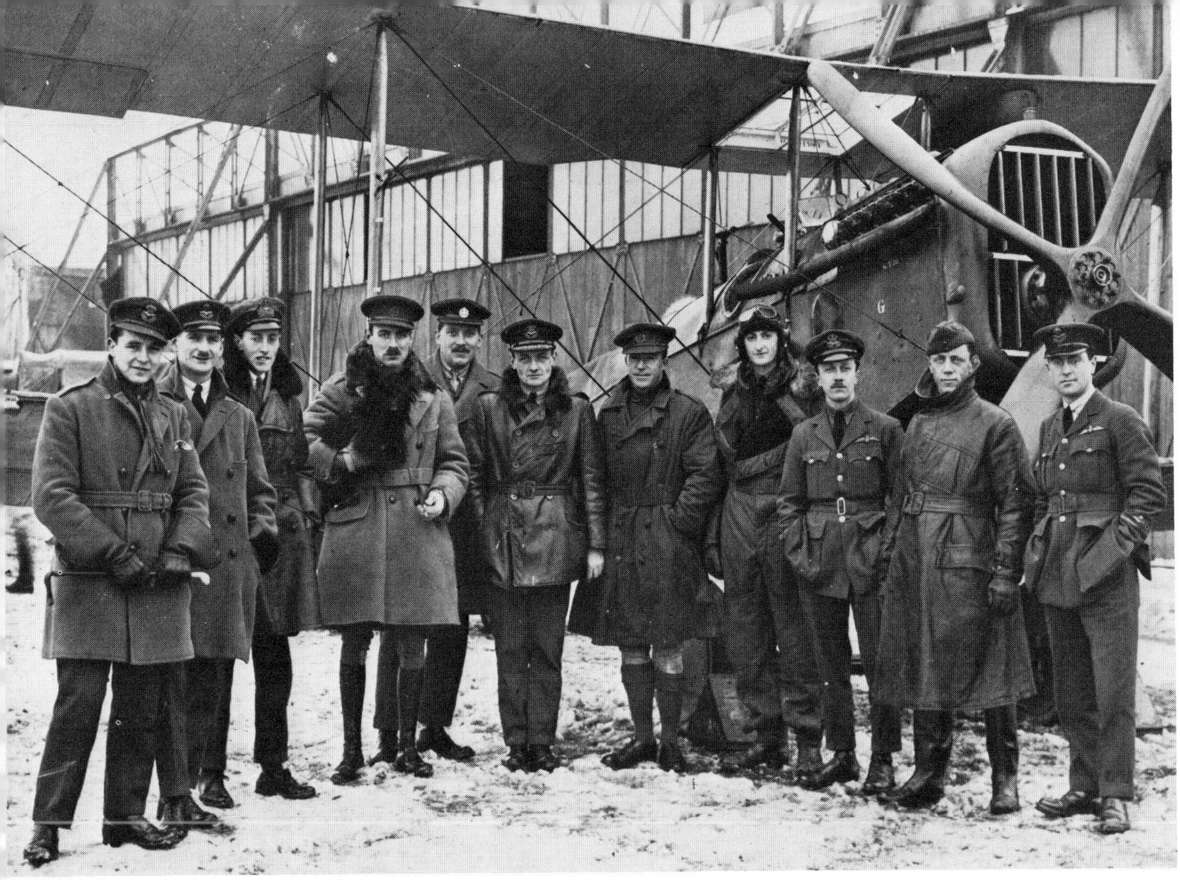

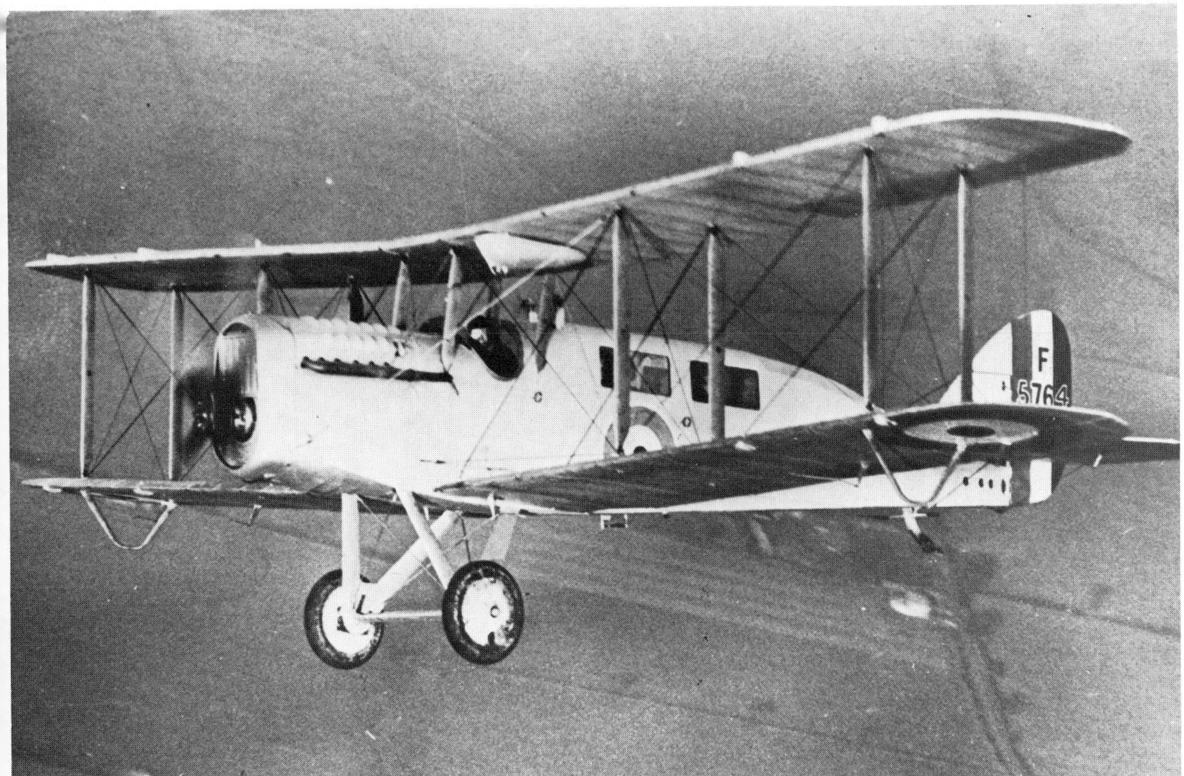
F
5764

**Left: DH4A, showing seating arrangements.** / *Central News Ltd*

**Below left: One of the Martinsyde F4 Buzzards used by No 86
(Communication) Wing.** / *MOD*

**Above: HMA *Silver Star* with wings folded.** / *MOD*

**Below: Handley Page 0/400 of No 86 (Communication) Wing.**
/ *MOD*

A larger organisation was clearly needed to meet the Peace Conference commitment, and on 13 December No 86 (Communication) Wing was formed, also at Hendon, under Lt-Col W. Harold Primrose. Patteson was promoted major, and his unit became No 1 (Communication) Squadron. More aircraft and pilots were provided and several Handley Page 0/400 night bombers converted by the Royal Aircraft Establishment, Farnborough, to carry up to eight passengers. A suggestion that the DH4 might be improved for passenger work came from Mr Bonar Law, Lord Privy Seal, another regular passenger, with less enthusiasm for the open air life than the CAS. The Aircraft Manufacturing Co at Hendon first made a mock up passenger cabin from a crashed fuselage, and in late December the DH4A prototype (F5764) emerged. Surprisingly it was faster than the standard version, and on 14 January three more DH4s (F2663, 4 and 5) were allotted for similar conversions. Access to the cabin was through the hinged roof, and the two occupants sat face to face so that conversation was (just) possible. The idea was that the VIP and his secretary could continue urgent work during their journey, and the aircraft became popular with passengers.

From 14 December until 10 January 1919, the Paris service operated on an ad hoc basis, and no records of its early work appear to have survived. The only figures available, which are merely a continuation of those for the original squadron, show an overall total of 117 passengers and 100 mailbags carried in 136 sorties between 27 July 1918 and 15 March 1919.

No 1 (C) Squadron maintained a small detachment at Buc aerodrome, near Versailles, but to cope with the rapidly growing traffic, No 2 (C) Squadron was formed there on 1 March under Major C. R. Edwards, shortly afterwards succeeded by Major J. Ronald McCrindle. During February there had been a No 3 (C) Squadron at Hounslow for special high-speed work, but this task was transferred to the No 86 Wing Headquarters Flight. (The number 3 had earlier been earmarked for an F5 flying boat squadron to operate services to America, the Azores and Egypt, soon abandoned as unpractical. A less ambitious scheme to link with Scandinavian ports was studied, and No 4 (C) Squadron started to form for the purpose at Felixstowe in September 1919, but never became operational.)

In April, Kenley replaced Hendon as the London terminus, and from this time the wing's activities must be considered as a whole, since records of the two squadrons are inextricably mixed. By early summer each was established for 18 aircraft, divided into three flights of six — one each of HP 0/400s, DH4s and DH4As, though it is doubtful whether the wing as a whole ever had more than eight HPs. Aircraft were immaculately finished in silver dope, with a coloured fuselage band, and some carried individual names. DH4A No F2664 was HMA *Lady Iris* and HP No D8326 was HMA *Silver Star*. Other Handley Page names were *Silver Queen* and *Great Britain*. The Headquarters flight at Kenley had two Martinsyde F4 Buzzard single-seaters for express courier work, two Bristol Fighters for use in small airfields and two Avros for general duties.

Not on the official inventory were a few single-seat fighters which enabled pilots to maintain their flying skills on smaller and more agile aircraft. This form of continuation training combined with relaxation — operationally legitimate but difficult to justify before granite-faced finance officials — was first enjoyed by No 2 (C) Squadron. The weekend crowds of Parisians who watched the flying at Buc were often rewarded by the spectacle of French pilots performing hair-raising 'stunts' in fighters. This aroused deep frustration among the RAF pilots, who were not permitted liberties with their staid

**Above: DH9A E9707 of No 205 Squadron employed on the 'B' mail route, photographed at Verviers in early 1919; pilot, Lieutenant Wardlaw.** / *Chaz Bowyer*

**Bottom left: Handley Page 0/400 HMA *Silver Star* of No 1(C) Squadron about to leave Hendon for Paris, 1919. Passengers on this flight included Mr J. H. Thomas MP.** / *Philip J. R. Moyes*

transport aircraft. So to keep the British flag flying two Snipes and two SE5As were somehow acquired.

The Handley Pages themselves, as the earliest examples of large aircraft furnished to VIP transport standards, were in much demand, and on 23 March King Faisal made his first flight in one, accompanied by Col T. E. Lawrence ('of Arabia'), Brig-Gen P. R. Groves, and two Japanese Ministers.

Despite the problems surrounding the introduction of such an important service in the winter, No 86 Wing earned a high reputation for determination, and if pilots sometimes failed to reach their destination airfield, they usually managed to deliver the goods somehow. On 19 March Captain E. M. Knott left Hendon at 1600 in poor weather carrying a special despatch for the Prime Minister. Conditions worsened as he crossed the Channel and he was forced down at Boulogne/Marquise, but knowing the urgency, continued his journey by train and personally delivered the package in Paris later that night.

Meteorological reports were graded from category 'A' (perfect flying weather) to 'F' (gales, low cloud or fog) but on many occasions flights were successfully completed in 'F' conditions. 'Flying by Bradshaw' was an accepted technique, and from Kenley the route crossed Tonbridge, after which pilots followed that splendidly straight railway line to Folkestone. The route continued via Cap Griznez, Boulogne, Etaples, Abbeville, Poix, Beauvais and Pontoise to Buc. The DH4s normally took 2 hours 10 minutes for the journey — the fastest trip for the type being 1 hour 20 minutes — and the Handley Pages an hour longer. The record for the 245-mile journey — 1 hour 15 minutes — was flown by Primrose in a Martinsyde.

Inevitably there were accidents, and the first fatality occurred during the winter when an aircraft crashed attempting a forced landing in a hail storm, killing the pilot. The wing's worst spell — three fatals in four weeks — came later on when the kinder weather might reasonably have been expected to reduce flying hazards. On 22 April 1919, a DH4 returning empty from a special flight to Brussels disappeared, presumably lost at sea; on 3 May Knott was killed at Kenley and on 15 May a DH4A flown by Capt E. R. B. Jefferson and carrying the Netherlands Food Minister, Mr Aaronsohn, came down in the Channel during a fog and both occupants were drowned.

Knott's passenger, Sir Frederick Sykes, who had recently become Controller-General of Civil Aviation, escaped with eye injuries which left him with slightly impaired vision for the rest of his life. The engine of the DH4 seized when the aircraft had reached about 200ft after take-off because of an omission to fill the radiator.

Sykes wrote more than 20 years later:

'Parachutes were not carried in those days, and in any case they would have been useless. I did not feel frightened; I suppose there was not time, and I fully realised each phase of the accident — the stalling, sideslip, the nosedive and crash — and was intensely interested and not unconscious for a moment. Poor Knott was killed instantaneously, and I suddenly found that I could not see. My immediate fear was of fire, but this fortunately did not occur and I managed to pull Knott clear . . .'

Sykes had a previous lucky escape in February, while still Chief of the Air Staff. Although the weather was officially graded as unfit, Lt E. Drew, one of 86 Wing's Australian pilots, volunteered to fly him from Paris to Hendon to attend an important London meeting. They took off in a snowstorm, laboured up between thick cloud banks to about 10,000ft, and after two hours' flying in brilliant sunshine cautiously let down to check their position. As they broke cloud in blinding snow the engine stopped dead. There was no time to select a suitable forced landing spot according to the instruction manuals, and Drew managed to dive under some telegraph wires before crashing into a dyke. Both occupants were strapped in and unhurt, and over coffee in a nearby village, learned that they were about 15 miles from Ostend — 70 miles off course. They travelled to the port in a mule cart, only to learn that the weather had also stopped all passenger steamers. However, Sykes crossed to Harwich overnight in a freighter, and still managed to reach London ahead of the others in his party.

Various other accidents caused complete write offs — including that to Handley Page C9786 which crashed into a ditch on 16 August while attempting to land at Marquise in very low cloud — but there were no serious injuries.

A highlight of 86 Wing's short history was an experimental night flight carrying unsurcharged GPO mail from London to Paris. HMA *Silver Star* of No 1 (C) Squadron took off in the early hours of 15 May with letters posted in central London on the 14th. Another was on 28 June, when Primrose led four DH4As in a formation flight over Versailles during the signing of the Peace Treaty.

Bonar Law hurried away before the final ceremonies were concluded, carrying Lord George's formal notification to King George V of the signature. He flew to England in a DH4A captained by Lieutenant G. R. Powell which, according to Press reports landed at Kenley at 1930, but official files record as having put down near Guildford because of bad weather.

Traffic declined after the treaty signing and the Chief of the Air Staff ruled that to continue an essentially civil flying task was a luxury which the RAF could not afford with its slender financial and manpower resources. The decision to disband 86 Wing was made on 18 September, but because of a possible domestic requirement, execution was delayed for a few weeks and its last cross-Channel flights were made on 8 October. In all the wing had covered some 350,000 miles.

From the formation of the original Hendon unit on 27 July 1918 until 31 August 1919, the cross-Channel communications squadrons carried a total of 934 passengers and 1,028 official mail bags or despatches in 744 trips. These figures are sometimes wrongly quoted as the achievement of No 86 Wing itself from formation in December 1918, but as mentioned earlier, the first three months of the wing's activities appear not to have been separately logged. Detailed records maintained for the period 16 March-31 August show that flights were made on 142 of those 169 days (84%), and it is reasonable to assume that cancellations were due to the weather. In that period 817 passengers were carried.

Of the 38 uncompleted DH4/4A flights, 25 were

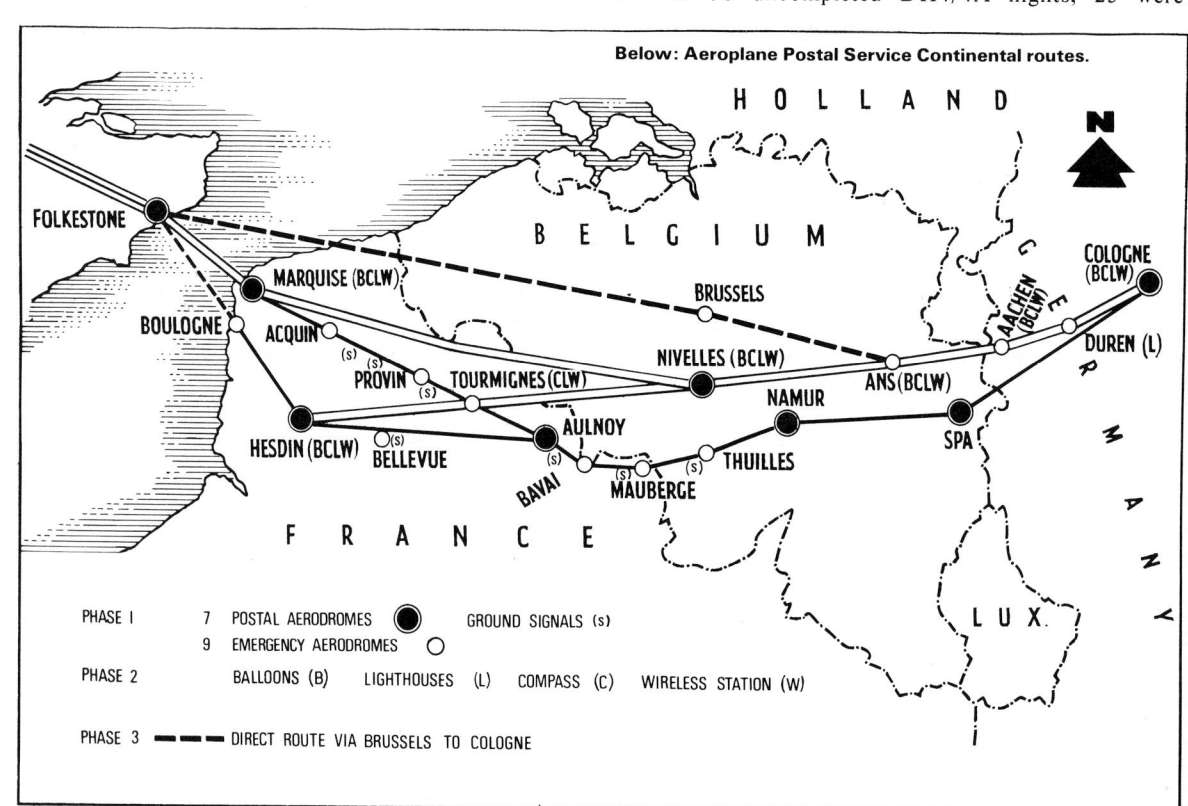

Below: Aeroplane Postal Service Continental routes.

**Operations by No 86 (Communication) Wing,
16 March-31 August 1919**

| Aircraft type | Flights started | Completed same day | Regularity % |
|---|---|---|---|
| DH4 and 4A | 491 | 453 | 92.3 |
| HP 0/400 | 92 | 81 | 88 |
| Martinsyde | 20 | 18 | 90 |
| Bristol Fighter | 4 | 4 | 100 |
| Avro | 1 | - | - |
| Total | 608 | 556 | 91 |

abandoned because of engine failure and other technical faults and 13 for weather reasons. Only four of the HP flights failed from technical causes, and seven through weather. The 7.6% weather failure rate for the twin-engined aircraft as against only 2.4% for the single-engined type seems surprising, but the Handley Page with its 100ft wing span was difficult to handle in high winds, in the air and on the ground. It cruised at only 70mph and its general unwieldiness made it unsuitable for the low flying which route operations often demanded.

One aspect of the Handley Page operation which exceeded all expectations was the performance of the radio-telephone equipment, R/T stations were set up at Kenley, Lympne, Marquise and Buc, and the aircraft's wireless operator could receive the 86 Wing weather reports and pass to the destination aerodrome details of passengers and mail, transport requirements and so on. The normal drill was for aircraft flying to Paris to remain in communication with Kenley, Lympne and Marquise until the Channel was crossed — and in the reverse direction to make similar contact before starting the crossing. Aircraft were often in good communication with Kenley when flying over Abbeville, and ranges exceeding 100 miles were frequently obtained. The Buc R/T station was affected by interference from the Eiffel Tower W/T installations and although on occasions direct speech could be exchanged with Kenley, regular working was not possible. On a special flight over London, speech from a Handley Page was passed via the Air Ministry switchboard over an ordinary telephone — a near miracle for the day.

The Air Ministry calculated that cost of the scheme as £30,585, which meant that a paying commercial air mail service might be operated for a charge of 1s 0½d per oz, though the figures are a little suspect. The squadrons were greatly overstaffed in aircrews to cater for the continual depletion caused by demobilisation (73 pilots flew with No 86 Wing in March-August, although the actual establishment was only 53 officers of all categories) and full allowance was not made for all aircraft written off or damaged in accidents.

The second of the post-Armistice transport commitments, formally entitled the Aeroplane Postal Service, was agreed at a War Office-Air Ministry meeting on 2 December 1918, and although considerably more demanding, was readily accepted by the Air Staff. Aircraft and pilots were plentiful, the RAF possessed vast operational experience and this was another opportunity for the new Service to gain prestige. It was a bold decision, for there were very real difficulties in starting such services

in the depth of winter with minimal navigation aids and aircraft by no means suited to the work. Apart from the direct hazards of snow, fog and gales the less obvious and insidious effects of icing on airframes and engines were little understood. Whereas a few abortive sorties had rarely prejudiced the success of wartime fighter or bomber operations — and VIPs could usually appreciate the reasons for a concellation — regularity was of supreme importance for postal schedules. Complaints would be quick and vociferous if the troops' mail was delayed.

An official mail service to France, using operational aircraft on delivery flights and proposed in 1917, was not adopted because regularity could not be guaranteed. Early in November 1918, when road links to the advancing Fourth Army were interrupted by enemy action, mail was flown from Le Cateau to Dinant and Marche, but for one day only before the war ended.

The new schedules were planned to start on 16 December, with an 'A' Service by Handley Page 0/400 bombers (Nos 207 and 216 Squadrons) flying between Marquise, near Boulogne, Valenciennes and Namur, and a 'B' Service linking British Army GHQ at Hesdin with Valenciennes, Namur and Spa, the Armistice Commission HQ — in effect a 'stopping service' fed from intermediate points. This more intricate network was flown by DH4s of No 55 Squadron based at Hesdin/St Andre and Maisoncelle, and No 57 Squadron with detachments at Namur/Spy, Nivelles and Spa; DH9s of No 99 Squadron at Valenciennes/Aulnoy and No 206 at Cologne/Bickendorf; and DH9As of No 205 Squadron based at Hesdin/St Andre and Maisoncelle. It was planned to extend both services to Cologne as soon as possible.

Extensively used as a day bomber towards the end of the war, the DH9 answered the criticism levelled at the DH4 by positioning the two crew seats close together. Unfortunately its 230hp Puma engine proved most unreliable and this led to severe operational losses. Later versions showed some improvement, and the aircraft finally came into its own when redesigned as the DH9A with the 400hp American Liberty engine.

The surprising omission of a cross-Channel link was simply because the Army postal authorities required a speedy alternative if bad weather should stop all flying. The current steamer schedules were such that by the time firm cancellation of the day's flying was decided, the last vessel had sailed, making a 24-hour delay inevitable.

The aerodromes at Valenciennes and Namur were at first unsuitable for large aircraft, so the 0/400s were adapted to air drop the mail. A chute was constructed inside the fuselage along which mailbags could be guided for release. They were enclosed in special containers made of aircraft fabric strengthened with wooden battens, and two or three of these could be hooked together, attached to a parachute and released through a side door. It was also found that four of an obsolete type of GPO parcel basket exactly fitted into the fuselage bomb bay and these could be para-dropped by a release gear controlled from the rear cockpit. In experiments with tins of corned beef to simulate mail, baskets dropped from 400 feet landed within 50 yards of the target marker — though in one practice the CO of No 216 Squadron scored an inadvertent direct hit on

**Above:** A No 57 Squadron DH9A, No F1023, named *Billy*, unloading mail at an unidentified aerodrome. This aircraft was flying on the 'B' route services in February 1919. / *E. F. Cheesman*

**Below:** Handley Page 0/400 used on the Marquise-Namur section of the Aeroplane Postal Service, December 1918, showing GPO parcel basket fixed under the fuselage. The ground crew men are displaying one of the fabric containers for the mail bags carried internally.

**Right:** Checking mail arriving at Hawkinge on the opening day of the cross-Channel link, 1 March 1919. / *T. C. Marvin*

**Below right:** Checking mail arriving at Hawkinge on the opening day of the cross-Channel link, 1 March 1919. / *T. C. Marvin*

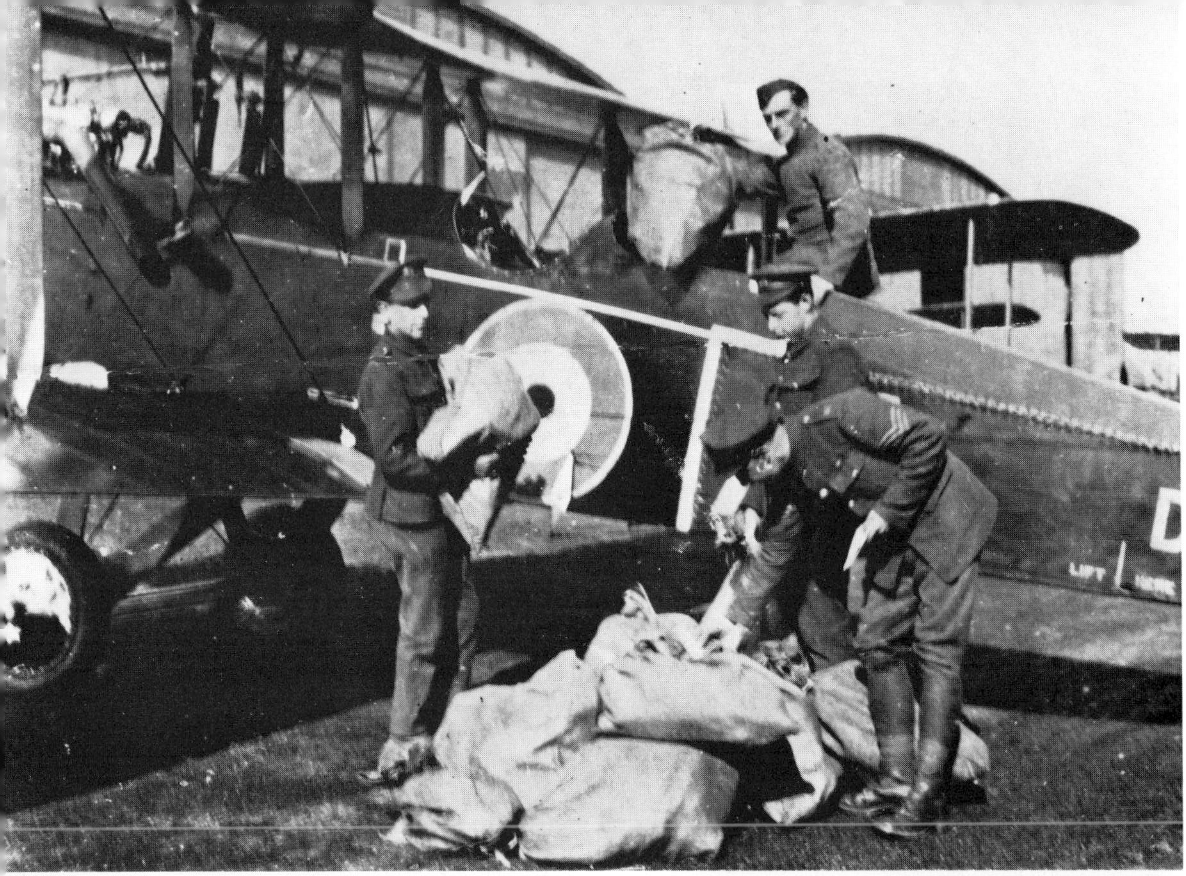

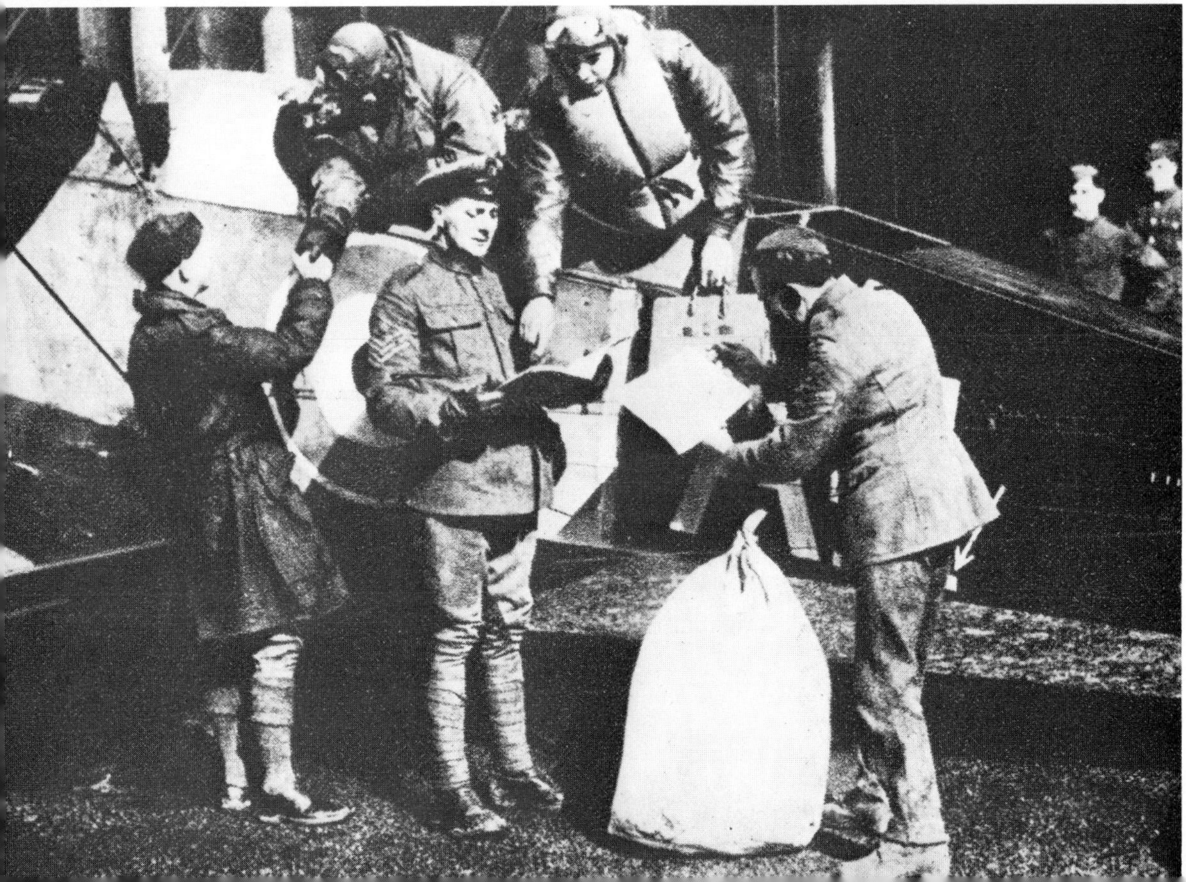

Rinxent church near their base.

Weather on the planned opening day was prohibitive for the Handley Pages at Marquise and very bad along the entire route, so a 24-hour postponement was ordered. This instruction seems not to have reached all bases — unless the keener squadrons viewed it with a Nelsonian blind eye — for at 1030 on 16 December, Lieutenant F. O. Thornton of No 57 Squadron, flying DH4 No H7148, took off from Namur/Spy with mail for Spa, landing back at base 1¾ hours later. This was the first mail flight by the RAF on an organised schedule. The squadron made another flight in the afternoon and No 99 also managed to get two aircraft away from Valenciennes/Aulnoy with mail for Namur, but conditions were too risky for landing and the mail was heaved overboard.

The service officially started on 17 December, when Handley Page 0/400 No D5410 lumbered off from Marquise laden with 37 mailbags. The weather was still poor, but 17 bags were delivered via the fuselage door to land fair and square in the middle of Valenciennes/Aulnoy aerodrome, and the remainder via the bomb bay baskets at Namur. Just after the 0/400 had dropped its mail at Valenciennes, five of the single-engined aircraft which had left Hesdin/St Andre at 1250 arrived. Altogether 83 mailbags were delivered along the 'B' Route, three aircraft crashed on landing and two others force-landed for reasons not recorded. Three days passed before the next Handley Page sortie could be flown, and on 20 December, D5410 dropped another 53 mailbags. After Christmas the intermediate aerodromes became fit for the large aircraft and following several trial flights, the 'A' Service was extended to Cologne on 5 January 1919. No 216 Squadron remained at Marquise and No 207 operated from Cologne/Merheim. The paradrop method had the obvious disadvantage that no mail could be collected from intermediate points, but offered a compensating saving in time — and as an Army report stated with brutal frankness 'the element of danger of crashing when landing is eliminated.' A Spa-Cologne section was added to the 'B' Route on 1 January.

During the early weeks all services were badly disrupted by severe weather. Less than a third of the Handley Pages were getting through, and flying was possible on only four of the first 16 days on the Hesdin-Valenciennes leg of the 'B' Service. Over this same period No 57 operating the more difficult Namur-Spa section amazed everyone by flying on 13 of those days, although landing was impossible on five occasions and the mail was thrown overboard. 'The only explanation apparent is that the pilots of 57 Squadron . . . were infused with greater enthusiasm and took greater risks than those responsible for the other sections' commented the report.

Special problems arose on the 'B' Service, which was like a rather complex relay race. Some pilots, perhaps over-enthusiastic to get airborne during short breaks in the weather, took off without waiting for the inbound aircraft bringing the mail along the feeder leg. Another indication of inadequate briefing down the line is discernible in an instruction from Brigadier-General E. R. Ludlow-Hewitt in January, requiring squadron commanders to ensure

'... that all members of postal crews can read their maps, are familiar with the landing grounds en route, can manipulate a forced landing with confidence and know how to dispose of their mail'. On 11 January, Lieutenant-Colonel C. E. C. Rabagliati, was appointed as mail routes supervisor and general trouble-shooter.

Mainly because of the appalling weather, irregularities over some sections caused the Army to revert to the railways, but to prevent the collapse of the whole scheme RAF mail continued by air and great efforts were made to improve the services. Various navigation aids, sophisticated for the time, were set up along the routes. Compass stations and lighthouses (the Handley Pages started night flying in January) were installed at main aerodromes, and balloons were flown from intermediate points. These were prominently numbered according to location, and when flying above cloud carried a 25ft triangular red pennant if the weather beneath was fit for landing, or a 12ft rectangular blue one if it was not. Names of towns were painted on large buildings and arrows of white stones on the ground served as pointers towards airfields. Some aircraft carried W/T equipment — and all had two pigeons to be released in the event of a forced landing.

A vigorous internal public relations campaign was launched to stimulate enthusiasm, and squadron commanders were asked:

'... to aim at regularity and speed in the delivery of mails, and to show what can be done in this respect by a first-class Service squadron ... to explain to all ranks that this is the first organised aerial post that has ever been in existence, and that the immediate future of aerial mail carriage will depend largely on their success or failure ... to impress on all concerned the importance and significance of the work upon which they are engaged'.

Some pilots — including men who had distinguished themselves in action a few months before — had made no secret of their dislike of mail flying, which they considered of minor importance. Others found it a satisfying challenge to their flying skills, but at the end of January it was decided that the mail crews should be volunteers. Rabagliati declared that only the very best and keenest would be selected for 'the highest honour to which a pilot could aspire'.

Despite the continued incidence of delays — on 15 February seven out of ten flights were not completed for weather or mechanical reasons — the Army was persuaded back into the fold that month. Meanwhile the schedules themselves were examined to see what improvements might be made, and the convenient introduction of an afternoon cross-Channel steamer from Folkestone provided the required standby if flying was impossible. Towards the end of February, No 120 Squadron moved to Hawkinge, ready to start mail flights to Maisoncelle on 1 March.

The improved service was preceded by a stirring Order of the Day from Major-General J. F. A. Higgins, Commanding the RAF in the Field, headed 'Our Aerial Future'. Part of it read:

'At present the papers are full of speculation as to what *may* be done, but as soon as we are in a position to state what has been done and is going to be continued, not only will the public interest be gripped, but other commercial schemes by aviation will at once begin to materialise. They are waiting for a lead. Let the RAF give it to them. By such an achievement the whole country will benefit, and the RAF add to its reputation. We want pilots and mechanics who are all out to make a success — and uninterrupted success — of this scheme. It is at the moment the best job in the RAF, and it is a job that will confer distinction on all who participate'.

The new link was designated the 'C' Service, No 120 Squadron operating the Hawkinge-Maisoncelle stage with DH9s and 9As, and Nos 110 at Maisoncelle and 18 at Cologne/Bickendorf flying the Continental stretch with DH9As. It began well, with four aircraft of 'B' Flight led by Captain A. F. Hordern leaving Hawkinge spot on schedule at 0915 on Saturday 1 March, with 24 mailbags. Then came another spell of exceptionally bad weather, and on 10 days in the month no departures were possible from Hawkinge. Severe conditions prevailed right across northern Europe, contributing to the wave of accidents which hit the services. Ironically, the first pilot to lose his life was Thornton, who was regarded as the outstanding bad-weather pilot, capable of flying through anything. His DH4 crashed near a remote Ardennes village on 6 March while returning from Cologne, and his observer, Captain P. S. Burnay, was also killed. On 20 March another 57 Squadron pilot, Lieutenant A. S. Smith, had a fatal crash on the same route. On the 26th an observer was killed at Vaals, just across the Dutch border in a crash-landing during a snowstorm, and next day a pilot flying from Cologne to Maisoncelle lost his life in a similar accident in the Meuse valley.

A technical point which emerged from the intensive all-weather flying was the need for metal-tipped propellers because up to an inch could be worn off the leading edges of unprotected wooden blades by heavy rain or hail.

As the weather improved and overall knowledge of the route increased, No 120 Squadron was allowed discretion to fly non-stop to Cologne, with a dramatic saving in time. Duration of the journey via Maisoncelle had averaged 4-6 hours, but one pilot soon made the direct flight in 1 hour 55 minutes. On the night of 14/15 May a twin-engined DH10 (F1869) made a trial night flight from Hawkinge to Cologne, which began the unquenchable legend that No 120 Squadron was equipped with this aircraft type. In fact the flight was made under No 18 Squadron auspices. July brought various changes; the French staging post moved from Maisoncelle to Marquise early in the month, and on the 16th Lympne became the English terminal because the Hawkinge sheds were required to store Handley Page V/1500 bombers. On 25 July the intermediate stop was eliminated altogether and No 110 Squadron withdrew from mail flying.

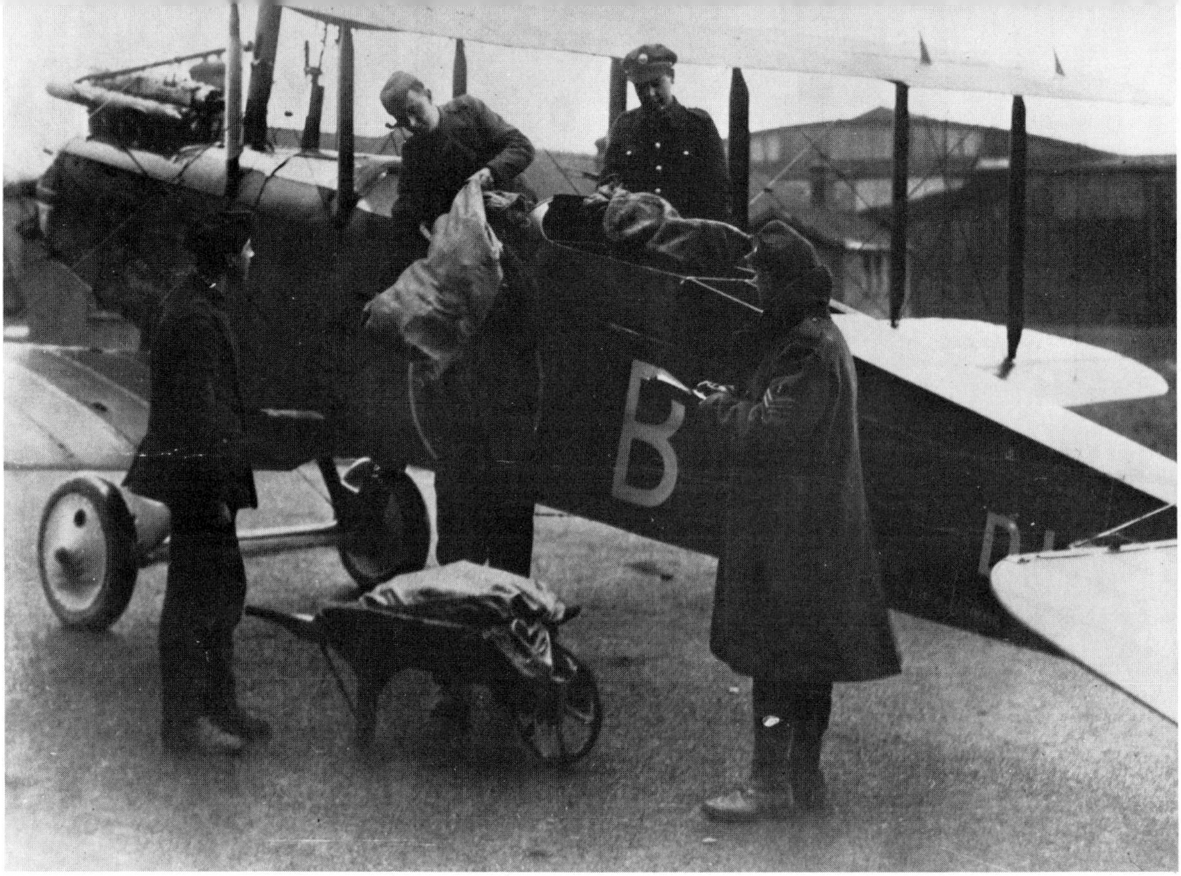
B

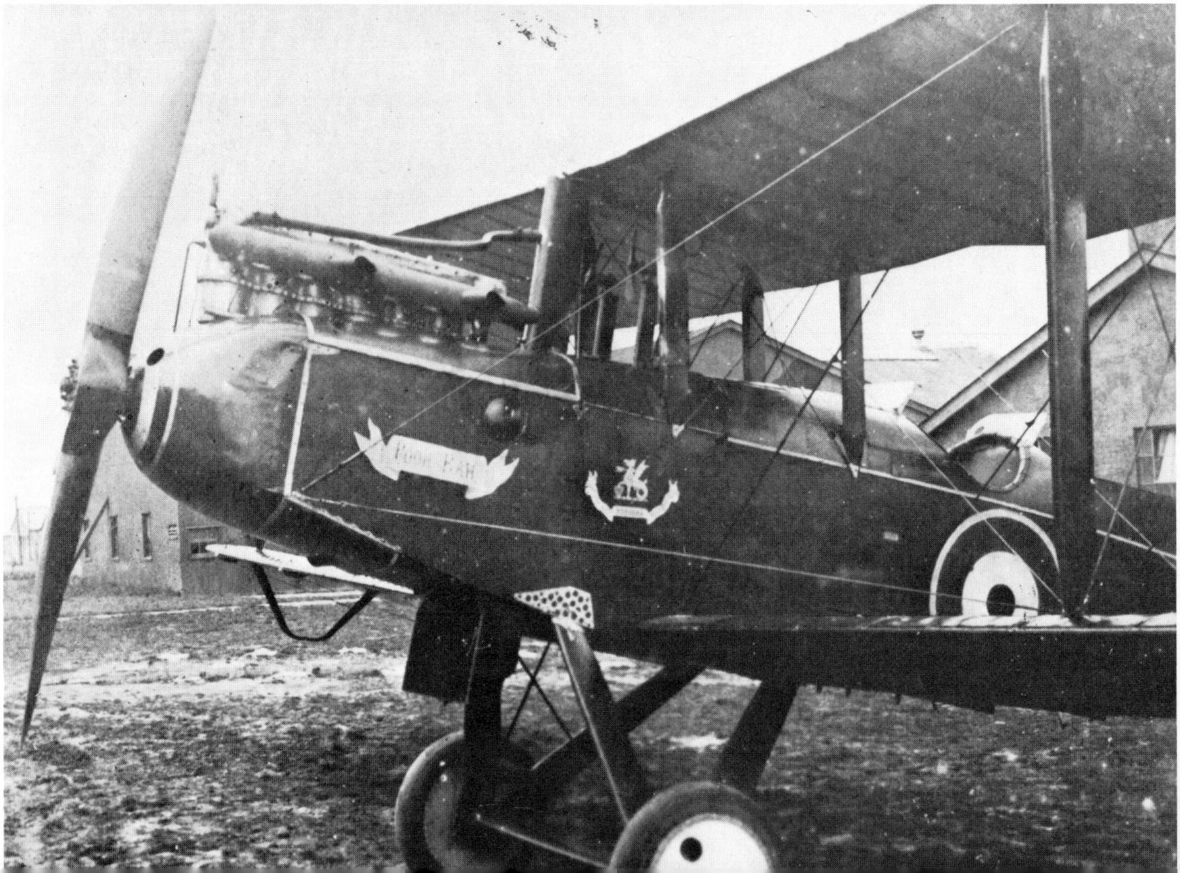

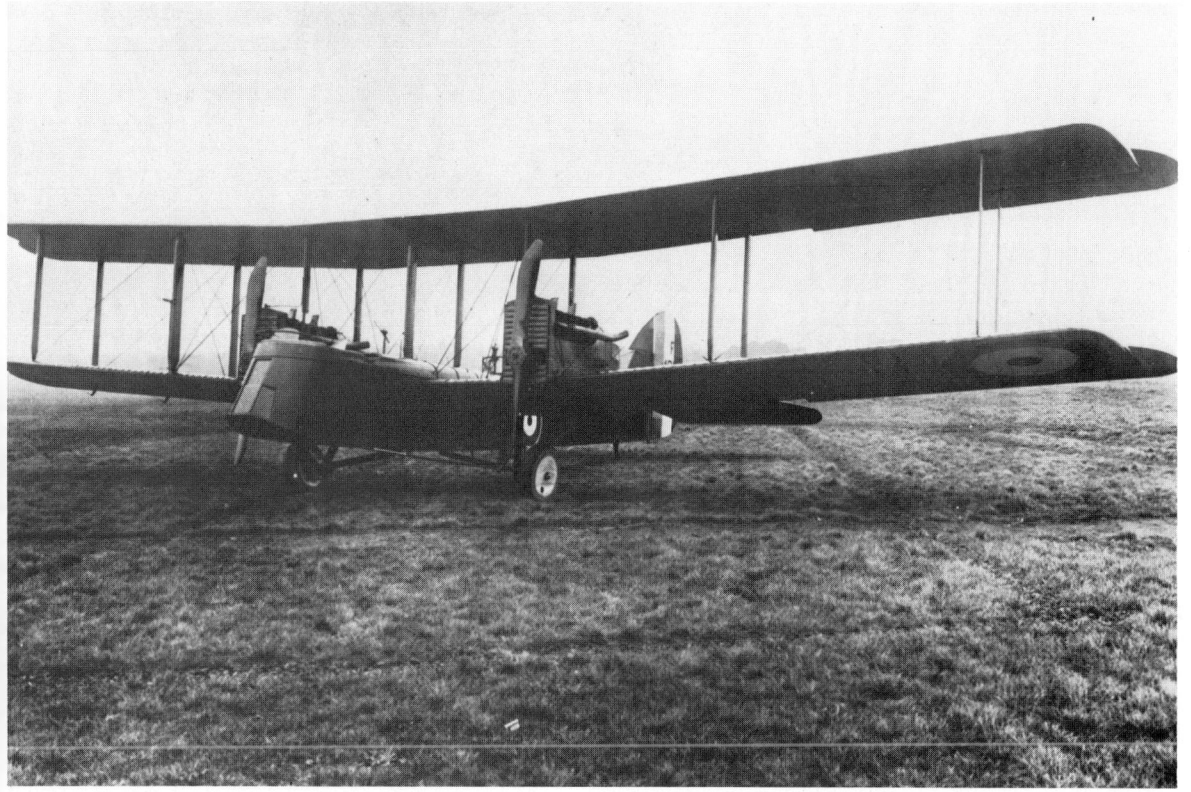

Above left: Loading mail into a No 120 Squadron DH9 at Hawkinge. Note sophisticated ground transport. / *T. C. Marvin*

Above: DH10A, believed to be F1869, which made the experimental night mail flight from Hawkinge to Cologne on 14/15 May, 1919.

Left: Captain A. F. Hordern's DH9, which carried the name *Pooh Bah*. / *T. C. Marvin*

The success of the 'C' Service rendered the 'A' Service virtually redundant and it was discontinued on 5 May. It had always been the least reliable schedule, and only 27½% of the planned sorties were completed. No fewer than 64½% were cancelled because of bad weather, and 8% failed through forced landings or technical reasons. As well as suffering the same disadvantages experienced in the Communication Wing, the heavy Handley Pages were often unable to fly from Marquise because the aerodrome was waterlogged. There were also reductions in the 'B' Service. Nos 55 and 205 Squadrons had ceased mail flying in January and February respectively, then Nos 99 and 206 were withdrawn in May and June pending redeployment further afield. No 57 re-equipped with DH9As and took over a general supporting role for the whole route, working from Nivelles and Maisoncelle.

Despite a marked improvement in general airmanship, navigation errors caused occasional embarrassments. Pilots seldom had the assistance of an observer, and one aircraft, well and truly lost en route to Cologne, landed in unoccupied Germany 80 miles east of Dusseldorf, where the mails were impounded for several days. In the reverse direction there were instances of pilots bound for Folkestone coming down at Dieppe and Le Havre. The pilot and mails from an aircraft forced to ditch many miles off course in the North Sea were picked up by a German fishing boat and put ashore near the Kiel Canal. For some reason the authorities would release the mail only on payment of a 1,000-mark deposit — perhaps for services rendered by the rescuers. To ease such problems — at least within Allied territory — pilots carried a card identifying them as authorised mail carriers, and instructions were issued that they should be given all possible assistance and consideration.

By June 1919 Nos 110 and 57 Squadrons had radio-telephony equipment by which pilots could communicate with the nearest one or two of the eight ground stations, and with each other, up to ranges of 15-20 miles.

Provision for mail stowage improved, and the DH9s and 9As were fitted with a plywood compartment aft of the observer's cockpit to accommodate about 18 mailbags. At first some squadrons simply stowed the load in the cockpit, but this practice was stopped after a bag was found wedged so far down in the rear fuselage of a 120 Squadron DH9A as to risk fouling the tail control cables. The DH9 could also carry up to 12 bags in the forward fuselage bomb cell.

In August the British Occupation Force was greatly reduced and the smaller mail commitment was handed over to civil aviation on the 15th. No 120 Squadron ceased mail flights on 24 August and No 18 on the 31st.

**ROYAL AIR FORCE.**

## AERIAL POST.

**TO BE CARRIED BY THE PILOT OF A POSTAL AEROPLANE.**

Extract from G.R.O. No. 819, dated 23rd January, 1919:—

"6104 AERIAL POST. In the course of long flights undertaken in connection with the Aerial Post, pilots are frequently forced to land, on account of weather conditions or engine failure, etc.

In such cases, pilots have been instructed to apply to the nearest unit, who will make every endeavour to provide transport to convey the mails to the nearest Military post office, with the least possible delay.

(254 (Q.A.), 23-1-19)."

*Name of Pilot* A. F. HORDERN AFC (Capt)

*Squadron* 120ᵗʰ AERIAL MAIL

*Location of Squadron* HAWKINGE

**RAF mail pilot's authorisation card.** / *T. C. Marvin*

The only figures recorded for the period 16 December 1918 to 28 February 1919 show that of the 1,023 flights started, 978 were successfully completed — 96%. This often quoted and impressive result is a rather rose-tinted way of stating a scheduled service achievement, since it takes no account of the many *planned* sorties cancelled for weather and other reasons.

From 1 March to 31 August, 1,842 flights were started and 1,775 completed — again 96% — with the causes of failure equally divided between weather and mechanical factors. The best figures were for the direct Hawkinge or Lympne to Cologne service, with 267 of the 270 flights started being successfully completed — 99% — an excellent result even allowing for the fact that it operated only during the summer months. For this second period the Air Ministry produced a rather more informative breakdown, recording the days per month on which services were flown, which shows a regularity trend even though the percentage of mail actually delivered on time was still not given. From Hawkinge/Lympne, flights were made on 146 of the 182 days (excluding two public holidays in July) — 80.2% — and from Cologne on 139 days — 76.4%. While the intermediate stop was being made, flights from Maisoncelle or Marquise were made on 113 of the 142 days — 78%. Monthly figures show that weather was the prime cause of cancellations, the percentage of flying days out of Hawkinge/Lympne rising from only 67.7% in March to a peak of 90.1% in June, and out of Maisoncelle/Marquise from 71% in March to 86.7% in June. From Cologne the April figure was the worst at 53.3%, while the June peak was 96.7%.

The Army postal authorities calculated that, averaged over these six months, about 70% of the mail was delivered on time — though towards the end the figure was obviously far higher. By surface transport, mail and newspapers leaving London in the early morning reached Cologne late the following afternoon — or in more practical terms, the troops could not read Monday's English newspaper until Tuesday evening. The air mail accelerated the process by a full 24 hours, but although this happened for seven days out of ten, there were the inevitable grumbles when mail did not arrive, or letters turned up out of sequence because of earlier delays.

The total tonnage of mail carried is not known, and a guess would be misleading since individual aircraft loads on the 'C' Service varied from 36 to 522lb. No 120 Squadron alone carried 7,164 mailbags weighing about 90 tons, and No 18 Squadron lifted 2,051 between April and July. From March to August the personnel establishment of the squadrons on 'C' service totalled 64 pilots, 26 observers, 13 ground officers and 455 other ranks, though the actual turnover of pilots was 115, mainly because of demobilisation.

Since the large red areas of the old British Empire disappeared from world maps it has not been easy to visualise the tremendous enthusiasm for the development of imperial air routes which sprang up after World War I.

Continental air services performed a useful function, but clearly the aeroplane would show its real value over longer distances, where surface communications were primitive or non-existent. Although not exclusively transport operations, two Handley Page flights of 1918-19 may be regarded as the beginnings of RAF long-range route flying, and also qualify for mention since they carried some token mail and had a few route survey commitments. Between 28 July and 7 August 1918 Handley Page 0/400 number C9681 captained by Major A. S. C. MacLaren made the first England to Egypt flight. (This was the aircraft used in the final stages of Allenby's campaign and mentioned in Chapter 1.) The same aircraft, with Captain Ross Smith as captain, left Cairo on 29 November and reached Baghdad via Damascus the following evening, carrying Major General Geoffrey Salmond, C-in-C RAF Middle East, on a visit to units in Mesopotamia. On 4 December it went on to survey a projected Imperial air route to India, reaching Delhi on the 12th, and later flew to Calcutta. The Manston to Cairo section over a route mileage of 2,592 had been covered in 36 hours 13 minutes flying time — 72mph — and the 3,233 miles from Cairo to Calcutta in 47 hours 21 minutes — 68mph. During October MacLaren had flown a second 0/400 to Egypt, and was awarded the Air Force Cross for his pioneer long-distance flight.

Meanwhile the first through flight to India had started on 13 December by one of the four-engined Handley Page V/1500s — 'Super Handleys' — built to bomb Berlin but delivered just too late for operations. MacLaren, a brilliant navigator whose war service had been mostly in the Middle East, was chosen as captain. Co-pilot was Captain Robert Halley, a vastly experienced ex-RNAS 0/100 and 0/400 pilot who, after winning two DFCs for bombing operations in No 216 Squadron, had been posted to No 166 Squadron at Bircham Newton, where three V/1500s had arrived a few days before the Armistice.

Archie Stuart MacLaren and Jock Halley — he was from Perthshire — presented an almost music-hall contrast in appearance, one being just over 6ft tall and the other a modest 5ft 3½in. Early in the war Halley was twice rejected for service because of his shortness and soon became reconciled to the incongruity of his long association with Britian's biggest bombers. He flew with great precision and expertise elevated by two extra cushions in the pilot's seat. The crew was completed by two fitters — Flight Sergeant Albert Edward Smith and Sergeant William Crockett, and a rigger, Sergeant Thomas Brown. Brigadier-General Norman D. K. McEwen, newly appointed to command the RAF in India, was travelling as a passenger.

Both McEwen and MacLaren had been educated at Charterhouse, so V/1500 number J1936 was accordingly named HMA *Old Carthusian*. With a wing span of 126 feet and powered by four 375hp Rolls-Royce Eagle engines in tandem pairs, the V/1500 had a cruising speed of about 85mph. In theory it could attain 10,000ft in 21 minutes, a claim which raised cynical smiles from those who flew the type. It was extremely unstable, requiring to be flown all the time, and the complicated plumbing of the four engines provided ample scope for leaks and other faults. The prototype had first flown in May 1918 — and crashed in June — and it speaks volumes for the RAF spirit of the times that men would happily set off on a 5,560-mile journey in a virtually untried aircraft.

As things turned out this was one of the most remarkable RAF flights of all time. Fate played every shady trick in her hand, and the crew were continually fighting first the weather and then mechanical failures. On at least three occasions disaster seemed almost inevitable, but skilled handling aided by a few belated strokes of good luck retrieved the situation. The final stage produced more drama than a writer of old-style boys' magazine stories would have dared to use.

Aircraft modifications for the journey included provision of a small table and stool, a cupboard for maps and other items, a windscreen for the front gunner's cockpit and two additional 75-gallon petrol tanks. The planned departure date of 28 November was deferred because of technical snags and after a spell of bad weather a start was actually made on 7 December, but an engine failure caused by a broken reduction gear forced an early return. On one air test the flimsy cups broke away from the vanes of the wind-driven petrol pump. Both these faults were to recur at inconvenient moments.

When they finally took off from Martlesham Heath at 0942 the crew pointedly avoided mentioning that it was Friday the 13th — but this was not enough to ward off trouble on the very first leg. They crossed the coast between Dover and Folkestone and a few miles over France encountered a solid bank of cloud which blotted out all ground features. They had no W/T or other means of obtaining a position fix and at 1140 cautiously let down to break cloud at 400 feet over unrecognisable wooded countryside. Suddenly, the side of a hill flashed past about 100 feet off their starboard wing and another loomed ahead, so MacLaren immediately opened up to get out of this unfriendly area. As he began to climb through the 2,000ft cloud layer he experienced a classic case of disorientation. His senses told him that *Old Carthusian* was on an even keel laterally but the compass bubble was swinging round and round and the air speed indicator rapidly moved up to 140mph — so thinking that he must in fact be diving he pulled the control column right back, with no result. He then decided that the aircraft had perhaps entered a fast left-hand spiral which might rapidly develop into a spin, so shut down all engines and centralised the controls, with the result that it flattened out almost at once. He resumed the climb, realising that they had been within an ace of making 'mystery air disaster' headlines and decided to return to England and await better weather.

As they flew northwards a few breaks appeared, so MacLaren let down again and immediately spotted a good aerodrome, where he landed at 1250. This turned out to be Bergues, near Dunkirk, and next morning they pressed on to Le Bourget — a very important staging post for personal reasons. On returning from Egypt some weeks before, MacLaren had been obliged by British quarantine regulations to leave his beloved Maltese terrier 'Tiny' wit friends in Paris. This was in the days before any RAF rule and regulations about canine passengers, and MacLare claimed that with 170 flying hours 'Tiny' was the world' most air-travelled dog, and planned to take him on to India On meeting his master the terrier was so overcome that th only adequate way to express his rapture was to roll i some evil-smelling muck — whereupon McEwen decree that he could join the crew only after a thorough bath.

They left Paris on the 15th, and after further force landings for weather reasons at Beaune and Pisa, their pla to fly from Rome to Athens on the 19th had to be change after *Old Carthusian* could not be coaxed high enough t clear the Apennines safely. It was decided to follow th coast round the toe of Italy, and in trying to avoid th worst of the weather some stretches were flown at height of only 200 feet. Passing through the Straits of Messina th turbulence was such that both pilots were hanging on to th control wheel, and Tiny came up forward to see what wa going on. With daylight fast fading and fuel getting low i seemed prudent to land at Catania, in Sicily, bu unfortunately the aerodrome which looked so good fro the air proved to have soft boggy patches, and after th Handley Page had ploughed to a standstill at 1527, nearl nosing over in the process, its four great wheels relentlessl sank in to their axles. A day's work by a 100-stong team o Italian soldiers, spurred on by no less than a general, wa

KEEP CLEAR OF THE
PROPELLERS

required to dig the aircraft out, and it made a rather nerve-racking take-off for Malta on the 21st.

Free at last from European weather hazards *Old Carthusian* left Malta at 0255 on 22 December on the 1,150-mile leg to Cairo. The polo field at Marsa served as the aerodrome, and its 800-yard run with rising ground at the end was barely adequate for a safe take-off with full fuel load. For a few anxious seconds it seemed that they were not going to make it, then a ridge in the surface bounced *Old Carthusian* off just in time to clear a stone wall and she gradually clawed her way into a safe climb. Conditions over the Mediterranean were ideal, and after about three-and-a half hours the unmistakeable African desert smell indicated that the mainland was near. The coast was sighted at 0630 and 20 minutes later they crossed it a mere two miles south of their planned landfall at Benghazi, and began to think that fortune had decided to take their side. The, at 0925 ominous noises came from the rear starboard engine which ground to a stop. They knew from test flights at Martlesham that the V/1500 could comfortably maintain height on three engines, so decided to make for Alexandria, a plan which was abruptly abandoned at 1045 when the other starboard engine also failed. This called for an immediate forced landing which Halley successfully accomplished on flat scrub about 50 miles west of Mersa Matruh, a little south of the coast road. The time was 1055 and the 850 miles from Malta had been covered in exactly eight hours.

Inspection showed that the engine failures were due to broken reduction gears — and that two tyres had been punctured in the landing. They seemed to be miles from any visible human activity — then, within minutes three Arabs materialised apparently from nowhere in that

Left: Handley Page 0/400 No C9681 on arrival at Aboukir on 7 August 1918 after completing the first England-Egypt flight. Left to right: Maj A. S. C. McLaren (holding Tiny, claimed to be the world's most air-travelled dog of the time), Sgt Goldfinch, Air Mech Francis and Brig-Gen A. E. Borton (co-pilot). / *Guy Slater*

Above: Handley Page 0/400 (C9681) on arrival at Delhi on 12 December 1918 after making the first flight from Egypt. The aircraft was shortly afterwards written off having sustained severe damage in a storm. / *J. C. Moss*

uncanny way which became familiar to the troops in World War II. They showed more interest in bully beef tins and Halley's shoelaces than the aircraft, and encouraged by a golden sovereign each — McEwen had obtained 200 from the Treasury for just such contingencies — padded off to get assistance. The crew's lunch was washed down by the last bottles of champagne remaining from the crate presented by the Italian general at Catania. The Arabs were good as their word, delivering the message by 0830 next morning, and help arrived later that day. The Air Ministry blandly announced that the aircraft had 'arrived in Egypt', and on 29 December a fullscale RAF servicing party arrived from Aboukir with the necessary spares.

One feature of the V/1500 which did earn unqualified praise was its robust undercarriage, and at 1300 on 31 December *Old Carthusian* took off easily for Heliopolis where it was given a thorough inspection. The 3,085 miles from Martlesham had been covered in 35 hours 8 minutes flying time, at an average speed of 88mph.

Departure from Heliopolis was at 0330 on 8 January 1919 with the intention of reaching Ahwaz, Persia, in one hop. After passing over the Sea of Galilee they climbed to 5,000ft above an extensive cloud bank and saw nothing of the ground until 1005 when they let down to check their position. MacLaren's navigation had again proved faultless and they were on course east of Damascus, having flown directly over the city above cloud. About an hour later, soon after they had passed the ruins of Palmyra on their port side, two of the engines began to show signs of distress, shortly to be joined by the remaining two, until the revolution counters were 'doing a sort of clog dance', as MacLaren wrote in his diary. Halley and Smith furiously pumped fuel from the main tank while Crockett took out the tank filters one by one and found them choked with dirt and water. Cleaning these produced some improvement, but the carburettor filters could not be reached and at 1245 the port front engine stopped completely. This was not so much alarming as exasperating, since it put paid to their planned long non-stop flight, and having established their position by the Euphrates, headed for Abu Kemal where they landed at 1400.

All the filters were checked and cleaned of quantities of dirt and water, and at 1515 they took off for the 220-mile run to Baghdad. Progress was very slow because of headwinds and by 1730 it was getting dark, while a solid bank of black cloud illuminated by intermittent lightning blotted out the horizon to the east. It was nearly half an hour before they found a desert track near Khan Baghdadi which appeared suitable on which to land for the night, and Halley crawled forward to wake up McEwen, fast asleep in the front cockpit, and break the news that they were about to make yet another forced landing.

They camped by the aircraft and flew the 110 miles to Baghdad early next morning. During inspections it was found that some of the petrol pump wind vane cups had blown off and slightly damaged one of the rear propellers. Its leading edges were given a new layer of reinforcing tape, but on running up the engines for take-off next morning this stripped off and a 24-hour delay was agreed in order to make a more thorough repair. The scores of visitors who came to see the aircraft included the typical inquisitive little old lady. This particular one was intrigued by the pitot head. Quick as a flash Bill Crockett gave her the answer — 'That little spikey thing Ma'am? That's for when we feel hungry on a long flight. If we see any wild fowl we chases 'em and impales 'em on it'.

An SE5A and a Bristol Monoplane accompanied *Old Carthusian* for 45 minutes after take-off on the 11th, and the five hour flight to Ahwaz, during which headwinds reduced their ground speed to about 50mph, was enlivened by moments of drama. At 1140 MacLaren noticed that an aluminium stay piece on an engine bearer had become loose, which if it broke free and hit a propeller could mean serious trouble. He therefore decided to try and climb out and break if off. With Smith's help he unlaced a section of the fuselage fabric, but as he squeezed through the gap into the slipstream he was blown backwards against a strut and could make no progress. Meanwhile the madly flapping loose fabric was likely to tear off, and the whole project did not seem quite such a good idea after all, so he fought his way back inside. The stay held in place and was fixed at Ahwaz, where they noticed that once again some of the wind vane cups had blown off — and there were no more spares.

Between Ahwaz and Bushire they indulged in a glorious burst of low flying, racing across the desert at heights between 10 and 100 feet. Their excuse was that winds were more favourable low down, and in any case the whole area was one vast natural aerodrome. Occasional tribesmen gaped with astonishment as the 14-ton monster hurtled past, and one terrified man fell flat on his face in a stream where he was washing clothes. Head winds were again encountered on the Bushire-Bandar Abbas leg flown on 12 January and it took 6 hours 20 minutes to cover the 400 miles.

A month had now gone by since *Old Carthusian* had left England, and there was some debate as to whether they should spend 24 hours on giving the engines another thorough overhaul or press on next day with the final non-stop leg to Karachi. True, it would again be the 13th, but a Monday, not Friday, and since they had already suffered just about every misfortune in the book they decided to go.

For the first time in several days the weather forecast promised favourable winds, and they took off from Bandar Abbas at 0702 in high spirits and full of optimism. At 1125 they passed Charbar and as the day wore on, with the temperature climbing well into the 70s, even the roar of the four unsilenced Eagles could not entirely dispel feelings of drowsiness. The rear starboard engine was not entirely happy, running noticeably below its prescribed revolutions, but it was the rear port which at 1408 blasted everyone into instant wakefulness. A piston had seized, driving a cylinder adrift from the crankcase and causing damage beyond any hope of repair. With another engine already playing up there was nothing for it but to land.

They had been flying about three miles out to sea and turned inland to hit that inhospitable coast at probably the best spot for a hundred miles in either direction — at Ormara, a fishing village 170 miles west of Karachi. It was located on a rocky peninsula which sloped down to a long spit of sand, and *Old Carthusian* put down on an adjacent track. As the three big propellers whickered to a stop there was silence apart from the distant noise of the waves and the occasional tick from the cooling engines. The crew looked at each other, nobody daring to say the first word. At last one of them spoke, then wearily they climbed out and discussed the options open. McEwen felt that if the aircraft remained for any time exposed to that climate the wooden structure would soon warp beyond recovery, and it must therefore be dismantled and shipped out — unless spares could be obtained quickly.

McLaren, on the other hand, did not rule out the possibility of flying off on three engines. While they talked the local inhabitants sprang up like mushrooms, and among the first on the scene was a smiling, English-speaking official from the nearby Eastern Telegraph Company station — who was promptly given more urgent messages than he had handled for months. He proved a tower of strength in other ways, organising accommodation in the house used by visiting political officers, providing beds, carpets and a cook.

On the 14th McEwen was suffering from sunstroke, possibly the result of his dozing in the front cockpit, and MacLaren started stripping the aircraft of everything easily removable — some parts of the useless engine, floorboards and so on — and drained off all but the 220 gallons of

**Above: Handley Page V/1500 HMA *Old Carthusian* at Martlesham Heath before leaving for India.** / *MOD*

**Below:** *Old Carthusian* being serviced at Baghdad, **9-10 January 1919. The somewhat shapeless appearance of the port rear propeller is caused by the repair in progress.** / *via Philip J. R. Moyes*

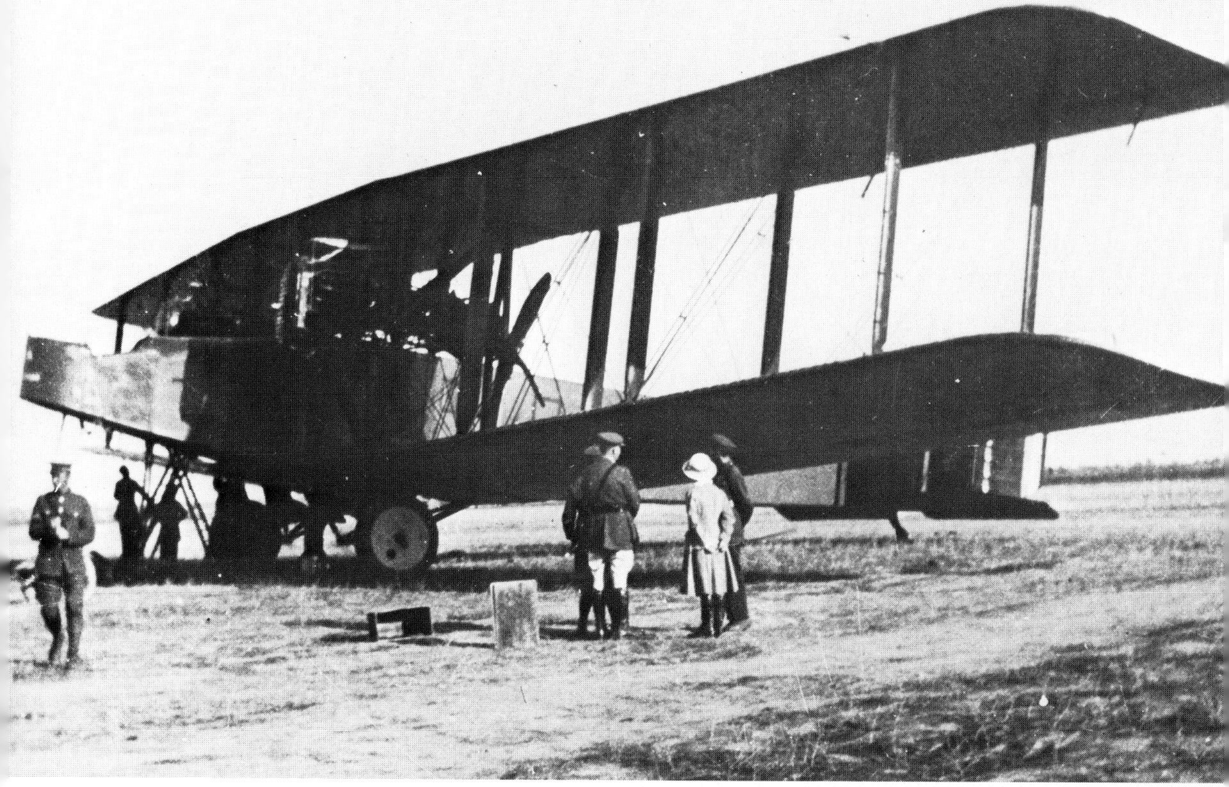

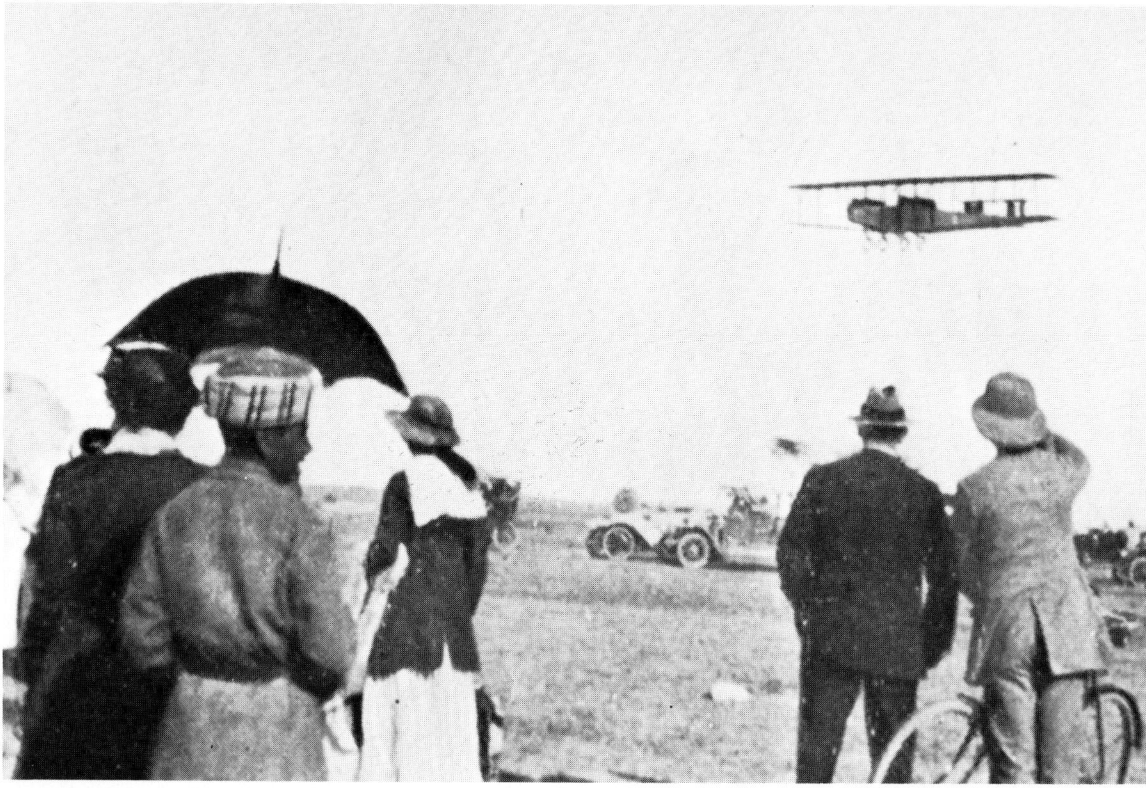

**Left: Another view of *Old Carthusian* during overhaul at Baghdad, 9-10 January 1919.** / *via Philip J. R. Moyes*

**Bottom left: Handley Page V/1500 HMA *Old Carthusian* at Delhi, January 1919.**

**Above: HMA *Old Carthusian* on show at Delhi, 23 January 1919.**

petrol required to get them to Karachi should they decide to take off. The two fitters gave the three good engines a thorough check and Halley reconnoitred the area to see whether it was possible to taxi through the sand dunes to the beach. During the afternoon answers to McEwen's cables started to arrive. Cairo said that spares could be at Karachi in perhaps three weeks, while the Air Ministry declared that engines and propellers previously shipped should already be there — if not they should await further instructions. Karachi signalled that help had been sent in the shape of HMS *Britomart*, which would arrive next morning.

The ageing 710-ton gunboat duly arrived at 0800 on the 15th, but since she could offer little more than a few comforts and moral support, decided to leave in the afternoon with the mail and heavy baggage. McEwen reluctantly decided to travel in her since he was not yet fully fit, had already overshot the date for taking up his new appointment, and felt that he could do more good sorting out the spares situation in Karachi.

MacLaren was quite determined that they should get airborne from Ormara. Although the flight had started in secrecy the details had soon leaked out and there was something humiliating in the thought of *Old Carthusian* immobilised for several weeks almost within hailing distance of their destination. Throughout the morning he and the fitters worked on the engines while Halley organised a shovel party to clear a taxiway to the beach and also removed a telegraph pole which presented a possible hazard. The rear port engine stubbornly refused to give full power, but late in the afternoon after the magnetos had been dismantled and cleaned it finally delivered the requisite 1,600rpm.

Although McEwen had been the ideal passenger, never interfering on flying or technical matters, his departure had

clearly removed a factor which could have inhibited the pilots in making their decision. Any doubts in MacLaren's mind vanished when for the first time in two days a brisk wind blew up which would greatly help a take-off. McEwen's last words had in effect been 'play it by ear' until the spares situation had clarified, and nobody had forbidden a take-off — though the pilots had no doubt whatever that there would be the most searching inquiry if anything went wrong. They decided to go.

To reduce weight only one of the NCOs could travel — he was in fact needed in the tail cockpit to give the correct trim for take-off — and Smith won the toss. While Halley dashed back to get their kit and pay the bills, MacLaren taxied his way between the dunes as fast as he dared to avoid getting stuck in the soft sand. The tide was right out leaving a two mile strip of firm, damp beach. There was a slope across its width, but the pair of sound engines was on the side to counteract any tendency to swing. Today, a three-engined ferry take-off by a four-engined aircraft from a concrete runway is a routine piece of operating procedure, and with the substantial power reserves of a modern jet transport presents no hazard. The crew of *Old Carthusian* were — as far as is known — doing it for the first time in aviation history, in a hot climate, from wet sand in an aircraft considered underpowered even by 1919 standards.

MacLaren opened up the three Eagles and at 1745 the aircraft slowly rolled away, gradually picked up speed and was airborne after a run of about a mile. Twenty minutes later they had reached 1,000 feet and were passing the *Britomart* on their starboard side. Her smoke was still a smudge on the horizon when their justifiable elation was rudely shattered as both starboard engines gave a few splutters and then stopped, leaving them to defy gravity by the sole efforts of the front port. The crew's immediate diagnosis was the right one — the wind-driven pump for transferring fuel from the main tank to the starboard gravity tank had finally shed all its miserable little vane cups and given up the struggle. Halley dived back to the engineer's station and strenuously attacked the emergency pump with both hands, wondering how he could attract Smith's attention. The engines picked up again and Halley hastened back to the cockpit. He had just managed to get through to Smith — 60 feet to the rear — by sign language when the engines again stopped, and again Halley rushed to the pumps. As the engines picked up for the second time, Smith came crawling down the fuselage and thereafter they took turns to man the pumps.

At 1845, just as the last light had faded, and with about 35 miles still to go the rear starboard engine began to lose revolutions, its temperature shot up and there was no alternative but to throttle it right down, then switch off completely. The seizure was due to a broken oil pipe, and nothing could be done in flight. Since they were providentially left with an engine on each side they retained reasonable control though it was impossible to maintain height. The next half hour seemed like an eternity. With both remaining engines at full throttle and their temperatures reading only 5°C below boiling point, MacLaren held the aircraft barely above the stall, and with the airspeed indicator showing 52mph she staggered along, losing about 10 feet of vital altitude with every minute that passed. They just scraped over the ridge of hills to the west of Karachi, but very soon they must hit the ground and there was no possibility of circling around looking for the city's temporary aerodrome.

By some happy chance the priority departure signal despatched by Brown from Ormara had not only arrived but was sent straight away by runner to the senior Royal Engineer officer who was playing hockey. He immediately appreciated the need for urgent action, grabbed some men and hastily improvised flares from petrol and rags, and for good measure fired off a few pyrotechnics as soon as the faint drone of engines was heard to the west. From the flight deck of *Old Carthusian* the crew peered at the myriad lights of Karachi still some miles away and wondered where they could safely put down. Then Halley gave a wild shout and pointed straight ahead. He had spotted one of the signals, and faintly twinkling on the ground almost dead in line with their heading was an obvious flare-path. They were now frighteningly low down and the straight in approach had to be exactly right, first time. It was precisely so and when the Handley Page rolled to a halt at 1915 the pilots climbed out, grabbed one another by the arms and literally danced for joy.

'Until that moment I thought that dancing for joy was just a figure of speech', recalls Halley, 'but we did it — though since we were such an oddly sized couple, the onlookers probably thought we were quite mad. They had seen us make a good and apparently normal landing, but knew nothing of our harrowing experiences'.

Present day jet passengers bothered by the effects of long distance travel on their circadian rhythm or body clock may care to reflect that this first England to India flight over a distance of 5,560 miles was accomplished in 72 hours 41 minutes, at an average speed of 77mph.

That night Halley underlined the impression that flyers were eccentric people by arriving for dinner with the Governor of Sind half an hour late and wearing a dinner suit nearly a foot too long in the sleeves and leg. He had fallen asleep in his bath from sheer fatigue — and was not the easiest fit when it came to borrowing clothes.

When McEwen arrived and heard the full story he promptly forestalled any criticism of the pilots by signalling Air Ministry, saying that he could not speak too highly of their enterprise, grit and determination for successfully completing the flight in the face of so many difficulties, particularly during the final 170 miles — over 50 of which there was no possibility of landing.

Despite only once being able to land at the aerodrome designated on their flight plan, the crew had nearly always managed to notify some authority of their whereabouts before anxiety was aroused. The aircraft was for a short time posted as missing after the forced landing in Egypt, since it had not been sighted after passing Sollum, and HQ Middle East was about to launch a major search when the message reporting its safety was received.

MacLaren was made an OBE and Halley awarded the Air Force Cross in recognition of their achievement and the NCOs the Air Force Medal for their no less important part. *Old Carthusian* was fitted with four new engines and flew to Delhi on 23 January. Meanwhile the third Afghan war had started and on 24 May Halley flew the aircraft to bomb Kabul. 'This raid was an important factor in producing a desire for peace at the headquarters of the Afghan government', said the official despatch on the campaign. Halley won a second bar to his DFC and became known as the only RAF officer who had stopped a war single-handed. According to the late C. G. Grey, the distinguished founder-editor of *The Aeroplane*, he also struck a notable blow for women's lib in Afghanistan, when one of his bombs breached the walls of the King's harem.

# Baghdad Air Mail

## 4

Most of the V/1500's troubles on the India flight were attributable to its untried state, and the older 0/400 had covered a generally similar route with no serious difficulties. Results were sufficiently encouraging for the RAF to consider spreading its wings over the Middle East and beyond. The Service felt a justifiable sense of achievement over its European mail and communications flying of 1918-19, but was fully aware that air routes further from home, where the time savings over surface transport would be dramatically greater, would require detailed organisation and a high state of crew training.

A firm Air Ministry proposal for weekly RAF services to carry 1,500lb of mail between Egypt and India, using two Handley Page 0/400 squadrons, and costing £100,000 for essential airfield works was evolved in May 1919. Salmond returned to India to discuss details, but the Air Staff argument that the route would permit rapid air reinforcement in the event of trouble, plus a valuable mail link, produced a predictably lukewarm response from the Treasury. Trenchard pressed the matter, and although Churchill obtained provisional Cabinet sanction in October, the scheme was shelved. Second thoughts were perhaps prompted by the unfortunate outcome of what should have been an impressive mobility demonstration in April-October. Of 51 Handley Page 0/400s from Nos 58, 214 and 216 Squadrons which left France for Egypt on redeployment, at least 15 were written off in accidents, others were damaged and eight crew members were killed.

India did briefly feature in the early history of RAF mail flying when DH10s of No 97 Squadron started a service between Karachi and Bombay on 24 January 1920. This was terminated on 9 March having proved uneconomic.

An RAF mail and passenger service over the Cairo to Baghdad section — where the surface route via Aden, Bombay, and Basrah took 18 to 28 days — was proposed in January 1920 by the very air-minded Civil Commissioner in Mesopotamia, Lt-Col A. T. (later Sir Arnold) Wilson. A year earlier he had reduced his travelling time to the Paris Peace Conference by departing from Baghdad on 25 February 1919 in an RAF DH4 to join his ship at Port Said. This he achieved — after three forced landings and three changes of aircraft — five days later. In May 1919 he was the passenger in the DH9A which made the first Baghdad to Cairo flight (with refuelling stops at Ramadi and Damascus) in a single day. The Air Ministry was attracted by Wilson's suggestion, and AVM Sir Geoffrey Salmond (the new rank titles of the RAF were introduced in August 1919) arranged weekly trial flights over a route of comparable distance between Heliopolis and Wadi Halfa to gain general hot climate scheduled flying experience. The scheme was abandoned in May for financial reasons.

On 12 March 1921 a high level conference assembled in Cairo to discuss the maintenance of law and order and general administrative problems in the former Turkish controlled territories mandated to Britain by the Peace Treaty. It was chaired by Churchill, who had become Colonial Secretary, and Trenchard was there to advise on air matters. The RAF already had squadrons in three of the territories — Mesopotamia (which became Iraq in September), Palestine and Transjordan — and maintained bases in Egypt. Trenchard claimed that the previous year's air operations in Somaliland had, for relatively little expense (later put at about £250,000) produced results which would have cost £6-7 millions to achieve by land forces, and urged adoption of the Air Ministry scheme for control by air, first put to the Government in 1919. The best training for the high mobility and rapid reinforcement capability essential to such a scheme, he said, would be the operation of a regular Cairo to Baghdad mail and transport service.

The conference agreed in principle to RAF control of Mesopotamia, though the takeover from the Army was deferred until October 1922, and immediately accepted Trenchard's air route proposal. Functions of the route were defined as, first, a direct means of supplying Mesopotamia with aircraft flown from Egypt instead of shipped via the Red Sea and Persian Gulf; second, to form the first stage of a Cairo-India-Australia air route; and third, a rapid communications link between Baghdad and Cairo — and on to the UK.

HQ RAF Middle East signalled Baghdad the go-ahead for the route on 12 March 1921, and planning started without delay. Previous flights had been via French-controlled Syria, but a regular RAF service must clearly fly over British-controlled territory. Route mileage between Cairo and Baghdad was approximately 860, of which the 540 from Amman onwards traversed desert country. This was not the golden, undulating sand of romantic fiction, but more an arid plateau lying at an average height of 2,000ft above sea level. The surface varied from a thin soil supporting the spiny camel thorn and other simple vegetation to a flinty gravel, and about halfway across there was a forbidding stretch of black volcanic rock. Then

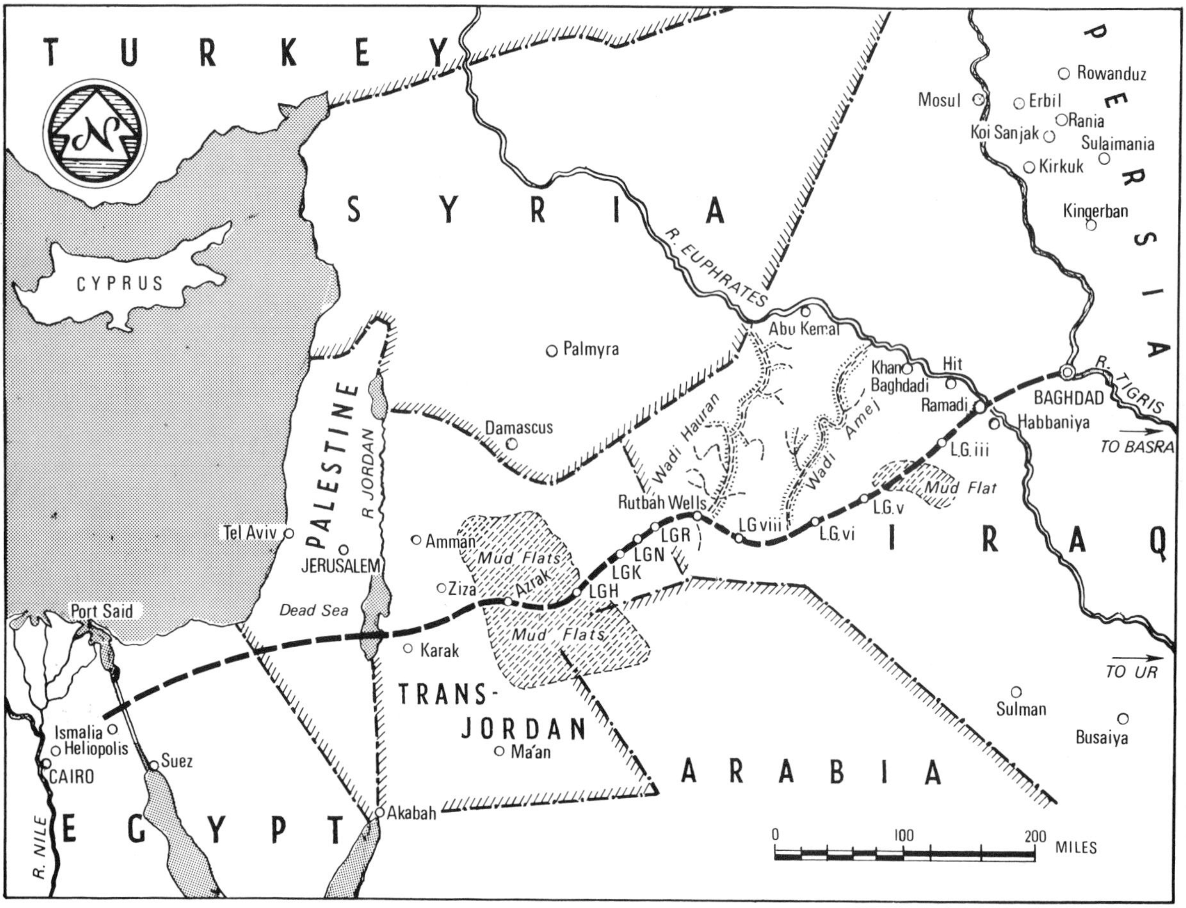

Map showing the region including TURKEY, SYRIA, IRAQ, PERSIA, PALESTINE, TRANS-JORDAN, ARABIA, and EGYPT, with the air route marked.

CYPRUS

TURKEY

SYRIA

PERSIA

Mosul ○ Rowanduz ○ Erbil ○ Rania Koi Sanjak ○ ○ Sulaimania Kirkuk ○ Kingerban ○

R. EUPHRATES

Palmyra ○

Abu Kemal

Khan Baghdadi ○ Hit ○ Ramadi ○ BAGHDAD R. TIGRIS

Damascus ○

Wadi Hauran

Wadi Amej

Habbaniya
TO BASRA

L.G. iii

Rutbah Wells

Mud Flat

L.G. v

Tel Aviv ○

JERUSALEM

Amman ○

Mud Flats

LGR
LG viii
L.G. vi

IRAQ

Azrak
LGN
LGK
LGH

Ziza ○

PALESTINE

R JORDAN

Dead Sea

Mud Flats

Port Said

Karak ○

TRANS-
JORDAN

Ma'an ○

ARABIA

TO UR

Sulman ○

Busaiya ○

Ismalia ○ Heliopolis ○ Suez ○ CAIRO

Akabah ○

R. NILE

EGYPT

0          100          200
MILES

ame 120 miles of plain which gradually rose to some
8,000 feet hills, and finally a 200-mile 'downhill' stretch to
Ramadi, a small market town on the Euphrates. At
intervals there were wadis, mud-flats and lakes varying in
appearance according to season, but generally showing
such similarities as to mislead all but the most experienced
pilots.

The RAF had gained sufficient experience of peacetime
flying to appreciate that regular schedules along this
apparently straightforward route presented a formidable
challenge. Navigation and radio aids were in a primitive
state, engines were still temperamental and forced landings
inevitable. Refuelling stops were necessary if any
worthwhile payload was to be carried. Thus essential
requirements included easily located intermediate landing
grounds and some means of ensuring that aircraft would
not stray from the route. On the western section conditions
were easier, the only stretch offering natural hazards being
that between Amman and the Dead Sea, where the rugged
3500 feet Judean hills fell away steeply to the water's
surface 1,286 feet below sea level.

It was decided that car convoys starting from Amman
and Baghdad should select and mark suitable landing
grounds at roughly 20-mile intervals, meeting at El Djid
about halfway across. The party from Amman was to letter
sites from A to R (omitting I and Q which could be
misread) and that from Baghdad to use Roman numerals I
to XI — but employing the Arabic 8 instead of VIII. As a
preliminary step, a small RAF group under Flight
Lieutenant R. C. Jenkins joined a railway survey expedition
led by Major A. L. Holt, RE, which left Ramadi on 6 April,
and the first supporting air sortie was flown by Flying
Officer W. Bentley of No 30 Squadron in DH9A number
H109 on that day.

The main surveys began in May, and the Amman
convoy of all-white personnel under Squadron Leader
W. L. Welsh was the more elaborate because it had to
conquer the gruelling volcanic stretch. It comprised six
Crossley tenders, three Rolls-Royce armoured cars — and
one motorcycle. Air support was provided by DH9As of
No 47 Squadron and Handley Page 0/400s and Vickers
Vimys of 70 Squadron. The Baghdad convoy of six
Model T Fords was again led by Holt, and the only other
white members were Flying Officer F. R. Wynne, Sergeant
Lowery and a political officer. To save weight the
Englishmen decided to live on the less elaborate rations
which catered for the six Indian drivers and four Arab
guides. No 30 Squadron again provided the air support.

In the event the two parties never did meet up as
planned, and the more flexible Baghdad convoy made two
journeys to El Djid before the Amman group had battled
its way through the lava belt, eventually reaching Baghdad
on 25 June. At one point the going was so bad that
abandonment of the expedition was seriously considered.

A suitable means of marking the landing ground was
found almost by accident. At first the corners and numbers
were white washed, then flattened and painted petrol tins
were pegged down as marker strips at selected points, but
both methods proved ineffective. When the AOC from
Baghdad first flew to visit El Djid his formation was
actually seen from the ground, but the pilots failed to locate
the aerodrome or the convoy and were obliged to try again
next day. The solution emerged in casual conversation,
when a pilot remarked that they very seldom spotted any
markings — only the Fords' wheel tracks from time to
time. From then on the LGs were marked simply by driving
the vehicles several times round the perimeter.

In July both convoys travelled in company back to
Amman, then the Baghdad party returned to its base and
the job was finished for the time being. Throughout the
operation the ground parties had been entirely supplied by
air, No 30 Squadron alone flying 645 hours, representing
nearly 50,000 miles. Some RAF historians suggest that
from the outset the route was marked by a furrow literally
ploughed across the desert. As planned, the Amman
convoy did in fact include a plough, though this was soon
discarded as not practical. The successful ploughing and
straightening of some sections in October 1922 followed a
proposal by Flying Officer J. J. Lloyd-Williams of No 70
Squadron, who conceived the idea while bathing one
afternoon. Noticing the effective work by a Fordson tractor
and Oliver plough on a riverside Government farm, he
suggested that similar equipment could perhaps mark the
desert route. Tests were highly successful, and Lloyd-
Williams was rewarded by command of the plough convoy
— which in fact he thoroughly enjoyed. It left Baghdad on
4 October and reached LG 'R' — 390 miles to the west —
on the 18th. Lloyd-Williams then inspected his brain-child
from the air, and likened it to 'a pencil mark drawn across
the desert from horizon to horizon'.

The Air Ministry regarded the route as having opened on
23 June 1921, when three 47 Squadron DH9As supporting
the eastbound convoy reached Baghdad to end the survey
phase. Other authorities consider 30 June more
appropriate, since this was when the first aircraft crossed
the entire route, three DH9As of 30 Squadron leaving
Baghdad at 0430 and two of them reaching Heliopolis,
Cairo, at 1945 hours the same day. On 9 July a 47
Squadron aircraft (with AVM Sir Geoffrey Salmond as
passenger) completed the Cairo-Baghdad trip in one day
for the first time. The first official air mail left Baghdad on
28 July arriving in London on 9 August, and the first
eastbound consignment left London on 4 August, arriving
in Baghdad on the 17th. The service was opened to the
public on 8 October at a surcharge of 1s per oz, later
reduced to 3d. Aircraft departed on Thursdays, fortnightly
in each direction, the schedules being arranged to connect
with sailings from Port Said.

Squadrons tasked for route flying — which was in
addition to normal operational commitments — were
Nos 30, 47 and 216, the last named having started ad hoc
passenger and mail flights at Kantara in 1919 and recently
moved to Heliopolis and converted from Handley Page
0/400s to DH10 (Amiens) aircraft. The DH10 bomber,
completed just too late for wartime service, was as different
from the HP 0/400 as chalk from cheese. Whereas the HP

**Above: DH10 of No 216 Squadron.** / *MOD*

**Above right: Vimys J7444 and J7454 of No 216 Squadron at Rutbah Wells — with Iraqi police officer in left foreground.** / *via Philip J. R. Moyes*

was sluggish and slow, the DH was highly manoeuvrable, quick on the controls and its two 400hp Liberty engines gave it a genuine 110mph cruising speed. The HP pilots found conversion training rather difficult, and numerous crashes did not improve squadron morale. According to some pilots the DH10 rudder was inadequate to correct a tendency to swing on take-off, and in addition the starboard engine was liable to stop suddenly just as the aircraft became airborne, demanding instant reaction from the pilot. It was some time before this trouble was traced to an obscure defect in the petrol system — but meanwhile a basically first class aircraft had acquired a bad reputation which probably helped to shorten its RAF service life. It carried two people in addition to the pilot and had ample fuselage stowage space for mail and luggage. It could reach Baghdad in about 10 hours' flying and make the return trip in an hour less, usually completing the journey in a single day.

The single-engined 'Ninacks' — also powered by the 400hp Liberty — carried only one passenger, and their normal 110mph cruising speed was slashed to 80-90mph by external loads festooned about the airframe. Up to a dozen four-gallon petrol tins were lashed to the bomb racks, luggage to the upper surface of the bottom wing and a spare wheel under the fuselage. The mail was stowed in the rear fuselage, behind the observer's seat. The number of aircraft making the trip at any time depended on the mail load and priority passenger bookings, but was never less than two, since regulations required that a wireless operator and a fitter should always travel. With kindly winds a 'Ninack' could fly Baghdad to Amman non-stop, but an intermediate landing for refuelling — laboriously funnelled from the tins — was usually required, and the night spent at Amman. Flying eastwards the prevailing winds often enabled the entire Cairo-Baghdad journey to be completed in a day.

Little has been recorded about the earliest scheduled flying over this historic route beyond a few figures, which show that in the first 12 months four-and-a-quarter tons of private and official mail were carried, said to represent some 175,000 letters. The first civil consignment from London was only 57 letters, though the figures had risen more than tenfold by Christmas 1921. From February to September 1922, 120 passenger were carried.

The route really entered its stride in 1922, when new aircraft were introduced. No 216 Squadron received the Vickers Vimy, another twin-engined bomber produced too late for the war and best known for the Alcock and Brown Atlantic crossing and the Smith brothers' flight to Australia in 1919. Although slower than the DH10, it carried a substantially bigger load. More important was its transport derivative, first built for the civil market in 1919 as the Vimy Commercial and later introduced by the RAF as the Vernon.

No 70 Squadron rearmed with Vernons towards the end of 1921 and moved to Baghdad in January 1922, followed by No 45 similarly equipped in April, after which the DH9A squadrons ceased regular route flying. The Vickers Vernon, great-great-great-grandfather of the VC10, was the first real RAF transport aircraft and most of the 55 constructed were flown by 45 and 70 squadrons. It was of Junoesque build, and its oval-section cabin accommodated up to 11 passengers in some austerity — indeed the early versions had metal gauze windows. Heavier than the Vimy, it was powered by two 375hp Rolls-Royce Eagles, which gave it an honest cruising speed of around 65-70mph although reference books may be more generous. Excellent engines though the Eagles were, they simply had not sufficient power for operating the Vernon to the best effect over the hot, turbulent desert stretches and the mountainous regions of Kurdistan. Even when carrying 500lb below the permitted maximum weight, the rate of

imb was less than 100 feet per minute. Another difficulty as that the Vernons shrank. There was no previous xperience of maintaining sizeable wooden aircraft in such ot and dry conditions, and it soon became necessary to nsert additional washers under nearly every bolt in the tructure. The main wing spars contracted by at least $\frac{1}{8}$in ausing control wires to slacken, and rectification required he cutting of no fewer than 88 holes in the wing fabric — nd then repatching at vast expenditure of man-hours. In ne respect the Vernon was ahead of its time — the cabin oor opened downwards and incorporated built in steps for assengers' convenience.

The year 1922 saw the careful planning begin to pay ividends, and the first examples of what became standard rocedure — the air supply of spares and servicing parties o stranded aircraft. On 14 February three Vimys flew to he aid of a DH9A at LG 'X' about 260 miles west of aghdad. One of them carried, slung under the bomb bay, replacement engine for the 'Ninack' probably the first me that an engine had been externally transported in this ashion. In August three Vernons performed the same ervice for a Vimy in a similar plight. The drag of spare ngines thus exposed to the airflow, and the weights arried, demanded that aircraft must frequently operate far eyond normal limits. A typical experience was that of light Lieutenant G. Martyn of 216 Squadron, on 0 August after delivering an engine to a Vernon marooned t LG 'P', 570 miles east of Heliopolis. He had left base vith two brand new Eagles just installed in his Vimy, but he amount of full throttle punishment he had been obliged o inflict in maintaining heights over the hills near Amman orced him down with one of them completely wrecked. So he signals started to crackle and the whole tedious process egan again, to supply a replacement engine for Martyn's Vimy.

One day a weary, sweaty pilot landed at Amman after a particularly tiresome trip and happened to enter the operations hut while the station commander was earnestly discussing some aerodynamical point about performance and wing areas. He glanced up, noticed the Vimy pilot and remarked, 'Ah, Jones — just the chap who can tell us! Had a good trip by the way? What is the loading of the Vimy?' Flattered by this high level interest, he answered from the heart — 'Just as much as they can bloodywell stuff inside the fuselage, sir, plus anything else which will hang outside'.

Events of the year included the squadrons' move at the end of May from Baghdad West to Hinaidi, about six miles out of town, east of the Tigris, where the original aerodrome had been expanded into a large cantonment. During September, relays of Vernons flew stocks of petrol to establish a dump at LG 'V', about 170 miles west of Baghdad, and thus eliminate the need for the mail aircraft to sacrifice payload by carrying their own fuel reserves.

An Air Ministry costing exercise in June-November 1922, covering 41 mail flights — 36 Vernon, 4 Vimy and one DH9A — provided some revealing figures. In 482 flying hours the aircraft carried 81 passengers and 7,407lb of mail, and even allowing a notional figure for fares, receipts were well below the £17,273 operating cost. There were 42 forced landings, and salvage operations required another 513 flying hours and 3,192 miles running by motor transport.

An important operational landmark was the engine refit programme for the Vernons. The 450hp Napier Lion had already proved successful in an ambulance version of the Vimy and was the obvious engine to improve the regular squadron aircraft. The Vernon's appearance suffered, the elegant octagonal radiator of the Eagle giving place to one of rectangular shape, and its noise increased sharply. The Eagle was a relatively quiet engine, but not so the Lion, which really roared its challenge across the desert, and is to this day commemorated in No 70 Squadron's official badge. From the ground a pair of Napier Lions produced a sound which once heard was never forgotten — and very difficult to describe. It was first noticed in the distance as an unsynchronised, musical hum, rising and falling, swelling almost imperceptibly as the aircraft made its snail-like approach. One pilot called it a low, sobbing rumble.

No 70 Squadron's Vernons were the first to be re-engined, and although at least two were converted by

September 1922, it was another year before the process was complete. The Lion Vernons soon showed themselves far better suited to the route, so No 70 flew the mail from the summer of 1923 until September 1924, when No 45 began to get the more powerful engines and took over until February 1926. During this period No 216 continued to operate every third schedule with its Vimys.

In the 1920s the RAF was very much the *corps d'elite* envisaged by Trenchard, and many of the mail pilots names have a familiar ring. Commanding Officer of No 45 in 1923-24 was Squadron Leader A. T. ('Bert') Harris, and his flight commanders were Flt Lts Robert Saundby and Ralph Cochrane. In World War II when Harris was C-in-C of Bomber Command, Saundby was his deputy and Cochrane one of his Group Commanders (and later, C-in-C of Transport Command). No 45's next CO was Wing Commander Roderic Hill, who, as C-in-C Air Defence of Great Britain in 1944, made the crucial decision which gave mastery over Hitler's V-1 flying bombs. Among his pilots were Flight Lieutenants Basil Embry and Alan ('Uncle') Lees, who were also to become commanders-in-chief. Hill's book, *The Baghdad Air Mail* gives a fascinating account of the route and the various problems it posed.

Despite what present day airmen would consider almost intolerable conditions and inedible food, morale on the Iraq transport squadrons was remarkably high. This was largely because the ground crews were visible members of the team — flying on operations when everyone, officers and airmen, had to muck in for engine or wheel changes and other eventualities requiring sheer hard work — and not just shadowy, oil-stained figures briefly glimpsed at the home base.

The aircraft themselves had personalities — and their own names, as befitting vehicles authorised to display His Majesty's mail pennant. Among them were *Valkyrie* (J7134), which during the tenure of Harris and Hill was the CO's aircraft, *Vagabond* (J7135), *Vesuvius* (J7137), *Morpheus* (J7138), *Aurora* (J7141), *Ancaeus*, *Argo*, *Assyrian*, *Claribel*, *Golden Gain*, *Pelican*, *Stormcock*, *Unity*, *Vaivode*, *Vampire* and *Venus*.

Vernons normally operated the route with a crew of four — pilot, second pilot, engine fitter and wireless operator. The mail weighed 200-350lb and the general servicing kit about 300lb of small spares, fabric, dope, washers, cable, wheel jack, foot pump and picketing gear — plus chewing gum for plugging leaks in the engine water cooling system. There was also a spare wheel, smoke candles to indicate wind direction for a forced landing, fabric strips to lay out ground signals and a telescopic aerial and hand generator for the wireless. Three days' emergency rations and 10-15 gallons of drinking water were carried. A highly important item was the pilot's 'desert box', containing cooking equipment, utensils and favourite food items to improve meals at unscheduled night stops or add savour to those taken in flight. Typically, Harris had battled with the Air Ministry for improvements to the inadequate and unimaginative route flying ration scale, but these were slow to materialise. When all essentials were stowed aboard there was seldom room for more than three passengers — who were each allowed 35lb luggage in summer, and 55lb

in winter, thanks to the higher operating weight.

With full fuel load the Vernon had nearly seven hour endurance, and route flying time varied from 9½ to 16 hours according to weather. Aircraft operated in pair and a typical 1925 pattern was for the westbound flight to leave Hinaidi on Thursday afternoon and night stop a Ramadi. This was to permit a full load take-off in the coo air of first light, giving a reasonable chance of reachin Ziza without refuelling. Ziza, about 20 miles south o Amman, although not the geographical halfway house, wa the logical operational one, but it could not be reached non stop from Baghdad. Aircraft usually night-stopped there though if they arrived well on schedule they might press o to Heliopolis. Originally, the mail aircraft staged at RA Amman, set among steep hills 2,700ft above sea level, an Ziza was marginally better for the Vernons being 300 lower down in a basin partly fringed by gentler slopes. O the return trip, aircraft left Heliopolis at first light, an completion of the journey in a single day often depended o the take-off conditions at Ziza.

Pilots always felt a sense of relief on clearing the blea volcanic area in north-east Transjordan, which had strange, almost haunted atmosphere. Not far from th track were traces of habitation by some early people whom wandering Arabs referred to as 'the ancients'. It wa not until the 1970s that excavations began to uncover large urban settlement showing evidence of grea engineering skill and dating back to around 3500BC.

Compared with the severe weather faced by squadron flying the Continental air mails in the winter of 1918-19 the desert route was altogether kinder, and a pilot meetin one of the sudden seasonal storms could usually land safel on a level stretch to await a clearance, with little mor trouble than punctures from camel thorn. But the hea produced its own hazards in the shape of violent vertical a currents — known to the pilots as 'dunts' — which coul toss the ponderous Vernon like a child's paper glider. A cruising heights of 3,000-4,000 feet these 'dunts' coul bounce an aircraft up and down as much as 1,000 feet i seconds and caused little more then discomfort. On ingenious individual devised a 'dunt indicator' from 2 gallon petrol cans connected to a pressure gauge whic showed the presence of rising air, enabling a skilled pilot t remain in an up current, and even find it again when los Currents were particularly prevalent in certain areas wher experienced pilots claimed that they could sometimes rid them to maintain height with minimum throttle settings.

Discomfort became danger nearer the groun particularly during take-off and initial climb, because eve with the extra 150hp conferred by the Lion engines, th Vernon was still underpowered for its demanding role. I particular, take-off from Ziza could be critical during th heat of the day, when summer temperatures migh

*Top right:* Eagle-engined Vernons of No 45 Squadron lined up at Hinaidi in 1925. Individual aircraft names are carried on the panels below the cockpits. / *MOD*

*Right:* An Eagle-Vernon of No 45 Squadron and a Vimy of No 216 at Heliopolis. / *MOD*

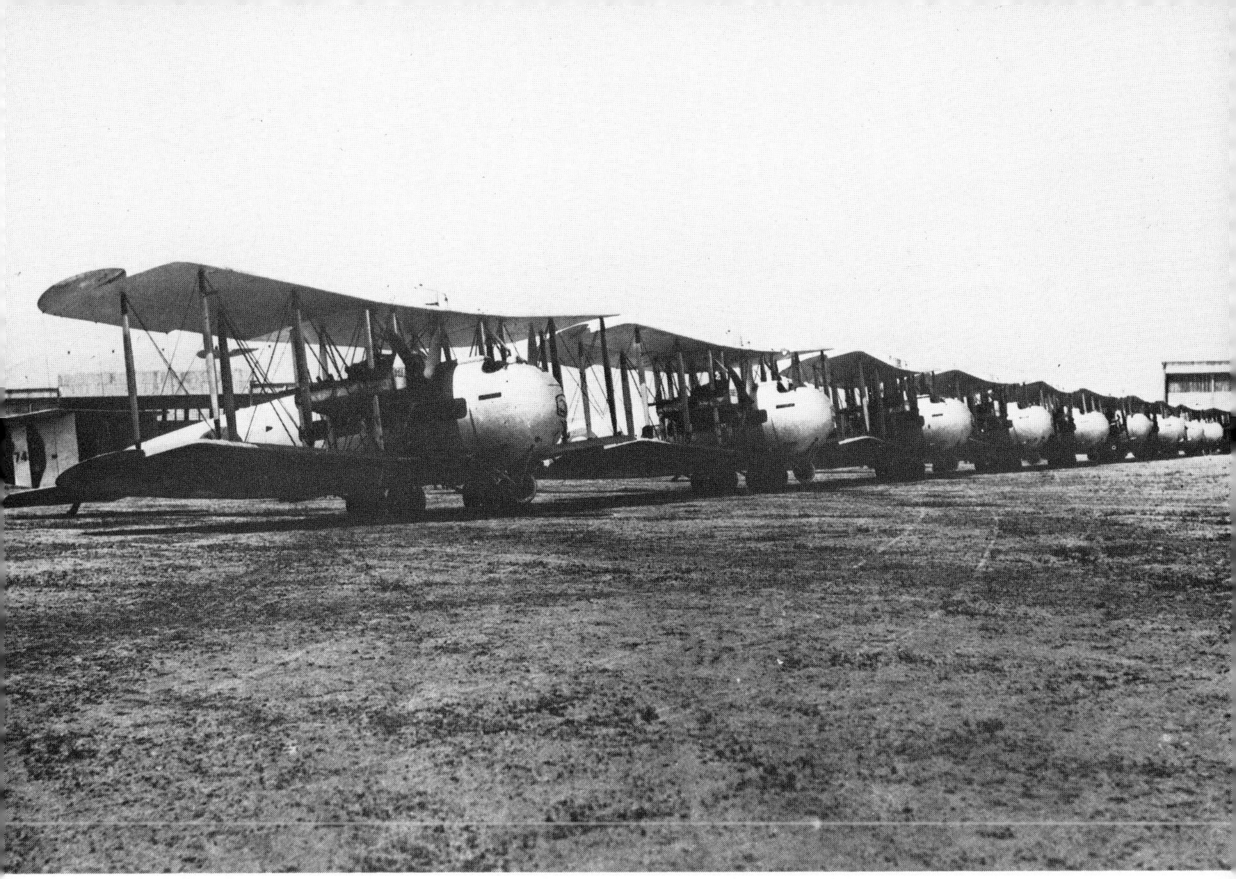

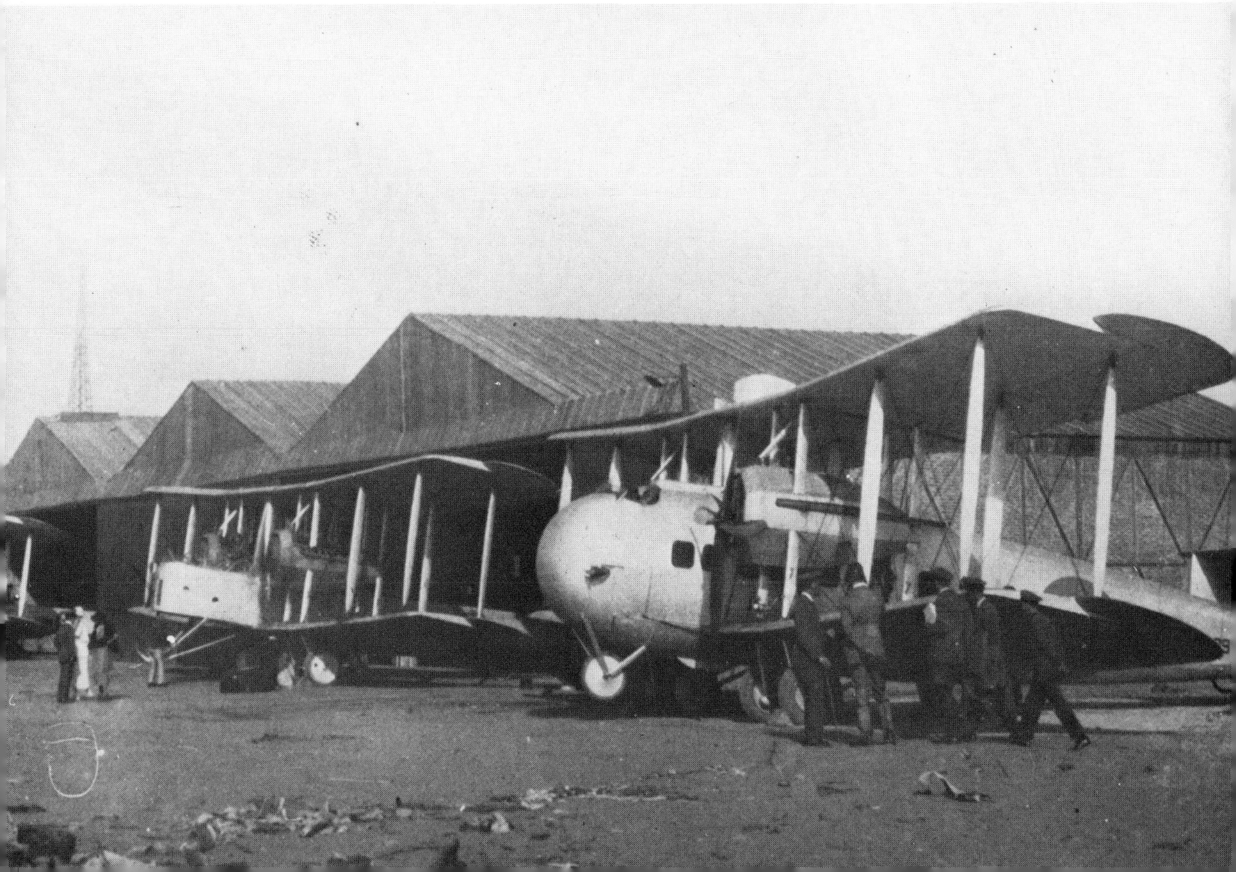

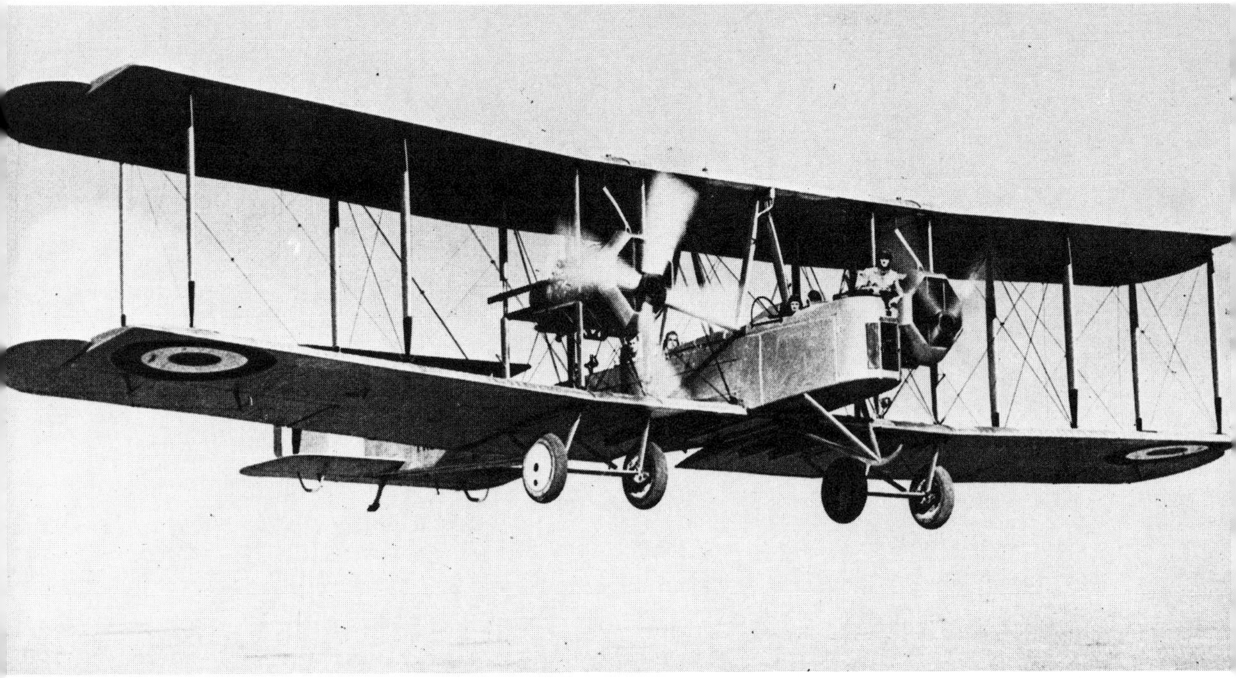

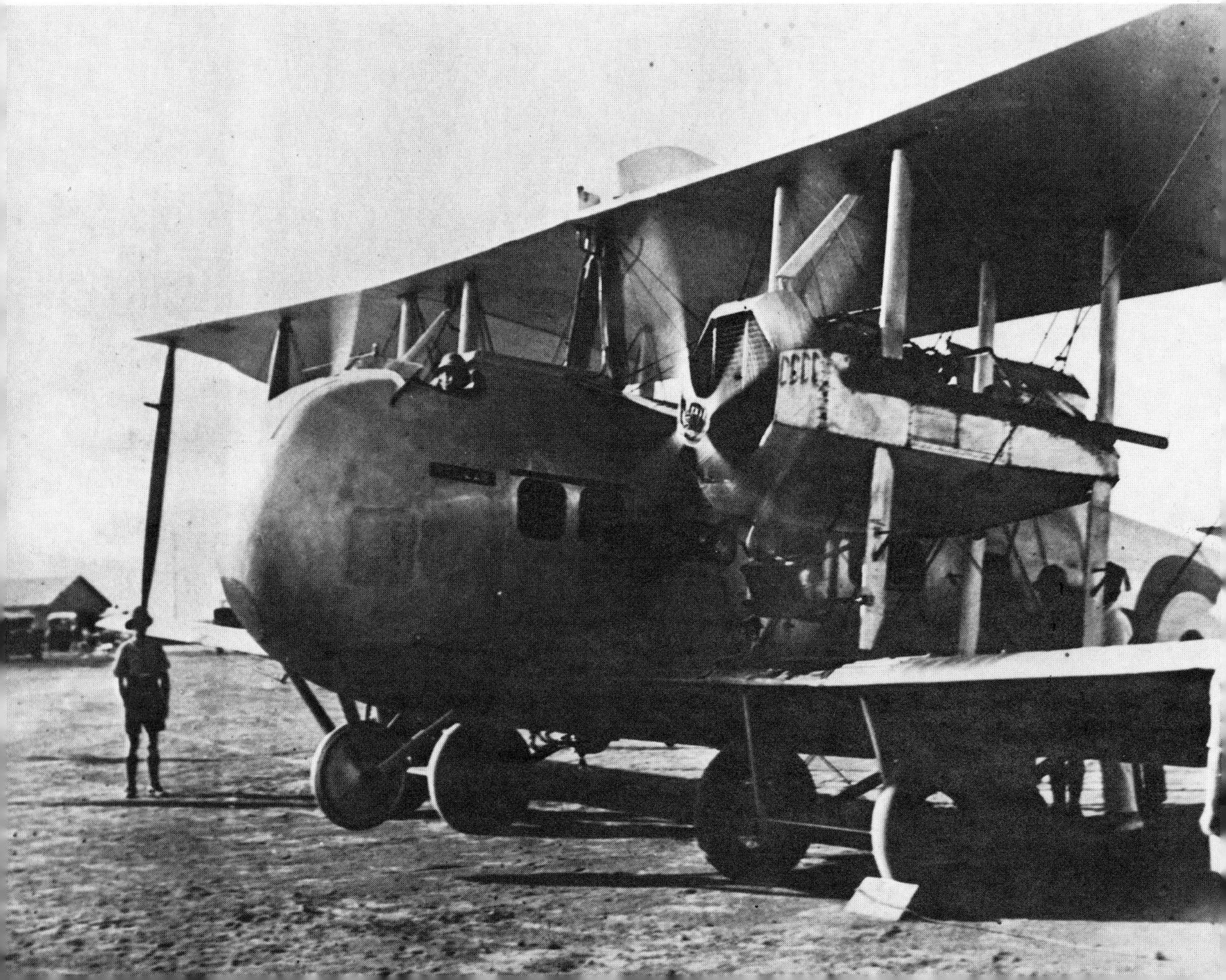

Left: A Vickers Vimy — probably of No 216 Squadron — flying over Middle East desert territory in the early 1920s. *MOD*

Bottom left: King Faisal of Iraq in the cockpit of No 45 Squadron Vernon, *Pelican* at Hinaidi in the early 1920s. *MOD*

Right: Lord Thomson, Secretary of State for Air (left) arrives at Hinaidi by Vernon in September 1924. With the S of S are AVM J. F. A. Higgins, AOC Iraq, and Sir Henry Dobbs, High Commissioner for Iraq. / *Public Record Office*

Below: Sir Samuel Hoare and Mr Leo Amery are passengers on board No 70 Squadron Vernon JR6904 photographed at Samawa in April 1925. The aircraft made an unscheduled night stop en route from Hinaidi to Basra because of dust storms at the destination airfield. The Red Cross indicates that this aircraft was one used for aeromedical work. *Chaz Bowyer*

approach 100°F. In July 1925, Hill, who had been a Farnborough test pilot for some years and was probably among the dozen most knowledgeable pilots in the Service, narrowly escaped disaster there. His co-pilot was Sqn Ldr Freddie Stent, of the HQ engineer staff, travelling the route to see at first-hand some of the operating problems. Hill was, as usual, flying *Valkyrie* and had left Heliopolis shortly after dawn. By the time he had refuelled at Ziza it was nearly midday, and after debating whether to wait for cooler air, he decided that the thermometer reading of around 90°F guaranteed textbook conditions to demonstrate the Vernon's shortcomings without risking life and limb.

Ziza aerodrome had a distinct gradient and Hill chose to take-off up the slope, into the slight wind. He ran up the engines by the disused railway station buildings, raising the usual dust storm, and causing *Valkyrie's* 5½ tons of wood, metal and fabric to quiver in anticipation of departure. He taxied to the far end, tested the flying controls, opened the throttles and the aircraft lumbered off, gradually reaching unstick speed and started to climb away normally. Hill described the agonising 15 minutes which followed as something quite outside his 9½ years' flying experience. When *Valkyrie* reached about 70 feet over the point where the ground began to drop away, she, too, sank like the proverbial lead balloon, embraced by an invisible down current against which the engines bellowing at full throttle were pitifully ineffective.

Hill was faced with the choice of carrying on in the hope that the aircraft would gain height before reaching the slope ahead, or attempting a turn while natural, rather than human, forces were still in control. He chose the latter, and *Valkyrie* drifted into a sickening flat turn, then plunged crabwise down wind, still sinking until the starboard wingtip was only 10 feet from the ground. Despite all his test-flying expertise it was only by using almost brute force on the controls that he managed to regain a more normal flying attitude, then a providential up-current bestowed a few score feet of altitude. After 12 more minutes of wallowing around the immediate neighbourhood of the aerodrome, at one point attaining 200 feet only to be slapped down again, *Valkyrie* was still barely 50 feet up and Hill decided to abandon the attempt. But even to land at this altitude and temperature with full load (there was no provision for fuel jettisoning in those days) meant touching down at a speed much faster than normal, with no throttling back for a thistledown three-pointer, and Hill managed to fly *Valkyrie* on to the ground at about 60mph.

In February he had fought a slightly different duel with the elements when flying westwards from Ziza. Strong winds had blown him some miles off course, and he was unable to climb above the winter clouds brushing the peaks of the Judean hills. By using full power he managed to coax *Valkyrie* through a narrow layer of clear visibility between the surface and the cloud base. For 10 minutes he battled against the wind, making minimal progress through an area of violent turbulence, one moment dropping to within a few hundred feet of the jagged ridges below and the next being thust upwards, lurching along where the highest peak occasionally disappeared in the racing cloud.

Above: Hinaidi aerodrome, 1924. The Vernons of Nos 45 and 70 Squadrons occupied the hangars at the top of the picture. *C. A. Sims*

Left: Vernon JR6904 of No 70 Squadron photographed after October 1925, when the Red Cross marking was discontinued. *MOD*

From 1923 the Nairn Motor Company's weekly trans-desert car service had enabled some surface mail to reach Baghdad as quickly as the fortnightly air mail, and despite the reduction of the surcharge to 3d, air mail loads were nearly halved in 1924. Answering suggestions that the RAF should use faster aircraft and accelerate the somewhat leisurely schedule, The Under Secretary of State for Air, Sir Philip Sassoon, said on 18 February 1925:

The primary object of the operation of the desert air route is not the carriage of mails but the affording of a training exercise to pilots and ground personnel of the RAF in long-distance flying under conditions similar to those of active service and the employment under the same conditions of various standard types of aircraft and engines. This object would not be attained if the operation of the route were restricted to a few highly specialised personnel or to any one particular type of machine. I would add, however, that the delays due to engine or other failures of aircraft flying over the route have decreased progressively since it was initiated'.

In August 1925 the RAF carried the surface mail for several weeks while the Nairn service was suspended because of tribal raiding in Syrian territory. Occasionally the mail aircraft went to the rescue of foolish motorists who broke the strict rules about travelling in convoy. On 5 October 1923 a Vernon spotted a stranded Ford and occupants near to LG 3, and on landing alongside found that they had just finished the last of their food and water, having been there for three days. Baghdad was signalled for a rescue aircraft which also picked up from LG 2 the missing driver, who had tried to walk to Ramadi.

The Vernon offered a more dignified form of air travel for important personages than the open-cockpit two-seaters, and on such occasions special seats were installed. The first recorded Vernon VIP flight was on 21 March 1922, when Sir Percy Cox, High Commissioner in Iraq, made an aerial inspection tour and visited Sheikh Fahad beg Ibn Hadhal, chief of the Amarat tribe, at his headquarters 30 miles north-west of Hit. In a report the following year Sir Percy commented; 'Without air transport the niceties of administration and military touch are impossible . . . perhaps the greatest achievement of air control in Iraq during the six months under review has been the introduction of this inestimable asset'.

The RAF 'control without occupation' experiment in Iraq attracted VIPs from England, and in September-October 1924 the Secretary of State for Air, Lord Thomson, made the Heliopolis-Baghdad return trip by Vernon. The following March the new S of S for Air, Sir Samuel Hoare, with his Colonial Office counterpart, Mr Leo Amery, made a 3,500-mile aerial tour of the Middle

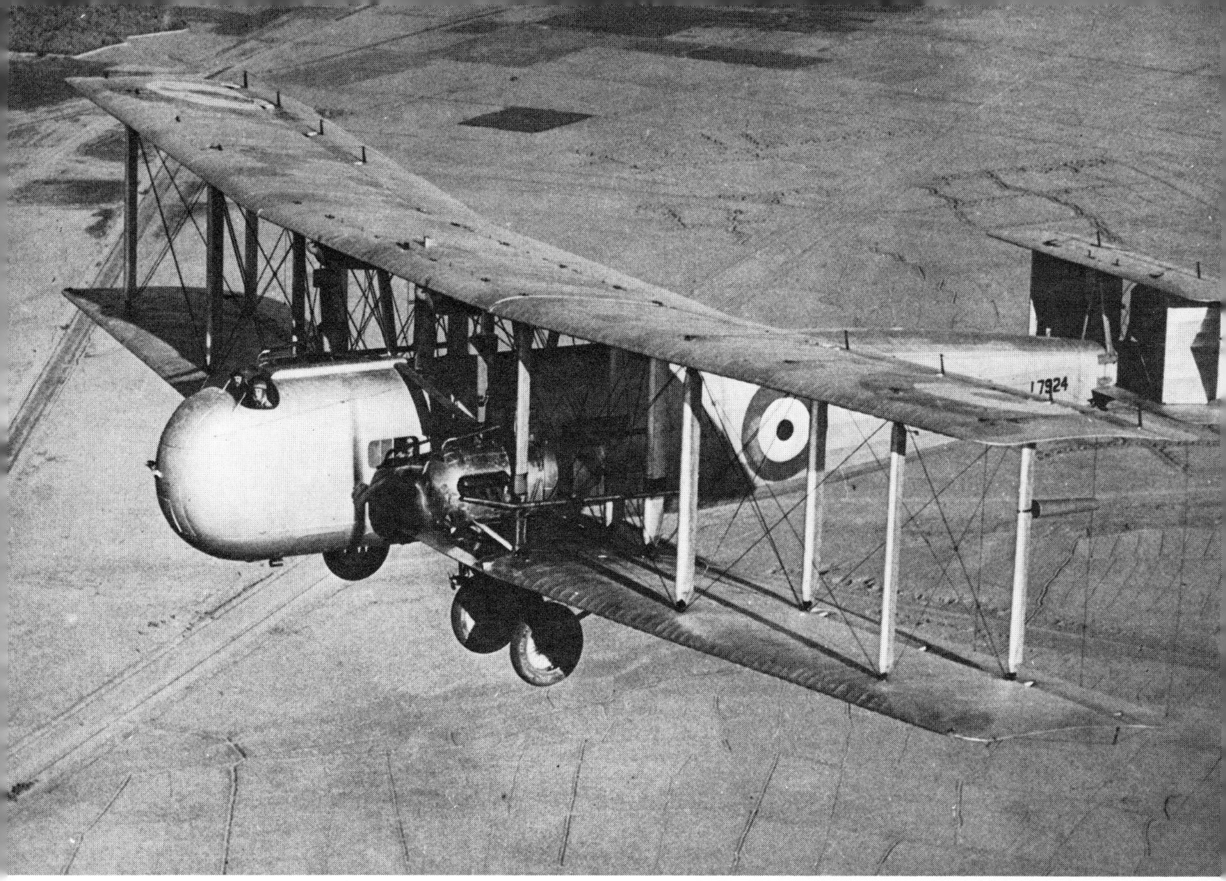
17924

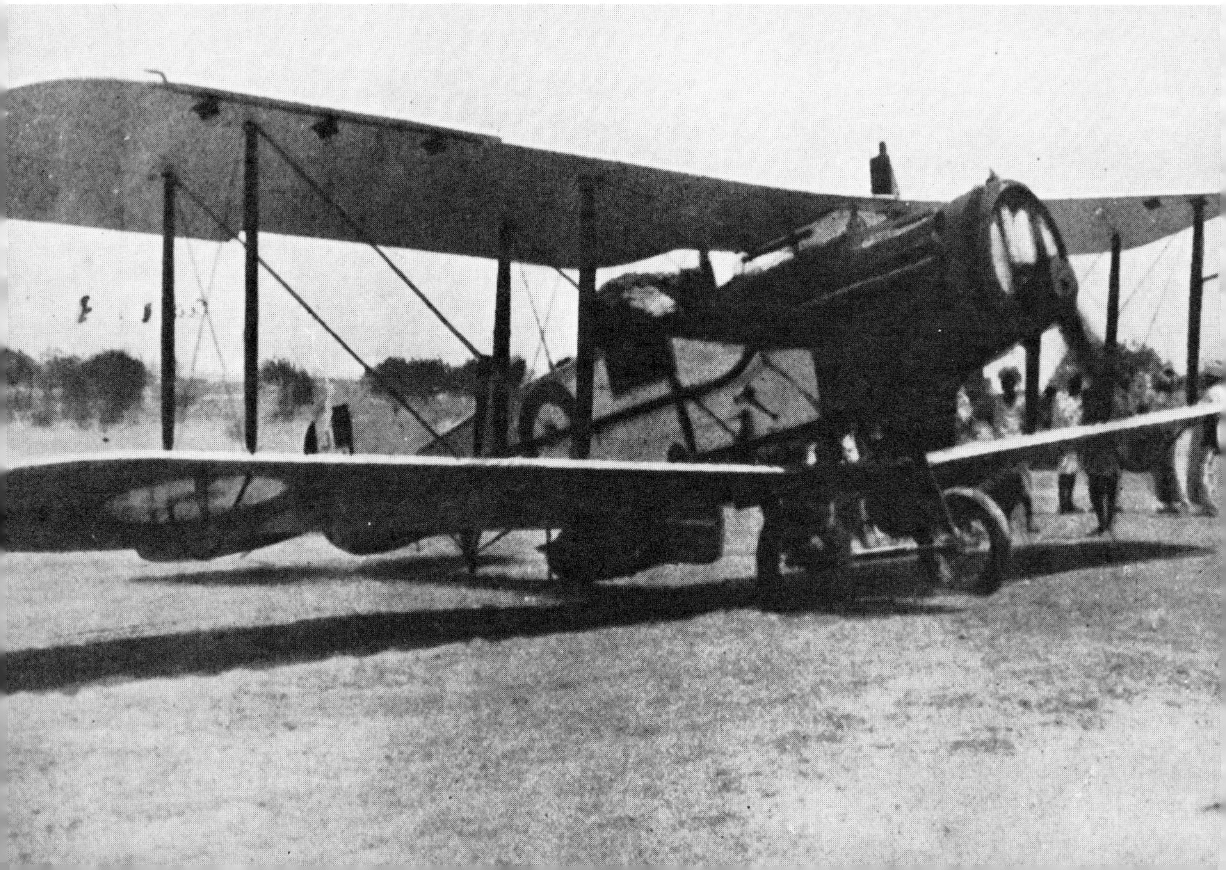

ast, and three Vernons carried the party over the mail
oute. In his book *A Flying Visit to the Middle East*
(Cambridge University Press) Hoare gave this description
of VIP flying, Vernon style:

'A journey of seven hours in a shut machine, even though
you sit in a comfortable chair and can normally read and
write without inconvenience, is a trying business. The noise
of the propellers in the air, the noise of the two great
engines on each side of you, and the monotonous outlook
of the wide distances and limitless desert, combine to make
you feel deaf and tired, when, without a moment for
recovery, you are expected to leap lightly from the machine
and say a few bright words to the guard of honour and the
local notables who have come to meet you at the
aerodrome'.

Another side to this visit — when the pilots grasped a
providential opportunity to air their grievance about the
poor rations — is described by Air Chief Marshal Sir Basil
Embry in his book *Mission Completed*. When Hill raised
with his pilots the matter of an appropriate VIP lunch to be
served in the air, 'Uncle' Lees acidly quoted the MP who,
returning home after a short stay with the High
Commissioner, had spoken of brown-kneed young
servicemen living in a land of luxury. 'Let the blighters eat
the luxuries we're supposed to thrive on', he argued. So,
when one of the private secretaries fluttered round before
take-off to check the lunch menu he was blandly shown a
cardboard box full of the official ration delicacies — bully
beef, hard biscuits and raw onions. He reeled away
speechless and anxiously boarded the Vernon in the wake
of his master. When lunch time arrived, suitable
sandwiches and cold drinks were magically produced —
but the point had been made.

The summer of 1926 saw the final change of aircraft on
the mail route before it was 'civilianised' to become part of
the Imperial Airways service to India, when Nos 70 and
216 Squadrons began to receive the Vickers Victoria.
Developed from the Virginia bomber, the prototype
Victoria had first flown in 1922 and went to Iraq for
operational trials two years later. The production version
could accommodate 20 passengers, and although at first
was powered only with similar 450hp Lion engines, its
more generous wing area enabled it to cope far more easily
than the Vernon with the trying Middle East conditions.

By September No 70 had received four of the new
aircraft and operated the mail route until the end of 1926
when Imperial Airways' DH Hercules took over. The
squadron's farewell gesture to scheduled route flying was to
provide two Victorias to accompany the Hercules which
left Baghdad on 1 January 1927 carrying the Air Minister
on the inaugural flight to India. A month earlier 45
Squadron had ceased operations prior to reforming in

another role, its Vernons being transferred to No 70 to
soldier on a little longer.

The following figures show the quantity of civil mail
carried by the RAF during the five complete years of the
Baghdad air mail service — though the totals for 1922 and
1925 are estimates since available Post Office Records for
those years are incomplete: 1922 — 8,150lb; 1923 —
18,900lb; 1924 — 10,000lb; 1925 — 10,150lb; 1926 —
10,982lb. To these should be added the official mail, which
appears to have averaged some 3,500lb per year, so,
allowing for the mail carried in 1921, the total for the entire
duration was about 35 tons.

The Vickers Vernon deserves a place in any top twenty
list of RAF aircraft where versatility and hard work
performed are the criteria for selection. It was ugly and
unglamorous, its performance was unexciting and
somehow its greatest achievements never hit the headlines,
but it was a forgiving aircraft and in crashes the occupants
were seldom badly hurt. As far as can be traced the only
Vernon disaster was on 26 July 1926, when a 45 Squadron
aircraft crashed into the stores hangar at Hinaidi causing
the deaths of six RAF men and one civilian.

The RAF maintained periodic training flights over the
route and No 70 Squadron twice went to the rescue of
Imperial Airways machines. In October 1930 a Victoria
picked up the passengers from a Hercules forced down with
engine trouble 100 miles west of Rutbah Wells, and in 1936
two Valentias performed a similar service for the Handley
Page 42, *Horsa*, stranded in the desert some 700 miles
south-east of the squadron's normal operating area. The
Valentias were despatched to Bahrain with Vincents of
No 84 Squadron to search for the four-engined air liner,
which was found by a Vincent on 29 August. The Valentias
flew out the exhausted passengers, most of the crew and the
mail that afternoon, and the remainder on the following
day. When they returned to base they had each devoted
more than 25 hours' flying time to the operations.

No 70 Squadron's final association with mail flying came
in 1938, when Imperial Airways was unable to cope
with unprecedented Christmas mail loads. Between
19 November and 27 December, Valentias made 17 flights
between Amman and Habbaniya carrying 25,500lb of
mail.

The Valentia, like its predecessors, was in frequent
demand as a VIP transport and in April-May 1939 was
used for a Royal flight, carrying Princess Alice and the Earl
of Athlone on the final stages of their journey to Teheran
for the wedding of the Crown Prince of Iran. Valentias of
No 70 Squadron picked up the Royal Party on 16 April at
Tel Katchek on the Syria-Iraq border and returned them on
9 May to Mosul, having completed 150 hours flying in Iraq
and Iran on the entire commitment.

The inter-war years produced one other short spell of
mail-carrying by the RAF, in a different theatre. In August
1930 severe flooding of the Indus river cut the railway line
between Jacobabad and Sukkur, and for several weeks
Bristol Fighters of No 31 Squadron flew the mail over this
stretch. With no observer or guns carried, the long suffering
Bristols were able to lift up to 590lb of mail — 150lb in
each of two containers fixed to the bomb racks — and the
remainder in the rear cockpit.

# Kirkuk and Kingerban

## 5

The ending of World War I brought no immediate peace to the Middle East, and British Forces were for many years to be embroiled in a host of minor operations designed to contain dissident elements, to show where necessary that crime did not pay and generally to maintain law and order. The presence of air squadrons transformed the entire planning and conduct of these operations, and from the outset the Air Staff appreciated that air transport would have an important role — and a vital one in the scheme for air control in Iraq. Between the wars all the large transport squadrons were deployed in the Middle East, which became the proving ground for virtually every type of military air transport activity and also set the pattern for the essential co-operation between ground and air forces.

During the 1920's and 1930s different classes of aircraft could not be justified — nor were they strictly necessary — for what later became recognised as specialised strategic and tactical transport tasks. Thus the Vernon doubled up as the contemporary equivalent of the VC10 for long range strategic route flying and the Hercules for tactical air lift and supply work. In an emergency the single-engined Bristol Fighters and DH9As of the army co-operation and bomber squadrons were detailed for light transport duties and tasks which today might call for a helicopter. Conversely — at the instigation of Harris — the Vernon was adapted with a prone bombing position to drop ten 112-pounders, nearly three times the load of a DH9A. Successors to the Vernon were better equipped for this dual bomber-transport role, but their strike operations lie outside the scope of this book.

Inevitably, the RAF was criticised during this period, and since little news of its activities was publicly released, its friends had sparse ammunition with which to reply. Some elements were bitterly opposed to spending any of the British taxpayers' money on a presence in Iraq and others protested against the 'brutality' of RAF bombing — ignoring the immense trouble taken to minimise casualties. In 1924 on completion of his tour in command of British Forces in Iraq AVM Sir John Salmond defined the British policy thus: 'Air control achieves its result not by its severity but by its certainty and swiftness and its deterrent effect'. There were also those few traditionalists in the older Services, reluctant to admit the need for the RAF at all, who damned with faint praise its achievements, particularly in the air supply and transport field.

The first postwar air transport operations in the Middle East were probably those of X, Y and Z Squadrons, hastily formed in Egypt from Training Brigade resources during the Nationalist rising of March 1919. Aircraft flew mail between Cairo, Alexandria, Port Said and Suez, and dropped food and ammunition to isolated British units threatened by armed rioters.

A rather different exercise was the first heavy tactical air lift demonstration staged for the Army on 21 September 1920 by No 70 Squadron at Heliopolis, which involved the loading and carriage in two Handley Page 0/400s of a 1,176lb mountain gun, with 98 rounds and a team of six gunners. The aircraft flew to Almaza where the gun was unloaded, reassembled and fired its first round seven minutes after doors-open time.

Most of the action took place in Iraq, and for more than 10 years it largely centred around the activities of the colourful Kurdish leader, Sheikh Mahmoud — to such an extent that he became known to the squadrons as 'Director of Air Force Training'. He had fought — unsuccessfully — against the British as far back as 1915, and the Turkish administration later appointed him Governor of Sulaimaniya. After the war Britain made him Governor of Southern Kurdistan, but in May 1919 he was deposed and interned after leading an unsuccessful rising against the administration. Meanwhile Turkey was fomenting trouble, notably in the Mosul area to which she laid claim, there were tribal disputes in other regions and from 1920 onwards British Forces were dealing with acts of rebellion in many parts of the country.

On 9 and 11 July 1920 six Bristol Fighters of No 6 Squadron dropped 350lb of food and nine boxes of ammunition to the besieged British garrison at Rumaitha on the Euphrates south of Baghdad, and later staged a diversionary attack so that the troops could make a temporary break out and forage for themselves. On 12 August a No 6 Squadron Bristol made two sorties to pick up the Political Officer and an Army officer from Qila Sikar, where serious trouble was threatening. There was a tragedy on 22 September, when an 84 Squadron DH9A was shot down near Khidr by snipers' fire while dropping food to an isolated river gunboat, and its crew of two murdered by tribesmen.

Major transport operations did not start until 1922 when one of Mahmoud's followeres, Kerim Fattah Beg — 'KFB' to the RAF — started trouble. The murder of two British officers in June by fanatics of his Hamawand tribe held the prospect of triggering off a wider uprising, and happened to coincide with infiltrations by Turkish groups

**Below: Lion-Vernon at Hinaidi. Experience proved that the engine cowlings made a negligible improvement in performance and aircraft usually flew without them.** / *Chaz Bowyer*

**Bottom: Vernons of No 70 Squadron at Mosul — proving that the entire surface of Iraq was not covered by desert.** / *W. H. Cox*

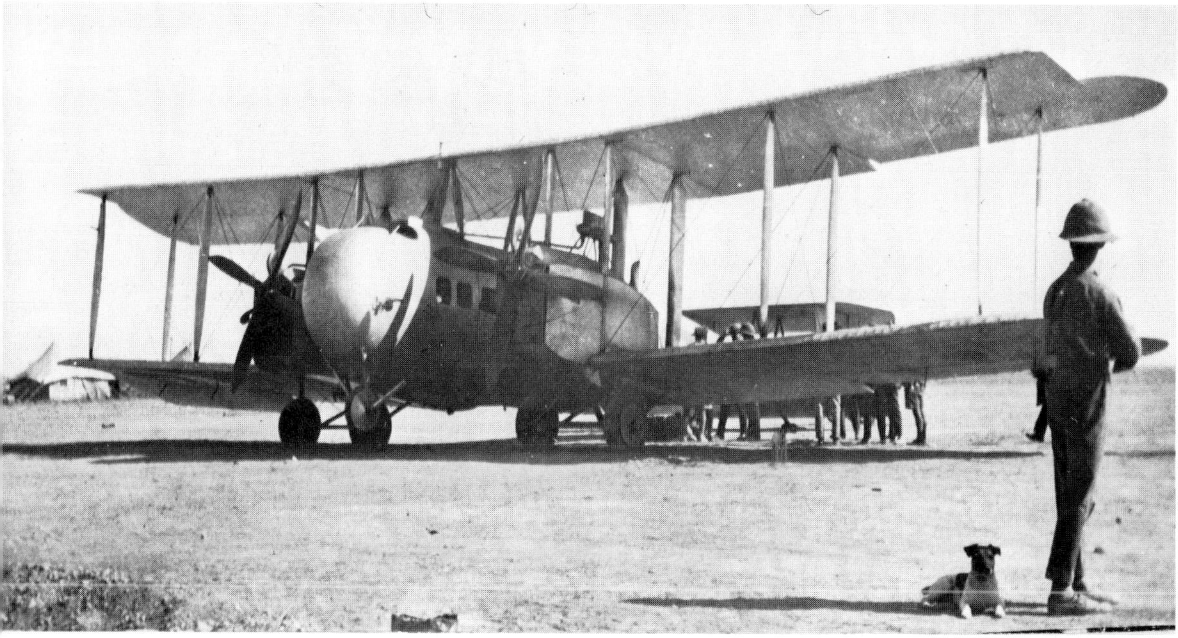

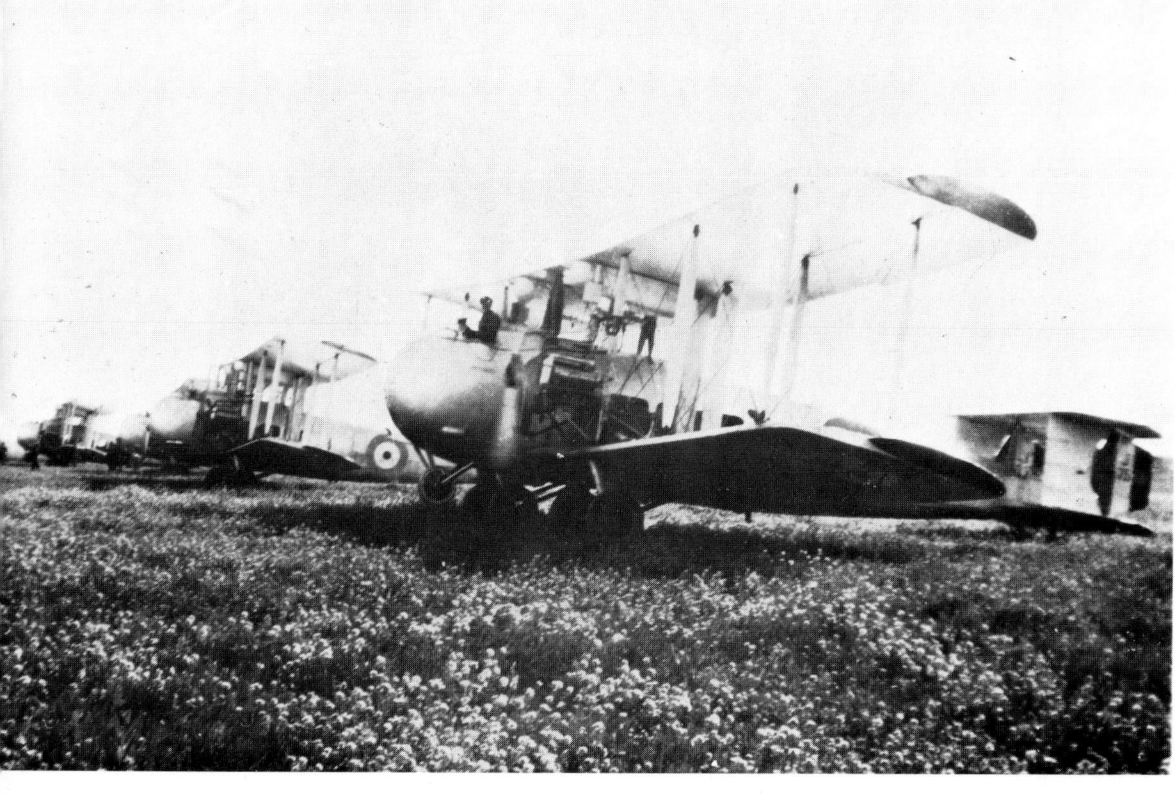

into Kurdistan. Operations were planned to deal with both nuisances — to seek out Kerim Fattah Beg and to thwart any Turkish-inspired moves.

A reinforcing detachment of DH9As from No 30 Squadron was sent to Kirkuk and on 19 and 23 June, Vernons flew in ground W/T equipment and wireless operators. During the following weeks considerable quantities of spares and supplies were also delivered by air. But the column of British troops and levies advancing to deal with the rebel groups encountered many difficulties, forcing it to withdraw, and towards the end of August, Sulaimaniya was threatened.

All British subjects and pro-British officials who wished to leave the town were given the opportunity to do so in the first ever RAF evacuation air lift, mounted on 5 September 1922. Surrounded by steep hills and gorges and lying under mountains frequently capped with snow, Sulaimaniya had only a small sloping aerodrome with its approaches obstructed in most directions. A force of 29 aircraft was assigned to the lift — 24 DH9As, two Vickers Vernons and the three Bristol Fighters of No 6 Squadron already on the aerodrome. It had hitherto been considered unsuitable for Vernons, but these were the first two Lion-engined versions, with extra power to provide an acceptable safety margin.

The lift was spread over six hours to avoid aerodrome congestion and minimise any impression of abnormal activity which might spark dormant anti-British elements into some response. Passengers were instructed to arrive by dawn, given breakfast at the aerodrome and those awaiting

their turn to fly kept occupied by helping with the luggage and other turn-round chores. The DH9As were capable of taking two adults squeezed into the observer's cockpit, but the pilot of the first away at 0635 later claimed a type record of five passengers. These were a Persian official, his wife and their two babies — plus the unborn child carried by the heavily pregnant wife. The manifest for a Vernon taking off at 0820 recorded '12 Assyrian levies and a dog'. In addition to the evacuees a considerable quantity of valuable and portable equipment was flown out.

As the morning wore on strong winds blew up, gusting with sufficient force to wrench the windsock from its pole and calling for extreme care in flying and taxying. Aircraft touching down heavily on the short, rough surface were plagued with punctures — a dozen wheel changes were required — and altogether it was a strenuous day for Squadron Leader E. R. Manning, CO of No 6 Squadron and Flying Officer F. R. Wynne, of No 30, not long back from his route-marking expedition, who were in charge of aerodrome activities. Fortunately, there was no trouble in the town, and the fruit sellers could be seen happily trading with levies manning a few discreetly positioned defensive sites. At 1235 the last aircraft departed for Kirkuk carrying

**Below: Vernon J7541 of No 70 Squadron over Baghdad. Note wing patches where the fabric has been cut for servicing.**

**Right: The prototype Victoria which took part in the 1924 troop lift to Kirkuk.** / C. A. Sims

the 67th passenger and the dust began to settle. Then Manning and Wynne left, the latter carrying Major H. A. Goldsmith, the Political Officer, and this pioneer, almost forgotten, air lift was over.

'KFB' faded into the background (he died of wounds received during a tribal skirmish in June 1926) and in a perhaps forlorn attempt to restore the overall situation in Kurdistan, Mahmoud was reinstated on his promise of good behaviour. By early 1923, however, he had reverted to his old game of plotting with the Turks, and British intelligence received reliable reports of plans to attack Kirkuk, Arbil and Koi Sanjak as a prelude to general insurrection.

An immediate British countermeasure was the mounting of the first RAF troop airlift. The initial threat was to Kirkuk, which maintained only a small garrison of Assyrian levies, a few armoured cars and the Bristol Fighters of No 6 Squadron — clearly insufficient to deal with the considerable rebel forces reported to be approaching the town. Reinforcement by surface means, involving a 12-hour railway journey from Baghdad to Kingerban followed by a four-day march to Kirkuk, was ruled out as heavy rains had made the track virtually impassable. Two companies of the 14th Sikhs therefore went by train to Kingerban, where 10 Vernons — five each from Nos 45 and 70 Squadrons — were assembled to start the onward lift at 0830 on 21 February 1923. Force Commander was Squadron Leader F. P. Don, CO of No 70, who had returned to flying despite the loss of an arm when shot down over the Western Front in 1917 by the German ace, Werner Voss. The ebullient Harris was there with the 45 Squadron contingent of Eagle-Vernons, though his own flying was curtailed after his aircraft had been damaged on the ground by a wildly, cavorting DH9A which landed down-wind in error. Legend has it that Harris immediately placed the offending Ninack pilot under open

arrest — in which state he remained for the rest of his RAF career since Harris forgot to either formally charge or release him.

With the ponderous dignity of outsize bumblebees the Vernons droned busily back and forth, making 28 round trips of 140 miles, finishing the job on the 23rd. They had covered a total distance of 3,920 miles, carrying two British officers, 320 Indian other ranks and 11 specialist support personnel, plus 30,000 rounds of small arms ammunition — a total weight of 76,260lb. This timely air lift produced an effect out of all proportion to its modest size. Rebels who had infiltrated into some areas of the town and were seeking easy pickings in the bazaar fled at the sight of the turbanned Sikhs, and RAF prestige soared as local gossip greatly magnified the operation, spreading the story that the reinforcements had flown all the way from India or England.

Mahmoud had ignored both a summons to Baghdad and a follow up ultimatum, so his headquarters at Sulaimaniya were bombed, causing him to retreat to the hills to conduct a guerilla campaign. With the object of achieving some final settlement of the Mahmoud problem and clearing Turkish troops from the country, mounted and infantry columns comprising nearly 6,000 British and Indian troops, and levies, left Mosul between 18 and 29 March, reaching Koi Sanjak and Arbil on 4 and 5 April, and then pressed on to Rowanduz, a town of great strategic importance commanding the road links with Turkey and Persia. They met sporadic opposition from forces estimated as 700 tribesmen and 340 Turks and frequent sniping from the hills, but by the end of April all Turkish elements had retreated across the Persian border — though the Mahmoud situation was still unresolved.

To avoid risking any repetition of the previous year's failure the columns had far stronger air support, and between 18 and 27 April there were 257 aircraft

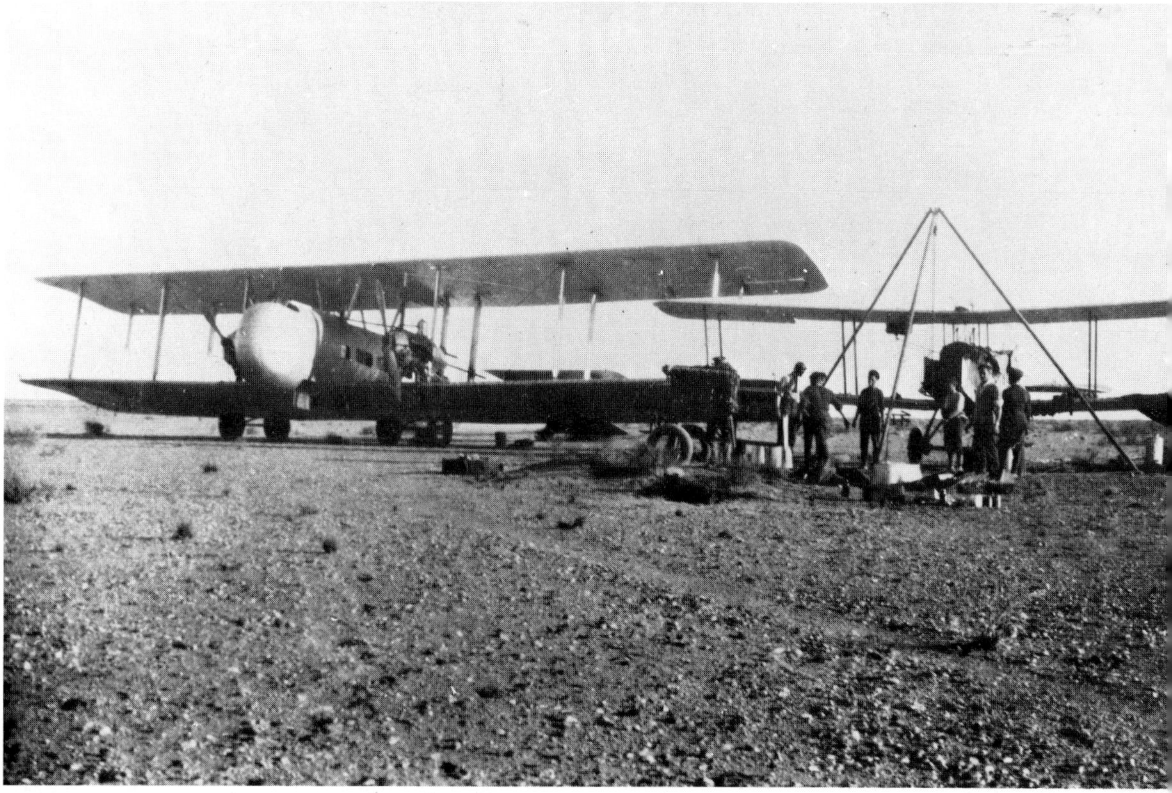

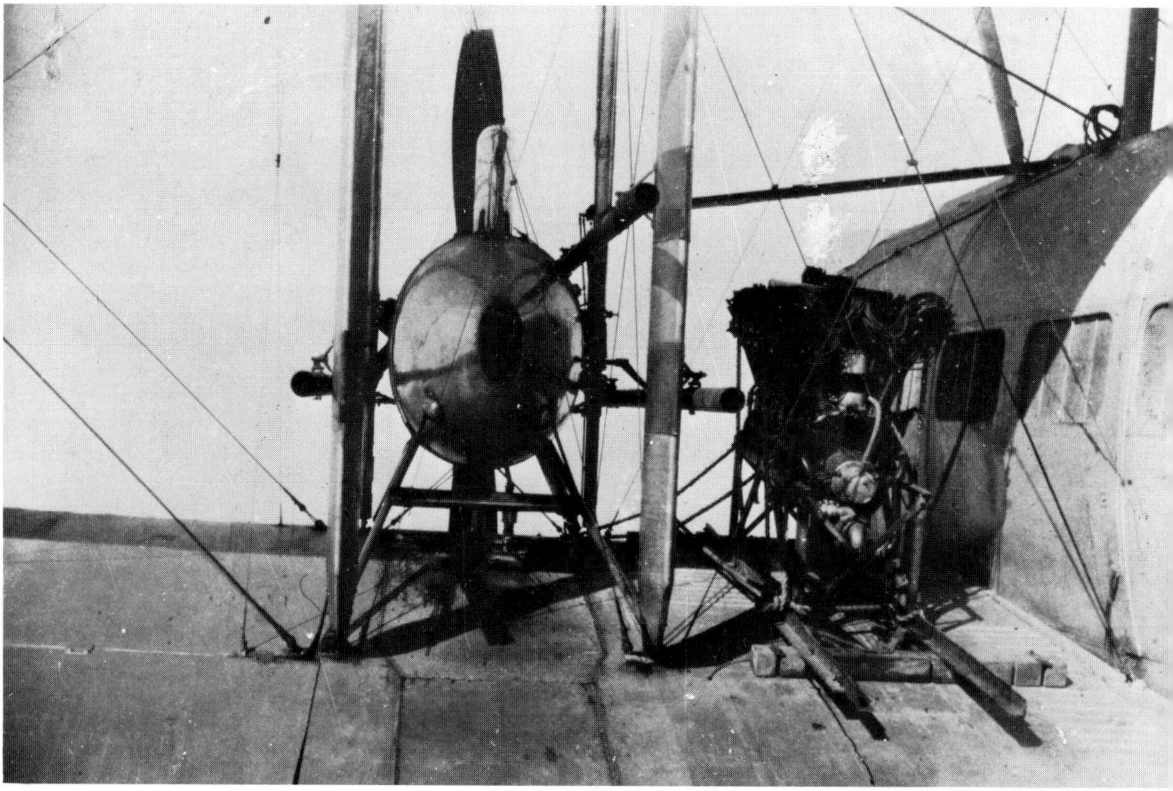

movements from Arbil alone. In addition they had been promised far greater flexibility and speed of movement by means of air supply. It was the first military operation of its kind to depend primarily on the air for essential supplies and for sheer variety of goods delivered this air lift probably stands by itself. Squadron Leader Raymond Collishaw, CO of No 30 Squadron, one of the outstanding World War I fighter pilots and a widely experienced officer, was appointed RAF liaison officer with the ground forces and the entire operation marked a significant advance in Army-RAF co-operation. The air lift operated between 4 April and 5 May 1923, intensifying as the columns approached Rowanduz, where a speedy occupation was essential. During the early stages the Vernons and other types were able to unload on the ground, and Collishaw rode ahead to select suitable landing areas. As the troops moved up through winding gorges into the higher mountainous regions where landing was no longer possible, aircraft dropped the stores using parachutes made in the squadron workshops — and when the supply of parachutes began to run short, packages were free dropped.

The low-flying aircraft were often the target for snipers' fire, which caused no more damage than a few holes in fabric and plywood but added to the pilots' problems when attempting accurate approaches through severe turbulence to small dropping zones in the awesome territory. The first experimental 1500lb free drop from a Vernon was made on the evening of 21 April to a site near Benawi, followed by three more the next afternoon. Largely owing to the nature of the ground these were disappointing, as indicated by this signal to RAF headquarters from Colonel Berkeley Vincent, commander of one of the columns:

'Only about one-third of stuff dropped on both days could be retrieved. Many loads dropped in rocky wooded ravines, some over a mile from camp. Both days Vernons bombarded the camp itself dangerously, especially yesterday when three tents were hit and some animals. Fortunately the column had not arrived. No portion of the 600lb atta (wholemeal flour for chupattis) was found and little barley retrieved as sacks burst on the rocks. Even some boots were split'.

Packing methods were improved and on the 23rd the Vernons flew four sorties in the morning and four more in the afternoon, dropping four tons of barley and other foodstuffs — rice, oatmeal, flour, sugar, tea etc — to make up a day's ration for the column. Another four flights were made on the 24th. This particular phase of the lift was flown by Flying Officers Ernest W. Nicholson, William H. Markham, Robert D. V. Howard, Marion H. Aten and Sydney A. Lane, all of No 70 Squadron.

The rough going for the troops was aggravated by heavy rain and melting snows which turned some stretches into seas of mud, while the general dampness caused materials to rot and disintegrate. This is reflected by the aerial delivery of 1,000 pairs of boots, 3,000 pairs of socks, 100lb of boot repair materials, 4,000 shirts, 500 pairs of shorts and 500 pairs of puttees. Other supplies included 24 sun helmets, 1,400 bars of soap, 270 tins of dubbin and 500 fathoms of rope for bridging a river. Nor were the animals excluded from this airborne bonanza, and 1,000 horseshoes, 7,000 horseshoe nails and 1,200 new nosebags were provided. The greatest calamity to strike the column was the defection of the locally enlisted canteen staff, who melted away into the hills one night with most of the stock. However, the RAF came to the rescue and on 29 April dropped 2,000lb of cigarettes, sweets, chocolate, biscuits and other goodies — 'which did much to promote contentment with all ranks' in the words of Collishaw's report.

Regular arrivals of the aircraft meant more to the troops than mere physical subsistence and a few minor comforts, for they also brought that greatest of all morale sustainers — the letters from home.

Before making delivery flights to the columns on the move, the Vernons had previously conveyed most of the stores from Baghdad, Mosul or Kirkuk to the forward despatch aerodrome at Arbil, and the total tonnage lifted during the entire operation must have reached several hundreds, though no complete record appears to have survived. 'The magnitude of the air achievement has never been equalled', wrote Collishaw. 'Pilots flew regularly, with their machines heavily burdened with exceptionally bulky loads, through threatening storms to make their deliveries'. Yet this remarkable, pioneer air support operation, like the evacuation of Sulaimaniya, was barely mentioned at the time — possibly because of communications delays and a general low key policy as regards Iraq operations — and is dismissed in an few lines in subsequent RAF histories.

Surprisingly the next Iraq troop lift — also to Kirkuk — was not precipitated by any Mahmoud activities. On 4 May 1924 an argument between three Assyrian levies and a Moslem shopkeeper rapidly developed into a serious disturbance, with two levy companies roaming the streets and shooting Moslems on sight. To prevent this from escalating into a major conflagration the urgent presence of British troops was vitally important, and since the nearest were at Baghdad, 150 miles, and by surface travel five days away, only air transport could meet the situation. The news reached Baghdad around midday, Nos 45 and 70 Squadrons at Hinaidi were alerted, and the Royal Inniskilling Fusiliers ordered to prepare a company for an immediate move.

Aircraft departed at intervals during the afternoon — four Vernons and the prototype Victoria, which carried 20 compared with only 12 in the older aircraft — and by early evening the first 66 officers and men of the Inniskillings were patrolling the town and a potentially ugly situation was under control. On 6 May the remaining 79 men of the company were flown in. The troops travelled with their basic equipment of rifles, ammunition and two blankets — plus a Lewis gun section — and found air transport

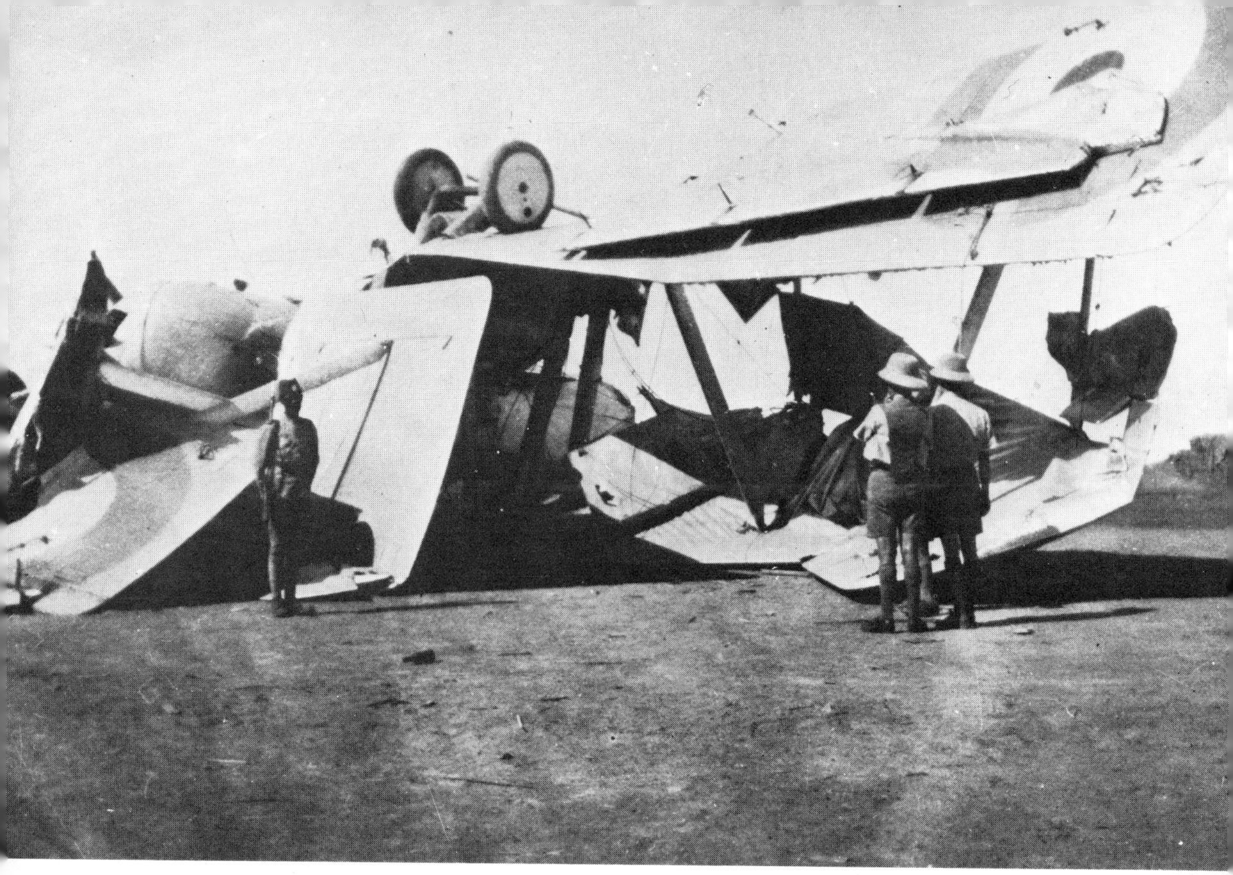

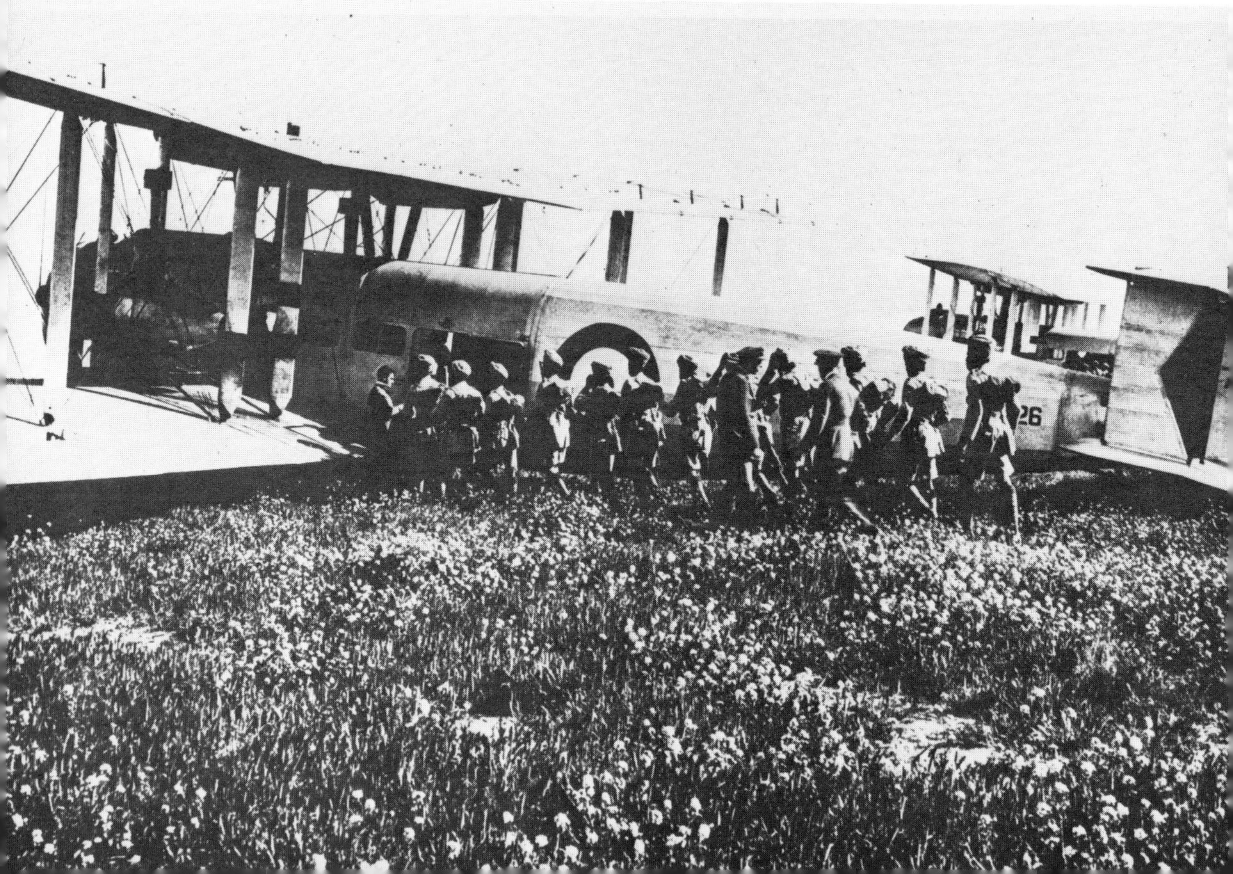
26

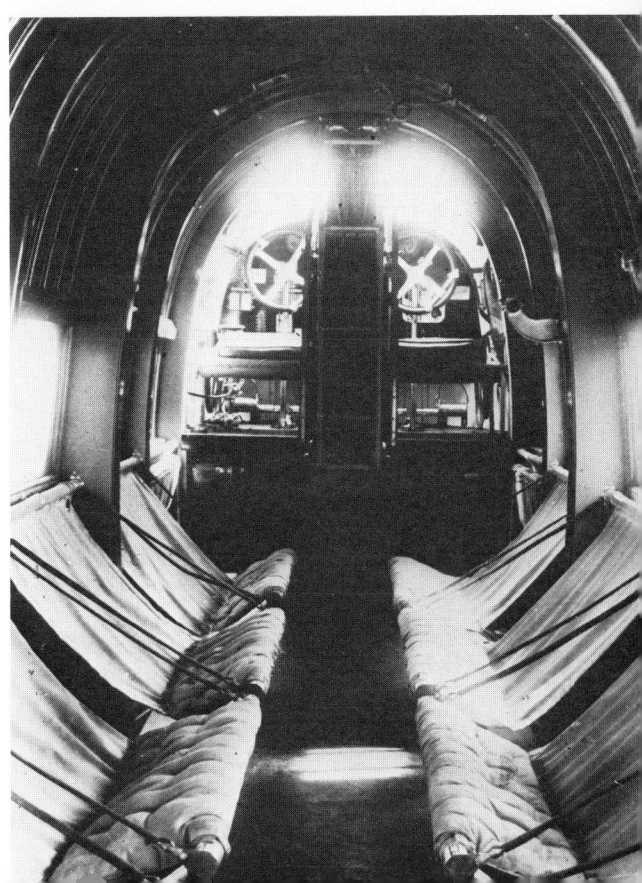

Above left: Victoria of No 70 Squadron destroyed during a dust storm at Ur while taking part in the Akhwan operations of 1928. / *W. H. Cox*

Left: Punjabi troops emplaning at Hinaidi in No 70 Squadron Victorias for an exercise, February 1927. Aircraft J7926, in foreground was written off after a forced landing during the Kabul evacuation air lift in January 1928.

Above: Victorias of No 216 Squadron near Nicosia on 23 October 1931 immediately after landing with troop reinforcements during the Enosis troubles. / *Sir Malin Sorsbie*

Right: Vickers Victoria interior.

eminently preferable to the dusty and tiring surface journey with all its cooking and other chores.

Mahmoud, who had again been bound over on promise of good behaviour for the past year, seized upon the Kirkuk incident as a pretext to declare a *Jihad* or holy war against Britain and the Assyrians. After due warning to minimise casualties, Sulaimaniya was bombed and in July occupied by British forces, some detachments being flown in by the Vernons of Nos 45 and 70 squadrons. The elusive sheikh spent the next two years flitting between Iraq and Persia and on 16 June 1926 six Vernons of No 45 Squadron answered an urgent call to transport servicing personnel and spares of No 1 (Fighter) Squadron from Hinaidi to Sulaimaniya. A large force of Mahmoud supporters was posing a serious threat in that area and the Snipes were required for ground attack work, departing at less than 24 hours' notice.

One of 45 Squadron's last Vernon operations was between 13 and 22 October 1926, when six aircraft spent 15 days in the Rutbah Wells area, supporting a flight of 55 Squadron DH9As countering the activities of Shammar tribe raiders. The Vernons totalled 230 flying hours and lifted 30 tons of fuel, rations and other stores during these operations.

With the introduction of the more effective Vickers Victoria, RAF air transport overseas achieved a sort of middle-aged maturity and its efficiency was almost taken for granted. During the next 10 years hardly a month passed without some activity, occasionally of a dramatic nature but usually rather mundane. The squadrons widened

their experience with training flights and 'cruises', covering several thousand miles over routes pioneered by smaller aircraft in as many days as the modern jet would require hours — but providing crew enjoyment and satisfaction of a kind which may have diminished since flying became less of a challenge. Routine work included deployments of other squadrons' ground staff and spares about the theatre on exercises and operations, surveys for new routes, movements of replacement engines, wings and other components for stranded aircraft of all types, search and rescue, VIP flying and aeromedical work.

In January 1928, a year after No 70 Squadron had taken over all air transport work in the Iraq theatre, it started the largest and most prolonged air supply operation mounted by the RAF up to that time. For some eight years peaceful tribes in southern Iraq and Kuwait had suffered vicious sporadic raids by the Akhwan — a fanatical group from the Nejd pledged to purify Islam — and all diplomatic efforts to reach a solution had failed. Substantial operations were therefore planned by the RAF, firstly to deny the raiders access to water-bearing areas and then drive them back across the border. For this purpose several units were selected to operate under a special headquarters at Ur, and designated Akforce. DH9As of Nos 55 and 84 Squadrons were detached to desert airstrips at Busaiya and Sulman, 100 and 150 miles from the Ur railhead, to provide the reconnaissance and strike capability, while six armoured car sections and an MT column gave ground support. No 70 Squadron was positioned at Ur, and success of the operations depended upon air supply, since it was planned

**Above left: Troops of the 1st Northamptonshire Regiment emplaning at Ismailia for Hinaidi, June 1932.** / *MOD*

**Above: For this relief much thanks: The first wave of reinforcements from the Northamptonshire Regiment arrives at Habbaniya on 22 June 1932. The flight from Ismailia, via Ziza and Rutbah Wells, was completed in daylight. JR8920 (farthest from camera) captained by Flying Officer Pelly, was delayed en route by engine trouble.** / *Philip J. R. Moyes*

to use some advanced locations inaccessible to motor transport.

On 8 January six Victorias and three Vernons (later replaced by Victorias) flew to Ur with the Headquarters staff and servicing personnel, some of whom slept in the aircraft until adequate tentage arrived. Heavy gales prevented flying the next day, but between 10 and 13 January, four days' rations and nearly 8,000 gallons of fuel were air-lifted to Busaiya and Sulman. During the next four months the Victorias operated an almost daily service from Ur to both bases and other more remote temporary landing areas, at peak periods lifting five tons a day. Each Ninack squadron used 450-900 gallons of petrol a day according to the extent of flying and on a fuel sortie a Victoria carried 56 four-gallon tins of petrol, 10 five-gallon drums of benzol and five five-gallon drums of oil. Freight loads varied from 2,100 to 3,200lb according to destination. By 29 May, when Ibn Sa'ud gave a formal undertaking that raiding activities would stop and Akforce started to withdraw, the Victorias had carried 517 tons of supplies and 1,192 passengers.

No 70 Squadron spent many hours on breakdown work and below is a typical 24 hours in the life of a Victoria:

5 March 1928: 1340 depart Shaibah with new Liberty engine for DH9A at Kuwait. Arrive 1445. Load u/s Liberty — servicing team help to instal new engine. Depart Kuwait 1705, arrive Shaibah 1815. Unload u/s engine.

6 March 1928: AM Shaibah to Ur. 1450 depart Ur with new Lion engine for Victoria forced landed in desert 45 miles south-west. Arrived 1555. Servicing team help to change engine. 1745 depart for Ur with u/s engine.

The weather was trying for both men and aircraft, being cold and wet — with even some snow — in the early weeks, followed by scorching summer heat and frequent dust storms during which the Victorias could not be taxied because their throttle barrels seized. When parked in high winds, all flying control surfaces had to be securely locked to avoid damage, and wheel chocks pegged down to stop aircraft from being blown backwards. The intensive spell of heavy freighting in hot weather caused cabin floor joists to shrink and split — with a risk of the floor collapsing and fouling the tail control cables — and new improved joists were made in the Hinaidi workshops.

Without the Victorias, said the official Akforce report, it

would have been impossible to maintain and operate the strike aircraft from advanced desert bases on such a scale, and the campaign would have been considerably protracted and complicated.

During the next three years No 70 Squadron mounted several lesser air transport operations of some historic interest, including the support of No 6 Squadron's transfer to the Middle East Command in October 1929. Five Victorias carried the advance party from Mosul to Ismailia between the 1st and 3rd, then from the 23rd to 25th three of them escorted 16 Bristol Fighters flying the same route in two waves, and two others carried the rear party. Rations were also flown to the main party's MT convoy.

Between 1 and 11 July 1930, Victorias flew three salvage sorties after one of the classic inter-war desert forced landing episodes when five Wapitis of 84 Squadron en route to Shaibah on 27 June were caught in a severe dust storm and forced down on soft sand. One turned upside down, three tipped on their noses and the fifth luckily hit a firm patch and was undamaged.

In October, No 70 Squadron pioneered night flying across the full length of the Baghdad-Cairo route. The first recorded trip was by Flight Lieutenant E. S. C. Davis, who left Hinaidi at 1800 on 10 October, reaching Heliopolis at 0700 on the 11th. He took off for the return flight at 1900, arriving at Hinaidi at 0645 on the 12th. Refuelling stops were made at Rutbah Wells and Ziza in both directions.

At about this time, after the announcement that Iraq would become a sovereign state in two years, Sheikh Mahmoud launched one last attempt to establish himself as leader of a Kurdish state. It ended with his final surrender, and on 15 May 1931 the erstwhile 'Honorary Director of Air Force Training' was flown from Sulaimaniya to Hinaidi in a Victoria piloted by 70 Squadron's CO, Wing Commander C. H. B. Blount, and later taken on to Ur and retirement.

There was a bizarre incident on 7 October 1931 when a 70 Squadron Victoria was returning from Cairo by night with a load of passengers which included several nursing sisters. The aircraft refuelled at Rutbah Wells, and about half an hour after take off the co-pilot came aft to announce that they must put down because of engine trouble. Everyone remained calm at the rather alarming prospect of a night forced landing, and LAC Ralph Fuller, following the drill for such emergency, started to open the cabin door. Somehow he slipped and fell 700 feet to his death. The Victoria made a perfect landing with no damage.

For the next historical milestone the setting switched from the arid deserts of Iraq to the more congenial Mediterranean area. Soon after No 216 Squadron at Heliopolis received its first Victorias in 1926 it had flown

**Below: Victoria of No 70 Squadron over Baghdad in 1932 — pilot, Squadron Leader Ryder Young.** / A. J. Blagden

**Below right: Assyrian refugees photographed inside Victoria K1310 of No 70 Squadron between Mosul and Hinaidi during the big airlift of October 1933.** / A. J. Blagden

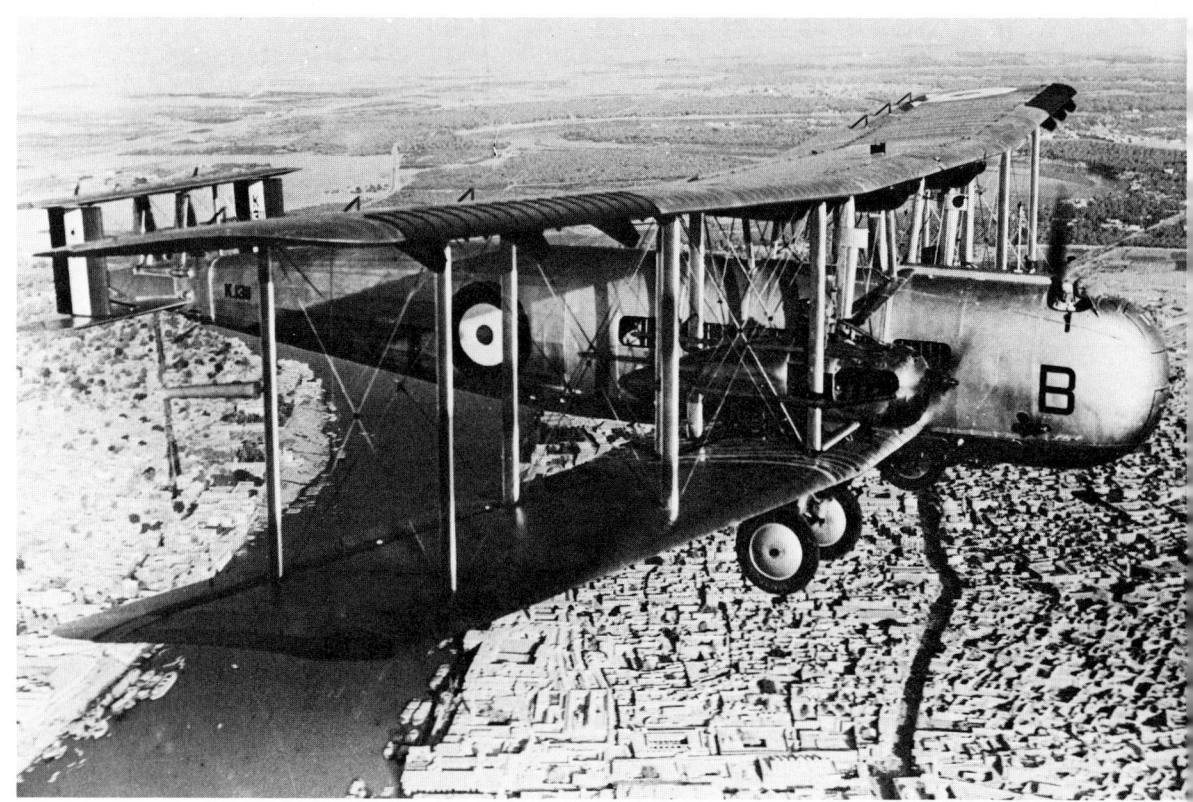

two of them to Aden and back, between 15 and 19 September, identifying a few performance shortcomings which were later rectified. On 24-25 August 1929 during Arab-Israeli disturbances, four Victorias carried 52 personnel of the South Wales Borderers, plus equipment and ammunition from Egypt to Kalundia (Jerusalem), the first lift departing at seven hours' notice.

In March 1930 the squadron began a small commitment, which dragged on for nearly a year, to supply a Trans-Jordan Frontier Force column and Fairey IIIFs of No 14 Squadron operating jointly against tribal raiders. The same month one of No 216 Squadron's Victorias was written off during a forced landing on the 'pan-handle' area in north-eastern Cyprus when returning from a training visit. Between 12 January and 11 March 1931 three Victorias made the 11,242-mile flight to Cape Town and back, the longest 'cruise' to-date by the heavy transports. It was completed on schedule throughout, the only minor mishap being a taxying argument with a tree stump. They exercised with colonial forces en route and gained valuable experience of operating in different environments — learning for example that not more than 12 passengers could be carried when taking off from the 4,300ft above sea level aerodrome at Entebbe.

But these were routine activities, and it was the pleasant island of Cyprus which hit the headlines. Since Cyprus had become a British Crown Colony in 1925 the underground movement for union with Greece — Enosis — had gained strength, and on the night of 21 October 1931 there were riots in Nicosia during which Government House was burned down. It was feared that the trouble might spread, and next day seven No 216 Squadron Victorias went to Ramleh, Palestine to collect a company of the 1st King's Regiment, which they flew to Cyprus on the 23rd, landing in fields five miles west of Nicosia at 1100. This 250-mile lift of 126 troops, and 23 airmen for servicing and communications duties, more than doubled the strength of British Forces on the island and earns a place in the record books because it was the first time the RAF had flown troops over the sea to a trouble spot. Official spokesmen at home highlighted this aspect, and probably due to the lack of hard facts, the press substantially exaggerated the performance. The naive attitude still held by the layman towards flying is shown by this extract from a *Star* report which was used by Vickers in an advertisement: '.... They were landplanes, so that their flight over 440 miles of sea was risky'.

On the 24th the Victorias flew over the main towns and villages in a show of strength, and during the next few days carried parties of troops about the island as required. Ringleaders were arrested and the situation calmed, and after a week, five of the Victorias returned to base. Two remained with a flight of 45 Squadron IIIFs which had flown in for general flag showing duties.

Two unarmed RAF technicians who accompanied the heavy wireless equipment shipped from Egypt, distinguished themselves during the crossing. They sailed in the 60-year old Italian-registered *El Gharib*, crewed by a cosmopolitan collection whose competence aroused serious doubts when the vessel managed to cover only 90 miles in

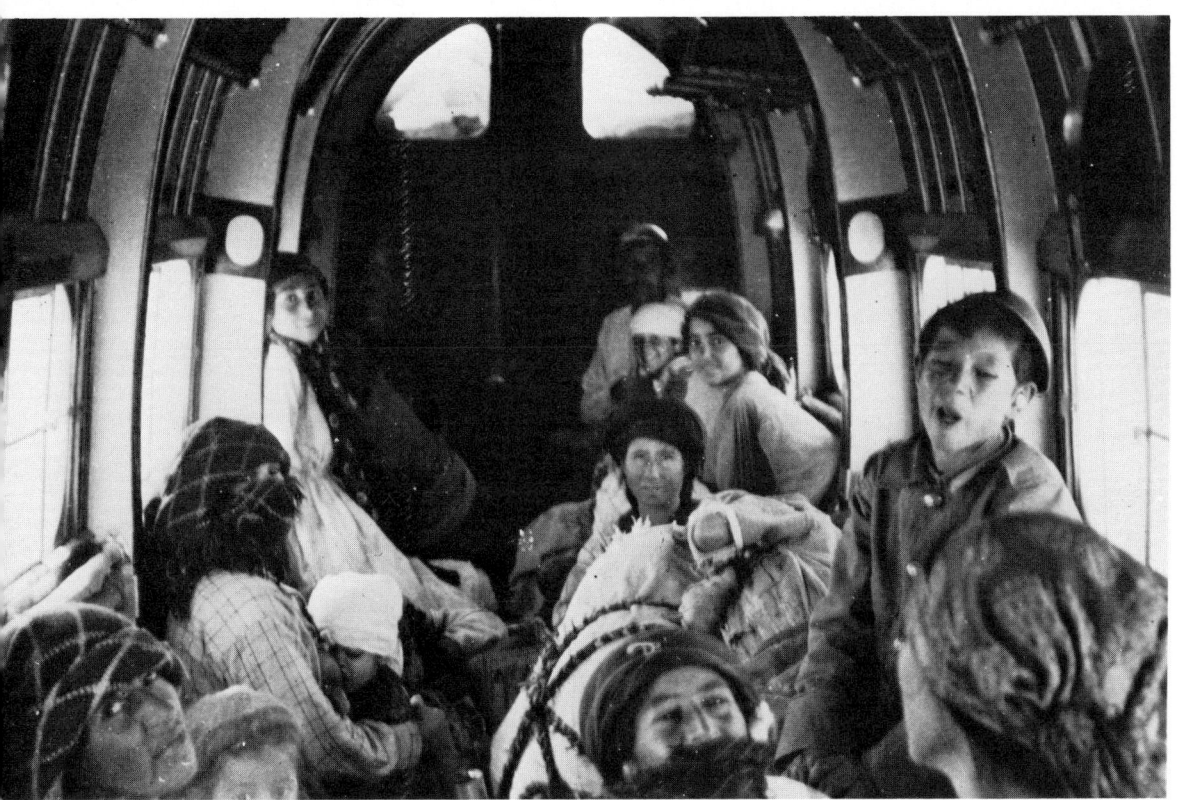

the first 70 hours' steaming. The airmen erected the W/T set and signalled HQ Middle East explaining their situation, and on eventually reaching Cyprus they were obliged virtually to take over the piloting and berthing arrangements to ensure a safe arrival in Famagusta harbour.

In Iraq meanwhile, the coming of independence brought no immediate reduction in the air transport task. Although internal security was to be primarily the responsibility of Iraqi armed forces, the air force was in its infancy and RAF assistance was still available. On 4-5 April 1932 after an Iraq Army column had met with a heavy reverse at the hands of Sheikh Ahmad's Barzan rebel forces, losing its baggage and supplies, 70 Squadron Victorias dropped food, ammunition, blankets and greatcoats. On 25-26 April a Victoria with 'sky-shouting' equipment flew over rebel villages at 2-3,000 feet broadcasting warnings that air action would be taken in 48 hours.

The independence issue was also the indirect cause of a large troop deployment and the biggest civilian air lift mounted by the RAF during the inter-war years. The Assyrian minority of some 3,700 people living mainly in northern Iraq claimed that Britain had failed to safeguard the future of the Assyrian nation after terminating the mandate. The 1,500-strong Assyrian levies, formed in 1921 and employed mainly for guard duties, were very much under the influence of the Assyrians' principal religious and temporal leader, the Mar Shimun, and on 1 June 1932 declared that they would terminate their service at the end of the month. To exert a stabilising influence and provide any necessary replacements for the levies, troops of the 1st Northamptonshire Regiment were flown the 800-odd miles from Egypt to Iraq. The British Government emphasised that no military operations were envisaged. The 25 Victorias for the lift were drawn from Nos 216 and 70 Squadrons, and 562 troops were carried in 36 sorties between 22 and 27 June.

On the first day eight Victorias of 216 Squadron left Ismailia between 0400 and 0440, reaching Hinaidi at 1650-1720 having refuelled at Ziza and Rutbah Wells. Meanwhile 70 Squadron aircraft were travelling westward in readiness to lift the second wave of troops on Day Two. And, so it continued, with remarkable regularity despite an almost unprecedented incidence of technical snags. There were ten forced landings which called for engine changes and several others with less demanding problems, and the two flying workshop aircraft positioned at Ziza and Rutbah each flew five breakdown rescue sorties during the week. However, nobody was hurt and replacement aircraft were speedily provided for stranded passengers. The technical failures, and severe dust storms extended the operation to six days instead of the planned five, but it was nevertheless an impressive achievement which strikingly vindicated the decision to maintain the old airmail route in being.

On reaching Hinaidi the troops were each given two bottles of lemonade and a packet of cigarettes — and the news was gently broken to the first arrivals that they would be travelling north by rail and road the next evening, as all aircraft were committed to the main lift. However, a few days later 70 Squadron flew six sorties to collect arms from the disbanded levies at Diana and Sulaimaniya.

The lift was planned in great detail, with aircraft timings staggered to avoid congestion at the staging posts, where the refuelling — by crew and passengers from four-gallon tins — was carried out in an area off the main landing ground. On landing, each aircraft was directed to its own fuel dump by a route which avoided blinding others on the ground with its taxying dust. Aircraft and medical teams were kept on standby at Rutbah and Hinaidi for emergencies. At the main bases airmen slept by day and worked right through the night to ensure maximum aircraft availability each morning. Among the useful lessons learned in this biggest troop air lift to date and the first involving aircraft of two commands, was the need to standardise procedures.

It was found that the Middle East and Iraq Command operating regulations for Victorias differed in important respects, including the amount of water, rations and special equipment carried on trans-desert flights, permissible all-up aircraft weights, forms of load sheets and so on. This meant that the load offered to the Army in identical aircraft of the two squadrons could be different. The average weight of each soldier with his kit bag, rifle and ration pack, worked out at 210lb and it was suggested that procedures for future lifts might be simplified by assuming a standard average weight for a fully-equipped soldier. Inevitably someone pointed out that there could be a significant weight difference between a Guardsman and a Ghurka, and no conclusions were reached.

On 29 June all the levy battalions had been disarmed without serious incident and by 12 July the 'strike' had been settled, the levies agreeing to continue service. It is an indication of the tight control even then exercised over defence expenditure that planning staffs were required to produce a scheme for the Northamptonshires to return by road and rail. This was complicated almost beyond comprehension, and to their CO's intense relief it was agreed that the troops should fly back to Egypt. During the outward trip the aircrews had suffered considerable fatigue after a week of intensive flying 12-14 hours' daily at the hottest period, nor were the conditions conducive to the arrival of the troops in a state of peak efficiency. It was therefore decided that the return journey should be in slower time, with No 70 Squadron flying the Hinaidi-Rutbah stage, and 216 Rutbah-Ismailia. The troops spent the night at Rutbah and thus avoided flying through the hottest period of the day, and in contrast to the outward move, the return was completed between 18 July and 12 August without a single forced landing.

The Air Estimates Memorandum of the following year described this episode as a 'striking demonstration of the mobility conferred by the use of aircraft as well as of close and effective co-operation between the Army and the Royal Air Force'. In a letter to the Chief of the Air Staff, the AOC Iraq (Air Vice-Marshal E. R. Ludlow-Hewitt) expressed similar sentiments — 'It was certainly an

**Top right: Assyrian refugees from Mosul arriving at Hinaidi, October 1933.** / A. J. Blagden

**Right: A Victoria Mk VI of No 70 Squadron over Baghdad.** / MOD

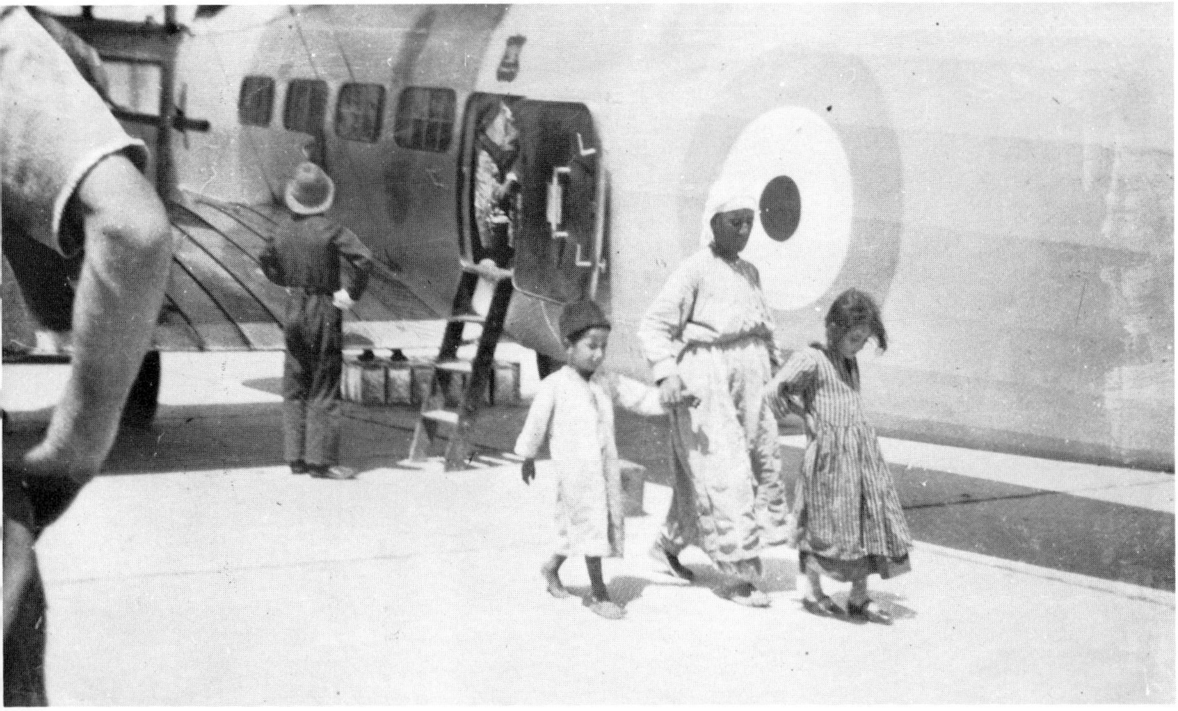

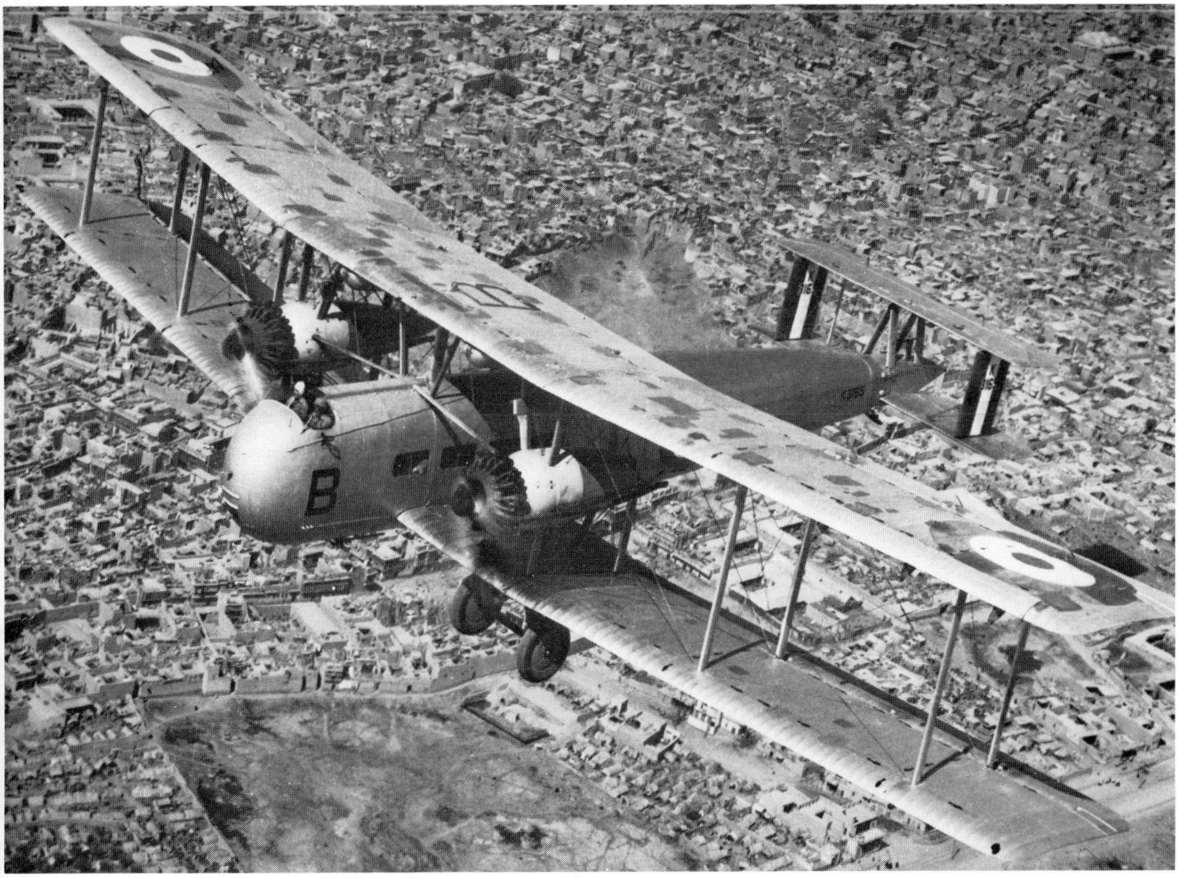
B

historical performance and has created a real sensation out here. Nobody ever dreamed that we could conjure a battalion out of the blue in that way'.

There was no further trouble among the levies, but the overall Assyrian situation became more confused and embittered, reaching a tragic climax between 4 and 11 August 1933, when hundreds of Assyrians in northern Iraq were killed in clashes and massacres involving the Iraq army. The RAF summer training camp at Ser Amadia, 110 miles north of Mosul, was closed on 7 August and the British and levy personnel flown out. By arrangement with the Iraq Government the Mar Shimun, his influential aunt, the Lady Surma Khanin and entourage were flown to Cyprus in a 70 Squadron Victoria on 18 August. A camp was opened in Mosul for dependants of those killed in the disorders and refugees from the devastated villages, many of them related to the Levies. In mid-September the Iraq Government eventually allowed the RAF to air lift these people to Hinaidi, where they were accommodated in surplus buildings in and around the camp. No 70 Squadron Victorias flew four sorties a day, and by 23 October no fewer than 790 refugees, mostly women, children and old men, had been carried south.

While this task was proceeding, three of 216 Squadron's aircraft had left Heliopolis on 13 October for an extensive West African cruise. They reached Accra on 6 November and were back at Heliopolis on 18 December, having covered more than 10,000 miles. Single-engined RAF aircraft had visited West Africa in the past, but this was the first time that large transports had made the journey. The flights planned for 1931 and 1932 had been cancelled because of a yellow fever epidemic in some territories, and economy considerations respectively.

In 1933 the Victoria gained a new lease of life. Since entering service in 1926 it had been improved in various ways — the Mark IV of 1928 introduced metal structure and the Mark V had the more powerful 570hp Lion engines — and performance and payload were enhanced. In 1928 the Air Ministry issued a specification for a larger bomber-transport capable of carrying 30 troops over distances of 1,200 miles which resulted in the four engined Gloster TC33 and Vickers 163 and the three-engined HP43 prototypes. None of these was ordered for quantity production, and financial considerations doubtless influenced the Ministry's decision to skip a generation and to meet the requirements of the next few years with a still further improved Victoria, the Mark VI with two 660hp air-cooled Bristol Pegaus engines, which had a maximum speed of 130mph. During the last quarter of 1933 Nos 70 and 216 Squadron began to receive Mark VI Victorias ferried from England by easy stages. Early in 1934 the

aircraft structure was strengthened to enable another 1,500lb of payload to be carried, wheel brakes were fitted and the tail skid replaced by a tail wheel. The aircraft was renamed the Valentia and in due course most of the Victorias were modified to Valentia standard, remaining in service well into World War II.

Neither squadron lost any time in trying out their Mk VI Victorias on major mobility exercises. Between 15 January and 17 February two from No 70 Squadron carried spares and servicing crews for four No 84 Squadron Wapitis on a 10,630-mile flight to Singapore and back, while between 26 February and 30 April four from No 216 Squadron performed a similar service for five No 45 Squadron IIIFs visiting Pretoria. Meanwhile a Victoria of the Bomber Transport Flight in India had accompanied four Hawker Harts of No 11 Squadron from Risalpur to Singapore and back between 1-25 February.

To a generation familiar with time scales of jet-age deployment exercises a Victoria pilot's logbook gives some idea of the more leisurely passage of an RAF biplane detachment down a continent then marked in the atlases so generously with red. Flying Officer (now Sir Malin) Sorsbie was captain of K2343 on the Pretoria flight which carried slung under the starboard bomb rack a spare Napier Lion engine for the IIIFs. Surprisingly this did not noticeably affect cruising speed but it did spoil the Victoria's flying characteristics in turbulence. Substantial spares packs and equipment were carried internally, and take-off with 500lb overload was authorised. On the outward journey there were night stops at Wadi Halfa, Khartoum, Juba, Nairobi, Moshi, M'beya, Broken Hill and Bulawayo — plus eight other intermediate stops, two of them unscheduled landings to check engine faults. Part of the return journey was over a different route, and air experience flights were given to local troops in Northern and Southern Rhodesia, Nyasaland, Kenya and Tanganyika. None of the African soldiers had flown before and those at Mombasa were firmly warned by their sergeant that any who were sick woud receive ten strokes of the whip. None was sick. Including air tests the aircraft made 70 take-offs and landings and logged 133.40 flying hours.

To meet the Italo-Abyssinian war situation of 1935-36 a number of RAF bomber and fighter squadrons were deployed to Africa and this generated additional work for 216 Squadron — which also undertook intensive training in the bomber role. Six Valentias were fitted with nose and mid-upper gun turrets, and gun positions were installed by the port side door and a starboard window. These excrescences caused no measurable loss of performance though the pilots' forward view was slightly impaired. Twenty-five airmen were trained as gunners and a scheme was devised for refuelling the aircraft in the air from tins which substantially increased the range.

While on detachment in Kenya the squadron established what was probably a height record for the Valentia. This arose from some discussion as to whether it was possible to fly over Mount Kilimanjaro, and on 15 July 1936, one aircraft reached a ceiling of 18,500 feet — still about 1,000 feet short of the peak.

When the crisis had subsided No 216 helped with the return moves of the UK-based squadrons, and on 2 August carried men and equipment of No 3 Squadron from Atbara, Sudan, to Aboukir. During this move No 3 managed to write off two of its Bulldog fighters.

In January-February 1937 substantial reinforcement and joint-Service exercises were staged in Singapore. Nos 84 Squadron (Vincents) and 203 (Singapore IIIs) flew from Iraq, and Nos 27 (Wapitis) and 11 (Harts) from India. No 70 Squadron provided nine Valentias to assist the small Indian Bomber Transport Flight in support of these moves, and including internal exercise flights while detached to Singapore, carried 185 passengers and nearly 16,500lb of freight. In January 1938 there was a similar exercise, but with different squadrons from India, and this time No 70 lifted 226 passengers and 8,000lb cargo. Since October 1937 the squadron had been operating from the large, new aerodrome at Dhibban, 60 miles south-west of Baghdad, which opened on 1 January. It was renamed Habbaniya on 1 May 1938.

The final months of peace passed with no major calls for RAF air transport in Egypt or Iraq. The summer of 1938 saw the first small moves towards trooping by air — which became standard procedure a quarter of a century later —

when five No 70 Squadron Valentias flew tour-expired airmen from Habbaniya to Aboukir to join their ship at Port Said. In September No 70 was busy supporting the Iraq bomber squadrons' deployments to their war stations during the Munich crisis. A year later, after repeating this operation, the squadron — less one flight — went to its own initial war base at Helwan, Egypt.

Since squadrons appear to have maintained their records largely according to the whim of the moment there are no consistent statistics to show the complete interwar transport achievement in the Middle East and Iraq. No 216 Squadron did record passengers carried between 1930 and 1934, giving a yearly average of 22,800, but failed to do so again until 1938, when the figure was nearly 23,800. Over the same period in Iraq, No 70 carried probably only half that number, because apart from its involvement in more operational bombing and freighting, it had fewer aircraft. The total passengers carried by the Middle East and Iraq squadrons between the wars was probably around 400,000, and this appears to have been achieved without a fatal accident involving a passenger on any transport, troop-carrying or mail sortie.

# Air Lift from Kabul

## 6

Compared with the extensive operations in the Middle East and Iraq, the early interwar years saw surprisingly little air transport activity in India, that other vast area so familiar to the British Forces, where the scope was even greater.

During the early 1920s the RAF bomber and general purpose squadrons in India were woefully short of spares and for some years after the end of World War I air transport was non-existent. The main reason for this situation was the peculiar financial arrangement whereby the cost of maintaining the RAF in India came from the Army C-in-C's budget. Although the Army in India initially viewed air transport with no great enthusiasm, and felt that any necessary supply-dropping could be done by the existing single-engined squadrons, they could not entirely ignore the excellent results being achieved in Iraq. They were, however, prejudiced against the Victoria, which they considered unsuitable for Indian conditions. In 1927, after some inter-Service bickering when the War Minister challenged the Chief of the Air Staff's claim that the Victorias operating in Egypt could carry 20 fully armed men for 200 miles, it was agreed to develop a transport version of the Handley Page Hinaidi bomber, to be paid for from Indian funds, and that in the meantime the prototype Hinaidi should operate as a makeshift transport. It was accordingly flown to India in 1928.

The value of air transport — and of the maligned Victoria — was to be brilliantly demonstrated sooner than anyone could have imagined. In 1927 King Amanullah, who ruled India's mountainous neighbour state of Afghanistan, had extensively toured Europe. He returned full of enthusiasm for Western ideas — universal education, separation of the church and state and the emancipation of women. But he was ahead of his time, and his plans outraged tribal and religious leaders, who fomented widespread disaffection.

On 14 November 1928 the Shinwaris, one of the principal tribes in Eastern Afghanistan, broke out in open rebellion against the King. Within hours they were rampaging through Dakka, looting, killing, destroying property, before taking up a position on the main road from Kabul to the Khyber. As a result all road and telegraph communication with India along this route was cut.

The following day a strong contingent was left behind to hold the road while the main body marched towards Kabul and attempted to seize control of Jalalabad. While this was happening the Afghan Mohmands, who as yet had taken no part in the uprising, moved a large number of men into the Jalalabad area; if the city fell they wished to share in the loot.

Meanwhile, disorder and chaos spread throughout the Southern Province where the Shinwaris had sent emissaries to urge the tribes there to rise in revolt. In the confusion the road from Kabul to Quetta via Kandahar became unsafe. The British Legation was now cut off by road and land line; their only means of communication with the outside world being with the Afghan Government wireless station at Kabul. This, however, was highly unreliable and likely to be severed by the advancing rebel forces.

On 14 December one of the principal rebels, Habibullah Khan advanced on Kabul with 1,000 tribesmen. After some bitter fighting with Royalist forces, he succeeded in capturing forts at Koh-i-Lula, one mile north west of the city. Many rifles and a considerable stock of ammunition fell into his hands. With their additional armoury the rebels established their position on the Asmai Heights, west and south-west of the British Legation.

It was unfortunate that the Legation stood on the plain between the city and the Heights. The Royalist forces, rallying in Kabul, were able to check the rebels' advance and both sides entrenched themselves firmly in their respective positions. The Legation became the unintentional recipient of a considerable number of shells and bullets directed at the rebel forces and from their direction came back an equal amount of wild and sporadic rifle fire.

By Tuesday 17 December the situation had changed rapidly to one of acute anxiety. The Legation staff were being forced to endure appalling conditions. Then, later that day, the only remaining link through Afghan Wireless ceased abruptly during the transmission of an urgent message from the British Minister, Sir Francis Humphrys; he wished to have the women and children evacuated as soon as possible. He requested that a reconnaissance aircraft be sent to Kabul.

In fact Air Vice-Marshal Sir Geoffrey Salmond, AOC India, had already reacted to a preliminary warning from Humphrys on 5 December that evacuation might be needed. He arranged for the immediate return of his Hinaidi from Baghdad, where it was positioned for a VIP flight, and when this was delayed by an engine change the AOC Iraq agreed that the substitute No 70 Squadron Victoria should remain in India to meet any Kabul requirements. Squadron Leader R. S. Maxwell, the highly

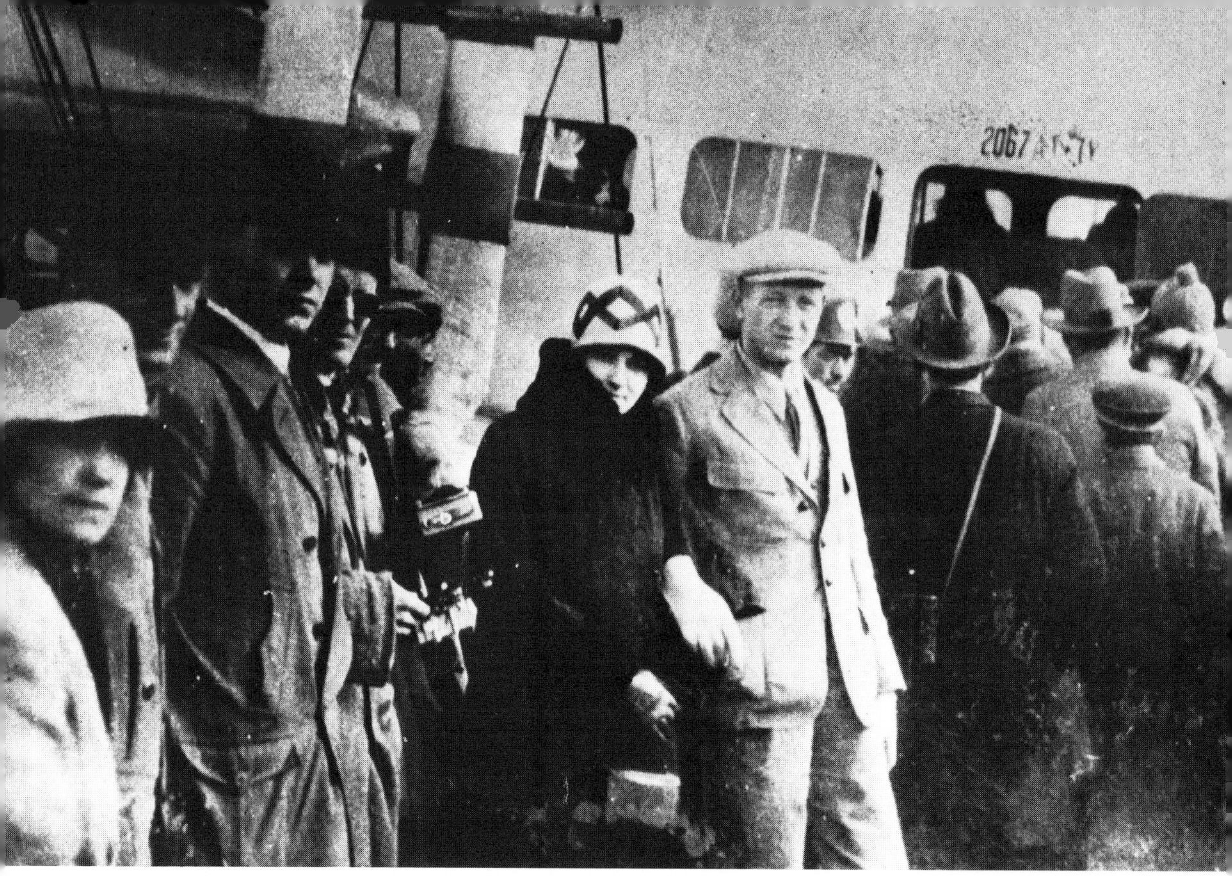
2067

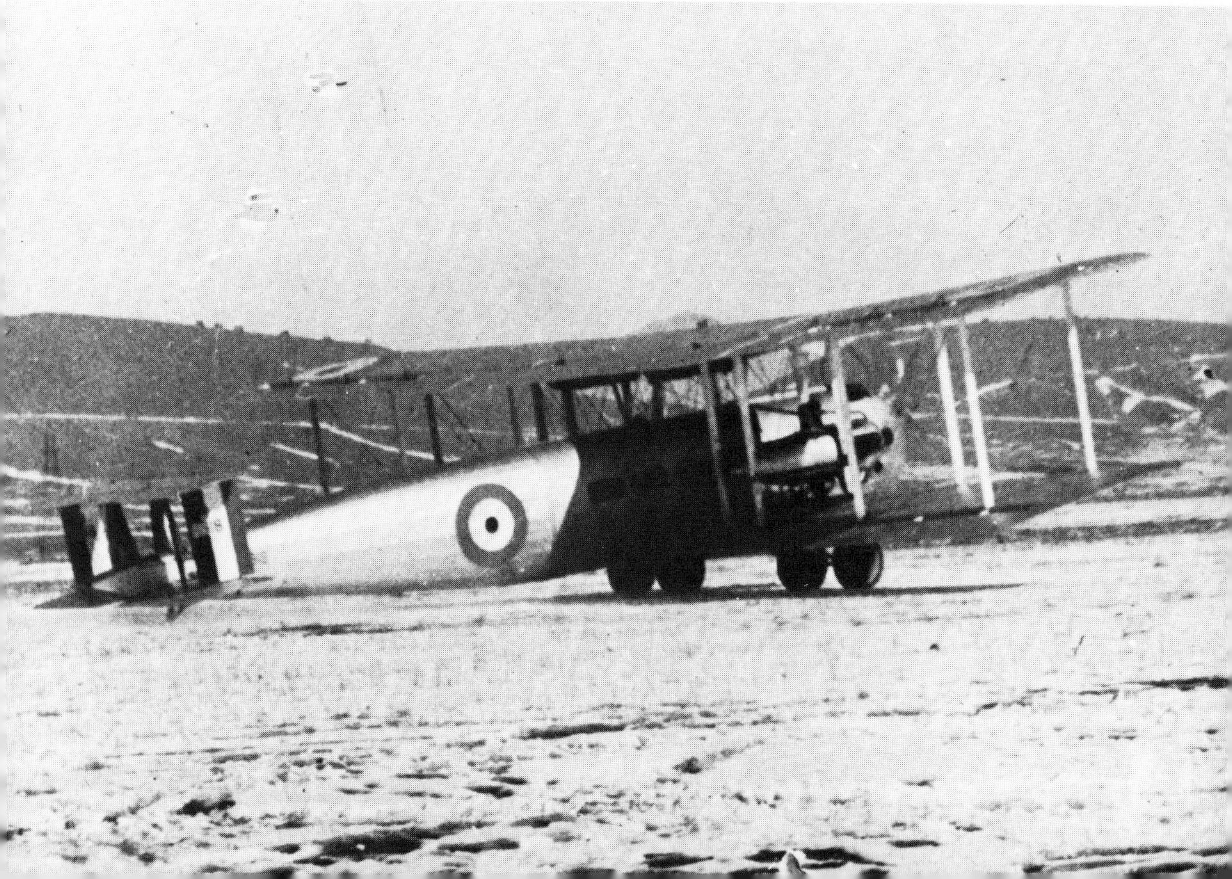

**eft: Evacuees from Kabul boarding a Victoria at Sherpur erodrome.** / MOD

**ottom left: Victoria of No 70 Squadron at Kabul during the vacuation.** / J. W. Burley

xperienced captain of the Victoria, had no personal doubts at it would cope with the high altitude conditions in fghanistan, and his belief was strengthened after a test limb to 12,400ft from Hinaidi before departure on the 6th. He reached Karachi next day and on the 18th flew or further tests to Quetta, which lay at 5,900ft — pproximately the same altitude as Sherpur aerodrome, abul. With a crew of two and petrol for three hours the ictoria was airborne against a very light wind in 400 ards, and climbed adequately.

That morning a No 27 Squadron DH9A, crewed by lying Officer C. W. L. Trusk and Leading Aircraftman ieorge Donaldson, was despatched to Kabul to drop a nessage and a Popham Panel (a device for visual Morse ignalling) in the Legation grounds. While running in for ie drop the Ninack was hit in the engine, and Donaldson ianaged to transmit a message before gliding in to herpur. The two RAF men were treated well, but were nable to make immediate contact with the Legation. A econd aircraft was successful, and saw ground signals eporting that all was well with the residents. Further )H9A reconnaissances were flown during the next four ays, and ground signals emphasised that no landings hould be attempted. On the afternoon of 22 December Amanullah's forces drove the rebels back from the utskirts of Kabul, the British Legation's radio facilities vere restored, and Humphrys signalled for the evacuation o start next day.

On 23 December the Victoria flew from Risalpur and eturned to Peshawar with 21 women and children, seven if them British. Three DH9As between them lifted out 90lb of baggage. Maxwell experienced no particular ifficulties at Sherpur, though the take-off demanded care nd concentration as there were obstructions or high round on all except the eastern side of the airfield and the 'ictoria's rate of climb was reduced by the altitude. On Christmas Eve the Victoria evacuated another 7 passengers — mostly French and German — while 1 Ninacks each carried one. After a break on Christmas )ay flights were resumed on the 26th, which saw the only assenger mishap during the entire operation. Despite epeated warnings a German woman, Frau Beitz, ran orward to inspect her luggage strapped to the under-wing ontainer of a DH9A and was struck on the head by the lling propeller. She received a nasty gash, but made a ,ood recovery and was well enough to be flown out six veeks later. The aircraft required a new propeller.

On 27 December the Hinaidi became serviceable and wo days later a second Victoria arrived from Iraq. By January 1929 the number flown out of Kabul had eached 134, which included all the women and children rom European legations. The situation in the town was elatively calm, though still tense and unpredictable. On 0 January Habibullah's forces counter-attacked, urrounding the Royal Palace and causing Amanullah to

abdicate on the 14th in favour of his brother, Inyatulla, whose reign lasted for only 72 hours. Encircled by rebel forces needing little excuse for starting a bloody massacre, Inyatulla stood down and gave way to Habibullah. Humphrys arranged for the three-day monarch and his household to be flown out on 18 and 19 January, and they later joined Amanullah who had departed by road.

Although Habibullah's behaviour towards the British had been highly correct, there was no telling how long his rebel government would last, and there seemed little justification in maintaining the British Legation. Before it withdrew, however, Humphrys obtained the Afghan authorities' approval for a progressive air evacuation of all foreign diplomatic staffs and nationals who wished to leave. The estimated number of several hundreds clearly required greater air lift capacity, and the Air Ministry authorised the transfer of more Victorias — bringing the total to eight — from No 70 Squadron in Iraq.

The last phase of the operation began on 29 January and soon settled into a steady routine. The biggest problems were caused by the severe cold, with air temperatures down to minus 3°F and ground temperatures at Sherpur of 0°F. These led to engine troubles with the Hinaidi, which were cured by blanking off the oil coolers and lagging oil pipes. Although it was normal drill to keep engines running during turn-round at Sherpur this was not always possible, and if engines had to be started from cold it was necessary to run them for 30-40 minutes to raise oil temperatures to the required figure. To maintain adequate temperatures in flight the Victorias' radiators were partly covered with fabric. During February the lift was briefly interrupted by a 17-inch snowfall at Sherpur, but within 24 hours a 600 × 20 yard runway was cleared. One problem not identified until it had caused the forced landing and loss of a Victoria — fortunately with no serious injury to the crew — was the presence of water in the petrol system which froze and blocked the filters.

Heroes of this episode were Flight Lieutenant Ronald Ivelaw-Chapman — later to become Air Chief Marshal and Vice-Chief of the Air Staff — and his co-pilot, Flying Officer A. R. S. Davies, who set off in Victoria J7926 from Risalpur at 1000 on Tuesday, 29 January, for Kabul. The cabin was empty, apart from the 10 blankets for their return passengers, and the two pilots had no extra kit with them.

For the first two hours all was normal, but as the Victoria approached the east of the Lataband Pass both engines started to fade rapidly and eventually stopped. The aircraft was at 3,500ft, and despite the efforts of the two pilots it was impossible to restart the engines; gradually the Victoria lost height.

Ivelaw-Chapman turned north towards the Kabul River, searching desperately for a flat piece of ground on which to land. Fortunately, he spotted what looked from the air to be a small flat area and just managed to land on it although, with the force of the impact, the port undercarriage and port lower plane were damaged and the tail skid and skid post broken off. Neither of the two men was hurt except for a bruise on Davies' knee where he struck his leg against the instrument panel.

As Ivelaw-Chapman wrote in an official report on the

incident, which he submitted later to his commanding officer:

'I found we were on a small plateau roughly sixty yards square, undulating and strewn with small boulders, with a steep drop of about two hundred feet on three sides and about two miles from the village of Sarobi.

'From the air the surrounding countryside had looked entirely deserted, but within a few minutes of landing we were surrounded by a seething mass of wildly shouting, heavily armed, excitable Afghans who surged round and in the machine and were raising a veritable babel in their highly pitched Pushtu!'

Neither Ivelaw-Chapman nor Davies could understand the language, although they did have some knowledge of Urdu. Try as hard as they could there was no one in the crowd who could speak this tongue. The airmen produced their 'ransom chit' — a document which informed anyone taking the time to read it that they were engaged on a peaceful mission and that they should be given safe conduct; unfortunately, no one in the milling throng was able to read. Ivelaw-Chapman wrote:

'However, they showed no outward sign of hostility and, as far as we could gather, they were making wild speculations as to our nationality. At this stage, a man arrived wearing a military greatcoat, who restored order, quietened the pandemonium, took over our "ransom chit" and generally took the situation in hand. We discovered later that this man was Noor Mahomed Khan, a "Brigadier" in that part of the Royalist Army then loyal to Ali Ahmed Khan. Unfortunately, however, he could neither speak nor understand Urdu and for the first thirty-six hours that we were in Afghanistan all our conversation had to be in sign language; nor were we able to find out among which political faction we had fallen'.

Noor Mahomed Khan was apparently satisfied with the contents of the pilots' 'random chit' and led them off down the slope, accompanied by several armed men. Sentries were posted on the aircraft. In a farmhouse at the foot of the hill the airmen were given green tea and chupattis while Khan wrote a letter in Pushtu, then sent it off to an unknown destination.

Ivelaw-Chapman and Davies were searched, but allowed to return to the aircraft to drain off the water and remove any valuable articles from the interior of the cockpit. These were taken into Khan's safe custody.

Some time later, their valuables and other personal effects having been returned, the two pilots left Sarobi with an escort of 12 riflemen and one officer. Ivelaw-Chapman reported:

'The leader of the escort and our two selves were mounted while our escort were on foot. It was during this journey that we discovered that our destination was to be Jagdallak where Ali Ahmed Khan, later Governor of Jalalabad, was mustering a strong army to march on Kabul.

'The journey that day, though only some thirty odd miles was very tedious and tiring, particularly for Davies who was in the saddle for eight hours almost continually with a knee which had swollen up badly during the previous night and must have been causing him considerable pain. The going was particularly bad — winding stony track partially covered in snow — the gradients were steep and the wind bitterly cold. The journey, however, went off without incident, except in a small village just short of Jagdallak where a large crowd gathered and obstructed our passage; however after a little time, our escort had convinced them of our British nationality and the nature of his mission and we were allowed to proceed, being given a chupatti each, presumably as a token of good faith'.

Ali Ahmed Khan's headquarters were in an old Rest House at Jagdallak on the main Khyber-Kabul road and it was into this building that the two pilots were led. They were shown to a room just large enough for two camp beds, two tables and a couple of chairs.

Khan's second son, Noor Ahmed Khan, announced that he was in charge of them and, although hospitable informed the airmen that he intended to treat them as political prisoners.

On the fifth day of their confinement a man got through
n foot from Kabul, bringing with him some cigarettes,
uit and a note for Ivelaw-Chapman from the British
Minister, Sir Francis Humphrys. The next day the pilots
ad their first meeting with Ali Ahmed Khan. Ivelaw-
Chapman wrote:

He assured us of his staunch friendship towards Great
Britain in the past, present and future; he promised to keep
guard on our aeroplane in Sarobi; he gave us despatches
r the Chief Commissioner in Peshawar and for the
'iceroy. He then bade us farewell.
'Outside the Rest House we found a Chevrolet van

awaiting us and we took our departure in this,
accompanied by a large armed escort. It was a great relief
to get out into the open again and the first part of the
journey towards the Jagdallak Pass was most picturesque.
The first hour or so passed without incident, but when the
road left the pass we started to encounter small gangs of
tribesmen at frequent intervals, all of whom stopped the
car, but in each case one or other of our escort was able to
establish friendly relations with the tribe in question and the
car was allowed to proceed'.

About three miles past Nimla they were again halted by
about 200 armed tribesmen who immediately started a
fierce row with the leader of the escorting soldiers.
Apparently, the tribesmen were completely opposed to the
Ali Ahmed Khan faction and considered that if anybody
was going to be recompensed for the safe conveyance of
the airmen through their territory then they should be the
ones to receive such a payment.

During the disturbance the Indian driver was made to turn the van round so that it faced back towards Jagdallak and for a time it looked as though the two sides would come to blows. On several occasions half-hearted shoves of annoyance were made by several members on both sides. How the matter was settled was something which always remained a mystery to the two pilots, but after about two hours of continuous shouting the van was allowed to resume its original direction; the leader of the tribesmen blocking the road then signalled that it could proceed.

'I then noticed that our party had been swollen by several of the tribesmen who had stopped us and no doubt they were eventually rewarded by the British Consul at Jalalabad. This increased load — there were now twenty-three persons in a van made to carry twelve — reduced our speed considerably, but the rest of the journey to Jalalabad went off peacefully, despite one or two false alarms and a barrier of boulders stretching right across the road and carefully placed just round a bend'.

At Jalalabad the pilots were informed that the British Consulate had been forced to leave when the rebellion had broken out in November and that it was now under the protection of the Pir Sahib of Baghdad within the surrounds of his fort at Charbagh, about six miles from Jalalabad. Ivelaw-Chapman, Davies and the extra large party of tribesmen lurched on along the road until they reached the fort. There they met the Consul.

The following morning the Consul informed Ivelaw-

Chapman that the road between Jalalabad and Khyber was still unsafe for travellers; he emphasised that this situation was likely to last for some time to come. There was only one way out of the country and into India — by air.

With the aid of a horse, lent by the Pir Sahib, Ivelaw-Chapman set off to search for a suitable landing ground as near to the fort as possible. He reported:

'After a long search I selected what I considered to be the only plot of ground within three miles of the fort which would in any way lend itself to the purpose. With labour offered by the Pir Sahib, I decided that it could be made fit in four days for a Victoria or Hinaidi, though not for a single-engined machine. That evening I wrote a lengthy letter to the Chief Commissioner, Peshawar, describing the situation fully and enclosing a detailed report as to the site, nature and the limitation of the landing ground and suggesting that either a Victoria or Hinaidi should come over the following Sunday and take us away.'

This letter, together with some consular despatches, was sent off to Peshawar by a special messenger on foot on the morning of 6 February.

As Ivelaw-Chapman and Davies waited for rescue, word reached them that Ali Ahmed Khan's camp at Jagdallak had been looted, the Rest House burned to the ground and Ahmed Khan forced to flee. He had only been able to slip unnoticed through the marauders by disguising himself as a mullah and getting away into the hills. All this had happened within a few days of the two men having left the Rest House.

Khan's downfall had come as a result of combined tribes of Shinwaris and Khogianis marching into his camp in full strength, ostensibly to give their allegiance to his cause; within hours they had turned on their hosts, killing them and looting the supplies.

On the Sunday morning — 10 February — Ivelaw-Chapman and his companion, accompanied by an escort, rode out to the makeshift landing ground to await the arrival of the rescue aircraft.

'To our surprise, two Bristol Fighters and a DH9A appeared and one of the former detached itself from the formation and, unfortunately, attempted to land. The undulations of the landing ground, however, as I had feared, proved too much for its tail skid which collapsed and in doing so broke the skid-post and fuselage cross members and damaged lower fin, tail-plane bracing and lower half of the rudder. It was obvious at once that it could not fly again that day so, on the advice of the consul, the two of us and Flying Officer C. R. Hancock, the pilot of the Bristol, left the large crowd that had collected around the machine, leaving Pir Sahib's men on guard, and rode back to the Fort to discuss the situation and to get off another letter to Peshawar explaining what had happened'.

Within an hour of the Bristol crash-landing the Shinwaris and Khogianis followed up their coup at Jagdallak by entering Jalalabad. They ousted the garrison and then proceeded to loot the city. From the airmens' point of view there was clearly little time to lose before they could make good their escape.

After a plan of action had been worked out Ivelaw-Chapman, Davies and Hancock returned to where the Bristol sat unhappily on the rough ground; there was no crowd peering and prodding at the machine — everyone had gone. The news of the rebel victory only six miles away had indeed travelled fast.

With the aid of the Pir Sahib's head carpenter, working with only a few primitive tools, the repair work got under way. One or other of the three pilots would explain what was required; the old man would shake or nod his head slowly, although always appearing not to understand. However, on every occasion, the broken part was repaired

**Below left: Some of the last passengers leaving Kabul in a No 70 Squadron Victoria.** / *J. W. Burley*

**Above: Victorias of No 70 Squadron and the Hinaidi of the Heavy Transport Flight lined up at Delhi for inspection by the Viceroy and the AOC-in-C after the Kabul evacuation, 27 February 1929.** / *W. H. Cox*

**Below: Inspection of the Kabul air lift aircraft and crews by the Viceroy at Delhi on 27 February 1929.** / *MOD*

satifactorily, or a new piece made to workable specifications.

'Towards evening when everything was going well, our work was suddenly curtailed by an inter-tribal fight over a small matter of loot which had been waging in the distance for some time, but was now moving rapidly nearer. We took shelter temporarily in a neighbouring fort and from that vantage point watched the scene of battle ominously close to the Bristol. At one time some of the tribesmen were sheltering behind the fuselage while the shots from their opponents were hitting the ground dangerously close to the machine.

'When the fighting was over we were advised not to return to the Bristol and so made our way back to the Pir Sahib's sanctuary just before dark'.

In the distance a bright red glow lit up the darkness. Jalalabad was on fire. Shortly before dusk the arsenal had been blown up by a time-fuse left behind by the fleeing

Below: The Handley Page Hinaidi of the Indian Heavy Transport Flight. / W. H. Cox

Right: The crew of an Indian Bomber Transport Flight Handley Page Clive at Lahore display the sartorial styles of the 1930s. Centre is Flight Lieutenant J. R. (later Air Marshal Sir John) Whitley. / AM Sir John Whitley

Below right: Troops of the 2/10 Baluch Regiment about to emplane in an Indian Bomber Transport Flight Valentia at Chaklala for the Chitral relief, September 1936. / AM Sir John Whitley

Royal garrison. Eight hundred people died in the explosio which sent a column of foul, black smoke almost 4,000 fee into the air above the city. Isolated fires sprang u everywhere and soon Jalalabad was ablaze from end t end.

The following morning the airmen went back to thei repair work and were surprised to find that the battlin tribesmen had not inflicted any damage on the Bristo Throughout the day they toiled and, surprisingly, wer unmolested; despite the fire in the city there was still muc looting to be done.

After another night's uneasy rest, with the sound c sporadic rifle fire ringing in their ears, it was back again t the exposed landing ground and down to work on th Bristol. By one o'clock the machine was ready to take off.

Davies went first with Hancock who had instructions t return in five days time to collect Ivelaw-Chapman. By tha time he hoped to have the landing ground in bette condition.

On Monday 18 February Hancock returned in th Bristol and this time made a perfect landing, using only ha of the extended strip prepared by the Pir Sahib's men unde Ivelaw-Chapman's direction.

At 1100hrs the Flight Lieutenant was back at Peshawa — exactly 20 days after having taken off from Risalpur o his transport mission.

With no aircraft to fly, Ivelaw-Chapman occupied hi time by completing his report and when this was finishe the air lift was almost over. On 24 February the evacuatio of the French and Italian legations was completed, leavin

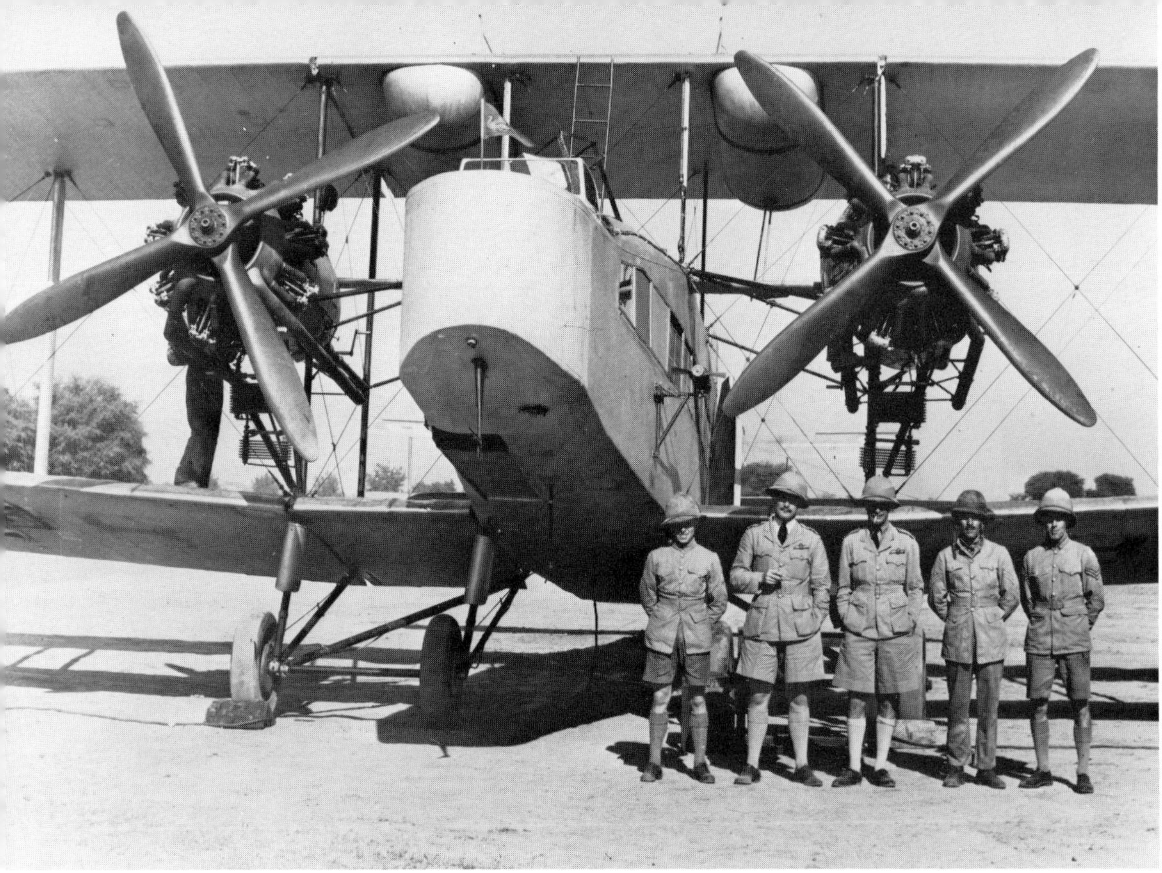

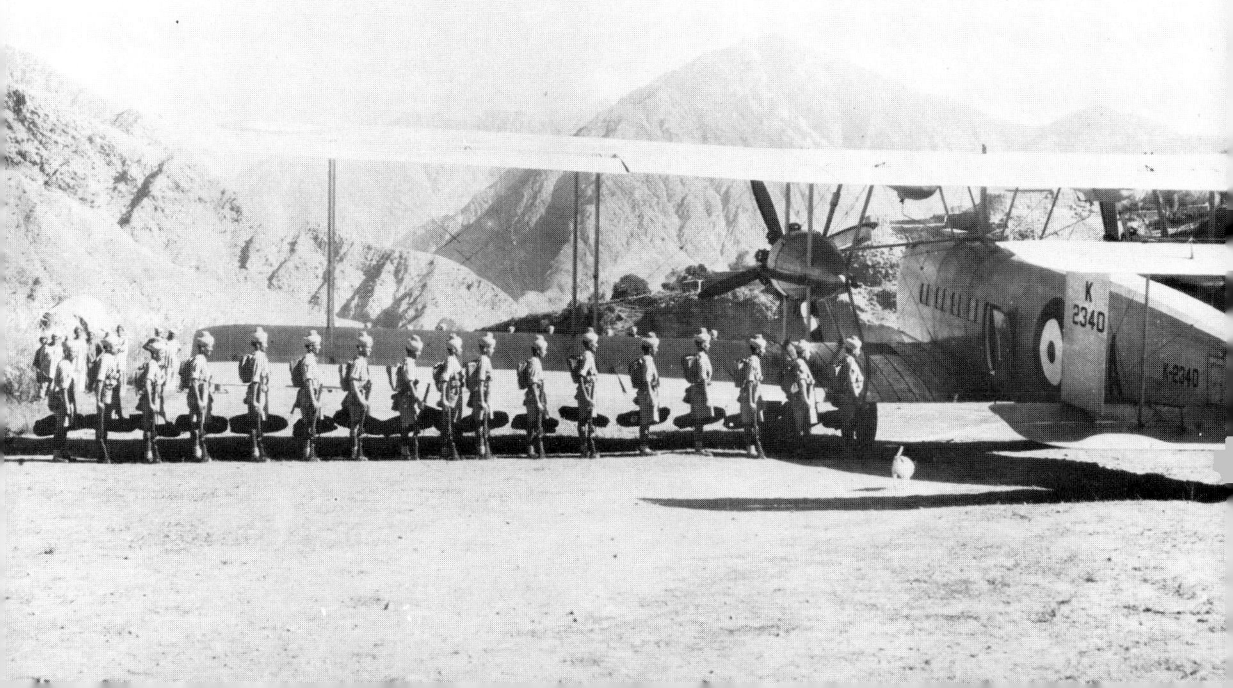
K
2340
K-2340

only the British. On the 25th, starting at 0745, seven Victorias and the Hinaidi left Risalpur for Kabul. By 1200 they were back at Peshawar with 39 passengers and nearly 2,000lb of baggage. In the last aircraft were Sir Francis Humphrys, Flying Officer Trusk, who had acted as a sort of airport manager, and LAC Donaldson, who had shared the essential wireless operating with an Army NCO flown in to assist.

Passengers flown out totalled 586, and their baggage weighed more than 24,000lb. Mileage covered on the actual evacuation flights came to 28,160, and if the positioning flights from Iraq and other supporting operations are added, the figure was 57,438.

Humphrys signalled the Foreign Office, praising the RAF's historic achievement in completing an air lift of such magnitude in the depths of winter across 10,000ft mountainous country. King George V, just recovered from a serious illness, sent a message of hearty congratulations on the great feat of rescue. *The Times* wrote:

'In those winter months — surely destined to become famous for ever in the history of the Air Force — the great aeroplanes went to and fro in all weathers over mountainous country of the most forbidding kind, where landing was practically impossible and any sort of failure in skill or material must have meant disaster. There was no disaster... It is a great thing to have won the Schneider Trophy. It is a greater thing, greater for the country and for the future of travel by air, to have effected the rescues from Kabul.'

On 27 February the aircraft flew to Delhi for inspection by the Viceroy and the Commander-in-Chief, then the Victorias returned to Iraq. Although Salmond's report stressed the value of having more large transport aircraft based in India, the sheer efficiency of the whole operation, with its demonstration of RAF flexibility, to some extent nullified his plea. Eight Victorias had been switched 2,800 miles from Iraq to the North-West Frontier of India, and their place taken by aircraft of No 216 Squadron transferred eastwards from Egypt, with no fuss or bother and apparently without prejudicing any important tasks in the Middle East.

There was no magical transformation in the Indian air transport situation over and above what was already in train. In 1929 the first of the new Handley Page transports — now given the type name of Clive — joined the Hinaidi at Lahore to operate as the Heavy Transport Flight, renamed the Bomber Transport Flight in April 1932. In 1930 the flight received two of the improved all metal Clive Mk IIs. The Hinaidi was eventually sold for scrap — according to local legend for the sum of 53 Rupees and ending its days as a shop — and in March 1933, when one of the Clives was destroyed by fire, it was replaced by a Victoria. By 1935 the flight was operating two Valentias, and a few Wapitis were available for communications flying.

From 1930, when the Hinaidi accompanied two Wapitis from Delhi to Singapore and back on 2-21 November, the transport flight made an annual Far East visit to support the bomber squadrons' reinforcement deployment training.

A regular army exercise offering great scope for air transport was the biennial changeover of the 1,400-1,700 strong garrison at Chitral in the North-west Frontier province. The Chitral Relief involved a 36-day march, and also tied up an escort and support force of even larger size. As early as 1927 a convincing case for using aircraft was argued in a paper to the United Services Institution of India by Squadron Leader E. J. Hodsoll, who calculated that four contemporary transport aircraft, such as the de Havilland Hercules, could complete the changeover in only 28 days, and eliminate the lavish escort arrangements. There was no need for the Army to consider seriously this piece of gratuitous advice on how to conduct a traditional land operation — which incidentally provided excellent training facilities — because there were simply no aircraft for the job.

RAF assistance was given in September 1930, however, when the column of 1,400 troops and 850 animals marching over difficult country from Dargai to Chitral was maintained for two days entirely by the Wapitis of Nos 11 and 39 Squadrons from Risalpur. About three tons of rations and forage were dropped each day at prearranged night halting points. The supplies were parachuted in specially made 56lb containers carried on the bomb racks and each Wapiti averaged four sorties a day.

For the 1936 Chitral relief not only was motor transport used for part of the route, shortening the journey by about a week, but one company (less two platoons) of the 3/11 Sikhs was flown from Chaklala, near Rawalpindi, to Drosh, the aerodrome for Chitral, and the 2/10 Baluch carried on the return journey. The flights crossed the 10,000ft Lowari pass and were made on 18-20 September by two Valentias. There was a repeat performance two years later, starting on 12 September, when a total of 28 troops and 32,300lb of equipment was flown between Risalpur and Drosh.

Sandwiched between these two Chitral reliefs were major operations in Waziristan, mainly against fanatical followers of the Fakir of Ipi. These underlined the value of air transport in no uncertain fashion, and with some 400 tons of supplies and more than 5,750 troops carried, represented the biggest combined freight and troop air lifts of the inter-war years. Although operations were spread over nearly 18 months, being governed by the sporadic and violent outbursts of rebel activity, and flights were mostly over short stages, the terrain was always difficult and spells of the most intensive flying were demanded.

The insurgents were more numerous and notably better organised than those encountered in Iraq during the 1920s as may be seen from the 1937 casualty figures of 21 British and Indian troops killed and 555 wounded. Hostilities started in November 1936 and during the next six months many supply dropping sorties were flown, about which few details are recorded. On 9-12 October four tons were dropped to troops advancing up the Khaisora Valley.

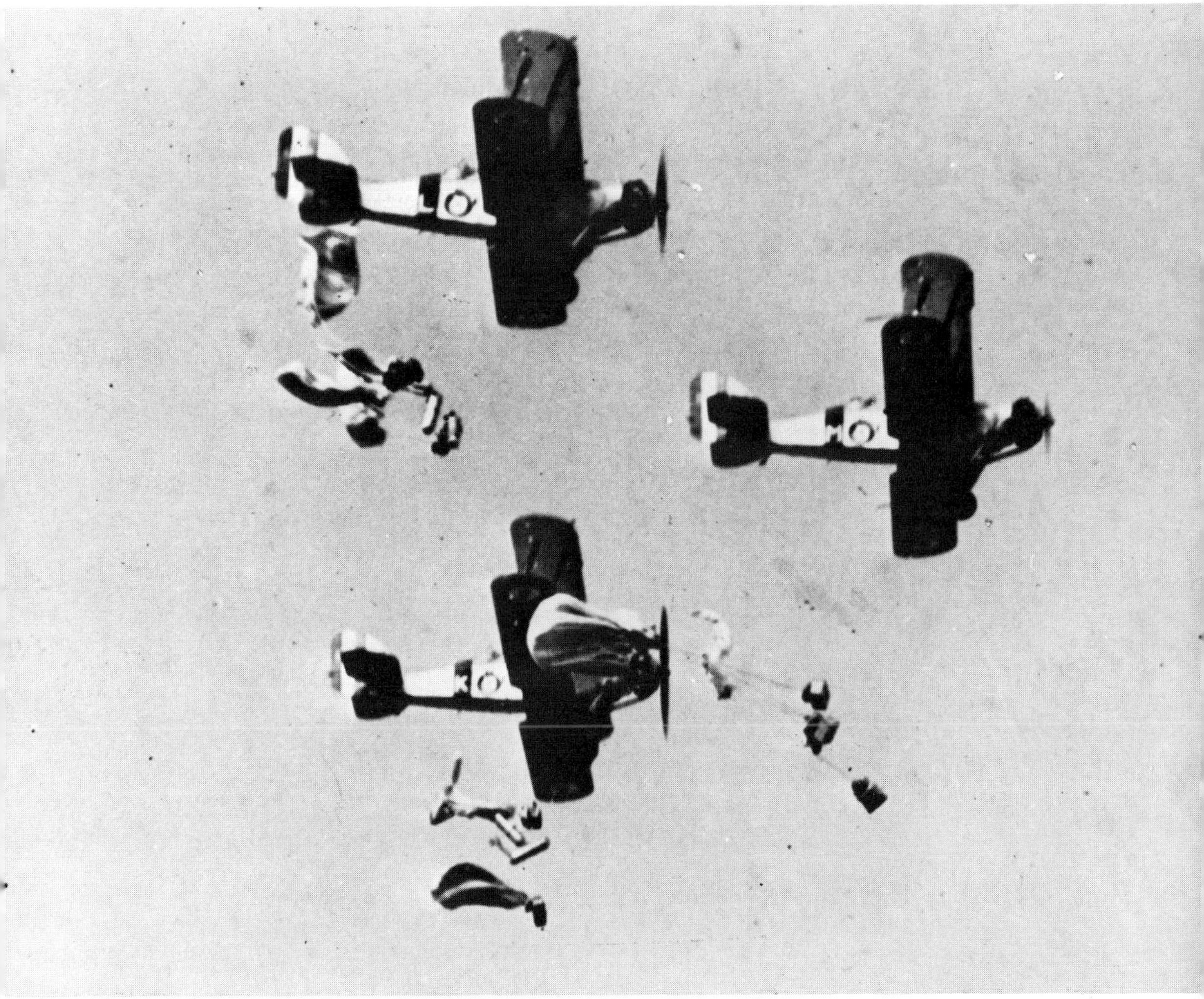

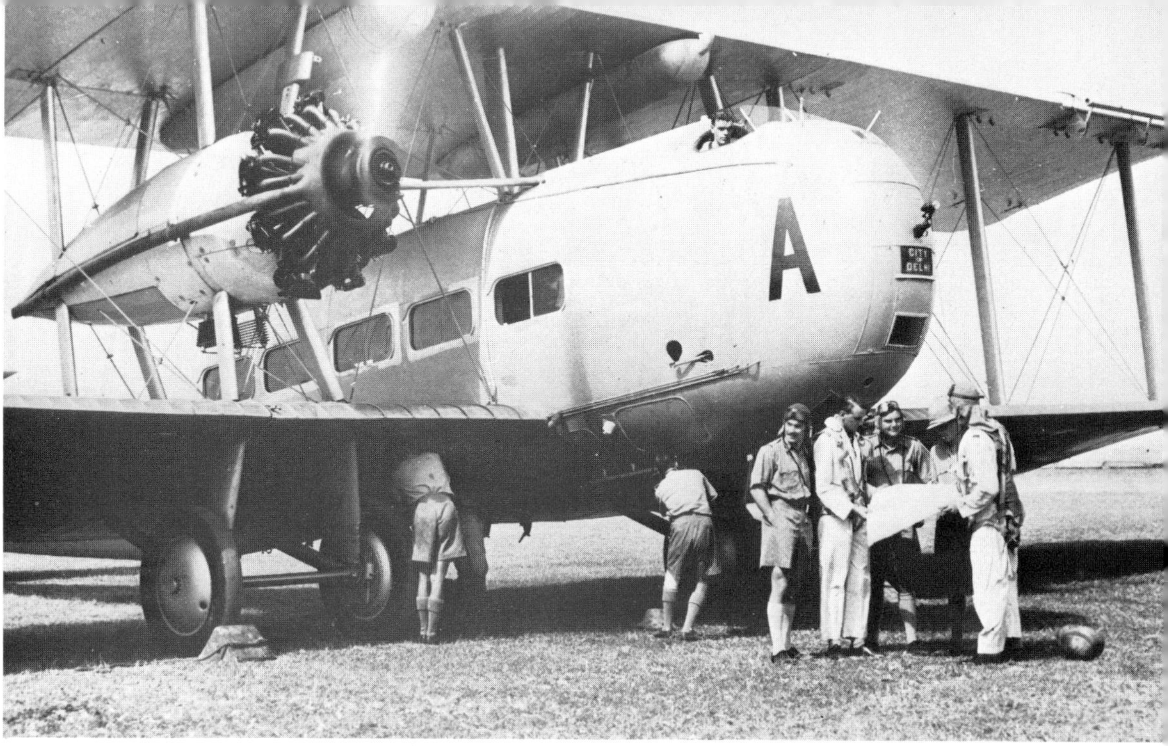
A
CITY
OF
DELHI

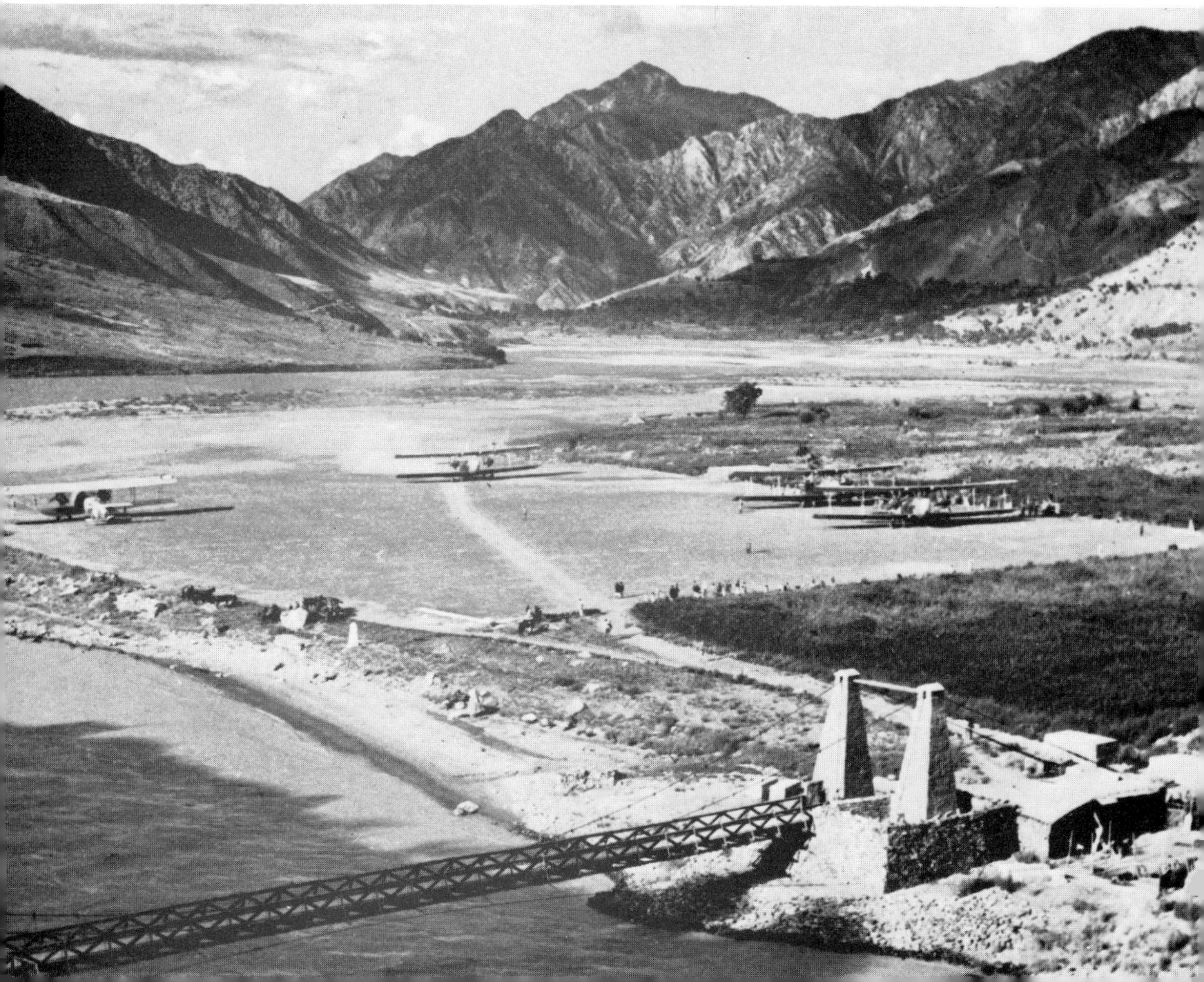

ter heavy rains had made the road impassable to motor
ansport, and on 9 January 1937 there was another rations
rop of more than 3½ tons.

Attacks were on a limited scale until 9 April, when a
0-lorry convoy escorted by four armoured cars was
mbushed in the Shahur Tangi gorge on the road between
e railhead at Manzai and the forward garrison base at
ana. Thirty-six men were killed — including seven
ritish officers. The 60-odd miles of winding mountain
ad offered ideal conditions for surprise attack and there
as no immediate alternative but to suspend road
ovements for a time while the garrison lived on its
eserves. Despite the short distance this was clearly an
pportunity for air transport, and between 19 April and
May two Valentias of the Bomber Transport Flight made
5 return trips between Manzai and Wana — plus other
ghts to Bannu, Kohat and Rawalpindi — carrying
0 tons of supplies and an unspecified number of
assengers which included 25 casualties.

Road transport was then restored and on 13 May the
alentias switched to para-dropping a day's rations to
oops moving across the Shammar Plain. The aircraft
arried 12 packs of 100lb on their bomb carriers, and
dditional loads for despatch through the side doors, the
arachute static cables being secured to the cabin floor.
ach Valentia flew two sorties and the total weight dropped
as 13,000lb. The location of the dropping zone,
urrounded by precipitous hills, called for the utmost flying
kill — and the turbulence caused some odd behaviour
mong the parachutes. One pilot saw a lightly loaded
arachute float upward to a height of 3,000ft above his
ircraft before it started to descend.

Two weeks later the BT Flight was back on the Manzai-
Vana run, where the road had again been closed by rebel
ctivities, putting in the most important air transport effort
f the whole campaign. Between 26 May and 4 June they
arried 114 tons of supplies and 601 troops. Ground crews
iled in shade temperatures of 118°F to keep the aircraft
erviceable and the aircrews sometimes flew five sorties a
ay, the Valentias bouncing prodigiously in the turbulence
s they staggered slowly up from Manzai, which lay at
,500 feet above sea level, to Wana, at 4,500 feet.

The air lift commitment had now grown beyond the
capacity of the India Command to maintain for any length
of time and at the end of May four of No 70 Squadron's
Valentias from Iraq were brought in to assist. Between
1 June and 25 July the 70 Squadron flight carried 135 tons
of stores and 1,664 troops, including about 50 casualties.
The apparent discrepancy between the amounts lifted
during these last two phases is explained by the fact that
the Iraq Valentias, with Pegasus IIL3 engines could only
carry about 2,800lb pay load, compared with the 4,000lb
lifted by the Indian aircraft which had the medium-speed
supercharged IIM3 engines.

Towards the end of July there was another lull in guerilla
activities and in early August the Iraq aircraft were
released. In September, however, the road was once again
rendered impassable and the BT Flight returned to the
familiar task, carrying about 60 tons and 2,764 troops until
the road was considered safe in early December. One
special operation was the relief by air of a mountain battery
at Wana on 17 November.

The last sustained transport operations of the Waziristan
campaign were in April-May 1938, when Bomber
Transport Flight Valentias carried 707 troops and 25,800lb
of equipment over the Manzai-Wana route. In the same
period there was an air drop of 500 empty sandbags to help
the defences of a Tochim Scout post which was under
bombardment by one of the few small rebel artillery units.

The campaign added much weight to the India
Command's case for a larger air transport force, and the
first improvement was the arrival on 16 November 1938 of
two twin-engined Airspeed Envoys to form a
communication flight at Lahore and thus free for their
prime operational duties the single-engined bombers
hitherto used. The Envoys had left England on
3 September, one of them being flown by Air Officer
Commanding India, Air Marshal Sir Philip Joubert. More
important was the conversion of No 31 (Army Co-
operation) Squadron to the bomber transport role on
1 April 1939. It took over the Bomber Transport Flight,
and additional Valentias were transferred for its use from
No 216 Squadron in Egypt, but for a time it still retained
one flight of Wapitis.

Final confirmation that RAF air transport in India had
come to stay was given when the 1940 Chitral Relief was
carried out entirely by air. Hodsoll was probably far too
busy at home to even notice that what he had advocated so
long ago had come to pass. Shortly before the start of
World War II he had become the British Government
adviser on air raid precautions.

# Home Affairs

## 7

The delay in disbanding No 86 Wing, mentioned in Chapter 2, was a precaution to meet a threatening industrial situation on the railways, culminating in a strike which began on 27 September 1919. Next morning a comprehensive air transport network was put into operation for carrying Government despatches to 76 places in the British Isles, with seats available on some aircraft for Government officials on urgent business.

Packages were collected in London overnight by RAF vehicles and mostly taken to Kenley, whence No 86 Wing aircraft flew them to Stonehenge, Birmingham, Tadcaster, Newcastle and Edinburgh. Various local services radiated from these centres, and parachute dropping zones were selected for 16 towns having no convenient aerodrome. Consignments for south-eastern England were distributed from Northolt.

On 28 September the first aircraft left Kenley at 0540 for Newcastle and was back by 1330. Next morning the loads included official mail for the King, flown from Edinburgh to Kenley. Fog badly affected operations on 2 October and is likely to have contributed to at least one of the accidents that day. Flying Officer F. H. G. Shepherd, who left Kenley at 0537 in a DH4, ran out of fuel near Newcastle, where he was due to land at the Town Moor aerodrome, and in attempting to put down on a football field, one of his wings hit a building and the aircraft crashed in a street at 0845. Shepherd died from a fractured skull, but his observer, Lt Page was uninjured and arranged the disposal of the mail. Later in the morning a DH4A was written off in a take-off crash at Newcastle, which caused no serious injuries, and there was a third accident between Bolton and Preston. The fog also prevented a Calshot-Plymouth mail flight by seaplane.

On 4 October five Handley Page 0/400s and a Vickers Vimy distributed a 5,000lb load of Government posters and handbills to various places, and there were plans to reinforce 86 Wing with similar aircraft if the strike was prolonged. Fog agains disrupted operations on 5 October — the last day of the strike — and many incoming flights had to be diverted from Kenley. In eight days the RAF flew 4,270 official packets from London and about 1,800 on the return trips.

The GPO policy regarding the carriage of public mail is somewhat obscure. On 29 September they announced that mail would be flown at a surcharge of 2/- per oz, and that all necessary RAF aircraft were being provided. Between 1 and 3 October mail was in fact flown both by the RAF and by various civil aircraft firms, but from 4 October onward the entire commitment was handled by the Service. The volume of mail was clearly far below expectations, and the RAF carried just over 1,600 letters between London and Glasgow, Manchester, Birmingham and Bristol, while the quantity officially recorded as having been flown by civil aircraft was even less. On all strike flying 62 RAF aircraft were employed, with the appropriate regional Group supporting the effort of No 86 Wing.

With the rail strike over and no foreseeable transport tasks ahead, No 86 Wing and its squadrons were disbanded, No 2 on 14 October and No 1 on the 28th. But before long the need arose for some central facilities to supplement the service offered by the various Area HQ communication flights, and on 1 April 1920, No 24 Squadron was reformed at Kenley for VIP flying and certain training tasks. No 24 had been the first RFC fighter squadron on the Western Front, and achieved a distinguished record. For its new role it has a mixture of DH9As, Bristol Fighters and Avro 504Ks, and apart from one experimental 'coupe' Bristol Fighter, passengers flew in open cockpits. All the DH4As had been sold on the civil market after the disbandment of 86 Wing.

Although a communications squadron, No 24 was controlled by HQ Fighting Area, and Squadron Leader William H. L. O'Neill, squadron commander in 1925-27 tried to make the most of this. When the fighter squadrons began to adopt characteristic unit markings, he devised bold red and blue zig-zags running the length of the fuselage for his aircraft, only to be told that these must be removed, as markings were for single-seater fighters only. However, a telescoped version comprising one 'zig' and one 'zag' painted on the tail fins was permitted and used by 24 Squadron until the outbreak of war in 1939. O'Neill seemed fated to conflict with authority and although he also lost the next skirmish, squadron morale was, if anything, raised. In 1926 he entered a team of six Bristols for the Fighting Area dive-boming competition which progressed to the final at Upavon and scored 94% — seven more than the runners up. All set to celebrate winning the

**Top right: DH4A of No 86 Wing at Tadcaster on a mail flight during the railway strike, September 1919.** / *RAF Museum*

**Right: A Bristol Fighter — squadron unknown — at Biggin Hill on a mail flight during the 1919 railway strike.** / *MOD*

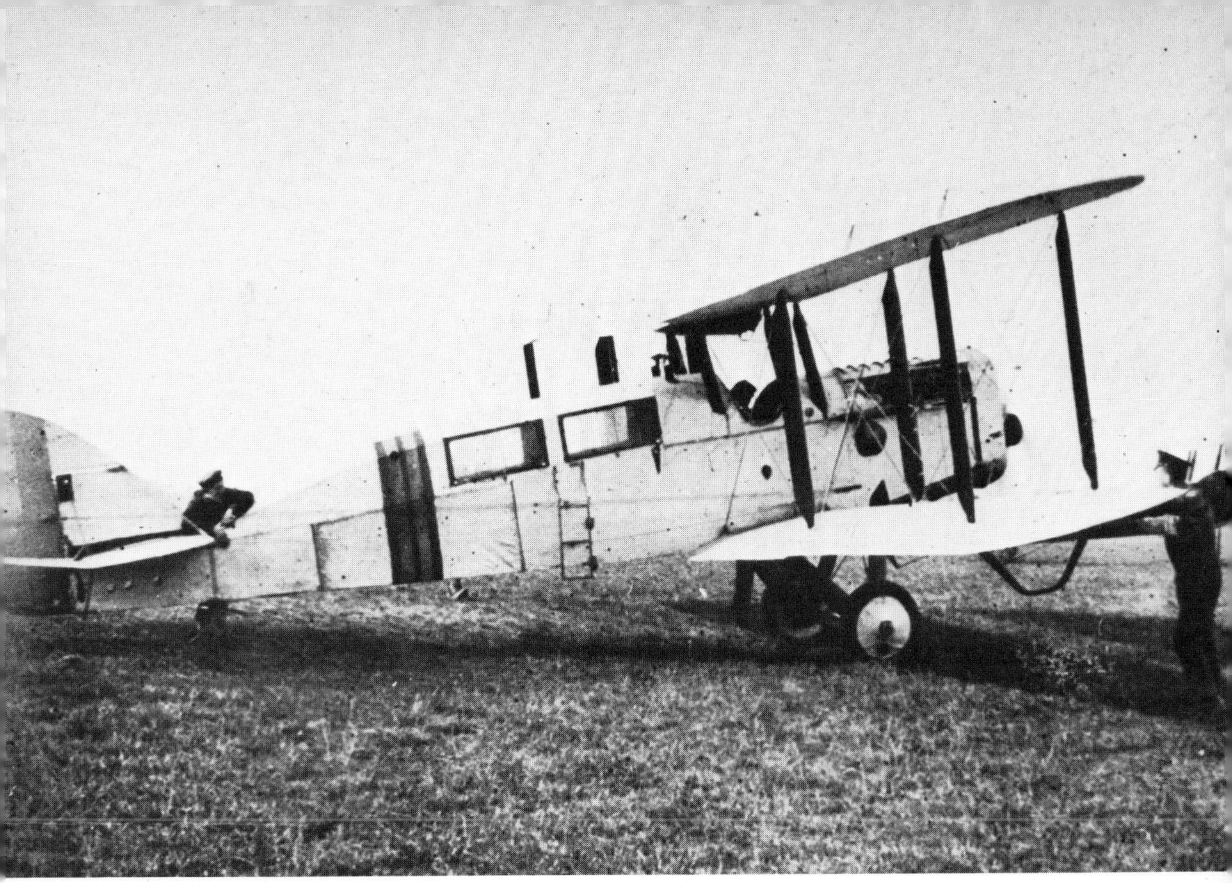

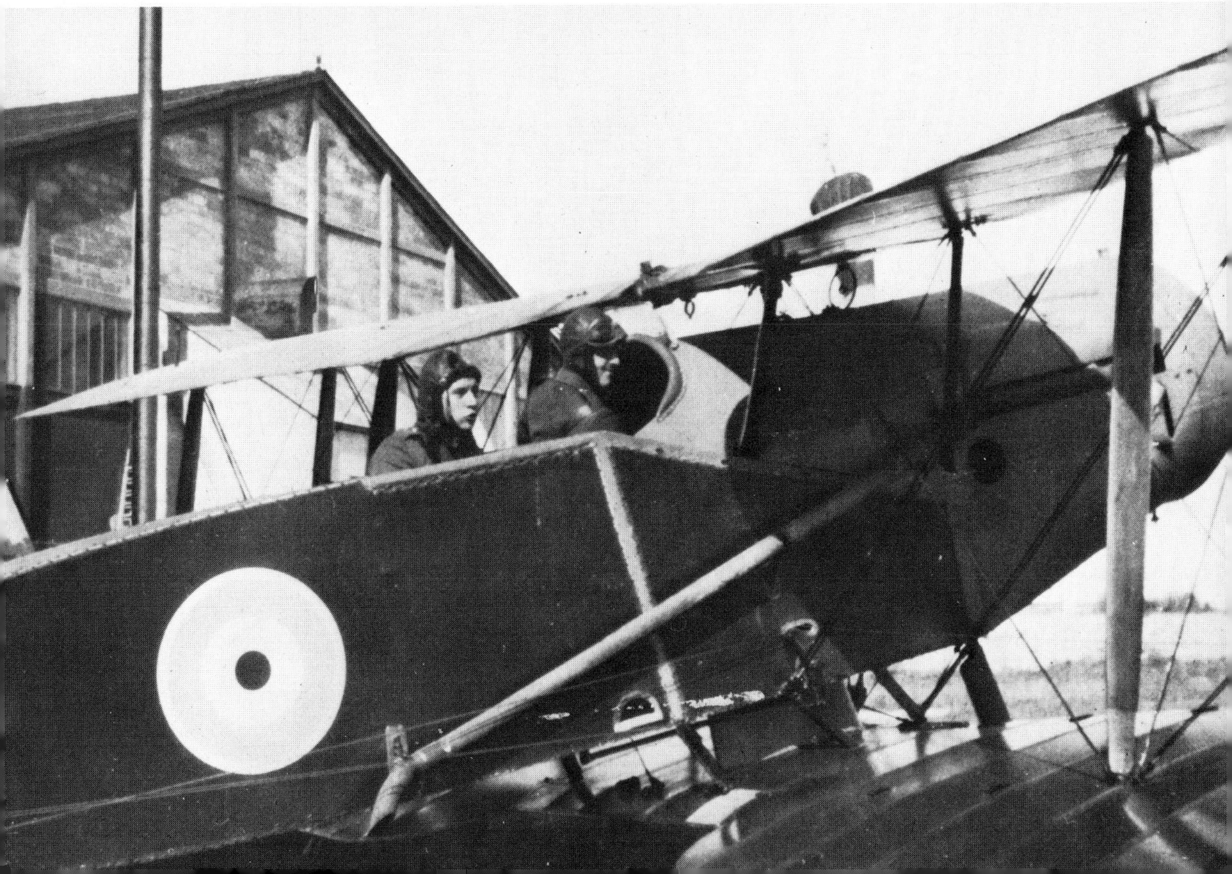

**Above:** 'Coupe' version (H1460) of the Bristol Fighter used by No 24 Squadron for a short time in 1920. / *Chaz Bowyer*

**Left:** Bristol Fighter of No 24 Squadron showing the zig-zag marking devised by the squadron commander but later disallowed by authority. / *MOD*

**Below:** Bristol Fighter J8430 first used by the Prince of Wales on 24 April 1928, piloted by Flying Officer G. C. Stemp. The abbreviated No 24 Squadron marking is shown on the tail fin. / *C. H. Barnes via Chaz Bowyer*

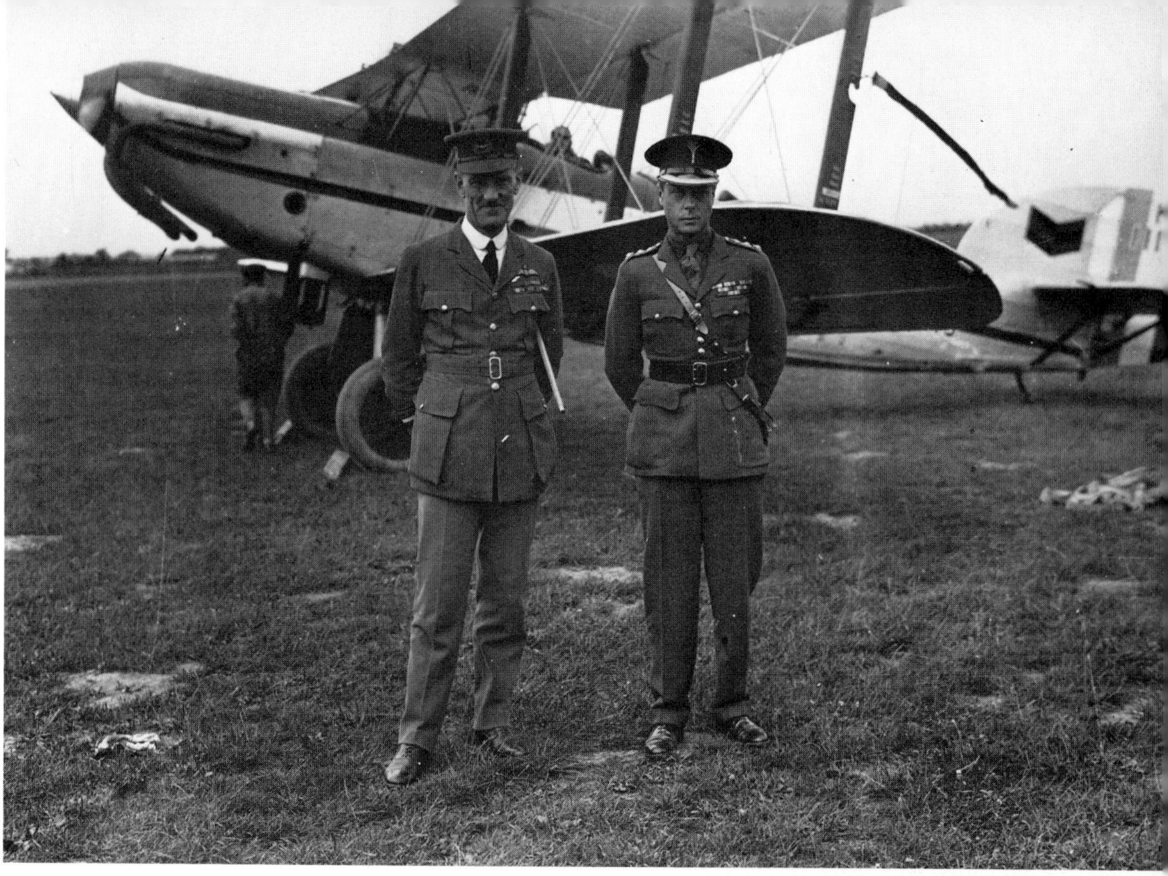

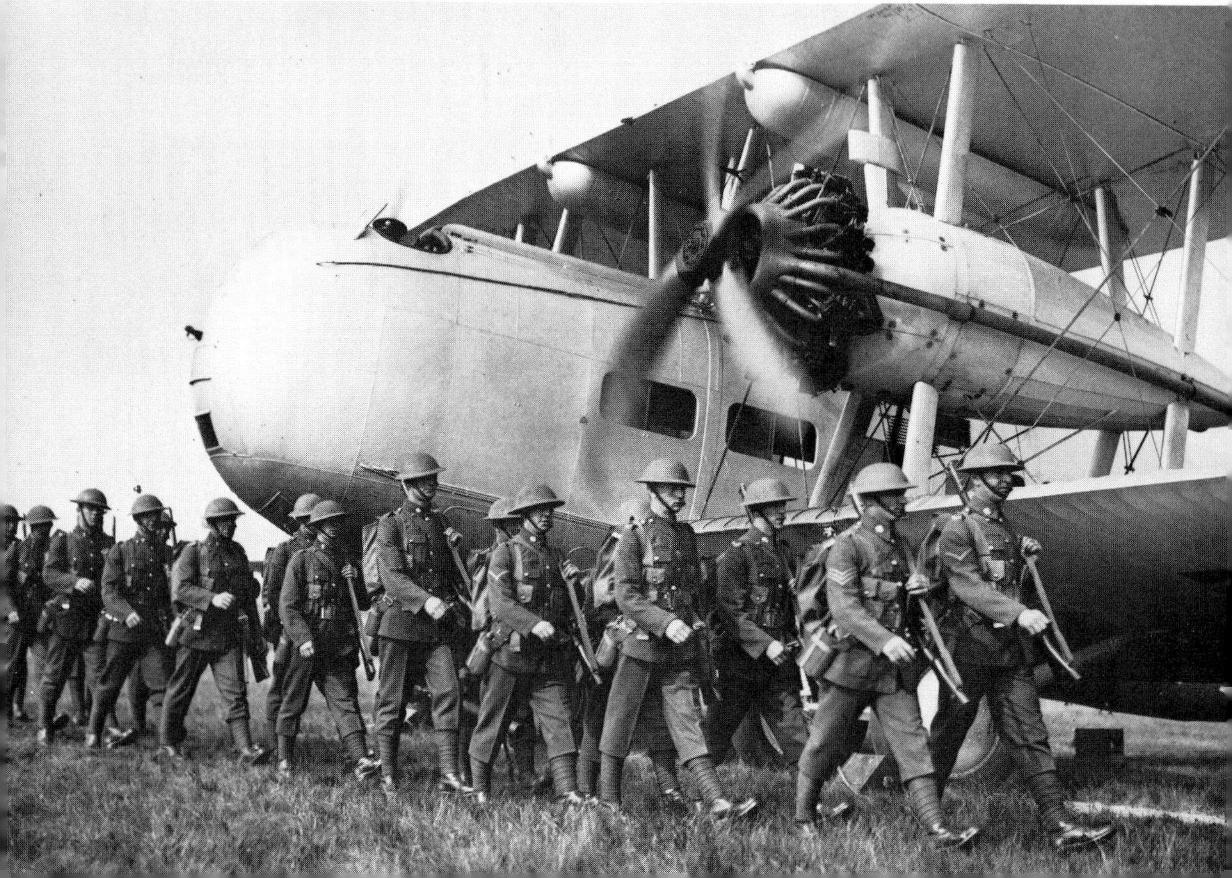

Left: The Duke of Windsor, when Prince of Wales, photographed with AVM Sir John Steel in front of a 24 Squadron VIP Fairey IIIF (K1115) while visiting Andover on 3 August 1930 during air exercises. / *Flight*

Bottom left: Coldstream Guards display traditional sang-froid in alarming proximity to a Valentia propeller during exercises, 1938. / *World Wide Photos*

coveted Sir Philip Sassoon Cup, they were belatedly disqualified, because the contest was supposed to have been confined to the single-seater fighters. However, the planned guest night was held, and O'Neill gave his crews miniature cups in consolation.

The next major air transport task at home also originated from industrial unrest — the General Strike of 1926. To co-ordinate air transport for urgent Government despatches, material and officials a special Air Ministry cell of six officers was formed under Air Vice-Marshal Robert Brooke-Popham. There was still no home-based transport squadron, so the work was shared by No 24 and other units.

The arrangements were similar to those of 1919, and No 24 Squadron flew official mail from Kenley to Castle Bromwich, Filton, Gosport, Halton, Norwich, Old Sarum and Spittlegate, then other aircraft took it on to 14 main distribution centres for ultimate delivery by road. The service began on 4 May, the first four aircraft leaving Kenley between 0525 and 0540. The next afternoon brought a touch of drama when Flying Officer Harry Schofield force-landed his DH9A near Sutton on the return flight from Spittlegate. Considerable ground haze had already caused one pilot to lose his way but Schofield established his position by the old Crystal Palace towers, and was approaching the Caterham valley in a relaxed frame of mind. Suddenly, there was a sharp bang from the rear, and looking round he saw something caught on the tail fin and flapping in the slipstream. The aircraft swung to the right, and corrective treatment revealed some major obstruction in the rudder movement. An immediate landing was advisable, and fortunately there was a reasonable field straight ahead, occupied only by a few cows. Schofield gingerly let down over some trees and rolled to a stop about six feet from the hedge. The object wrapped around the tail turned out to be a canvas engine cover which had blown from the rear cockpit. The curious cows surrounding the Ninack were soon joined by the inevitable crowd, which included several rather clinical looking gentlemen in white overalls. 'Glad you managed to miss that', said one, indicating a low building nearby. 'That's our explosives store — we're . . . .'s fireworks'.

The distribution of an official Government newspaper, *The British Gazette*, started on 5 May. Seven Vickers Virginia bombers — and a solitary Victoria transport — of No 58 Squadron were positioned at Northolt, where the staff of Inland Area Communications Flight organised the ground handling and loading of *Gazettes* flown to Sealand, near Chester. Virginias of No 9 Squadron flew from Biggin Hill to Catterick, and Fairey Fawns of No 100 Squadron took some packages on to Newcastle. On Sunday 9 May a Handley Page Hyderabad bomber of No 99 Squadron and four Fawns of No 100 carried 40,000 Newcastle-printed copies of the *Sunday Times* from Catterick to Northolt, which prompted other newspapers to demand similar facilities. The immediate ruling was that no more commercial newspapers should be air lifted, but there were second thoughts and a rationing scheme was under consideration when the strike ended.

Bristol Fighters of Nos 4 and 13 Squadrons, Fawns of No 12 and Virginias of No 58 assisted the Army by carrying personnel, small tank parts, wireless valves and other items.

Staff at some Navy establishments in Scotland could be paid only after the RAF flew £30,000 in Treasury notes from London to Edinburgh. A service by Supermarine Southampton flying boats was started between Calshot and Plymouth, and five Vickers Vimys were taken out of storage at Kenley and air tested against possible requirements, but the strike came to an end on 12 May.

The General Strike flights, which carried 39 tons of newspapers and 785 mailbags, had occupied an average of 19 aircraft daily and covered some 56,000 miles with excellent regularity, only one flight being delayed by weather. Other strike flying accounted for an additional 11,000 miles.

In January 1927 No 24 Squadron moved to Northolt, where for the next six years it continued VIP and general communications flying with a variety of aircraft types. On 24 April 1928 the Prince of Wales was given 30 minutes' local flying in Bristol Fighter J8430 by Flying Officer G. C. Stemp, and during the next three months made several official journeys in the same aircraft, flown by Flight Lieutenant D. S. Don who became his personal pilot. The DH9As had departed the previous June, but the Bristol was an even older design and there were some misgivings in high places about the Heir to the Throne's travels in such a veteran. In fact the Bristol Fighter was probably one of the safest aircraft ever built. However, in June, two new Westland Wapitis (J9095 and 6) were allotted to the squadron and these machines, with two Fairey IIIFs, delivered at about the same time, were used by HRH for most of his 20-odd flights during the next two years until he acquired the first of a series of civil registered aircraft. His longest trip was on 25 April 1930 in Wapiti J9095, flown by Don, from Marseilles to Smith's Lawn, via Lyons and Paris, after an African tour. The total journey time was 8 hours 10 minutes.

Another of 24 Squadron's regular VIP passengers was the Prime Minister, Ramsay MacDonald who frequently travelled by IIIF between London and his home at Lossiemouth. Pilots admired his willingness to start a flight in the face of a poor weather forecast, and, even more, his patience and lack of pique if a diversion or precautionary landing became necessary. On 24 August 1929 his IIIF flight from Lossiemouth took nearly nine hours, with landings at Newcastle and Catterick to await weather clearances and several detours round storms. In contrast, his fastest time for the journey, on 1 April 1931, was 3 hours 15 minutes.

The Westland and Fairey types were both single-engined day bombers, and beyond the provision of windscreens and a few modifications to the gunners' cockpits those in 24 Squadron made few concessions to passenger comfort. It was not until 1930 that the Air Council appears to have considered cabin travel for VIPs — for the first time since 1919 and again with a de Havilland aircraft. In November 1930, a three-seater Puss Moth went to No 24 Squadron for trials, but the type was not adopted for Service use.

On 10 July 1933 No 24 moved to Hendon, still with assorted two-seater aircraft — IIIFs, Harts, Moths and Tiger Moths — but two years later it began to assume more the appearance of a transport squadron with the allotment of a 10-seater DH89 Dragon Rapide. In 1938 it had two of the larger four-engined DH86s, and during September, one of them made the squadron's longest-ever trip, carrying the Under Secretary of State for Air, Captain Harold Balfour to Nairobi and back.

To supplement the communications and VIP work of No 24 Squadron a few bomber transport aircraft at home were used for troop familiarisation flights, special exercises and research. From the mid-1930s two Valentias were usually made available for a few days every year to fly parties of soldiers from Farnborough, and in the summer of 1938 a more ambitious programme was arranged, during which 5,250 troops — including 1,200 Territorials — were flown. Although much had been learned from overseas transport operations the programme included various exercises to study more precisely some of the points which had emerged — such as the effects of air transport on combat efficiency, and free drop techniques for use when parachutes were scarce or unavailable. In one phase 40 men of the 1st Battalion Coldstream Guards flew from Odiham to Catterick, where they immediately engaged in a mock battle. Half of the party flew before lunch and the remainder after their meal. Contrary to popular belief of the time, 50% of the men flying on empty stomachs suffered from air sickness, whereas none of the second group was affected.

In free dropping trials at Turnhouse loads were released from the side doors of Valentias at various heights, and it was confirmed that the lower they could be dropped the less they were damaged. In packages of corned beef, about 10% of the tins were damaged sufficiently to make their opening difficult, while official issue biscuits were substantially broken but still edible. It was calculated that in European conditions one Valentia could carry a day's food for 980 men.

# Air Ambulance 8

One factor contributing to the heavy mortality in World War I was the inevitably long time taken to move the seriously wounded from the front line to hospital. Doctors looked longingly towards the aeroplane, but there was no practical way of using it as an ambulance in the trench warfare of the Western Front.

It is therefore logical that the earliest British casualty evacuation flights should have been made in the Middle East, where despite longer distances and more tedious surface journeys to base hospitals, the type of warfare and terrain enabled aircraft to land and take off much closer to the scene of fighting. The first recorded 'casevac' in the Royal Flying Corps was on 19 February 1917, when a trooper of the Imperial Camel Corps whose ankle had been smashed by a Bedouin bullet at Bir-el-Hassana in the Sinai desert, was flown to Kilo 143 in the observer's cockpit of an unspecified aircraft in 45 minutes. A surface journey would have taken three days. In Egypt during the last year of the war experimental stretcher installations were made in various aircraft, including DH6, DH9 and Armstrong-Whitworth FK8. Flight trials of the DH6, with stretcher fitted, are believed to have been made in 1918 by Major A. D. Kennedy of the RFC Medical Service, but there is no record of operational aeromedical flights by any of these aircraft.

An opportunity to develop a more sophisticated air ambulance came in 1919, with the planning of operations against the 'Mad Mullah' in Somaliland. For 17 years the Dervish leader — Mohammed bin Abdullah Hassan, to use his proper title — had been fomenting unrest and generally flouting authority. To determine whether air power might succeed where conventional ground actions had failed, an RAF strike element of 12 DH9s, commanded by Group Captain Robert Gordon and entitled 'Z Force,' was shipped to Berbera in HMS *Ark Royal* to co-operate with the Camel Corps and the King's African Rifles in operations against the Mullah.

Since this was predominantly an air campaign, the senior Medical Officer, Wing Commander W. Tyrrell (later AVM Sir William) recommended that one DH9 should be assigned for ambulance duties, and sketched a layout to enable it to carry a sitting case and one stretcher behind the pilot. Aircraft D3117 was thus modified by the Royal Aircraft Establishment, Farnborough, and although rudder control was reduced and the stalling speed raised by the coffin-like structure on the rear fuselage, climb and cruising speed were hardly affected.

Operations began on 20 January 1920, and the RAF reconnaissance and bombing was so effective that the campaign lasted a mere three weeks, with only three native ranks killed. The 'blood wagon', 'hearse' or 'limousine', as the ambulance aircraft became known to the troops, was mercifully not required for combat casualties, but proved most useful for general light transport work. Then, a few days before the campaign ended it earned its keep medically. At about 0915 on 1 February Captain J. F. Godman, Intelligence Staff Officer of the Somaliland Field Force, was brought by stretcher party to the RAF advanced aerodrome at El Afweina — some 160 miles south-east of Berbera in a state of collapse and running a temperature of 104 degrees. He had been with a Camel Corps party for the past 36 hours engaged in a breakneck night and day final pursuit of the Mullah, when a septic toe had developed into general septicaemia. By chance the air ambulance had just arrived on a courier run, and at 0930 was airborne with the patient for the field hospital at Eil dur Elan, where Flight Lieutenant J. G. Skeet performed an immediate operation. The 75-mile journey took only 45 minutes, as against a 3½-day camel trek. A few days later Godman was flown the 95 miles to base hospital at Berbera, where the offending toe was removed. Seven other sickness cases made this flight during the withdrawal phase of the campaign. Tyrrell wrote:

'The air ambulance has proved that especially in operations over country where other transport is so tedious and trying, the aeroplane is a veritable godsend for sick and wounded. One officer ... owes his life, in my opinion, to his prompt and smooth evacuation by this machine'.

Apart from this immense benefit to patients, employment of the aircraft showed that the numbers of bearers, camels and other forms of surface medical transport on any similar expeditions in the future could be substantially reduced.

While the 'hearse' was proving its worth in Somaliland, an unmodified World War I aircraft type was making an emergency casualty evacuation flight some 1,750 miles to the north. This was at Abu Kemal, on the Syria-Iraq border, where a British detachment was under sporadic attack from dissidents. A few RE8s of No 6 Squadron were kept safe from saboteurs in the village square and wheeled through a gap in the walls when required for operations. During January 1920 (the precise date is unrecorded) the medical officer decided that even makeshift air transport

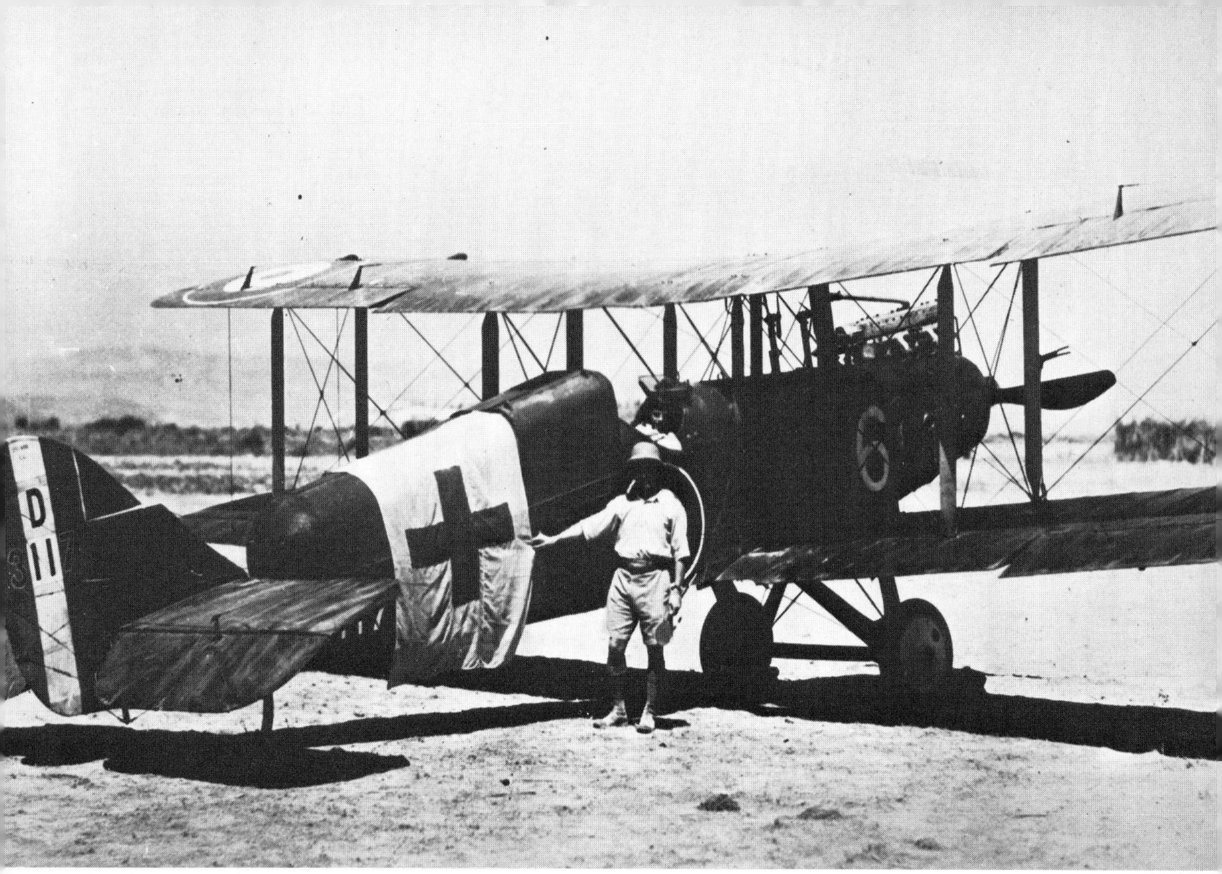
D
11
6

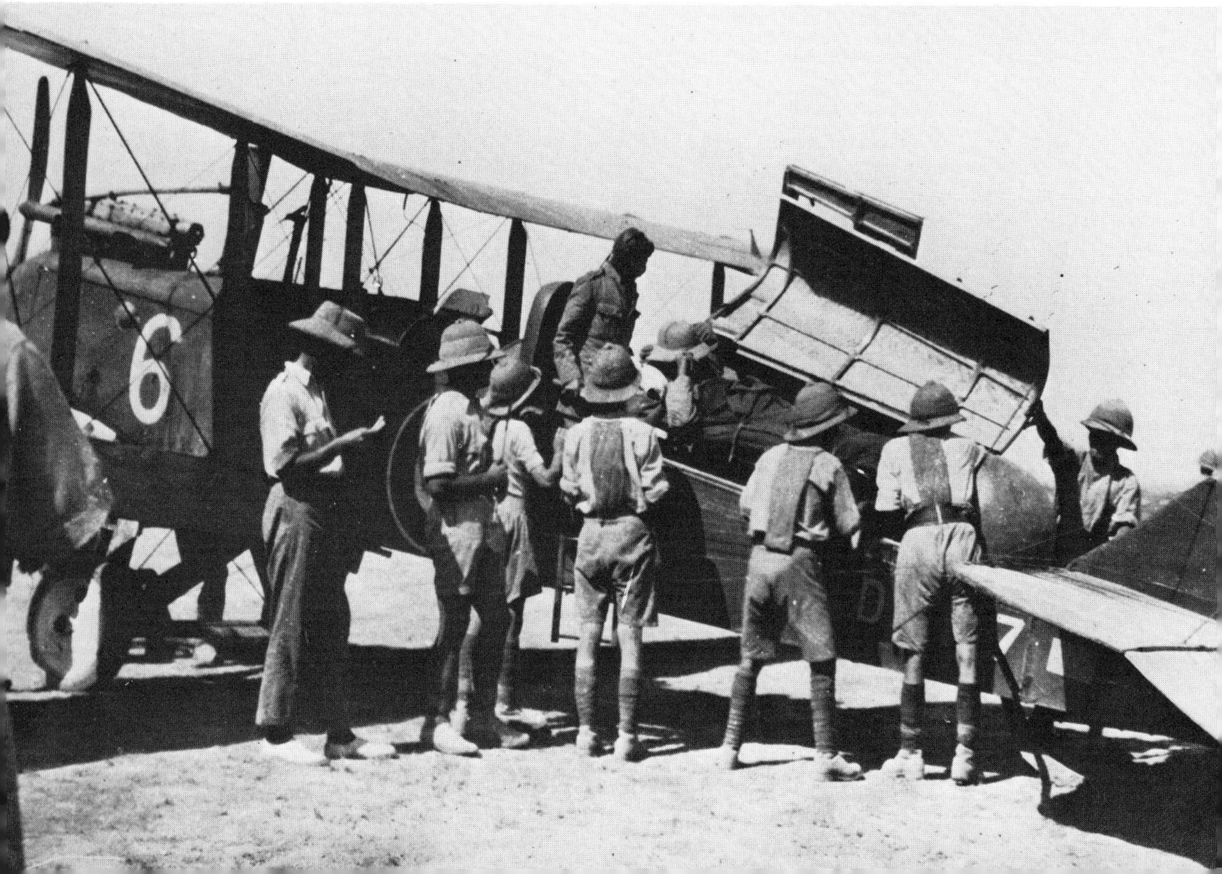
6
D

Left: DH9 converted by RAE for ambulance work, Somaliland, 1919. / MOD

Below left: The first aeromedical operation by a specially converted RAF aircraft. Captain J. F. Godman, of the Somali Camel Corps, being removed from the DH9 'blood wagon' at Eil dur Elan, 1 February 1920. / MOD

Above: The Z Force ambulance was also used for light transport duties — in this case the carriage of medical comforts! / Public Record Office

Below: The first of the Vickers Vimy ambulances (J6855) built for the RAF.

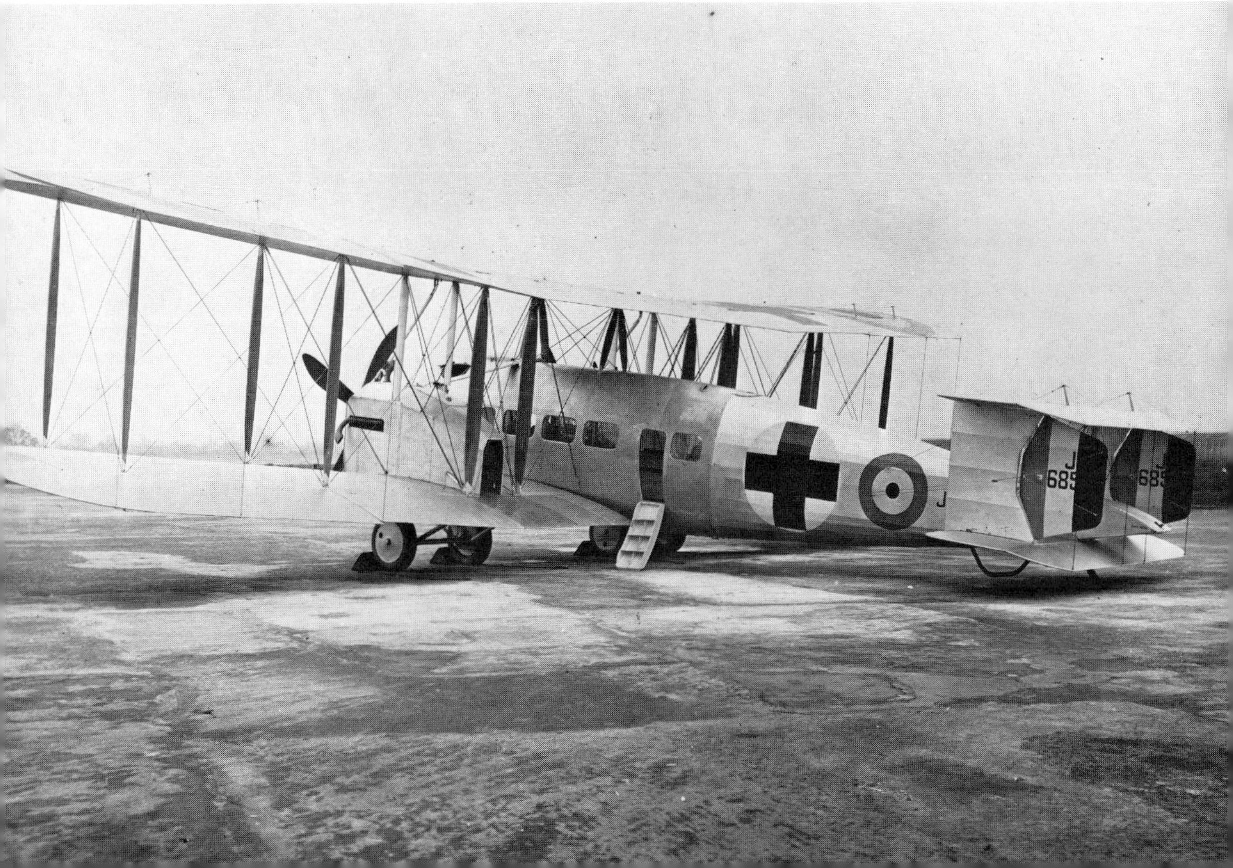

would give an officer with a severe bullet wound in the liver a better survival prospect than the exhausting journey over rough desert tracks in a Model T Ford ambulance. A car seat was rigged in an RE8 rear cockpit in an inclined position and the patient is reported to have slept for most of the 260-mile flight to Baghdad.

Nearly all the aeromedical pioneering took place in Iraq and on 20 July 1921 a Vickers Vimy of No 70 Squadron piloted by Flying Officer Herbert Seton Broughall, made the first recorded 'mercy dash' — to quote the headline nowadays used by the popular Press to describe a flight initiated or diverted to pick up a patient. In this case it was a VIP, Sheikh Murthi al Rifadi of the Aneiza tribe. The Baghdad-based motor convoy marking the desert air route had several cordial meetings with him during their early journeys, and on the final trip to Amman found his camp in some disarray after an attack by Beni Sekhr raiders from Transjordan. The young sheikh had an ugly back wound which clearly needed hospital treatment. After much parleying conducted by the invaluable Captain Holt, the tribal elders accepted the RAF offer to fly him to hospital, and Headquarters at Baghdad duly signalled their approval. During the afternoon the Vimy flew in to the nearest desert landing ground at Rutbah Wells — later designated LG4A — and after waiting for the better take-off conditions of the evening, departed for Baghdad where the patient made a full recovery. (In April 1938 Broughall returned to No 70 Squadron as its Squadron Commander.)

Most dramatic of the early Iraq 'casevacs' was that by two DH9As of No 55 Squadron, based at Mosul, on 12 September 1921. While co-operating with the Army in the Desht-I-Harir area on a low level reconnaissance, Flying Officer C. H. Teagle in aircraft H153 was hit by a rebel bullet and forced to crash land. This caused him further injuries and his observer was also hurt. It was the familiar situation requiring an air lift or a punishing surface trek to the nearest base hospital, and the troop signalled the next two Ninacks arriving for operations to land nearby. The pilots, Flying Officers Frederick Damant and Charles Spackman, thought it feasible to carry the two injured officers in the rear cockpits, but the displaced gunners would be little more than two extra mouths for the Army to feed. So these unknown heroes — doubtless airmen of humble rank — volunteered to fly out lying on the wings, with minimal moral and physical support provided by some rope lashings. It is sad to record that after this display of initiative and cool nerve, Teagle died of his injuries four days later.

During the following months various 'casevac' flights were made by Bristol Fighters and DH9As, both being adapted to carry the Neil-Robertson lightweight bamboo stretcher strapped to the top of the fuselage behind the pilot. This looked highly perilous, but was in fact safe and secure, and the technique was used until 1931, when Westland Wapitis were modified to take the stretcher inside the fuselage, thereby improving the patient's peace of mind.

The Air Ministry had been greatly impressed by the success of Tyrrell's first official air ambulance in 'Z Force' and lavish developments followed. In 1921 the RAF bought a Vickers Vimy Ambulance (J6855), based on the Vimy Commercial and powered by two Napier Lion engines. Intended for use in Egypt and Iraq, it had oxygen equipment for patients, cabin cooling fans, an electric kettle and a toilet. It was written off in a crash before it had performed any ambulance work, and in 1922 two more with less sophisticated equipment were sent to Iraq. These were also dogged by misfortune for many months. Apart from a nose-loading facility and internal stretcher fitting these aircraft were, to all intents and purposes Vernons and were usually known as such. In July 1923 while the specialist aircraft concept was still popular in the Ministry four passenger versions of the large single-engined Avro Aldershot bomber, adapted to carry 12 sitting or 6 stretcher cases, were ordered for use in the Middle East.

The first major medical air lift by the RAF took place in April-May 1923 when the troops sent to restore authority in the Rowanduz area (see Chapter 5) were on the return march. From mid-April a growing incidence of stomach troubles among the 2nd Cameronians and the West Yorkshires began to cause concern, and by the 26th the Senior Medical Officer, Lieutenant Colonel H. S. Roche had confirmed his worst fears — an outbreak of dysentery and severe diarrhoea. Some of the troops had recently come from service in India, they had undergone a tough march in bad weather on far from lavish rations and generally their resistance was low. The only possible way of moving the patients to hospital for immediate treatment was to fly them.

A suitable emergency landing area was found between the two high ranges of hills in the Beitwata valley near Serkhuma, and five Vernons carrying medical staff and equipment were ordered from Baghdad to join the seven already on supply work at Kirkuk. Nos 45 and 70 Squadrons were equally represented and Squadron Leader A. T. 'Bert' Harris, Co of No 45, was placed in charge of flying. The evacuation started on 28 April in weather which seasoned Bristol Fighter pilots of No 6 Squadron, well familiar with the region, described as the worst in their entire experience. To reach Serkhuma the aircraft had to cross the Adghir Dag peak at a minimum of 5,000 feet to avoid the worst turbulence — no mean struggle for an Eagle-Vernon — and the greatest care was devoted to aircraft servicing and preparation.

Despite all precautions nature claimed one victory. In the late afternoon of 28 April, Flight Lieutenant Ian Matheson, 45 Squadron, was staggering and bumping over the mountains with a full load of patients in Vernon J6882 when without warning the aircraft was gripped in the giant, invisible hand of a monstrous down current. Matheson applied full power but the Vernon was forced remorselessly and rapidly downwards through 3,000 feet. When nearly at ground level and only seconds from disaster there appeared miraculously in front of his eyes a small flat area amid the rocky outcrops. Matheson still retained some vestige of control and skilfully managed to deposit his rapidly sinking aircraft on to the surface in a flat attitude. Although the

**Top right: Interior of Vimy ambulance J6855. Note elegant toilet facilities.** / *Vickers*

**Right: Loading an ambulance Vernon at Hinaidi.** / *MOD*

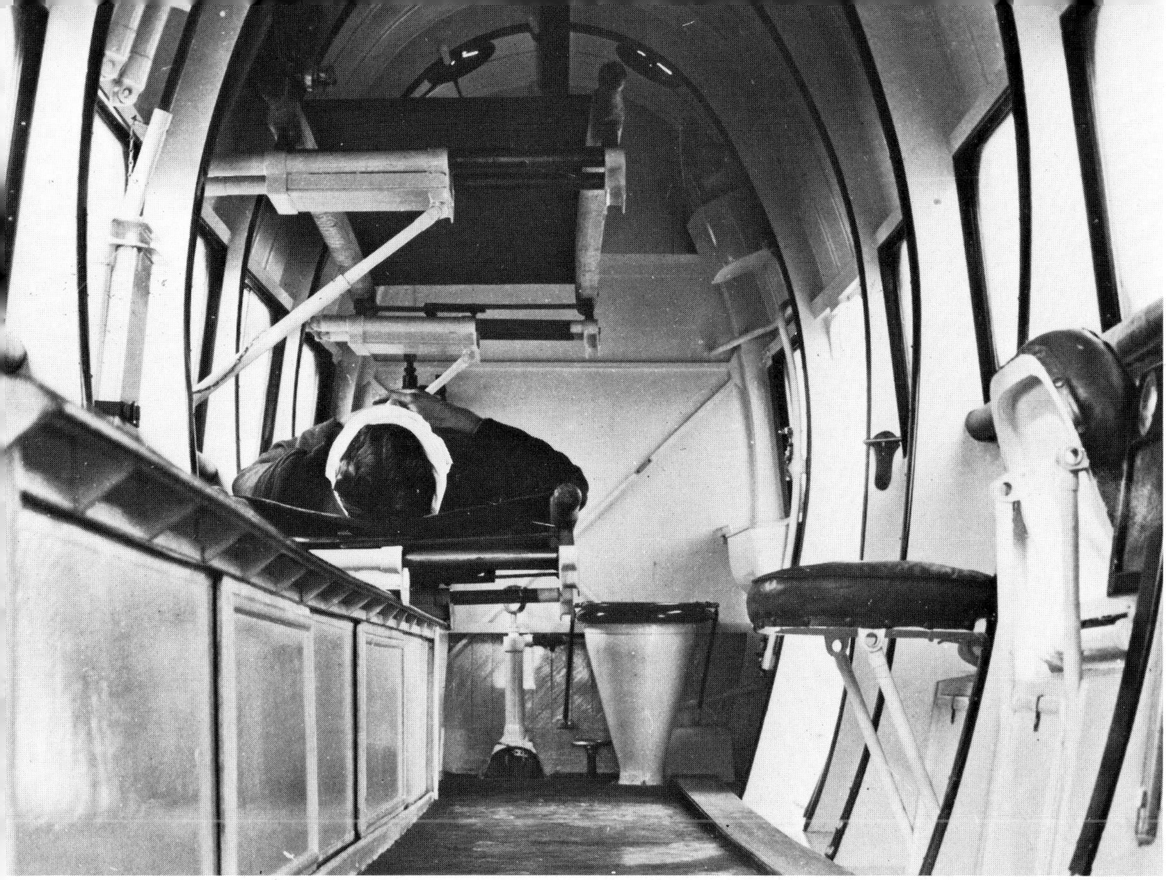

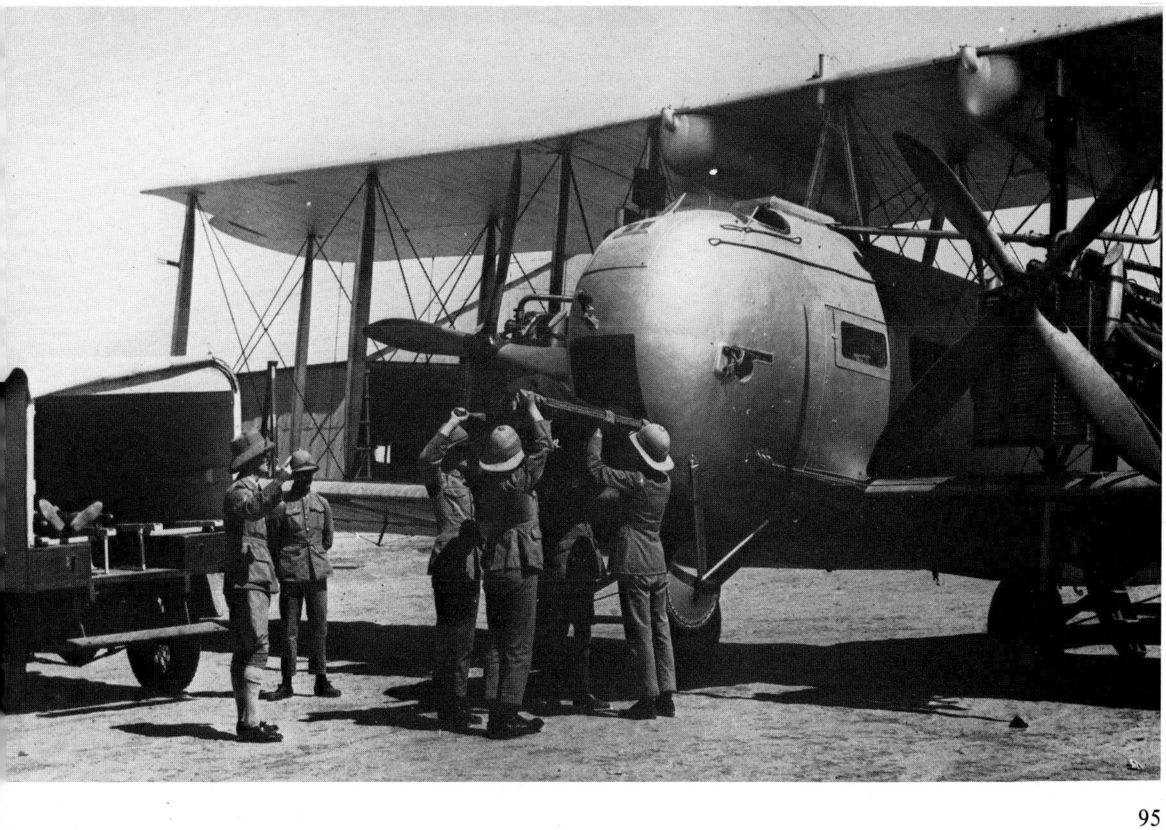

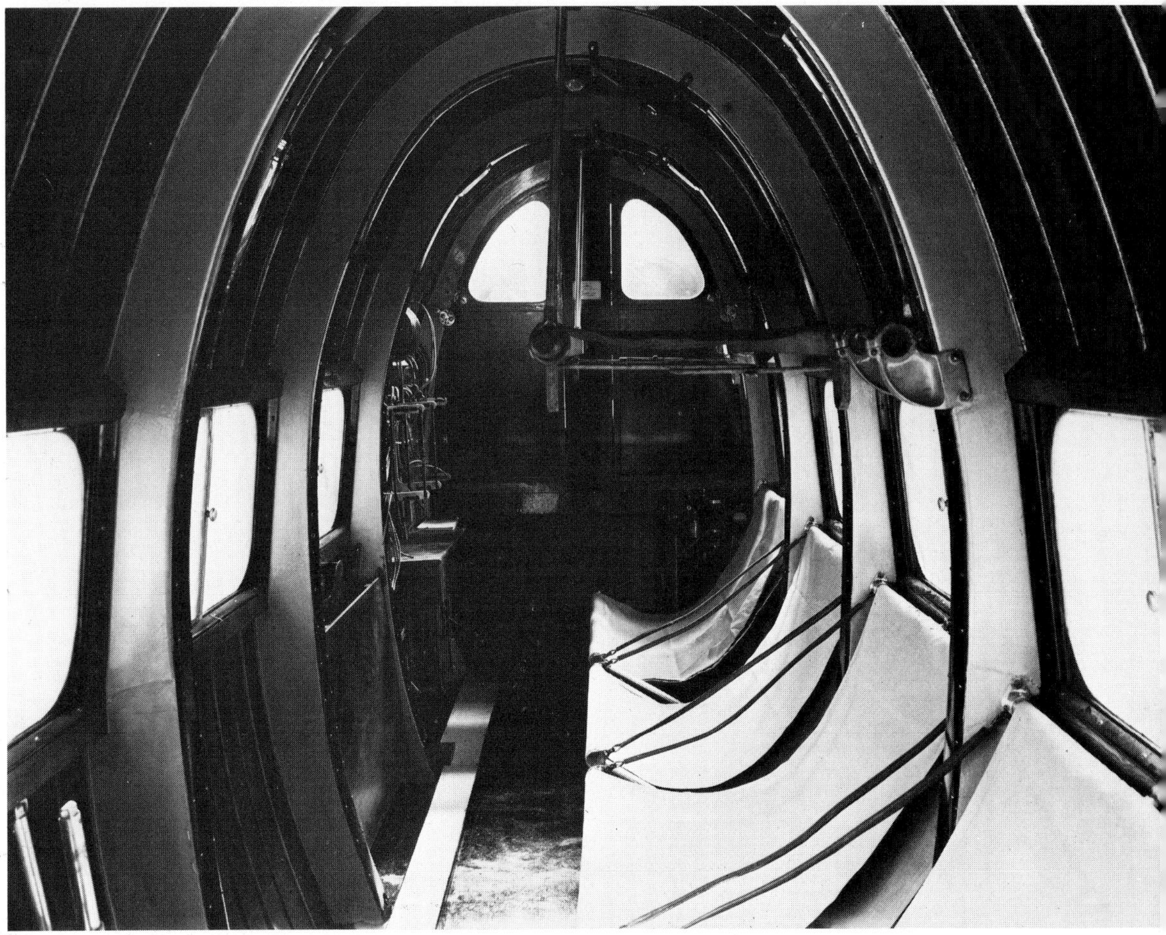

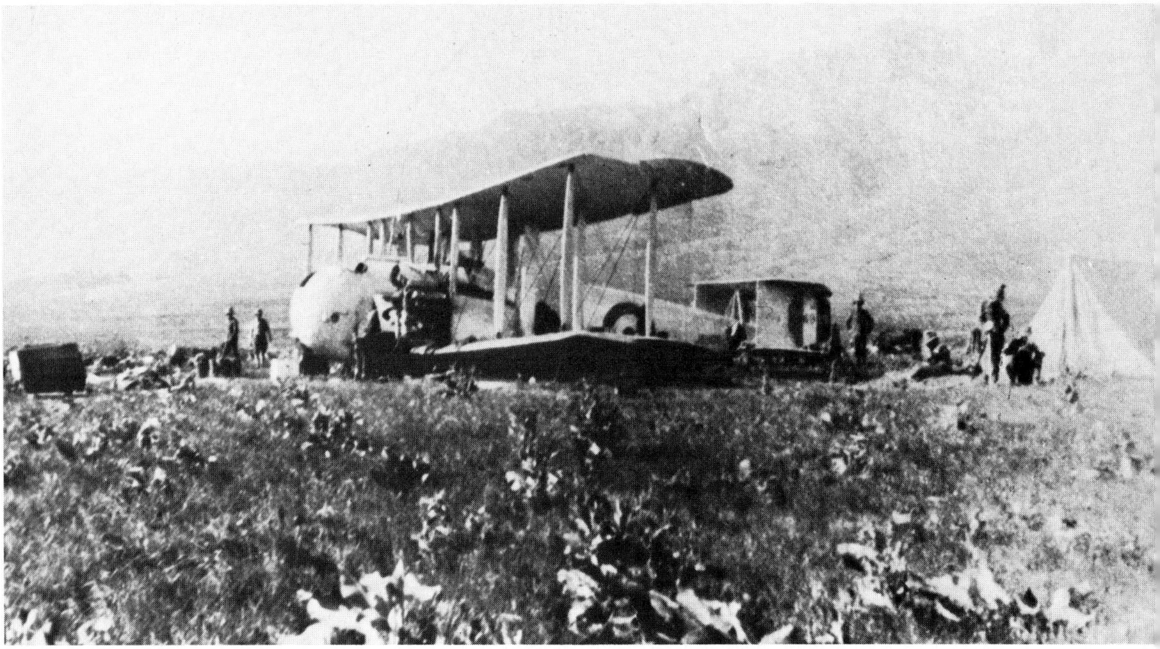

npact smashed the undercarriage and broke the fuselage
ft of the cabin, it was hardly felt by the passengers — one
f whom, fast asleep, had to be awakened and told to get
ut.

It was clearly impossible to fly the Vernon off again, but
n accompanying aircraft had seen their landing and
oubtless rescue would soon be organised. The wind was
usting strongly, everyone feeling cold and miserable and
here seemed little hope of any relief that day. Then, at
bout 1815 a Bristol Fighter appeared, circled a few times
nd started what they thought was the run in to drop
upplies or a message bag. It shed some height in a neat
ideslip, then, bucketing about in the turbulence with hardly
ny forward way, came lower and lower until finally to
veryone's amazement it put down near the Vernon. It was
own by one of No 6 Squadron's most experienced pilots,
light Lieutenant Elmer Peter Roberts, and in the back seat
vas Wing Commander Henry Treadgold, the Deputy
rincipal Medical Officer from Baghdad who had been at
Kirkuk to supervise the aeromedical operations. Treadgold
vas worried by the condition of one patient, and Roberts
onsidered that by moving a few boulders there was
nough space for a take-off with a passenger. This was
uccessfully accomplished in the last remaining light, and
wo more patients were similarly flown out next morning.
The Vernon was burned, and Treadgold, the crew and
emaining patients made the six day trek to Koi Sanjak on
onies and donkeys with the ground party which had
arrived at the scene.

Harris in his report on the operation considered that
Roberts' superb flying from what had seemed an
mpossibly small piece of ground undoubtedly saved on
atient's life. Surprisingly, there was no immediate
ecognition of his feat and it was not until May 1926 that
ie was awarded the DFC for general operations in Iraq.

The Vernons shuttled back and forth until 2 May,
ringing 198 patients from Serkhuma to Kirkuk in 15 trips.
They were then flown on to Baghdad, making the entire
ourney about 215 miles. With all the positioning and
upport activities, the aircraft covered 9,615 miles in 128
lying hours. During the earlier stages of the campaign,
vhich had started in March, there were four 'casevac'
lights by Bristol Fighters, one by a DH9A and one on 12
April by a Vernon to lift four wounded from Rania.
Towards the end some sickness occurred among the
11th Sikhs, and on 18 May four No 45 Squadron Vernons
lew 48 of them from Koi Sanjak to Kirkuk, making a total
of 255 cases carried during the entire operation.

Ironically the one serviceable ambulance Vernon, of
70 Squadron, had crashed on 27 April during a positioning
light for the Serkhuma lift, helping to underline the fact
hat standard transport aircraft had completed with
outstanding success the biggest aeromedical operation in
RAF history. This initiated a change of policy, and in 1924
he Air Council accepted a proposal from the Air Officer

Commanding Iraq that all future transport aircraft should
be easily adaptable for casualty work. There remained the
problem of what to do with the new Avro, now named the
Andover, which seemed likely to be something of a white
elephant. At a meeting on 10 September 1924 Trenchard
vetoed the Andovers' allotment to the Middle East on the
grounds that there was little prospect of operating
efficiently overseas with so few examples of a new aircraft
which also had a new type of engine (the 650hp Rolls-
Royce Condor). At the same time he ruled that no more
specialist ambulance aircraft were to be ordered.

It was eventually decided to use two Andovers (one of
the remaining Andovers was allotted for trials on civil
routes and the other to the Directorate of Technical
Development) on an experimental internal air ambulance
service operating over a radius of about 100 miles from
RAF Halton, Bucks, which housed one of the main RAF
hospitals. Thirteen aerodromes were nominated as
collection points and the aircraft were to be called upon
only when their use would save time compared with surface
transport to the nearest hospital. The service opened on
1 June 1925 and perhaps because of this rigid proviso, only
three cases were carried in the first four months. It was
clearly not an economic proposition and ceased on
18 December.

Meanwhile, in the Middle East theatre, aeromedical
flying had become routine, and during 1925-35 the number
of patients flown to hospital in Iraq, Egypt and Palestine
averaged about 120 a year. In Iraq the bomber transport
squadrons maintained a standby crew for the work, and
whenever possible flights were arranged to give patients the
greatest comfort by avoiding the heat of the day. In
October 1925, the red cross was removed from the
ambulance aircraft since this restricted their use for general
transport work. One of No 45 Squadron's Vernon pilots
specialising in aeromedical flying was Flight Lieutenant
Basil Embry, who was awarded the Air Force Cross for his
skill and determination in flying against adverse weather
and other difficulties to collect urgent cases.

A flight by two No 70 Squadron Victorias on 7-8 April
1929 carrying 13 patients on the first stage of their journey
to specialist treatment in England marked the beginning of
what eventually developed into the present day scheduled
RAF aeromedical services. Such patients would previously
have suffered that hot and tedious rail journey to Basrah
and the equally trying sea passage through the Persian Gulf
and Red Sea. Instead they were flown from Hinaidi to
Amman, where they night-stopped, and then on to Abu
Sueir to join a troopship sailing from Port Said. Later the
night stop was eliminated by flying from Hinaidi to Ramleh
and shipping patients from Jaffa. Even the most serious
cases were found to suffer no ill effects from the air
journey, and the scheme was continued on an ad hoc basis,
16 stretcher cases and 36 sitting patients being carried in
the first 18 months.

During the later interwar period the major RAF
aeromedical tasks arose in India where air transport
resources were the smallest. At three minutes past three on
the morning of 31 May 1935 a devastating earthquake
struck the pleasant garrison town of Quetta, in what is now
Pakistan, close to the Afganistan border. In about 30

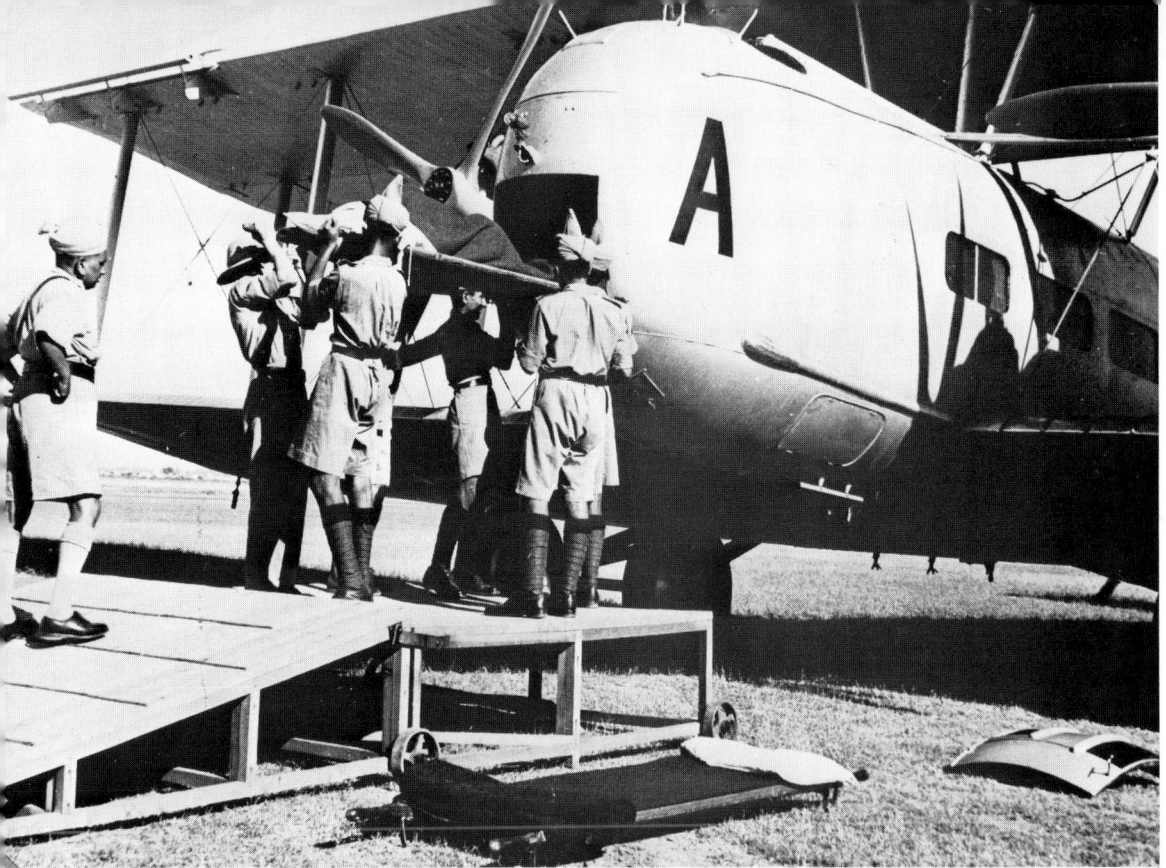

econds large areas were reduced to rubble and estimates of ¡e dead ranged from 24,000 to more than 30,000. The ⅃rmy cantonment was almost unscathed and there were no ⅃eaths among the 12,000 garrison, but No 3 (Indian) Wing ǂ the RAF was less fortunate with 53 killed, mostly from ⅃o 31 Squadron. All radio communication was cut and ⅃oon after daylight the only three Wapitis which remained ⅃rviceable from the 27 aircraft of Nos 5 and 31 Squadrons ⅃ew to various places with the news.

The fortunate escape of the British army cantonment ⅃ith its manpower, medical facilities, food reserves and ⅃ther resources, plus the relatively small proportion of ⅃juries to deaths, reduced the requirements for immediate ⅃utside help to something less than might be expected in a ⅃isaster of such magnitude, but during the next three weeks ⅃AF aircraft made 21 sorties from various bases bringing ⅃ medical unit of 15 Army medical officers and 11 nurses, ⅃,750lb of medical supplies and tinned food, 4,300lb ⅃othing and consignments of anti-tetanus serum. This was ⅃e first time that a British medical unit had been moved by ⅃ir. During the same period 136 casualties — including ⅃ree stretcher cases — were flown to Karachi, Lahore and

Risalpur, mostly in two Victorias of the Bomber Transport Flight. The majority of the 88 adults and 48 children carried were suffering from minor injuries and shock.

Two years later as the result of extensive operations in Waziristan the number of aeromedical cases flown in India for the first time exceeded the Iraq and Middle East figures. Of the 298 total cases flown in 1937, 157 were from the Waziristan fighting, nearly half being carried in Valentias of No 70 Squadron which had been detached from Iraq to assist the Bomber Transport Flight. Despite the excellent work undertaken in Iraq for many years, the Army medical authorities in India appear to have shown little interest in the possibilities, though these were obviously limited by scanty air transport resources. In the spring of 1937, however, the frequent supply and troop carrying flights to the advanced base at Wana provided ample back lift for casualties. The army was operating against fanatical tribesmen, and the hazardous surface journey by road and rough track back to the railhead could be medically dangerous for the patient and was sometimes made impossible by road conditions or the immediate military situation. Air transport produced a quite remarkable improvement, and a number of lives were undoubtedly saved when seriously ill men could be flown to the fully equipped hospital at the Murree hill station near Rawalpindi in a mere 4½ hours, compared with at least two days required for the surface journey.

By the outbreak of war in 1939 about 2,600 patients in all theatres had been carried by RAF aircraft in flights totalling some 320,000 miles.

# Aiding an Emperor

## 9

The East African campaign, which followed Italy's declaration of war in June 1940, offered small scope for major air transport activities, and in any case aircraft resources were slender. There were, however, several enterprising and little known transport flights which almost certainly sowed the seeds for those bigger operations which later made history in other theatres.

The RAF in the Sudan flew a miscellaneous collection of aircraft including obsolescent Vickers Wellesley single-engined bombers and positively obsolete Vickers Vincent biplanes. The Vincent was a rugged three-seater with square-cut wings built to the old general-purpose formula evolved during the overseas peacekeeping operations between the wars, and apart from more power — it had a single 660hp Pegasus engine — and a general cleaning up in design it showed very little outward change from the aircraft of World War I. It was developed from the Vildebeest torpedo bomber of 1927 design and its top speed was 142mph. The pilot sat just behind the engine and the gunner's cockpit was located aft of the wings. There was a third seat in the fuselage tunnel between the two, which could also accommodate miscellaneous stores and another seat if required. On some squadrons pilot and observer communicated by written messages placed in tin cans fixed to a cord running between the two cockpits. For a time the Sudan Vincents operated as 'D' Flight of No 47 Squadron (which had Wellesleys as its main equipment), but in August 1940 most of them were concentrated into No 430 (Army Co-operation) Flight and employed on night bombing, transport of small freight to the forward landing grounds and casualty evacuation work.

Meanwhile, plans were formulating to assist the Ethiopian Patriot movement, and a small British Mission under Colonel D. A. Sandford entered the country overland in mid-August to establish a secret headquarters in the Gojjam area. It was in signal contact with Khartoum, but otherwise very much on its own. On the night of 17/18 November an attempt to air drop supplies and money — those ubiquitous Maria Theresa dollars* — failed because the aircraft did not see any ground recognition signals.

Haile Selassie, the Ethiopian Emperor, had been in Khartoum since early July hoping to make an early return to his country conquered by Italy in 1935-36, and substantial refugee forces from Ethiopia had also gathered in this area. Nothing could be done until there was some organisation and co-ordination among all the patriot

forces, and the man nominated by General Wavell, C-in-C Middle East, for this task was a remarkable soldier, Major Orde Charles Wingate. A deeply religious man, his parents had belonged to a sect of the Plymouth Brethren, Wingate had become an ardent Zionist, and Wavell had been impressed by the success of his unorthodox methods during prewar operations in Palestine. Wingate's unconventionality even extended to wearing that strange antiquated piece of headgear, the Wolseley helmet, long discarded by most officers in favour of the lighter, though unofficial, Bombay (or Baghdad) bowler.

Wingate made his number with Haile Selassie and soon became convinced that discussions with Sandford were essential before adequate plans could be made for effective patriot activities. The problem was to reach the No 101 Mission headquarters, located 150 miles inside Ethiopia near Sakala, some 35 miles south of Lake Tana. A parachute jump with no provision for the return trip was hardly practical and in any case it was intended that a leading Ethiopian from the Emperor's staff should accompany him.

The obvious method was to fly there, and Wingate found the RAF authorities surprisingly receptive to this startling proposal. It was put to No 47 Squadron, and Pilot Officer R. A. Collis suggested that the old Vincent, with its built in short airfield capability, offered the best prospect. Despite the thin single ring of his modest rank, Reginald Alan Collis was no brash beginner fresh from training school but a recently commissioned ex-sergeant pilot of some years' experience. He volunteered to make the undoubtedly hazardous flight, and argued that since the aircraft would be carrying an extra passenger, supplies for the mission and a full petrol load — and using a rough strip at high altitude — there would be additional advantage in employing a pilot of his something under 11 stone medium build rather than one of the squadron heavyweights. The observer chosen was Sergeant Frank Bavin-Smith, who had recently won the DFM for exceptionally skilled navigation during some of the squadron's successful raids against Italian targets.

Vincent K6364 was detailed for the operation and on the afternoon of 19 November Collis and Bavin-Smith flew from Khartoum to Sennar and next morning continued to Roseires, near the frontier, where they were joined by Wingate and Dejasmach Makonnen Desta, the Emperor's representative, who had travelled down by road. The two passengers squeezed themselves into the tunnel between

* The Maria Theresa thaler, or dollar, an eighteenth century silver coin originally used by the Austrian Empire for trading in the Levant, gradually became an international exchange medium over a wider area, including Ethiopia. It has continued in production, but all coins carry the date of Empress Maria Theresa's death, 1780.

ockpits, though once airborne, at 1230 on the 20th, Wingate spent most of the time standing up behind the pilot. The Vincent was also carrying several tins of petrol for the mission's radio generator, 1,500 Maria Theresa dollars, two bundles of propaganda leaflets, two Very pistols and cartridges — and four bottles of whisky.

Maps of the area were notoriously inaccurate, and Sandford had arranged for a smoke signal to be displayed near the selected landing site. The Vincent bumbled along eastwards, leaving the scrubland of the Sudan behind and climbing steadily as it penetrated into the hilly country across the border. After an hour's flying it was nearing the first prominent landmark, the flat topped Jebel Belaiya. Any attempt to cross this 10,270ft mountain was ruled out as the aircraft was overloaded and oil temperature had already reached 95°C, so Collis made a slight diversion northwards to fly between Belaiya and Dangvur, then turned south again passing over the River Beles and a high escarpment beyond. Oil temperature continued to rise but fortunately stopped at 97°. After crossing the Dangila road another prominent landmark, Jebel Makasanyin, became visible ahead, which meant that they were very close to the landing site, though matters were not improved by gathering storm clouds.

One mountain valley looked very much like another, and however accurate their navigation, some co-operation from the ground was essential. Suddenly, smoke was seen on the port side, but on investigation this proved to be a small bush fire. Collis decided that he must now have overshot and turned round, then after flying four minutes back along the original course, he noticed a small wisp of smoke on the summit of Jebel Wondagaz. As he watched, it rapidly developed into a huge column, and any doubt that this was the signal vanished when he saw dozens of waving figures around the fire. Slightly to the south, nestling between the hills, lay a green valley, and as the Vincent approached, several hundred tribesmen, many of them holding coloured umbrellas, moved from the trees to line the boundaries of the landing area, which was additionally marked with a white V facing into wind.

Collis made one circuit, thinking that even for a Vincent the strip looked a little on the tight side, but landed without difficulty at 1430. He taxied towards some tall trees on the south flank, where they were warmly greeted by Sandford and Captain R. A. Critchley of his staff. Also present was an important Ethiopian Patriot leader with some 400 armed warriors, whose enthusiasm was unquenched by the torrential downpour which had begun. Later on, when the rain stopped, the visitors were conducted to the chief's camp, about two miles up in the mountains, and lavishly feasted with well prepared meats and the native honey beer. The RAF men were deeply impressed by their friendly reception from these most awesome looking of all warriors who joined the Allied cause in World War II. Wingate was presented with a bullock, and after a mule-back journey through the darkness and renewed heavy rain, they spent an uncomfortable night in tiny tents at mission headquarters.

Wingate completed his discussions with Sandford and planned to leave at first light next morning. Collis had thoroughly inspected the ground, taking particular note of the steep drop into a ravine at the end of the only suitable take-off run, and after farewells all round Wingate climbed aboard to the sound of much excited murmuring from the large crowd. Makonnen was remaining in Ethiopia.

Collis was not too happy at the state of the surface after the heavy rains — nor did the prospect of remaining as a permanent member of No 101 Mission hold any appeal. Fortunately, despite the Vincent's near-Edwardian appearance a thoughtful Air Ministry had specified that it should be fitted with the relatively new-fangled wheel brakes, which made a lot of difference. He ran up the engine fully then released the brakes, allowing the Vincent to lurch forward, bumping and bucketing over the rough surface, and very slowly picking up speed. It did not require many seconds of this sluggish progress nor anything resembling the present day V1, V2 take-off liturgy, to convince Collis that they were not going to make it, and he applied full brakes in time to stop before the end of the makeshift runway.

Wingate clambered forward, thumped him on the shoulder, and demanded "Why did you stop? We must get off! We can't stay here!" From that first run Collis knew full well that a successful take-off was impossible but rather than argue he taxied back to go through the motions of

another attempt. He had no intention of risking a plunge down the ravine, and this time Wingate shouted for him to stop when they were rather closer to the end than before. Collis then explained the fundamental laws of flight which prevented even a Vincent from getting airborne at that weight, from that short, rough strip 8,000ft above sea level, whereupon Wingate remarked something to the effect: 'All right. I may understand the will of God, but you understand flying. See if you can work out something.' Collis taxied the Vincent back under the trees where it was hidden by branches from any prying enemy reconnaissance.

Sandford explained the position and the local chieftain immediately detailed his men to improve the ground. Under Collis' direction they worked to such good effect that by 1430 the worst bumps and undulations were levelled out and a reasonable strip about 800 yards by 20 was created. Collis felt that this should be enough to permit take-off, but after a meal and a rest he decided to make certain by lightening the aircraft. With ample fuel for the return flight in the main tanks, this could be best achieved by draining the large long-range tank fitted under the fuselage which still contained 60 gallons. However, as the mission had no means of storing this valuable bonus it seemed sensible to remove the tank altogether. It was not a simple drop tank and dusk was falling before all the fittings were disconnected in readiness for its removal.

Meanwhile Wingate and Bavin-Smith engaged in some productive tourism. With Makonnen they had visited the source of the Blue Nile and the historic Gishe Abai Mika-

Above: Emperor Haile Selassie of Ethiopia combines a final briefing with a pre-flight snack before boarding the No 216 Squadron Valentia which flew him back into his own country on 21 January 1941. The location is believed to be Roseires, Sudan. / IWM

Left: Wellesley L2673 of No 47 Squadron at Belaiya, Ethiopia, on 11 February 1941. In the centre group are, left to right, Capt Douglas Dodds-Parker, who was flown in, and Col Dan Sandford and Major Orde Wingate, who were lifted out. R. A. Collis

(Church of St Michael's Spring) and while there were baptised by the chief priests and presented to an influential Ethiopian princess and a leading patriot who had never been subjugated by the Italian occupying force. The physical presence of a British aircraft as an earnest token of aid to come made a deep impression on this chief, and there was much speech-making after which he and some of his followers insisted on returning with the British pair (each the richer by a presentation sheep) to see the splendid machine which had brought their Emperor's emissary.

After another chilly night in the tents the crew and passenger were up at dawn on the 22nd. A dozen Ethiopians helped to lower the fuel tank from the fuselage and the Vincent taxied to the down-wind end of the much improved strip. To help him in judging what was still a somewhat adventurous take-off, Collis arranged for the runway centre to be marked with white strips and for Critchley to stand at the far end waving an umbrella.

This time there was no difficulty. The Vincent was airborne at 0700, climbing away perhaps not like a bird but without any real anxiety. Collis set course for Belaiya, reconnoitring en route several potentially better landing strips for future use, and reached Roseires without incident at 0900. With a small garrison at Dangila, only 30 miles away, the Italians apparently heard about the exploit and not long after the Vincent's departure the Sakala area was bombed and strafed.

Collis was now the unchallenged Ethiopia expert and and became much involved in the activities which followed Wingate's return. On 4 December he led a flight of three Wellesleys to drop supplies and cash to No 101 Mission headquarters. With the faster, more powerful aircraft, plus first hand knowledge of Sandford's precise location, the operation presented no difficulties. The main supplies were parachuted, and 30,000 Maria Theresa dollars, double-bagged in smaller packages, were free dropped from very low altitude out of the bomb aimers' panels. After the drop the Wellesleys mountain hopped away to the south-west to avoid notice by the Italians at Dangila.

On 16 December Collis dropped supplies for some of the Sudan Defence Force troops who had moved into Ethiopia and also reconnoitred more possible landing sites. On 21 January 1941 Haile Selassie himself returned to his country being flown to Umm Idla, just across the border, in a No 216 Squadron Valentia. In addition to the defensive armament devised in 1935 the Valentia also carried two hand held Lewis guns and was escorted by two Gauntlet fighters to meet any possible Italian attack.

Five days later Collis flew another supply drop sortie to No 101 Mission HQ, and despite very bad visibility over the whole area, he was now sufficiently familiar with the various peaks and valleys to locate the dropping zone with great confidence.

He made his first Wellesley landing in Ethiopia on 11 February, the main object being to bring out Wingate — now a lieutenant-colonel — and Sandford for a much needed rest. Allied forces had progressed to the eastern side of the Belaiya massif, and with hand tools the troops hacked out a new landing strip. Although a larger aircraft, less suited than the Vincent to short-field operations the Wellesley had, by contemporary monoplane standards, a low wing-loading and difficulties were not anticipated. Nevertheless, the landing produced its excitement as the strip had a pronounced downhill slope and Collis could only halt the aircraft by turning sharply at the end, offering up sincere thanks to the designer for giving it a sturdy, wide-track undercarriage. The take-off downhill and into wind presented no problems.

On 16 April Collis demonstrated the Wellesley's capabilities at two other strips inside Ethiopia. He was carrying two staff colonels for conferences, firstly at Asosa, across the border about 100 miles south of the previous penetrations, then on to Gambela, another 120 miles still further to the south. Asosa proved to be extremely short, calling for great care in the approach and landing, and Gambela was no better. It was easy enough to find, being located beside the Baro river, and Collis made several very low passes to inspect the surface. It looked reasonable, and he approached across the river to land up hill into wind. The brisk wind did not change direction during the two days his passengers remained, and when departure time came he was faced with the difficult choice of taking off up the considerable slope into wind, or downhill, downwind towards the river bank. He taxied from one end of the strip to the other several times before deciding that the balance lay slightly in favour of the downhill run. He ran up the engine on the brakes until the whole aircraft shook and quivered, then released it to roll away down the slope, and even with 40° of flap it only just managed to stagger off in time, scraping over the river with about five feet to spare. However, as soon as the undercarriage was raised it climbed away serenely, proving once again that the Wellesley could do things undreamed of when it first entered service in home-based bomber squadrons before the war.

Altogether Collis made 19 flights into Ethiopia — apart from 60 day and night raids on enemy targets in the theatre; in due course his achievement was recognised by the award of a very well earned DFC.

Meanwhile the opening of the West African Reinforcement Route in October 1940 had created a growing demand for air transport to return ferry crews to Takoradi, in Ghana (then the Gold Coast) and to carry equipment and stores to the staging posts. The four Bristol Bombays of No 216 Squadron detached to Khartoum for this purpose proved inadequate, so on 30 April 1941, No 117 Squadron was formed. It took over the 216 Squadron detachment plus another Bombay, the miscellaneous aircraft of the Khartoum communications flight and later

acquired four Italian SM79s, flown to Egypt by Yugoslav crews after the German invasion of their country.

For the next six months the Bombays were mainly occupied along the West African route while the SM79s performed useful work in the Sudan and Eritrea, and squadron passenger loads ranged from 370 to 800 a month. On 4 June a Bombay collected the Duke of Aosta, the ex-Governor of Eritrea, from Gura and flew him to Khartoum en route to internment. A potentially tragic incident on 7 June aroused more amusement than indignation by the sheer audacity of some unknown Italian pilot. One of the SM79s, piloted by the squadron commander, Wing Commander W. E. Rankin, was flying from Addis Ababa to Khartoum with a load of staff officers, and although unarmed it was not considered to be at risk even in daylight, as the last remnants of Italian air opposition were thought to have been grounded. Suddenly 25 minutes after leaving Addis, a hail of bullets rattled through the fuselage, then soon afterwards came two more bursts from the rear, which miraculously caused no injuries or vital damage. Meanwhile, the crew, badly affected by fumes from severed petrol pipes and with no means of retaliation, dived for the ground and put the aircraft down at Karkoj, beside the Blue Nile. Nobody saw the attacker and it was assumed to be a Fiat CR42 from the Gondar area, somehow made serviceable. As the passengers somewhat sheepishly climbed out to survey the damage they realised that among their number was the most legitimate — and captive — target for their indignation, the HQ 203 Group Intelligence Staff Officer.

More interesting than No 117 Squadron's routine operations was the strange story of the rogue Bombay. During the war it was not unusual for a squadron aircraft to acquire an often quite unjustified reputation as a rogue and there were also rare instances where some real eccentricity of behaviour was eventually traced to an obscure assembly error. But No 117 Squadron never did find out what was wrong with Bombay L5826.

On 6 June 1941 Flight Lieutenant R. T. (Bob) Chisholm gave the aircraft a short test before leaving for El Fasher and all points west to Takoradi. Apart from a little nose heaviness — rectified by removing some ballast from the front gunner's cockpit — all was well, and the 14 passengers and some freight were loaded. The aircraft climbed in the hot, clear sky to 8,500 feet, when without warning and for no apparent atmospheric or any other reason it made a steep diving turn to starboard. With some difficulty Chisholm regained control, but it continued to fly in such an alarmingly unstable fashion that he turned back and landed after 45 minutes in the air.

He was so shaken by the experience which suggested some very major fault, that he felt unable to accept responsibility for flying the aircraft until the trouble was cured.

Chisholm was one of the steadiest and most reliable Bombay pilots, not given to imagining things, and within hours of his experience becoming known on the station corroborative evidence emerged from pilots who had previously kept quiet, perhaps fearing ridicule or thinking that their own flying had been at fault. The pilot who had delivered the aircraft from England to Egypt in May appened to be passing through Khartoum and he recalled very similar occurrence when nearing Gibraltar which ad almost caused him to lose control. One of No 117's ergeant pilots had also encountered inexplicable fficulties. Someone even recalled hearing that this ombay had caused problems for a test pilot before elivery to the RAF in November 1939.

There was no set pattern to the incidents, and L5826 ould apparently perform its dirty dart to the right quite npredictably, under any conditions of loading or weather. arying intervals elapsed between incidents and the aircraft uld never be persuaded to fly abnormally on a routine air st.

Rankin, a tall, down to earth Australian, immediately rdered the fullest possible examination of all rigging measurements, dimensions, angles and so on, and checked e details of loading and weight distribution on Chisholm's ight. Everything was well within prescribed tolerances and fter a thorough personal test flight he had no option but to rder the aircraft back into serivce.

The next time L5826 chose to misbehave Bob Chisholm vas again the victim. He left Khartoum on 20 July, was delayed by engine trouble at Geneina, and on 22 July at Maidugari successfully coped with that most heart-stopping emergency, an engine failure on take-off. The passengers were sent on to Lagos by road and rail rather than have them wait for the engine to be changed. During the subsequent air test the aircraft again for no reason produced its violent diving turn, and lost several thousand feet before control was regained by the combined efforts of both pilots.

Chisholm then remembered a Bombay of No 216 Squadron which had mysteriously crashed near Heliopolis on 17 December 1940 with total loss of life, and although a careful ground check at Maiduguri could trace nothing wrong, he decided to take no chances and ferried the aircraft back to Khartoum empty. Rankin reported the situation to Group HQ, and to ensure that L5826 could not be flown again in a hurry the engines were removed and used as replacements in other aircraft and it was parked on a hard standing, tethered to ring bolts set in concrete.

In keeping with the whole strange story, the finale too had its inexplicable aspects. To write off a physically sound aircraft for no better reason than a series of pilots' complaints that it was a rogue clearly invited awkward questions, but while the staff were pondering these, natural forces took a hand. At 1415 on 21 August a typical Sudan haboob — a severe storm with violent gusts whipping up sand and dust into conditions of almost nil visibility — swept through Khartoum, and after its passage L5826 had ceased to be a flyable aeroplane. The force of one gust snapped the three inch ropes like cotton, broke some of the

Below: An Italian Caproni Ca133 captured during the East African campaign in 1941 on arrival at Khartoum. This may have been the aircraft destroyed by a *haboob* on 21 August. *IWM*

steel ring bolts, lifted the aircraft up bodily then slammed it down vertically on its tail, after which it lurched over on to one side.

Of the five other transport aircraft picketed in the immediate vicinity and physically shifted by the haboob only one was damaged, this was a captured Italian Caproni Ca133. Obsolescent and unpopular, it had nevertheless been used until lack of spares and servicing difficulties rendered it something of a liability, and the question of its disposal was settled after the haboob had plucked it into the air and dumped it back upside down, another write off.

A pilot who saw the incidents reported to the Court of Inquiry in roughly these terms: 'I was driving along the tarmac when through the murk I suddenly saw Bombay 5826 rear up on its tail then start to come towards me. I turned my car around and retreated rapidly.'

Cynics may suggest that the squadron, knowing local conditions, could have been a little less than careful over the picketing, and planned this Machiavellian method of writing off two unpopular aircraft. But the affair is well documented and there is no evidence that all procedures were not according to the book.

# Habbaniya

## 10

As dawn broke on 30 April 1941 the 1,200 RAF men and 3,000 non-European levies and camp workers living at Habbaniya, Iraq, awoke to the not wholly unexpected realisation that they were besieged. The vast cantonment, with every imaginable amenity inside, or just beyond, its seven mile perimeter fence, housed No 4 Flying Training School. Habbaniya — the name in Arabic meant 'the place of the oleanders' — lay about 125 miles west of Kut, scene of that other historic siege in 1916.

Four weeks earlier, on 3 April, the pro-Axis politician Rashid Ali had seized power in Baghdad. The British Government did not intend to allow the coup to pave the way for enemy infiltration into this part of the Middle East, and began to make immediate reinforcement plans. On the 6th they notified Rashid Ali that under existing treaty rights British troops would be moving through the country, and next day a small advanced party of the 1st King's Own Royal Regiment arrived at Basra having flown by civil aircraft from Karachi.

The main air lift which followed was notable for the distance involved — about 1,200 miles from Karachi to Basra — and for the multiplicity of aircraft employed, including the first RAF use of transports built by the famous American Douglas company. Earlier accounts of the operations are confusing, largely because the squadron concerned, No 31, maintained no Operations Record Book for the period due to some long forgotten administrative oversight.

Western Desert commitments precluded the provision of significant reinforcements from the west, and the only RAF air trooping capacity from India was provided by No 31 Squadron's old Vickers Valentias. Five of these stately veterans carried detachments of the KORR from Karachi to Basra on 17/19 and 21/24 April, but more and faster aircraft were clearly desirable. Fortunately, suitable machines were available in the shape of several Douglas DC-2s bought in America on behalf of the Indian Government for Indian National Airways and Tata Air Lines which had just arrived in India. They had all seen a good many years' service with various American air lines, and their airframe hours ranged from 8,000 to 17,000 while engine hours were in the 2,000/10,000 hour bracket. By arrangement with the Indian civil aviation department four of these joined the air lift, flown by suitably qualified British pilots with RAF Reserve Commissions, though not under the auspices of any particular air line. Some troop flights were also made by civil Atlanta airliners, which

encountered numerous troubles en route. Four of these aircraft subsequently appeared in RAF markings, though they were not, as is often stated, operated by No 31 Squadron.

On 24 April four of the civil DC-2s and two Valentias — one from No 31 and the other from the Habbaniya Communication Flight — began moving the troops from Basra to Habbaniya, the faster DC-2s making two trips daily. Meanwhile tension was mounting in Baghdad and 230 British women and children living in the city were driven in RAF vehicles to Habbaniya where they would be safe from any mob violence.

More reinforcement troops sent by sea disembarked at Basra on 29 April and this may have been one of the factors which persuaded Rashid Ali that his patience was exhausted. Overnight some 9,000 Iraqi troops surrounded Habbaniya, and their 55 pieces of artillery were installed in dominating positions on an adjacent plateau. The Iraq Government refused to allow any food to be delivered to the camp and demanded that all flying should cease. In the face of this near ultimatum the British Government decided that the best form of defence was attack and authorised the RAF to follow that ancient precept. The airmen had not been idle during this build up period, having fitted suitable bomb racks, checked machine-gun installations and generally prepared the motley collection of 70 training aircraft for war. Unofficially christened the Habbaniya Air Striking Force, they went into action at first light on 2 May.

By this time 343 officers and men of the KORR, plus 30 non-European attached for various duties, had been flown from India, and the air lift of these troops and supplies from Basra into Habbaniya continued, despite some rather wild Iraqi artillery fire. Aircraft were, as far as possible, held off until one of the periodic lulls in the shelling, and were given the all clear to land by air traffic using the code word 'Fair'. They were then instructed to touch down close to the hangars and to taxi fast. British and Indian women and children were carried out on the return flights. The airfield proper lay between the camp perimeter fence and the Iraqi forces, and although rebel activity never stopped flying, aircraft did from time to time use the large sports field area which provided greater security.

The mixed civil and RAF air transport operation was a far from ideal arrangement, and it was decided that the DC-2s should be formally impressed into full RAF service. Accordingly, pilots of No 31 Squadron had begun conversion training on DC-2s at Drigh Road, Karachi on

Above left: Bombay L5832, believed to belong to No 216
Squadron, at Habbaniya in 1941. / F. G. Swanborough

Left: One of the Douglas DC-2s impressed for service with
No 31 Squadron photographed at Habbaniya in 1941, showing
its Indian civil registration as well as RAF markings and serial,
DG478. / F. G. Swanborough

Above: Showing a marked contrast to the more familiar silver
peacetime livery, this camouflaged Valentia (K3614) of the
Habbaniya Communication Flight, was photographed in 1941.
It was still flying in the spring of 1944. / F. G. Swanborough

6 April. The first two pilots to finish the short course were
Squadron Leader W. H. Burbury, 'B' Flight commander,
and Flight Lieutenant L. D. 'Duke' Mavor, and they made
the first two RAF DC2 trooping flights from Karachi on
4/5 May. These formed phase two of the troop lift, which
carried another 140 men of the KORR. Six of No 31
Squadron's Valentias and a BOAC flying boat were also
employed.

Meanwhile No 216 Squadron had been bringing limited
reinforcements from the other direction. Between 2 and 4
May, five Valentias and three Bombays had lifted men of
the Essex Regiment from Lydda, in Palestine, to the H4
pumping station on the oil pipeline.

By 5 May, after the 'Habbaniya Air Striking Force' had
started night attacks on their positions, the Iraqi troops
investing the camp decided that they had had enough, and

when the sun came up on the 6th they had melted away —
whereupon the aircraft took off to help speed their retreat
to Baghdad with some vigorous ground attacks.

However, the campaign was not yet over, and ironically
the rebels gained their greatest success — thanks to the
weather rather than any military masterstroke — only
hours after Rashid Ali's troops had ignominiously
abandoned the siege. The onward move to Habbaniya of
the latest reinforcements arriving from India was
continued, and soon after daybreak on 6 May six of No
31's Valentias left Shaibah in two flights of three. Each
carried 18 troops and ample fuel for a normal flight, but
severe dust storms near Habbaniya obscuring the ground
presented navigational problems.

Squadron Leader Dudley Burnside, 'A' Flight
commander, who was leading the first three, suspected that
he had overshot the airfield and decided to press on to the
H3 landing ground and wait there for a weather clearance.
Everything appeared normal as he approached, then as the
aircraft rolled to a stop he heard machine-gun fire and
realised he was under attack. He had received no briefing
that the airstrip was in rebel hands, but without more ado
smartly turned about and took off down-wind.

The pilot of the second aircraft, banking round on the
approach did not observe the odd behaviour of his leader,
and was greeted with heavier bursts of fire as he landed.
The Valentia was hit in a petrol tank, caught fire, and was
completely destroyed within moments of the passengers
and crew scrambling out. They were taken prisoner, but
released when the campaign was over. The third pilot gave

the strip a wide berth and joined up with Burnside. Both aircraft flew to Hit, about 60 miles north-west of Habbaniya, where they landed with tanks almost dry. The other three Valentias, following some minutes behind on the flight from Shaibah were more fortunate, arriving over Habbaniya when visibility had improved sufficiently for them to land.

That same day the situation took a slightly more ominous turn, when German aircraft staged through Vichy-controlled Syria en route to Mosul. Soon afterwards there were several small-scale raids on Habbaniya by He111 bombers and Me110 ground-attack fighters, and two Valentias and a DC-2 were written off as the result. On the nights of 12/13 and 14/15 May, three of the Communications Flight Valentias assumed their secondary function and retaliated by bombing Mosul airfield.

Probably more effective was an audacious operation by No 216 Squadron on 25 May. Captained by Flight Lieutenant C. S. Bartlett, Valentia K2803 took off from Habbaniya at 1515 with a party of 13 Royal Engineers whose task was to destroy an important bridge at Campaniya, just inside the north-eastern tip of Syria. This carried the Aleppo to Mosul railway, an important supply line for the Axis forces in Northern Iraq, and it seems not unlikely that the raid was laid on with the assistance of Free French agents. The Valentia desert-hopped at minimum altitude for most of the 300-mile flight to lessen risk of detection, and touched down on flat ground near the bridge just as daylight was fading. The Sappers knew their job so well that the bridge was blown up and they were back at the aircraft within 40 minutes. The only opposition was some erratic machine-gun fire as the Valentia took off for Habbaniya, where it landed at 2240. In an apparent reference to this operation the official British history of World War II surprisingly discounts contemporary German claims that the British were responsible and attributes it to sabotage by enterprising Free Frenchmen.

These were virtually the last warlike transport operations by Vickers Valentias, which despite more power and structural improvements had changed little from the Victorias of 1926. But these buxom old ladies of the RAF were by no means ready to put their feet up for good, and

could be seen pottering around the backwaters of the Middle East for another three years on training and communications work. Among the last in regular use were K3600, K3614 and JR8063 (which actually began its existence in 1926 as a Victoria III) belonging to the HQ Persia and Iraq Communications Flight at Habbaniya in the spring of 1944. Warrant Officer H. Dawson of that unit flew K3600 as late as 1 May, which could have been the Valentia's final bow.

By this time the No 31 Squadron aircraft situation had been further tidied up and more DC-2s destined for civil use in India were impressed into RAF service. By the end of May the squadron had 12, of which six were operating in Iraq. For a time some of these carried their original Indian civil registrations as well as RAF serial numbers. Throughout May the DCs and Valentias performed invaluable work on troop deployments, freighting and special flights, and No 31 Squadron alone recorded nearly 2,000 hours' flying, with 18 pilots — and no less important with only 18 maintenance personnel, who worked prodigious hours to keep the aircraft flying.

From the moment that Rashid Ali abandoned the plan to seize Habbaniya, his forces were restricted to relatively easily contained nuisance activities. It was not long before he recognised the failure of his schemes, and on 28 May he fled the country, enabling the previous regime to be reinstated three days later. At the time of the revolt more dramatic events elsewhere attracted greater attention, and in Iraq the main focus was rightly on the successful transformation of the normally docile No 4 FTS into an aggressive animal. But without air transport to bring in reinforcements, fly out the women and children and the few wounded, and generally provide the lifelines, the whole task would have been immeasurably more difficult.

With stability restored in Iraq, the only country still offering a springboard for Axis operations in the eastern Mediterranean was Syria. To ensure that nothing of this sort happened, Allied forces started moving in on 8 June and a month later the Vichy forces requested a cease fire. Nos 31 and 216 Squadrons were actively engaged on the transport side, but it was routine work with no dramatic highlights.

doubt if I shall live till the morning, I am getting weaker
d weaker every minute. I have only three gulps of water
d I have such a terrible thirst, I should go somewhere,
t where? I am completely lost. Goodbye, we shall meet
ere we all have to go one day . . .'
'Death is very near, I tried to take off, I have still ten
lons but the accumulators are flat. I looked for help but
w help will not come . . . Oh God, shorten my sufferings,
ere will be no help for me, let nobody land in the desert
ere there are no people, as there is no way out . . .'
'I hear an aircraft flying to the south, to my right, my last
pe, I cannot get up to have a look. My last minutes. God
ve mercy on me . . .'

ese grim, but poignant extracts are taken from the last
essages written on 9 and 10 May 1942 by Polish
rgeant Pilot Mikolajczak, a Ferry Command transport
ot after he had force-landed in the African desert. The
ttered log book, its pages dried and crinkled, the ink
ding rapidly, bombarded by a succession of whirling
ndstorms and the dominating blast of the unshaded fiery
n, in which a man's last fears and abandoned hopes were
pressed, was found near to where his body lay huddled
side the wreck of his partially covered aircraft.
Sergeant Mikolajczak died while flying on one of the
anscontinental routes which were part of the vast network
erated by RAF Ferry Command, formed on 20 July
41, to provide an adequate air bridge for men, supplies
d deliveries of new aircraft over the North and South
tlantics and across Africa to India.
The Atlantic Bridge, as it became known, came into
ing in 1940, when an agreement was signed between
anada and Britain allowing the inauguration of deliveries
American-built aircraft from Canada to Britain. It came
a time when Coastal Command were placing great
pendence on the American twin-engined Lockheed
dson aircraft.
Not only was the demand for these aircraft
erwhelming, but valuable time was being lost by having
em shipped over to Britain. On some occasions three
onths elapsed between an aircraft being passed as fit for
rvice after test flights in the United States and its delivery
a squadron. Because of the hazards at sea many aircraft
ere also being lost when convoys were attacked and ships
nk.
The British Government sought advice; Mr G. Woods-
umphery, a former managing director of the illustrious

Imperial Airways, was asked to prepare a report. He
judged that it was perfectly feasible to ferry new aircraft
across by air and advised that this should be done. Apart
from a number of other important considerations the time
factor was, perhaps, the one to which most emphasis was
attached; using the ferry method new aircraft could be fully
operational within 10 days of their test flight.

The task began in earnest in July, 1940. Captains A. S.
Wilcockson, D. C. T. Bennett, R. H. Page, and I. G. Ross
all from BOAC, together with Squadron Leader G. J.
Powell, of the Royal Canadian Air Force, a former captain
on the Atlantic route with Imperial Airways, went to
Montreal to co-ordinate the start of operations.

Finding the necessary men needed to provide a nucleus
of crews was one of their first and highly complex tasks. At
this time, because of the heavy pressure being exerted on
them from all aspects of war, the RAF was unable to
supply any pilots. But there was no shortage of candidates
from all walks of life, connected with aviation, willing to
take part in this great new adventure. Bush pilots, crop
dusters, airline pilots, from large commercial organisations
and small insignificant companies alike, business men who
flew their own aircraft, amateurs to whom flying was a
weekend relaxation — all wanted to have a go.

Although well-trained pilots were needed it was also
imperative to find expert radio operators. It was in this field
that the air bridge planners came up against their first
stumbling block. To fly across the Atlantic an aircraft
would require to use its radio equipment to the utmost —
the difficulty was that qualified men, used to flying, were
remarkably thin on the ground.

Canadian and American civil airlines had long since
dispensed with the services of radio operators, preferring to
rely on the following of certain paths defined by radio
beacons audible to the pilot. BOAC was asked to help and
Mr H. Jubb, a former Imperial Airways radio operator,
went out to Montreal.

In a cramped shack at St Hubert airport he began the
arduous task of interviewing and training likely candidates.
There was a steady trickle of volunteers, mostly from
remote outposts in the Canadian Rockies and members of
the Canadian Pacific Railway Company's radio operating
staff. To a man they were all full of infectious enthusiasm
and skilled in the use of morse; to a man they were almost
devoid of any knowledge of flying whatsoever. Some even,
through no fault of their own, had little idea of geography.
Their willingness to learn and the expertise and patience of

their two instructors, Jubb and a former airline colleague of his, G. C. Cunningham, worked wonders in surmounting what seemed to many to be almost impossible odds.

The Lockheed factory in California announced that the first batch of long range Hudsons would be ready for delivery in mid-September; fifty aircraft were promised over a period of two months. By the end of October the first Hudsons started to reach Gander in Newfoundland and the men who would ferry them over the Atlantic were preparing themselves for the most testing challenge of all — their very first long distance flight.

Gander, surrounded by magnificent forests of tall spruce and fir, had been used as a staging post for experimental flying since 1937. The air bridge across the Atlantic would ensure that it would become one of the world's busiest airports; whatever would happen in the future the single name, Gander, would never be forgotten when men gathered to talk of transatlantic flying.

The date of the first delivery flight was fixed for 10 November. Seven Hudsons were scheduled and prepared for take-off. The historic occasion was marked by a certain amount of ceremony and a Canadian military band turned out in strength to provide a musical send off. As the first Hudson rolled down the runway, the airport lights twinkled in the frosty darkness, the band played, patriotically *There'll always be an England.*

Slowly, the Hudson, piloted by Captain Bennett, climbed into the sky and before long only occasional flashes from the exhausts told that the aircraft had set course for its 2,200-mile haul across the Atlantic. The six remaining Hudsons followed at 10-minute intervals.

For a time the aircraft kept together in a rough formation, using their radios to help each other check and maintain their positions relative to the leading Hudson.

At 18,000 feet Captain Bennett's aircraft hit a warm front which caused severe turbulence. He ordered the pilots of the other Hudsons to spread out to minimise risk of a collision and went up a further 2,000 feet hoping to encounter better conditions. At 20,000 feet the turbulence was even worse and to make matters more complicated the Hudson nosed its way into a blinding snowstorm. Captain Bennett gave the order for his fellow pilots to continue on their own; the seven Hudsons broke formation. Radio Officer, C. M. Tripp kept a detailed record of his first momentous journey.

'Ralph (Captain Ralph E. Adams in charge of Hudson T9468) began to check over the ship and found oil leaking badly from one of the starboard tanks. I passed a message to the leader, Captain Bennett, that our oil tank had ruptured, but we were watching closely and would keep him advised. Our skipper, being in some doubt as to whether to go or not, held back. Finally he decided the oil flow was diminishing; and, deciding to go on, we found ourselves quite alone.

'Then my radio blew up by shorting in the antenna switch box and giving us all a good scare. Ralph hollered to me: "Shut the bloody thing off", but I had beat him to the gun. With that load of gas it isn't pleasant to have a fire skipping around the cockpit and the corona from that transmitter was really something'.

Above: Air Vice-Marshal Donald C. T. Bennett, best remembered as the commander of Bomber Command's Path Finder Force, was also much concerned with the early development of the ferry service to deliver American-built aircraft to the RAF. This was when he was flying with BOAC, between completing an RAF Short Service Commission and returning to the RAF at the end of 1941. / IWM

Above right: Lockheed Hudsons for the RAF on a transatlantic airfield awaiting ferrying to the UK. / IWM

After Captain Adams decided to press on he took the Hudson up to 16,000 feet and told Radio Officer Tripp to forget the problems with the radio for a time. Tripp comments:

'What with the excitement of the take-off and the leaking oil tank, I was glad to sit back and relax and I think I actually enjoyed myself. When I look back I can't feel I was actually relaxing, but at the same time it felt good just to sit there and try not to think of anything.

'If Ralph and Dana (Flying Officer Dana Gentry — the co-pilot) were doing the same thing we all snapped out of it at 02.07 hours when our bomb bay tank ran dry and both motors started cutting out. I was not expecting it and even if Ralph and Dana were, the way they went for that hand pump and gas valve made me think they didn't like it any better than I did. I don't think anything ever sounded so good to me as hearing those big Wrights hit their stride again and settle down to a steady drone'.

For a time the flight of Hudson T9468 was smooth enough

espite the fact that the transmitter was still out of action. Tripp felt it necessary to take a fresh bearing on Captain Bennett's aircraft. As he adjusted the radio compass the indicator snapped, rendering the instrument totally useless. Tripp's feelings were best described in his own words.

 really felt up the creek without a paddle. No transmitter r (radio) compass and out over the Atlantic Ocean! I idn't have the heart to tell Ralph the compass was on the um, but from then on I couldn't sit there and do nothing, o asked permission to go to work on the transmitter'.

t 03.40 hours Tripp succeeded in repairing the damaged ansmitter and from then on the morale of the three crew members improved.

At 0800 Captain Adams started his descent and at 5,000 et Flying Officer Gentry caught a momentary glimpse of shadow of land through a break in the clouds. Eagerly, he crew consulted their charts. Their decision was nanimous; below them was Catlin Island. A few minutes ter they flew over Lough Neagh in Northern Ireland and lmost immediately Captain Adams spotted the scattered uildings of RAF Aldergrove dead on the Hudson's nose. hey made one circuit round the airfield and at 0850 the ircraft dropped smoothly on to the runway. They were nird to arrive.

The last of the seven aircraft touched down at noon but ny thoughts the crews might have had for celebrating their chievement and seeing something of Britain were dashed hen a signal from Headquarters ordered them to embark

by 1500 on a ship bound for Canada later the same day. The frustration they felt at having to return to their base so quickly was partially relieved when the ship's embarkation officer produced a tray of whiskies and soda almost as soon as they stepped aboard.

In this way, at sea on board a ship heading out into the Atlantic Ocean, 22 men — nine Americans, six British, six Canadians and one Australian — drank a toast to mark the pioneering flight made by seven aircraft which would pave the way for the operation of a highly efficient ferry organisation and greatly increase Britain's strength — and later that of the Allies — in the toughest and most difficult days of the war in Europe.

The next development called for the ferrying of long range flying-boats, required to help in guarding convoys and assist in concentrated searches for enemy submarines. The Catalina was considered the best machine for these tasks and Bermuda was judged to be the most suitable place for launching them on a 3,400 mile long flight to the United Kingdom.

Seven Catalinas were delivered to the base at Darrell's Island, near Hamilton, in January 1941, where Squadron Leader Powell had worked ceaselessly for a number of months to provide facilities for handling aircraft and accommodating the crews. Detailed checking and cross-checking of all manner of likely difficulties went on for some time before everyone was satisfied that the attempt should be made. Because it was estimated that the Catalina might take anything from twenty four to thirty hours to make the flight it was agreed that two radio operators should be carried so that watches could be shared.

One by one the Catalinas — each weighing around 15 tons — lifted off the blue water. Six hours out near disaster struck the flying-boat flown by Captain Fleming with Captain Meikle as co-pilot.

The Catalina was cruising at 20,000 feet when, without warning, the automatic pilot jammed. The aircraft heaved violently, the fuselage vibrating with the sudden uneven pressures being exerted upon it. As the pilots struggled to release the auto-pilot the starboard aileron jammed full down. Immediately the Catalina plunged into a spiral dive.

Gyrating wildly, the aircraft fell through the pitch black night towards the sea. The pilots used all their experience in trying to find some way to put it back on an even keel, but the controls remained totally immoveable. The altimeter needles spun round in the phosphorescent gloom of their glass fronted cases, making it difficult to make an accurate immediate assessment of height.

Captain Fleming ordered one of the radio operators to send an SOS. Just as the operator started to transmit there was a loud, snapping noise followed by the sharp crack of metal lashing against metal. The radio aerials had given way under the strain of the buffeting slipstream. They were now coiled tightly around the fuselage.

The crew began a desperate attempt to jettison anything on which they could lay their hands in the fervent hope that a reduction in weight might help to bring the aircraft under control. Out went smoke flares, tool kits, spare parts and a varied assortment of personal belongings. A new tool kit, which had cost one of the engineers over £40 only a few days previously, was unceremoniously dumped.

While this was going on the Catalina, heaving and bucking, passed the 1,000 feet mark. The crew prepared themselves for disaster, but continued to reduce the weight while the two pilots wrestled with the controls. Less than 400 feet from the surface of the ocean their silent prayers were answered. Almost as if nothing untoward had happened the Catalina broke out of her spiral dive. The engines were slowly opened up, crackling and backfiring as they found power once more; the fuselage became still and soon the only hint of vibration came from the engines as they beat out a fresh rhythm.

However, the crew's troubles were far from over. Captain Fleming realised that both ailerons had probably been torn away during the dive because the controls felt sluggish. As a result the Catalina had no lateral control — she could only be flown straight ahead. To use the rudder without ailerons could easily put the aircraft into a flat spin; a fatal move at low altitude. Both Fleming and Meikle resigned themselves to the unpalatable thought that if the Catalina was to remain airborne she would have to be flown manually for the rest of the flight and this would require every ounce of strength which the two pilots could muster.

They had been in the air for six hours; to continue with the flight would mean another 22 hours, at least, with nothing below them but thousands of square miles of unfriendly ocean. Captain Fleming nonetheless decided to press on. The radio equipment was brought into use again by fixing up the trailing aerial; no SOS was sent — only a three word message, simple and undramatic in appearance,

but one which the staff back at Hamilton found hard to believe.

The signal read: 'Both ailerons gone'.

When dawn broke the crew were able to see for themselves that indeed the two ailerons had been torn away, but by this time they had become accustomed to the strain and thought little more about it. The Catalina was now back on course due to skilful manoeuvring on the part of the two pilots. Committed to keeping their hands firmly on the controls there was no possibility of chart work or navigation. Fortunately, Captain Fleming had memorised the original course, and very slowly it proved possible to inch the Catalina round from flying due south and back on to the proper easterly course.

22 hours and 50 minutes after their plunge towards the ocean the exhausted pilots brought the Catalina down on a stretch of choppy sea near Milford Haven in Pembrokeshire. They had taxed their physical endurance to the limit, but for them and their fellow crew members there was one further test they felt unable to endure — seasickness. The waves under the floats were making the seaplane lurch and roll with such abruptness that everyone almost simultaneously, felt his stomach start to rebel. Off they went again to fly, skimming the surface, to a spot nearer the moorings where the water was sheltered.

By February 1941, 24 RAF crews were operating from Montreal, ferrying Flying Fortresses and Liberators. Before 31 March 263 people including flying, ground and administrative civilian personnel were connected with the ferrying organisation. Operations seemed to be running reasonably smoothly, but one difficulty was soon apparent: all Atlantic ferry crews were returning from Britain by boat — a journey which took anything from 10 days to a fortnight. Because of this time lag there were several occasions when so many men were aboard ships at sea that there were none to fly the aircraft ready for immediate delivery. To combat this steadily worsening situation plans were laid to operate a return ferry service and several Liberators were put into commission for this purpose.

Although the pioneers, both the planners and the crew who eventually flew on this service, were not to know it they were making aviation history. The operation of these Liberators by British Overseas Airways, at times with mixed RAF and BOAC crews, inaugurated the first regular all-the-year-round transatlantic passenger and freight service.

The first eastbound flight on 4 May, 1941, carried four passengers and 200lb of diplomatic mail with Captain D. C. T. Bennett as first pilot. With a brief stop in Newfoundland the flight from St Hubert Airport, Montreal to Prestwick took 19 hours and 5 minutes. On the same day Captain Youell of BOAC piloted the first westbound Liberator; seven passengers, all members of delivery crews, were on board. Although this flight was delayed by weather at Newfoundland the aircraft was actually airborne for only 16 hours 44 minutes.

Because of this important development the ferry service expanded rapidly; political and military considerations in North America and Britain made it essential that full control would have to come under a British Government Ministry. The Canadian Pacific Railway, who had initiated nd nursed the service into fruition, were informed that their contract would be terminated in May 1941.

The Ministry of Aircraft Production took over the reins nd many CPR employees stayed on to serve under their ew masters. In June the President of the United States, Franklin D. Roosevelt, made it clear to Winston Churchill hat his country was prepared to help with the ferrying of ll aircraft destined for Great Britain.

It was agreed that American service personnel would fly elivery aircraft to Montreal or any other suitable espatching point; in doing so American civilian pilots vould be able to help fly the Atlantic; these, in turn, would elease British pilots for operational duties. The President vas emphatic on one point: the hand-over of aircraft had to e made to a military command instead of to a civil uthority.

On 20 July 1941, Atfero, as the ferry organisation was ow called, became Royal Air Force Ferry Command; Air Chief Marshal Sir Frederick Bowhill, in charge of Coastal Command, was made Commander-in-Chief.

In October, Ferry Command left the airport at Montreal nd moved into a giant base which had been created at earby Dorval. By now there were around 100 trained rews, consisting mainly of civilians, but it became obvious hat if the Command was to function efficiently this umber would have to be doubled.

In Canada, airmen from all over the world were being rained under the Commonwealth Joint Air Training Plan. After a year, following elementary, service, in some cases perational flying training many were ready to join perational units. Sir Frederick Bowhill put forward the aring suggestion that these newly trained crews should be given the job of delivering combat aircraft. The plan was ccepted and those who had completed their operational raining on Hudsons, with a total of 250 flying hours on all ypes of aircraft, were given an intensive course of lectures nd flying practice to prepare them for the Atlantic rossing. These 'one-trippers', as they were called, took on he Atlantic crossing even in winter in the face of much ead shaking by the experts.

One Hudson on such a flight had a particularly difficult ime. Shortly after take-off from Dorval one of the engines tarted to ice-up severely. Eventually this was sorted out nd with Sergeant Killip and his crew congratulating hemselves, ice started to form just as badly, in the other ngine. A short time later an oil pipe burst and the propeller ad to be feathered. By now they were almost halfway cross the Atlantic and the navigator set course for Ireland, he aircraft flying blind on one engine.

For six hours they flew on under reduced power; then uel began to run short. Sergeant Killip brought the Hudson own low, trying to break out of dense cloud in case it vould become necessary for them to ditch. When daylight ome he went down even further, until the Hudson was no nore than 50 feet above the waves. Killip put the Hudson nto a climb once more while he pondered the problem. He decided there was no course left open to him but to ditch. ust as he was about to issue instructions the co-pilot saw a aint blur of coastline through an isolated gap in the cloud. The trainee navigator's work had been perfect — it was the Northern Ireland coast. Immediately land was reached

Killip set the Hudson down in a small field close to the cliffs; the aircraft landed perfectly on its belly, suffering no more than a few minor dents and scratches to its fuselage.

To enable aircraft of shorter range to fly the Atlantic the idea of a northern route was put forward. In this way, by the establishment of a number of bases, there would be places to where aircraft could divert during bad weather or use as staging posts in the course of a normal flight. Survey flights over Greenland commenced in earnest and in a sandy plateau of muskeg and virgin forest in Labrador, construction work started on what was to become one of loneliest, the largest and most important of the long-distance air bases — Goose Bay.

Within a month three temporary runways, each about seven thousand feet long, were ready for use. It was now possible for aircraft to fly from Dorval, touch down at Goose, refuel, continue on to Reykjavik, in Iceland, and then set off on the final stage to Prestwick. The northern route was now open — a journey of 3,241 miles as against the crossing from Dorval to Prestwick, through Gander, of 3,467 miles.

Not only did this new route greatly increase the operational efficiency of Ferry Command for delivering American aircraft to Britain, but in 1943, there began a flow of delivery aircraft in the reverse direction, from East to West. Twin-engined Hampden bombers, superseded by four-engined Lancasters, were chosen for use as training aircraft at air schools in British Columbia. It was decided that ferry crews work their passage back to Canada by flying these aircraft over from Britain.

It was an arduous and hazardous journey, covering over 5,600 miles, but only one Hampden failed to get through because of severe weather and adverse winds.

The crew were Captain Robert E. Coffman, of Louisiana, Flying Officer Norman E. Greenway, RCAF, Alberta, and Radio Officer Ronald E. Snow of Digby, Nova Scotia. From Prestwick to Reykjavik the flight was smooth and normal. Captain Coffman took the Hampden on the next stage to Labrador and for two hours the aircraft behaved perfectly. Suddenly, as they approached the east coast of Greenland an engine failed; all efforts to start it again were in vain.

For another hour the Hampden flew on one engine, but gradually lost height, coming down from 9,000 feet to 4,500 feet. Without warning the aircraft went into a savage spin and fell a further 3,500 feet before Captain Coffman regained control. However, the strain became too much for the remaining engine. After a further 20 minutes it faded completely. In a long, slow glide the Hampden dropped towards the sea and made a copybook ditching.

SOS calls were sent but, although the crew did not know it, were never received, because during the period of distress, the aircraft was within what is termed 'skip distance' from possible interception points — two far away for the HF ground wave to reach, too close for the sky-wave.

With a box of emergency kit and rations the crew leaped on to a wing and scrambled into their rubber dinghy. Just 70 seconds later the Hampden sank beneath the waves. Fortunately, Captain Coffman knew his exact position and decided to steer the dinghy on a course which would take

1em to the Greenland shore, about 15 miles away.

All around them, in every direction, were icebergs of
arying shapes and sizes and for almost 20 hours they
teered a hazardous course through the ice field before
ighting land.

The resounding cracks made by icebergs colliding
ounded like bombs being dropped and for much of the
me the air was filled with the noise of cracking ice.
Although they could see the Greenland shore no more than
mile away it was impossible for them to reach it because
f a swift coastal current which forced their tiny craft back.
hey made their way to a large black rock, about 50 yards
ffshore and scrambled on to this. They had landed on the
,000-foot pinnacle of an 11,000-foot mountain below the
ea, known as Umanarsuk or, from the Eskimo, 'shaped
ke a big heart'.

They searched in vain for a cave or a hole into which
1ey could crawl to get out of the biting wind. The rock was
overed in snow and there was no vegetation or wood of
ny kind with which to light a fire. Dispirited by the
aunting turn of events they hauled the dinghy to a narrow
dge 100 feet above the sea and made a makeshift tent out
f it so that they would have some protection from the
eezing cold.

By now Ferry Command headquarters at Montreal had
itiated a full-scale air search. Aircraft droned over the
innacle of rock, but because of storm clouds were unable
 see the Very lights fired by the crew huddled beneath
1eir flimsy rubber protection.

To ensure their survival a schedule of rationing was
rawn up by Captain Coffman. Their supplies consisted of
5 malted milk tablets; 4 squares of barley sugar; a small
uantity of chewing gum; 12 sealed pints of water; a first
id kit; a yellow distress flag; a 4inch square metal mirror
ith an attachment for use as a heliograph and the Very
istol and 27 cartridges.

The men estimated they had enough to last for one week,
ut after several days with still no sign of rescue the rations
ere cut back. They were now reduced to an absolute
ninimum. For additional water they sucked mouthfuls of
now.

For almost six days they were subjected to intense
:orms; sleet and snow, driven on by gale force winds and
n one occasion they were forced to flee their shelter when
1e sea poured over the one hundred foot high ledge.

On the ninth day they sighted a small ship, but again the
:orm prevented them from using the Very pistol and flares
 the best advantage. The following day an aircraft flew
lmost directly overhead but once more, although distress
ares were fired, there was no response.

As they lay, huddled together for extra warmth, in the

slush beneath their upturned dinghy hope began to fade in
each man's heart. Captain Coffman later gave an account
of what they thought were their last hours of life:

'Someone drew attention to the fact that each of us had a
middle name beginning with the letter E; we thought that
was an extraordinary coincidence and talked childishly
about it interminably.

'We were desperately hungry but never mentioned the
fact, only reciting to each other stories of steaks and other
foods we had eaten when delivering bombers to different
parts of the world. When one of us dropped off in a coma
for a short while, he would mention on waking that he had
been dreaming about gargantuan meals in which dumplings
and thick gravy seemed to figure.

'We saw no prospect of rescue, but we made a point of
taking a vow every few minutes that we would never again
complain about food, even the abundance of carrots which
we get every time we fly into Britain. Every few minutes we
would also speak mournfully about a sea-lion which came
out of the sea to see us off at the start of our voyage and
whose blubber and meat would have been a godsend to us'.

At noon that day Radio Officer Snow spotted a two-
masted ship at anchor about eight miles away. For the next
three hours the castaways signalled with their helio mirror
and fired off flares; there was no welcome answer.

Aboard the vessel a US Army major came on deck to
look at the Greenland scenery through binoculars. As he
allowed his gaze to travel slowly over the distant landscape
he caught a momentary glimpse of a bright gleam. A few
seconds later he saw what at first looked like a puff of
smoke, followed by a sudden glint as if a gull was wheeling
in the sunlight. He then noticed that the glint plunged down
rapidly, in a vertical position, and realised that whatever it
was, it was no gull.

He focused his binoculars on the pinnacle of rock and
after several moments was certain that a bright flashing pin
prick of light was some kind of signal. He went to inform
the Norwegian captain. What he had seen falling from the
sky was the last Very cartridge which the stranded men had
in their possession.

The captain was suspicious. He felt that any messages
from the pinnacle of rock might either be a U-boat trick to
entice him inshore or a ruse by Nazi agents who might
have established a radio post on one of the Greenland
islands.

The major solved his problem. 'If that's the case, let's get
in there and capture them', he announced.

A small boat was launched carrying the major and three
Norwegian sailors, all armed with automatic rifles. In their
belts they carried revolvers and combat knives. When
within range of the rock they trained their rifles on it until
the major could take a closer look at what appeared to be
men on a ledge nearly 300 feet up.

A few seconds with the binoculars and he was satisfied.
The rifles were lowered and the boat went in. When the
sailors and the major reached the crew they found them
barely able to stand up, but making a brave effort to do so
by holding each other round the shoulders.

On board the ship they collapsed; they were still

unconscious when the vessel reached a quiet Greenland fiord where it was possible to put them ashore. An aircraft had been lost, but thanks to remarkable stamina and something little short of a miracle, the crew would live on to fly again across the Atlantic.

As the months went past Ferry Command increased its scope to enclose a vast network of routes. These were used for delivering aircraft to the Middle East, flying south via the Bahamas, down South America from Natal to Ascension Island, on to Accra, across Africa to Cairo, and through to India.

These new transcontinental routes had their own problems, but for the crews there was only one difference; should an accident occur and they were forced down it would be into thick and impenetrable jungle or thousands of square miles of burning sand instead of a cold and unfriendly ocean. In only one aspect did this new territory bear a similar resemblance to the Atlantic crossing — it was just as hostile, every bit as alien.

When Polish Sergeant Mikolajozak wrote in his log book, as he lay dying in the sun: 'Let nobody land in the desert where there are no people, as there is no way out', he could well have been summing up the feelings shared by his comrades who braved the all-powerful Atlantic Ocean.

This was something of which all who crossed the Atlantic Bridge were aware, but for the men of Ferry Command it was a thought which they had to suppress and conquer as they flew their lonely and unprotected missions.

# Operation Chocolate 12

Among the many brilliant and imaginative transport operations of World War II few exceeded for sheer audacity, a Western Desert air lift by Hudsons of No 216 Group on 12-13 November 1942. Officially known as Operation Chocolate, the Hudson pilots simply called it the LG 125 Stunt'.

The idea was put up by Air Vice-Marshal Arthur 'Mary' Coningham, AOC Western Desert Air Force, and set in motion inside 48 hours. The enemy was in full retreat after Montgomery's breakthrough at El Alamein and the RAF was doing everything in its power to speed that process. To confuse the Axis forces further Coningham proposed that a Hurricane wing be placed *behind* their lines to harry airfields and road transport in back areas which would expect to be immune from precision fighter ground attack.

No 243 Wing, comprising Nos 213 and 238 Squadrons was nominated for the job. The location chosen for their secret base was a barren stretch of desert about 100 miles south-west of Tobruk which has been used once, earlier in the campaign, and was known as Landing Ground 125. Although it was perhaps not more than 50 miles behind the rapidly receding enemy lines, its position well inland gave the fighters a short cut across the coastal bulge between Bomba and Benghazi to reach road traffic beyond their normal range.

On 11 November a Bombay of No 216 Squadron, captained by Flight Sergeant Vickery, flew into LG 125 to check its suitability for other aircraft types and to reconnoitre the area for enemy forces. On receipt of the Bombay's signal that the strip was useable, rapid plans were made for Hudsons to fly in sufficient fuel, water, rations, ammunition and so on for several days' operations. Squadron Leader G. D. Fleming of No 117 Squadron, who had gained considerable experience of low level desert navigation while flying DH86s on air ambulance work, was chosen to lead the transport force. The 12 Hudsons from No 117 Squadron took off from Amriya at 0835 on 2 November, were joined by another 16 from No 267 Squadron and three from No 216, and the whole force, loaded to the roofs, roared off in a loose V-shaped gaggle at zero feet. For the pilots this was exhilarating, heady stuff. Although they normally flew low in combat areas, they rarely did so in such strength, rising and falling in the bumpy desert air, with their shadows racing along just below and enhancing the impression of speed.

Fleming headed first 50 miles south of Sollum for Fort Maddalena on the Egypt-Libya frontier — an easily identified landmark — then turned south-west on a 150-mile leg further inland over the featureless desert. He found LG 125 without difficulty and all the Hudsons put down safely, unloaded their supplies and returned to base. Two Bombays of No 216 Squadron followed and a small ground party with radio equipment brought up the rear.

On Friday the 13th the Hudsons took off at the same time with more stores, tentage and about 60 servicing personnel, assembled into three loose formations and were joined by the 36 Hurricanes of No 243 Wing under Wing Commander J. Darwen. This time they flew at 2,000 feet, as their escort gave them immunity from enemy fighter attack and the extra height offered any Hurricane which might suffer engine failure a better chance in a forced landing.

Although Fleming had confidence in his desert navigation it was with immense relief that he saw in the distance the dark outline of the stores dumped the previous day. Whereas the Hudsons had sufficient endurance to spend some time looking for LG 125 if necessary, the Hurricanes were getting low in petrol. He had been haunted by the prospect of the entire wing 'lobbing down in the bundoo', out of fuel, with himself having to accept the responsibility.

The Hudsons unloaded and returned to base while the fighter ground crews got to work. In less than two hours, 27 Hurricanes were airborne to attack traffic on the Benghazi-El Agheila road. It was crowded with vehicles of all sorts, and parties of soldiers working on defence positions, naturally assuming that any low flying single-engined aircraft so far back must be from the Luftwaffe, waved gaily as the Hurricanes slanted in to the attack. For the RAF pilots is seemed almost like cheating — but after all this was war.

And so it went on for three more days. Flying 119 sorties the Hurricanes attacked the airfields at Jalo and Agedabia, an Italian artillery column and countless vehicles moving along the coast road, and their total claim was some 300 vehicles destroyed or severely damaged, 11 aircraft destroyed on the ground and one — a Savoia — in the air. Three Hurricanes were lost. Obviously the enemy must soon track down the location of this particular hornets' nest, and on the 15th contrails of high-flying reconnaissance aircraft were seen in the vicinity. A Ju88 had also made an abortive attempt to follow the Hurricanes to the landing ground, and since there were no air defences and no radar it was decided to withdraw.

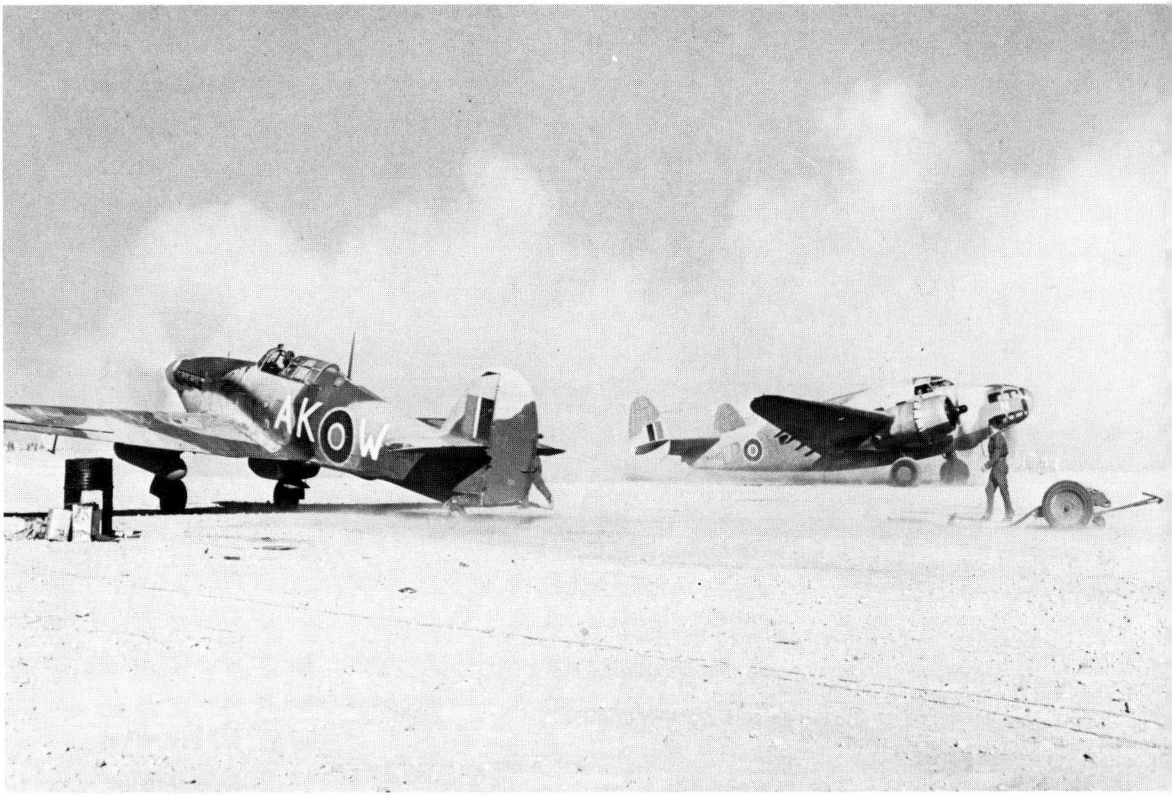
AKOW

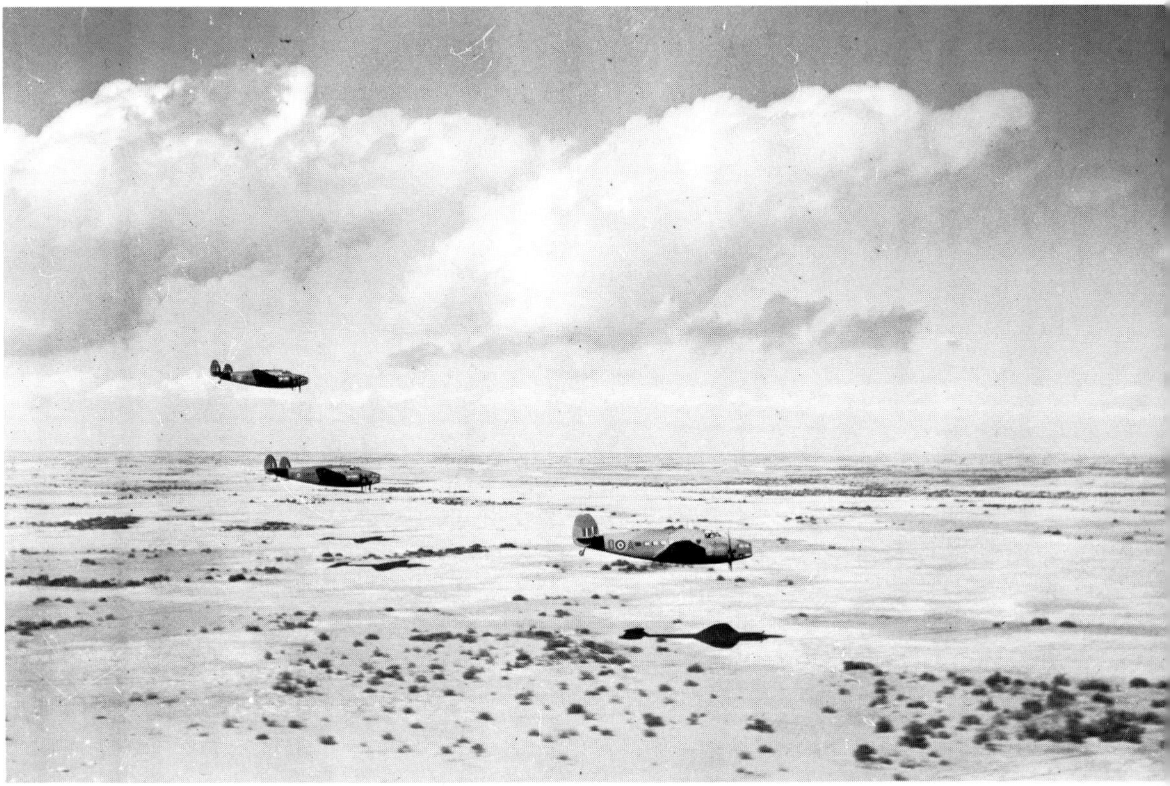

Around midday on the 16th the Hudsons came back, picked up the unused fuel, equipment and the servicing party, and by 1230 the entire detachment had departed. The dust settled, quiet descended on the desert and LG 125 was again empty, apart from a few nomadic Arabs scavenging for those valuable items which could be put to good use, discarded as junk by the 'Inglesi' in their casual, improvident fashion.

Nearly a year after the brilliant Operation Chocolate, No 216 Group was involved in a scheme which had a less happy outcome, though no blame could be attached to the air transport side.

With the prospect of Italy's capitulation, Britain had planned to gain a foothold in the Aegean by establishing a base on Rhodes. This plan (Operation Accolade) was abandoned shortly after the cease-fire, when German forces took control of the island, and the alternative Operation Microbe was substituted — the takeover of the Dodecanese islands of Cos, Samos and Leros. No 216 Group provided 22 Dakotas — 16 from No 216 Squadron and six from No 267 — to meet the air transport requirements.

On 13 September 1943 British forces landed on Cos, occupying the port and the airfield at Antimachia. A Spitfire squadron flew in next day, and three No 216 Squadron Dakotas operating from Nicosia, Cyprus, with a Beaufighter escort delivered fuel and ammunition. That night six more Dakotas from Nicosia dropped with pin-point accuracy 120 men of the Parachute Regiment 1½ miles north-west of Cos town to reinforce the Italian garrison. Between 15 and 19 September, 26 transport sorties landed men and supplies, some of the aircrews making two trips a day. Enemy reaction was rapid, and substantial Luftwaffe reinforcements arrived in the area. Five Dakotas were destroyed on the ground during strafing attacks, and another struck the surface of the sea while attempting to avoid interception. Such a loss rate was unacceptable, but night operations could not be conducted from the 900-yard rough gravel strip at Antimachia.

On the 21st the Dakotas were switched from Nicosia to Ramat David, Palestine, and started intensive night flying into a new and better strip at Lambia, which has been accidentally discovered by a No 267 Squadron pilot who put down on the first likely looking stretch he could find in order to evade enemy fighters circling Antimachia. By the 29th enemy bombing had damaged Lambia to the extent that it could no longer be safely used and the Dakotas began dropping their supplies. Five of them did, however,

The motto of No 31 Squadron, *In Caelum Indicum Primus* (translated as 'First into Indian Skies') was chosen to commemorate the fact that in 1916 it was the first air squadron to operate in that continent. Whether 'first' could also be used in the sense of 'supreme' is for debate by Latin scholars, but this would be most appropriate, since during the critical 12 months following Japan's entry into the war, No 31 was the only transport squadron operating in India and Burma. It was largely responsible for developing techniques in a theatre where the success of the entire campaign eventually came to depend upon air supply.

After its brief involvement in the Rashid Ali affair the squadron resumed routine flying in India, and in October 1941 eight of its DC2s were detached to Egypt to work with No 117 Squadron on supply and casualty evacuation in the Western Desert. They returned to India in February 1942 when air lift was desperately needed to assist the British withdrawal from Burma. The dismal overall transport aircraft situation in the RAF can be seen from the table below, compiled from figures produced for the War Cabinet showing strength as on 1 April 1942, when American transport aircraft purchases were under discussion.

**Aircraft Types and Locations**

| | UK | Middle East | India | Total |
|---|---|---|---|---|
| Douglas DC-2 | 2 | 7 | 12 | 21 |
| Bristol Bombay | 8 | 17 | - | 25 |
| Lockheed Lodestar/Hudson | - | 8 | - | 8 |
| Lockheed 10/12 | 3 | 4 | 2 | 9 |
| Vickers Valentia | - | 12 | 2 | 14 |
| Handley Page Harrow | 36 | - | - | 36 |
| DH Flamingo | 6 | - | - | 6 |
| DH86 | - | 6 | 1 | 7 |
| Percival Petrel/Q6 | 9 | 2 | - | 11 |
| Airspeed Envoy | 5 | - | 2 | 7 |
| | 69 | 56 | 19 | 144 |

The Percival and Airspeed types, and the smaller Lockheeds were hardly more than communications aircraft, and for this work, and courier flights, there were also 785 light single-engined aircraft not specified by type (606 in the UK, 160 in the Middle East and 19 in India). India, with 12 DC-2s could be regarded as best equipped with transports of modern design, though they were pathetically few in number and far from new. Towards the end of April No 31 Squadron also received the first of several DC-3s, which gave excellent service before the still more effective military version, the Dakota, became available to the RAF in 1943.

From February 1942 part of the squadron was operating from Akyab — where one of the old Valentias was destroyed on the ground by Japanese bombing on 27 March — then a detachment moved to Dinjan, in Upper Assam. The few aircraft mounted a tremendous effort to fly casualties and refugees out of Myitkyina, which had become the immediate goal for thousands fleeing westwards. While the pursuing Japanese were the main enemy for the refugees, the aircrews were also fighting a battle against the approaching monsoon. To reach Myitkyina they had to claw their way through the turbulence over the Naga Hills, which had peaks jutting to nearly 10,000 feet, and there was an ever present risk of attack from enemy fighters. Between 27 April and 3 May — and on two of those days bad weather prevented any flying — the detachment made 39 sorties, lifting 1,307 people out of Myitkyina with its three serviceable DC-3s and one DC-2.

The Japanese were now closing in and on 3 May the Air Officer Commanding (Air Vice-Marshal D. F. Stevenson) signalled to the squadron commander: 'Heartiest congratulations on the magnificent work your squadron is doing in Burma. Would you please convey this to all crews and maintenance personnel. Every sortie that it is practicable to be done during the next week or so will save lives that otherwise may be lost.'

Time was rapidly running out. On 6 May two of the DC-3s were caught in a heavy raid on Myitkyina airfield. D-Dog had begun to take off when a bomb landed just in front of its port wing and caused it to crash, mercifully with no injuries. E-Edward had just loaded but was badly damaged by a very near miss before it could start to taxi. The enemy aircraft followed the bombing with machine-gun attacks, killing two women passengers and a child and severely wounding two army medical officers. The Squadron Commander, Wing Commander H. P. Jenkins, who was among the passengers, carried a wounded Indian soldier to the relative safety of a bomb crater, and as the two pilots, Squadron Leaders W. H. Burbury and T. L. Howell, left by the front hatch Howell remembered to grab the Tommy gun they were carrying for emergencies. The Japanese attack continued for 10 minutes, and with little hope of causing any damage, Howell let fly at one aircraft making its final low pass. To his delight it began to trail

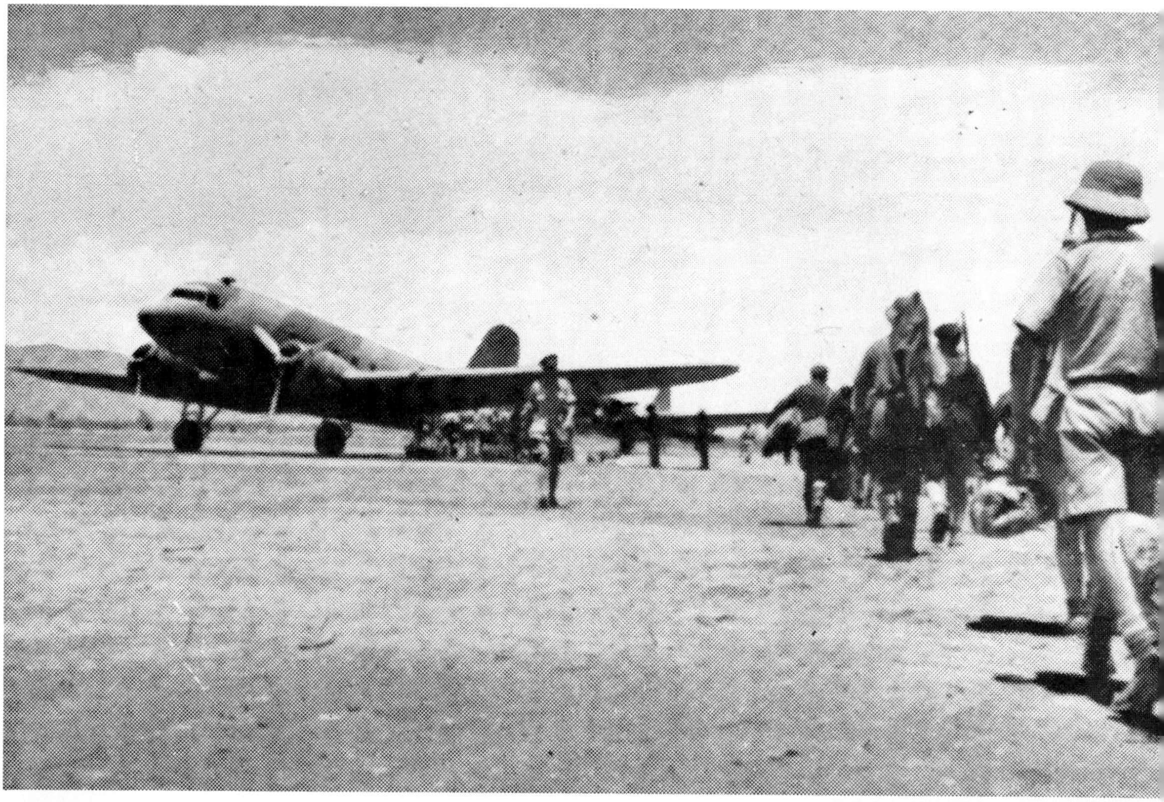

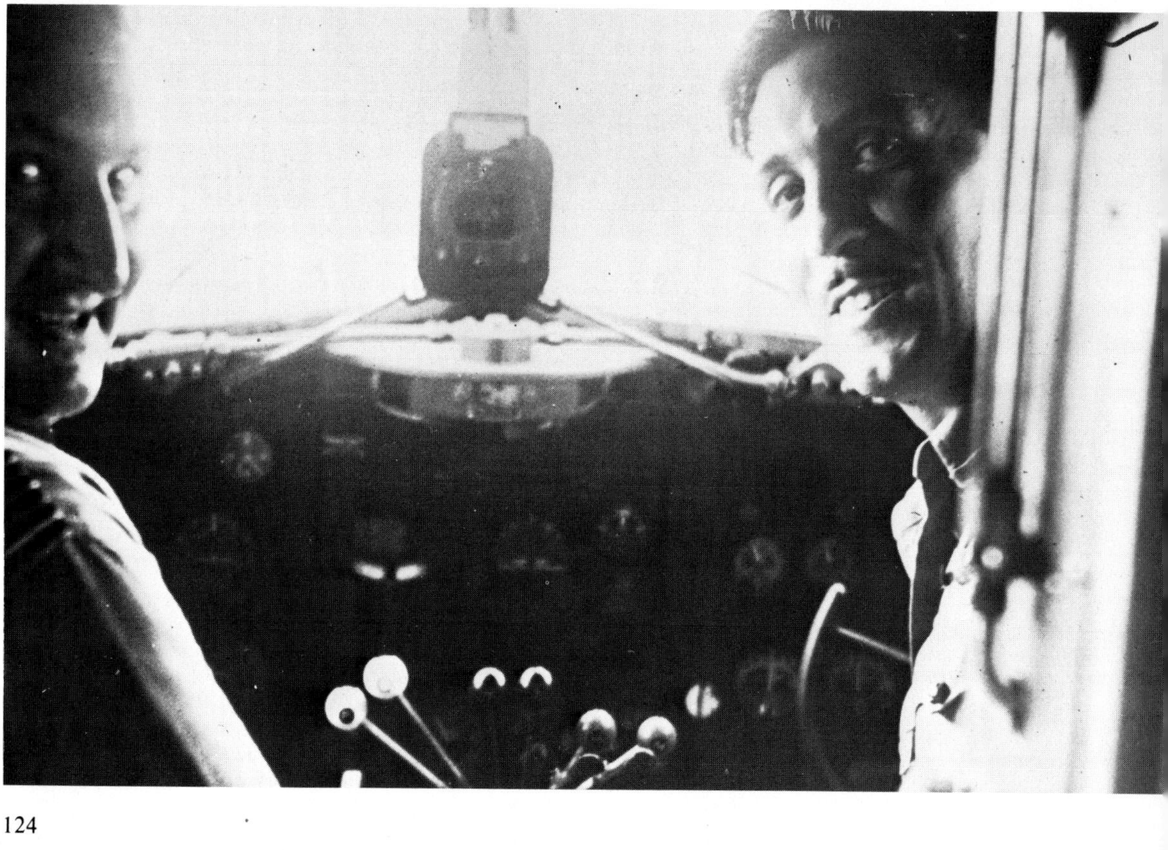

**Left: DC-2s of No 31 Squadron emplaning troops at Myitkyina, April 1942.**

**Bottom left: Wing Commander A. C. Pearson, CO of No 194 Squadron (left) in the captain's seat of a Dakota. The identity of the other squadron member is not recorded.** / IWM

hite vapour as it flew off and was believed to have crashed, though this was never confirmed. Evacuation flights were resumed later that day and on the last departure one of the ex-21-seat civil air liners left with an overload variously reported as 42 and 65 passengers.

Myitkyina fell on 8 May, and next day the aircraft began dropping food and other supplies along the three main routes over which civilians and soldiers were slowly struggling on their way into India. Apart from the aircraft lost at Myitkyina, several more had been destroyed in other enemy raids and the few remaining DC-2s and -3s were tested to the utmost. Spares were scarce and if all servicing procedures had been followed according to the book flying would have rapidly ground to a halt. It is said that some aircraft even flew with a 710hp engine from a DC-2 on one side and a 850hp unit from a DC-3 on the other. Fully realising the appalling plight of the refugees, the aircrews not only closed their eyes to these irregularities, but voluntarily increased their sortie rate, making up to five trips a day.

Another supply commitment was to the isolated garrison at Fort Hertz, bypassed by the advancing Japanese armies. By special request two landings were made, on 31 May and 3 June, to evacuate casualties and women refugees, and in August to deliver a specialist team to train Kashin levies in guerilla tactics, but the normal supply method was by parachute. Towards the end of 1942 the Fort Hertz supply flights were made from Tezpur, and the No 31 Squadron DC-3s were augmented by three Hudsons from No 194 Squadron, which were better equipped to cope with Japanese fighters. On one flight a supply pannier became caught on a Hudson's tail and the parachute deployed. For half an hour the pilot battled to retain control of his aircraft until eventually the parachute and load tore free. Two Hudsons were lost in the area but whether from enemy action or flying hazards was not established.

Throughout this period improvisation was the keyword, and perhaps without realising the fact, No 31 Squadron was re-inventing methods first used in 1916. Because parachutes were scarce many loads were free-dropped and grain supplies were packed in double or even triple sacks to avoid losses through impact bursts. The doors of the DCs were removed before take-off, and the moment for dropping was signalled from the flight deck by the 'fasten seat belts' signs. There were no specialist Army despatchers and up to 7,000lb of supplies were manhandled to the door by the wireless operator, assisted by the aircraft fitter and rigger. One dropping zone sited on a cone-shaped hill was little larger than a tennis court and it was a tribute to the skill and perseverance of the Douglas' crew that 50% of the supplies were recovered.

There are no detailed figures for the RAF air transport effort in Burma during this period, but it is known that of the 8,616 people — including 2,600 casualties — flown out of the country by the British and American transport forces, about half were carried by No 31 Squadron. The RAF took the major part in air supply work, and between May and December 1942 dropped 777 tons, compared with 212 tons by the USAAF and 108 by the Chinese National Aviation Corporation.

At this point the strange figure of Brigadier Orde Wingate renewed his association with the Royal Air Force. Despite his undoubted success in Ethiopia, Wingate's unorthodox methods and views were still far from universally acceptable, though Wavell, now GOC-in-C India, had never lost his faith in him and arranged his posting to that theatre. Wingate's approach was simple — the aeroplane provided the means of surmounting obstacles such as enemy territory, so use that capability intelligently, as he had done in Ethiopia. Had some more timid commander vetoed that hazardous flight in the old Vincent in November 1940, the history of the war might have been different. Wingate's plan was to provoke trouble and confusion behind the enemy lines by special Long Range Penetration Groups which would be supplied entirely by air. There was some scepticism, but Wingate had done his homework with great precision, and the aircrews who were to undertake the deliveries became infected with his enthusiasm. If he believed it could be done, they argued, let nobody say that the Air Force had failed. With the troops were to be RAF liaison officers, and radio equipment, so that supply matters could be handled with the necessary air expertise.

Wingate chose as his emblem the mythical winged lion, the 'Chinthe', guardian of the Burmese pagodas, which was additionally appropriate as symbolising supremacy on the ground and in the air. The official title of the force was the 77th Indian Infantry Brigade, and the name 'Chindits' was apparently coined by a British war correspondent after the operation was over.

The eight Chindit columns left Imphal in early February 1943 with pack mules, bullocks and even a few elephants. Meanwhile a detachment of 31 Squadron DC-3s and 194 Squadron Hudsons had moved to Agartala, the main base for the initial air supply programme, codenamed 'Vicki'. The troops crossed the Chindwin river in two main groups without opposition, and on 14 and 15 February Hudsons with fighter escort flew 10 sorties by day to drop 30,000lb of supplies to the southern group. On the nights of 15th, 16th and 18th, DC-3s and Hudsons flew 16 sorties to drop 71,000lb to the northern group near Myene. Night sorties had not been regarded as practical until shortly before the start of the expedition, when No 31 Squadron trials proved that on illuminated dropping zones in reasonably open country, acceptable accuracy could be achieved.

The feasibility of dropping into small jungle clearings was established by chance. On 24 February a prearranged dropping zone near Baw was found to be Japanese-occupied, so since their radio was unserviceable, the Chindits hopefully laid flare signals in a small clearing some miles to the north-west. The DC-3 crew saw these,

ft: The dramatic **PLANE LAND HERE NOW** message spelled
ith torn parachute fabric by a Chindit patrol in a jungle
earing, photographed from Flying Officer D. S. A. Lord's
akota on 25 April 1943. / IWM

ottom left: An informal de-briefing when Flying Officer
S. A. Lord returned to Agartala on 25 April 1943 with news
a Chindit patrol's request for a landing. Left to right: Wing
ommander W. H. Burbury (CO of No 31 Squadron), Squadron
ader E. B. Fielden (Flight Commander, 31 Squadron and later
O of No 62 Squadron), Flying Officer V. Barry (co-pilot) and
ying Officer Lord. / IWM

ut after dropping two wireless operators and packs
ontaining two days' rations the pilot developed a nagging
uspicion that the flares might be an enemy ruse and
bandoned the sortie. In fact the supplies were dead on
.rget.

Columns were at their most vulnerable while collecting
e airdropped supplies and to minimise the risks daylight
rops usually started at 1600. A zone was marked by
moke fires and the aircraft would make six or more runs
nce targets were normally too small for stick dropping.
he drop would take at least half an hour, with troops often
n the zone while it was in progress — strictly against the
iles and risking being hit in a free drop. Ghurkas proved
dept at climbing trees or throwing ropes weighted with
eavy stones to recover any containers caught in high
ranches. Outworn boots or clothing would be changed on
e spot, and the whole process of collection and
stribution might take up to an hour and a half. The main
nxiety then was to quit the area rapidly, and get as far
way as possible until darkness provided cover.

After completing their tasks, columns split into smaller
roups to return independently to friendly territory. One
arty signalled for equipment to assist them in crossing the
iver Shweli, and in reply No 31 Squadron delivered a
inghy and rope — almost a carbon copy of an operation
Iraq exactly 20 years earlier.

The troubles encountered by another column led to a
rilliant casualty evacuation flight by one of 31 Squadron's
)akotas — now replacing the DC-3s — which had far-
eached consequences. After a skirmish with an enemy
atrol these Chindits had managed to cross the Irrawaddy
a native craft seized while Japanese guard boats were
ccupied elsewhere. They had received no air supplies for
ur weeks and were desperately short of food. To make
atters worse the mule carrying their radio equipment
ollapsed and died, so they were obliged to abandon the set
fter signalling for a drop in a suitable area nearby. They
oved on, finding little to eat in the villages, and were
pproaching starvation point. Among them were men
rgently needing hospital treatment — several wounded,
ccident cases, and others with jungle sores, ulcers,
ysentery and malaria — whose survival prospects in the
ungle were minimal.

The spot chosen for the drop was an irregularly shaped
learing about 170 miles inside enemy occupied territory
nd 20 from a Japanese fighter airfield. Somebody jokingly
emarked that it seemed big enough for an airfield, at which
thoughtful look came over the CO's face.

Captain detailed for the flight on Sunday 25 April was
Flying Officer David S. A. 'Lumme' Lord, who had joined
the RAF in 1936, trained as a pilot two years later and
been with No 31 Squadron since October 1939. He had
reached the rank of warrant officer when awarded a
commission in July 1942. It is hardly necessary to explain
that this nickname derived from reversing the cockney
phrase 'Lor' lumme!' He was later to win a posthumous
VC at Arnhem.

The Chindits' smoke signal was located and the Dakota
began its drop. After about two circuits the crew realised
that the men on the ground were spelling out a message
with strips torn from the parachutes, and three runs later
this could be ready clearly: *Plane land here now*. The entire
crew was keen to have a go, but after two low passes Lord
could see that a landing might be disastrous without some
clearing of the roughest surface patches. Back at base,
Burbury, who had been squadron commander since the
previous June, felt that an attempt should be made and
Headquarters gave approval. Next day, during another
supply flight, instructions were dropped to mark out and
level a strip, preferably of at least 1,200 yards length.

Late on the 27th HQ somehow ascertained that the strip
was ready and that 20 casualties were awaiting pick-up.
'Lumme' Lord, perhaps the natural candidate for the job,
was not available and it was given to Flying Officer
Michael Vlasto, who had logged something over 1,000 DC
hours since joining the squadron. His home was Henley-on-
Thames, and he had enlisted and trained in India where he
was working in the jute trade when the war started. His
crew members were Sergeant Frank Murray, from
Kingston, Jamaica (co-pilot), Sergeant Jack Reeves,
RCAF, from Bradford, Ontario (wireless operator) and
Sergeant Charles Alfred May, from Leeds (rigger).

Dakota O-Orange left Agartala at first light on 28 April
with 5,200lb of supplies to be dropped before attempting
the landing, and called in at Imphal for a briefing with No 5
Squadron, which was providing a Mohawk fighter escort.
The Mohawks had insufficient endurance to remain
airborne while the Dakota was on the ground, so four made
the outward trip and another four were to take off later for
the return escort.

On arrival over the strip it was seen that the Chindits
had again exercised their spelling, and this time the message
read *Land on white line ground there vg*. The dotted white
line, marked with pieces torn from parachutes, extended for
perhaps 800 yards, with rough patches at each end, and its
centre passed through a narrow neck in the clearing where
the teak forest encroached to less than 100 yards on either
side. The trees at each end, some 80-100ft high, were
disturbingly close.

After dropping the main supplies in one corner, Vlasto
made a low, slow run down the strip. He climbed away and
turned over the trees, then, using every ounce of
concentration, made the steep approach which the setting
of the strip dictated, flared out precisely at the first marker
and greased the Dakota on to the ground. He braked hard,
turned and taxied back and before the engines stopped,
bearded and scruffy members of the Chindit column
looking like a band of cut-throats had swarmed from the
forest. After much back-slapping with the crew they

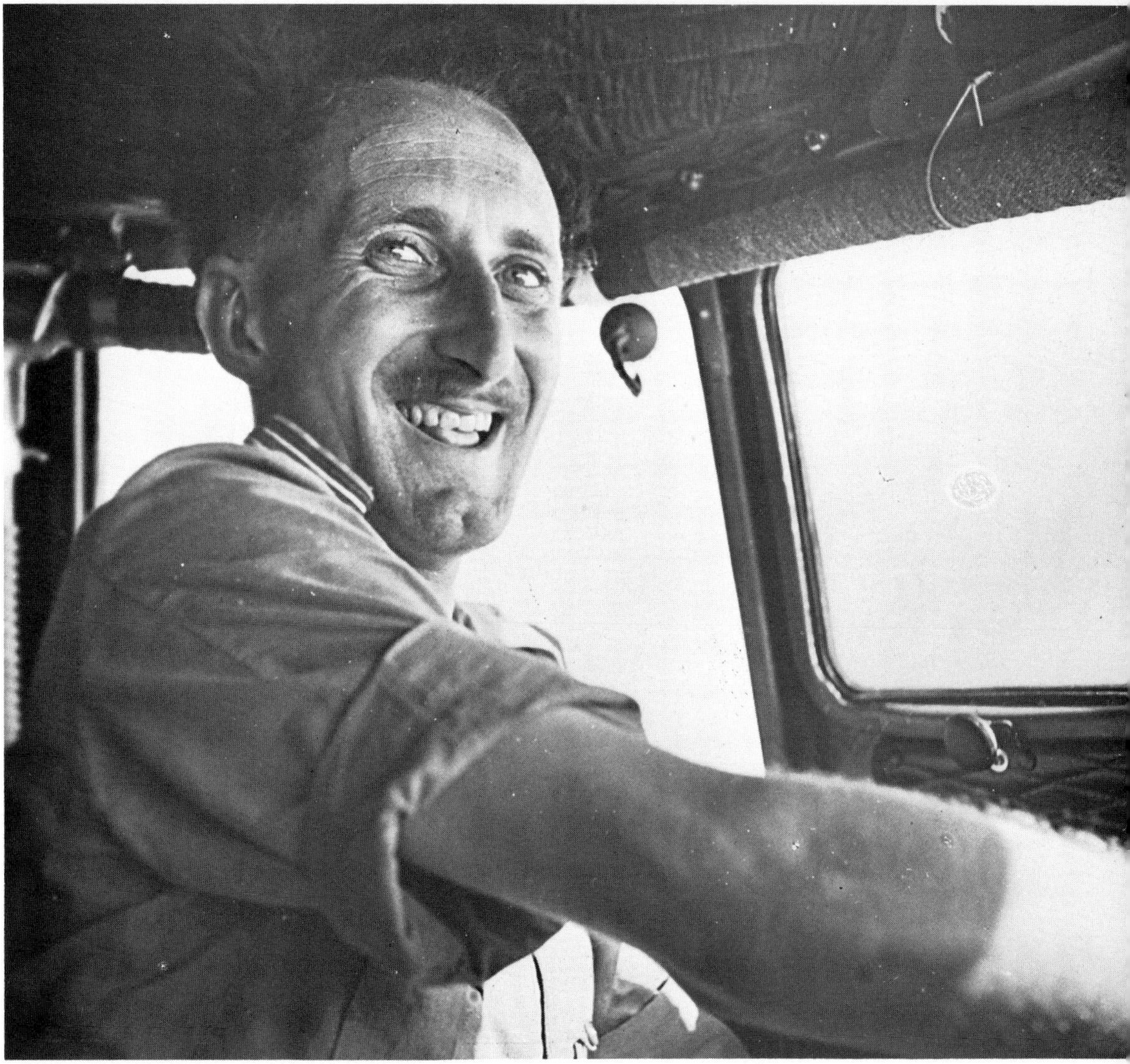

Above left: One of the escort Mohawk fighters of No 5
Squadron photographed from Vlasto's Dakota. / IWM

Left: Flying Officer Michael Vlasto, No 31 Squadron, who made
the historic landing in a jungle clearing behind the Japanese
lines on 28 April 1943 to pick up wounded Chindits. / IWM

Above: The jungle clearing — later named Piccadilly — from
which 17 sick and wounded Chindits were flown out on
28 April 1942. The dotted line of parachute material to mark
the landing direction, running diagonally through the neck of
the clearing to the top right-hand corner, is clearly seen in the
original print. / IWM

Right: A supply drop to a patrol during the first Chindit
expedition. / IWM

unloaded the more fragile stores, including a new radio set. Their general condition had much improved thanks to the rations drop three days before, but 17 still required urgent hospital treatment. There were no signs of envy among those left behind to continue their homeward journey on foot. Indeed, one man who would have been the 18th passenger persuaded his CO at the door of the Dakota that he was fit to carry on.

After about 15 minutes on the ground the co-pilot started engines, Vlasto exchanged a few final words with the column commander, then climbed aboard. Doors were closed and the passengers bunched up in the front part of the cabin for what might prove an exciting take-off. Vlasto ran up the engines, released the brakes and the Dakota lurched away over the rough ground. Its tail came up quickly, the bumps faded away and the wheels lifted just before the end of the strip. The co-pilot whipped up the undercarriage to reduce drag before facing the major hazard — those menacing tall trees so close ahead — but the Dakota was lightly loaded and, roaring exultantly rather than in protest, the superb Pratt and Whitney engines dragged it over with room to spare. Four more Mohawks appeared and the return flight to Imphal was without incident. Two Japanese fighters were seen, but showed no inclination to attack. Michael Vlasto was awarded an immediate DFC for this outstanding piece of flying.

In supplying the Chindits Nos 31 and 194 Squadrons flew 178 sorties and dropped 303 tons of supplies. The experience of No 7 column, which recovered 85% of the supplies dropped in six sorties between 20 March and 30 April, was probably typical of the operation as a whole. In their 1,000 miles' marching in three months the Chindits destroyed four bridges and cut or blocked the railway lines in more than 75 places.

The Army was unstinting in its praise, and on 5 May Wingate signalled to the RAF Commander-in-Chief: 'Throughout the campaign the RAF supply dropping has been nearly perfect and capable of astonishing performances. The men on the ground were first class. The w/t was as excellent as it was vital'. One of the column commanders said: 'I cannot express it more clearly than to put it in one word used by all the troops — wonderful'.

The Chindits lost about one-third of their strength and some later assessments of the net achievement were not uncritical, though none could doubt that the operation provided highly valuable experience. As to the RAF contribution, let the final word come from one of the Chindits, Brigadier Sir Bernard Fergusson, who, lecturing to the Royal United Services Institution in 1946 said:

'. . . the one really invaluable dividend was the proof of the efficacy of supply dropping. The whole force had been supplied by only five aircraft, and No 31 Squadron, Royal Air Force, were the heroes of that astonishing feat.

'I still have a soft spot in my heart for that unknown aircraftman who, at the end of every supply drop, used to chuck that morning's paper out of the aircraft on its last run.'

The first Chindit campaign highlighted the introduction

into the RAF of one of the great — some might say the greatest — aeroplanes of World War II, the Dakota. The merits of this and that fighter or bomber still produce endless debate, but in the transport category there can be no dispute. The DC-2, which began the RAF's association with Douglas transport aircraft, had a few awkward handling characteristics but many merits, including that of performing well in severe icing conditions. The DC-3 which first flew in 1935, was very similar in appearance though slightly larger and more powerful. It was a placid viceless creature, sometimes described as an 'old ladies' aeroplane'.

About 10,000 military versions were built, of which the RAF operated nearly 2,000 as Dakotas, and these had strengthened floors, bigger doors and various other differences to suit Service requirements. They served in every theatre of war and in virtually every transport role. The Dakota could be crashed by pilot error and was not immune from technical failure nor the hazards of weather but despite the abusive treatment it received it proved a durable, forgiving aeroplane with a superb safety record.

Even in the days when the Dakota was just one among dozens of piston-engined aircraft it had its own characteristic sound, and to the weary, sweating troops in the Burmese jungles this was music infinitely sweeter than any produced by the master composers. The last RAF Dakota was retired in 1970 and although civil DC-3s continued to fly they were something of a rarity in British skies. That swelling, throbbing hum of radial engines became a puzzling discrepancy when it occasionally intruded into the prevailing turbine sound, but always somewhere within earshot there would be a middle-aged figure pausing to look skywards, recalling that music which had made the jungle a little more bearable.

Fortunately the planners had not waited for the Chindit expedition to spell out with final precision one of the fundamental truths which was now emerging in the Burma theatre. The very nature of the country, with its mountains jungles and swamps, possessing limited communications regularly interrupted by weather during the monsoon, was already presenting a picture in which air transport offered the most promising method of successfully prosecuting war against the Japanese. Since the start of the campaign No 31 Squadron had borne the brunt of the RAF transport work and in 1943 it flew nearly 2,000 supply dropping sorties. More aircraft were already in the pipeline and when the Anglo-American Troop Carrier Command was formed on 15 December 1943 under Brigadier General William D Old, USAAF, the RAF was able to contribute No 177 Wing, commanded by Group Captain G. F. K. Donaldson and comprising four Dakota Squadrons totalling 100 aircraft. In addition, the Hudsons of No 353 Squadron were available to maintain a comprehensive network of passenger and mail schedules in India. Although this force was still not adequate to meet all the demands of the

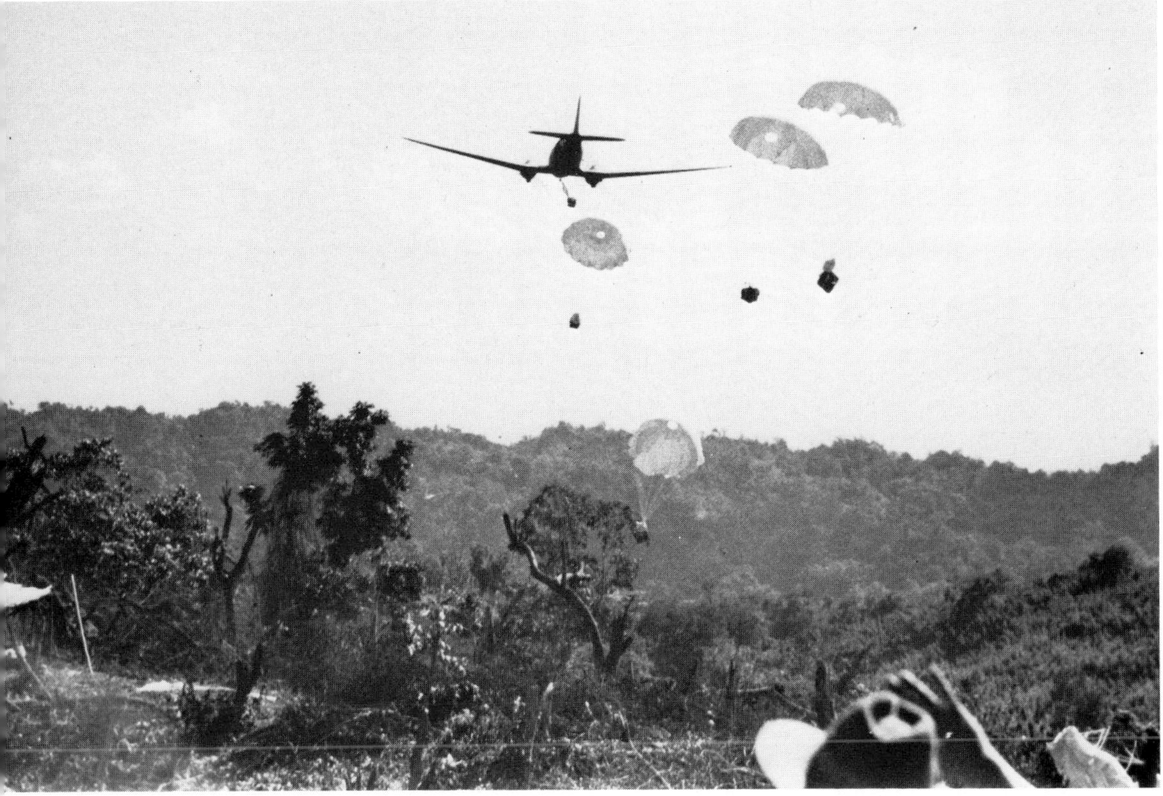

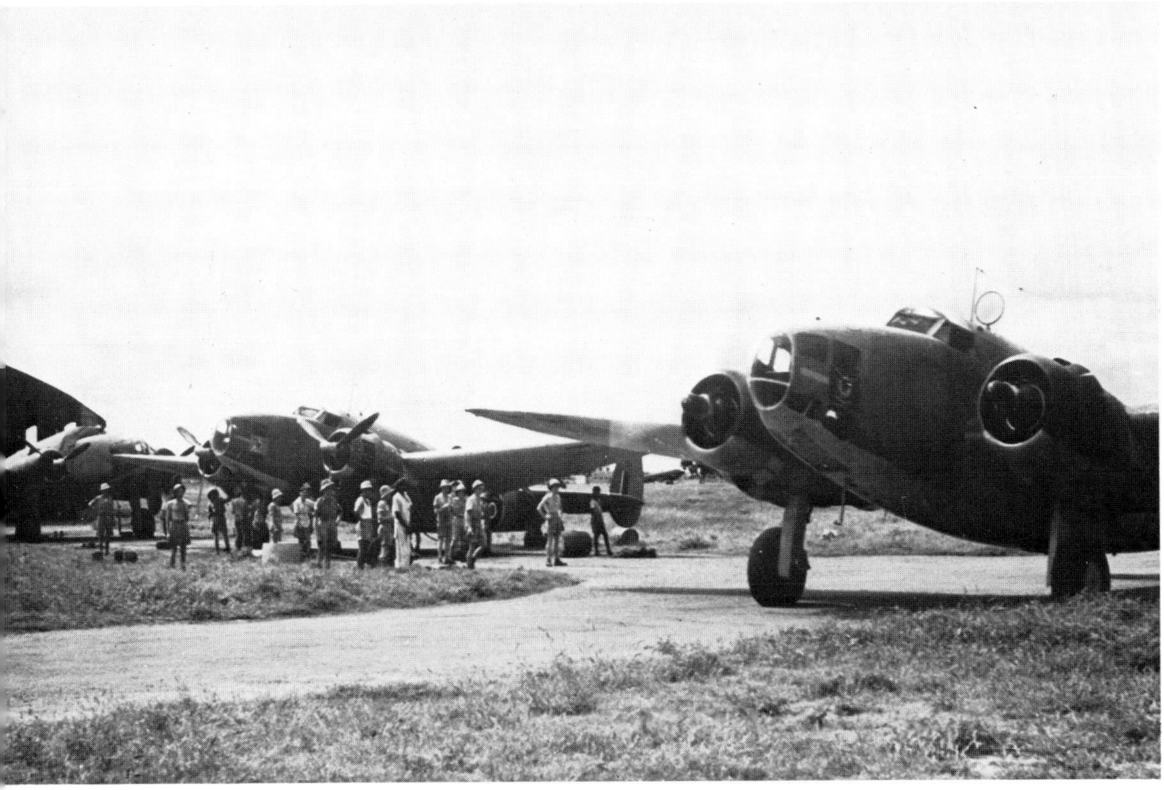

# Operation Thursday

Asked to name the most remarkable air transport feat of World War II many people would select Operation Thursday, the mundane code name allotted to the second Wingate expedition into Burma. It was, in fact, launched on a Sunday — 5 March 1944.

Wingate was now a major-general, whose unconventional tactics had gained him the ear of Churchill. His antiquated Wolseley helmet, and the beard which he had worn at intervals since the Ethiopian campaign were almost as well known as Montgomery's double-badged beret. With his flair for the unorthodox and his love of signalling operational instructions in the form of biblical quotations, he was fast becoming a legend.

The aim of Thursday was, briefly, to place behind Japanese forces operating in north-eastern Burma the equivalent of two divisions — some 12,000 men — no fewer than 10,000 of them to be flown to a point 120 miles beyond the area of Allied influence and some 270 miles from the main air base. Their functions included the creation of maximum interference with enemy supply lines, and the expedition was on a far larger scale than that of 1943. Air transport for the lift was to be provided by the RAF and the USAAF in approximately equal shares, under the general co-ordination of Air Marshal Sir John Baldwin, AOC Third Tactical Air Force. In addition to the regular RAF and USAAF transport squadrons operating under Troop Carrier Command, a specialised American force — No 1 Air Commando — had been formed to tow in the glider-borne spearhead which was to prepare the ground for Dakota landings. The commando also had light aircraft for casualty evacuation and bombers and fighters for other purposes. Its transport pilots were all former instructors who had volunteered for the job.

By a stroke of good fortune the Arakan operations had ended just in time to release the transports for Wingate's long planned foray, and all four RAF Dakota squadrons of No 177 Wing under Group Captain George Donaldson were deeply involved.

Several fairly extensive clearings had been selected for the landings, the two most important, codenamed Piccadilly and Broadway, being located about 20 miles apart. Piccadilly was in fact the strip used by Vlasto for his famous casevac pick up during the first Chindit expedition, which may well have stimulated Wingate's thoughts in the direction of similar landings on a much bigger scale. Operations on this Burmese D-day were primarily devoted to the glider landings. At the last minute it was decided that

in view of the limited experience of towing gliders, the tug Dakotas themselves should not, as originally intended, carry any load for paradropping on the landing site, so their cargoes were accordingly transferred to 10 RAF Dakotas.

The start of the operation provided one of the great dramatic moments of World War II. Senior officers at Lalaghat to see the glider force depart included General Sir William Slim, Air Marshal Sir John Baldwin, Lt-Gen George Stratemeyer, USAAF (Eastern Air Command), Brigadier-General William Old, USAAF, Air Vice-Marshal Thomas Williams (Troop Carrier Command), and Colonel Philip Cochrane (CO, No 1 Air Commando).

At about 1630, only minutes before the first Dakotas were due to start engines for take-off, one of the Air Commando's light aircraft landed and taxied rapidly over to the group. The pilot ran across and handed Cochrane a batch of prints, still wet from processing, of the three intended landing areas as photographed by a Mitchell two hours earlier. These showed that whereas Broadway and Chowringhee were clear, Piccadilly had been quite deliberately blocked by teak logs laid in rows down its length. When last photographed on 1 March all three areas had been clear. Wingate, who was checking some final loading points in his nearby operations tent was called over, and immediately demanded to know who had been breaking his specific orders that nothing should be done to arouse Japanese interest in the area. Cochrane explained that the few essential reconnaissance flights had been combined with bombing raids on targets in the same general direction, and that the pictures provided the proof of their value. Had gliders tried to land at Piccadilly there would have been complete disaster.

However, the vital and immediate questions were: did the blocking of Piccadilly mean that news of the operation had leaked? Had the Japanese blocked one clearing with the object of enticing the whole force to the other, where it could be ambushed? Or was it simply coincidence that the enemy had chosen this moment to deny a potential landing strip to the Allies? Had the Japanese just seen the picture of Piccadilly published in *Life* and *Illustrated* magazines the previous summer after Vlasto's landing?

Take-off was delayed while these matters were debated, and it was unanimously decided that the operation should proceed, but with all the gliders landing on Broadway.

The first Dakota with its two Hadrian gliders was airborne at 1812 and take-offs continued for nearly two hours, during which altogether 26 Dakotas and 52 gliders got away. There was only one failure, when a lead glider dug its nose into the runway and snapped the tow-rope. One Dakota plus gliders returned early with engine trouble, and before long other aircraft came in with stories of broken tow ropes and lost gliders. Spirits rose again when the first pilots to have released gliders at Broadway reported that everything appeared to be going according to plan. The Dakotas then left with a second wave but this time they towed single gliders to minimise the risk of further losses. Finally, the RAF Dakotas got away with their loads to be parachuted.

Official accounts vary as to the timing of subsequent events. Some say that a signal 'send no more ships', was sent at about midnight, followed two hours later by a message decoded as 'ground interference' (it was later decided that in fact this meant 'ground unserviceable'). Then at 0400 Broadway is said to have requested light aircraft for casualty evacuation, and at times varying from 0900 and 1100, eventually reported that all was well. Some of the discrepancies are probably due to confusion between local time and GMT, and the most probable sequence is that the prearranged code signal 'Soya Link' — meaning suspend all flights — was received at 0227 and 'Pork sausage' — signifying that all was well — at about 0630.

The precise timings of the messages are unimportant. The simple fact remains that Wingate was left for several hours in a state of agonising suspense, wondering whether the gamble had failed and whether the troops had indeed landed straight into an ambush. Fighter squadrons were stood by to meet any calls.

For the benefit of younger readers a short digression may be useful to explain the significance of these odd codewords. During World War II well-meaning experts at home worked on schemes to save shipping space and money, and rationalise odd facets of the war effort. Their successes were doubtless applauded in high places but not by the victims — usually the troops overseas who were too far away to answer back. One reviled product was the V cigarette, made in India and hailed (by the 'experts') as equal in quality to standard commercial brands. Another abomination was the stodgy soya link imitation sausage — doubtless packed with protein but apparently flavoured with sawdust and difficult to swallow unless swilled down with great gulps of tea.

A real pork sausage suggested well being and contentment, compared with the gloom produced by the sight of soya links on the menu, and any resemblance between the two was purely coincidental, existing only in the minds of the link's inventors. In rations, as in welfare amenities which Air Vice-Marshal J. D. I. Hardman described as 'pathetic' in comparison with the American provision for her forces, the troops often considered themselves poorly served, though whether this adversely affected morale is debatable. Perhaps some clever psychologist realised that in peculiar British fashion, the troops overseas took a perverse pride in their plight — without going so far as to accuse their American comrades of being pampered.

'Soya Link' had been signalled with every justification from Broadway, where the troops and engineers were facing many problems —though fortunately not of enemy

origin. The initial trouble was the unsuspected presence of ruts caused by logging operations and not visible in reconnaissance photographs. Some of the first gliders had crashed in these, others had piled into the wreckage while still others had simply crashed for a variety of reasons. In some cases loads had shifted in flight to affect the centre of gravity, some gliders were found to have been incorrectly loaded while a few had even been overloaded by as much as one-third. As to the tow-rope breakages en route, these were put down to the limited experience of the double-tow technique.

Of the 52 gliders in the first wave, 34 landed on Broadway and two nearby. Of the nine in the second wave, eight returned to Lalaghat after the 'Soya Link' recall, and the one which failed to receive the instruction managed to overshoot and clear the shambles on the strip. Several gliders hit tall trees barely 100 yards from the northern and eastern edges of the strip, and 23 men were killed in crashes while about as many were badly injured. Of the 10 RAF Dakotas detailed to drop supplies the two from No 117 Squadron and two from No 194 did so successfully, but the six from No 31 which left Agartala between 2200 and 0040 did not receive a recall message, and finding Broadway unlit, returned with their loads.

Despite the loss of some heavy grading equipment the engineers on Broadway were able to report by 1620 that the strip was fit to receive Dakotas. That night a second strip, named Chowringhee after Calcutta's main street, was opened up by teams of engineers landed in another dozen gliders.

From this point the RAF provided slightly the larger part of the air transport effort, and of the 83 Dakotas detailed for the fly in of troops, 47 came from the squadrons of No 177 Wing. They operated initially from Hailekandi and Lalaghat in Assam, then from Tulihal on the Imphal plain, which was some 90 miles closer to Broadway and Chowringhee.

By late afternoon of 6 March there was much activity at Hailekandi, where George Donaldson supervised operations. The British units were nominated to carry most of the mules and ponies and No 117 Squadron's historian described the scene;

'As the first string of mules came walking down the runway our crews cast anxious looks at the aircraft, remembering the days when they had carried generals, film stars and other such delectable cargoes, and wondering mournfully what the condition of the cabins would be at the end of this party. Their anxiety was groundless, for most of the animals took to the air nonchalantly, though they were not above expressing their impatience during the period before take-off by smashing the bucket seats and kicking out the odd window'.

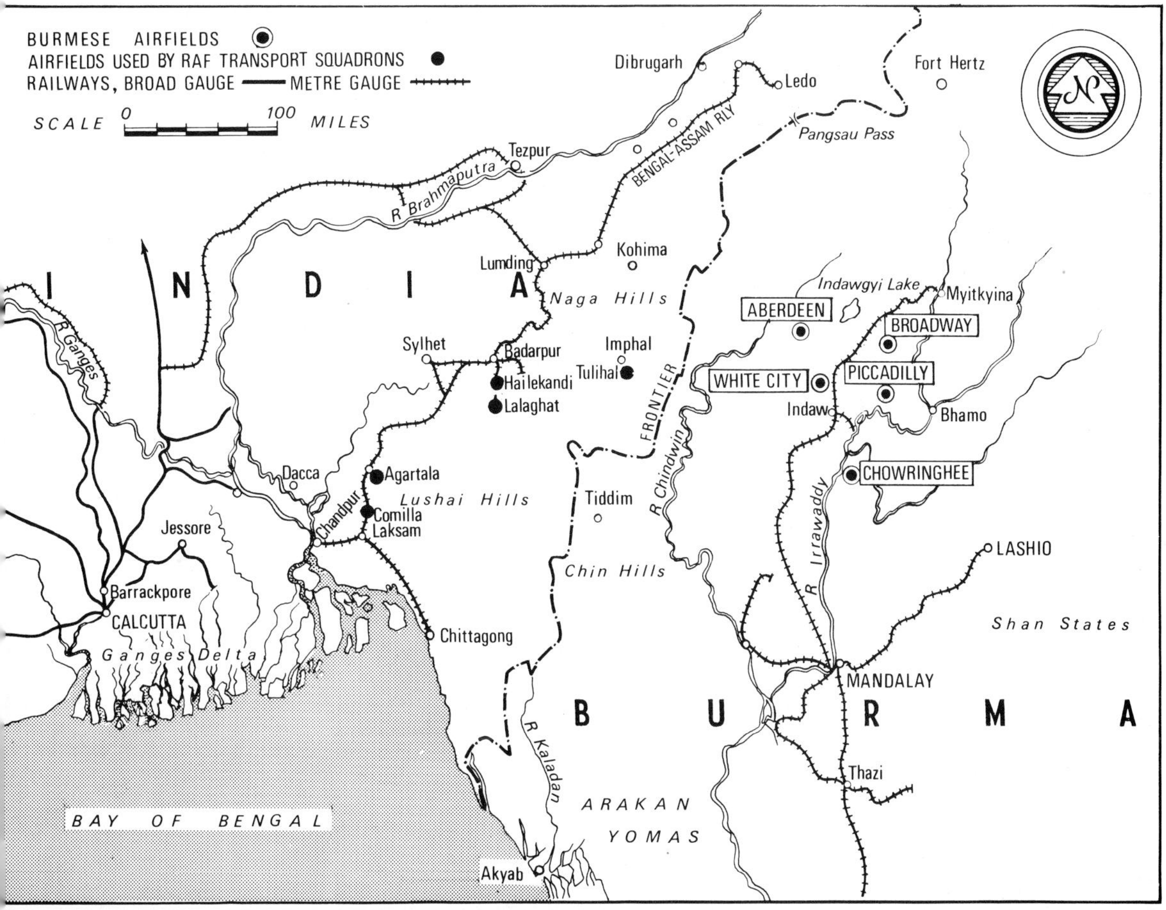

BURMESE AIRFIELDS ◉
AIRFIELDS USED BY RAF TRANSPORT SQUADRONS ●
RAILWAYS, BROAD GAUGE ━━ METRE GAUGE ┼┼┼┼

SCALE 0 ━━━━ 100 MILES

Dibrugarh
Ledo
Fort Hertz
Tezpur
BENGAL-ASSAM RLY
Pangsau Pass
R Brahmaputra
I N D I A
Lumding
Kohima
Indawgyi Lake
Myitkyina
Naga Hills
ABERDEEN
BROADWAY
Sylhet
Badarpur
Imphal
Tulihal
WHITE CITY
PICCADILLY
Hailekandi
Indaw
Bhamo
Lalaghat
FRONTIER
Dacca
Agartala
R Chindwin
CHOWRINGHEE
Chandpur
Lushai Hills
Tiddim
Comilla
Laksam
Jessore
Chin Hills
R Irrawaddy
LASHIO
Barrackpore
Shan States
CALCUTTA
R Ganges
Ganges Delta
Chittagong
MANDALAY
B U R M A
BAY OF BENGAL
R Kaladan
Thazi
ARAKAN
YOMAS
Akyab

Wingate, who was visiting the airfield, watched the unavailing efforts of 35 men to load one notoriously intractable mule, known as 'cushy Charlie', and personally walked it around, hoping to relax it sufficiently to climb the ramp into the Dakota. But Charlie even defeated 'the Beard', which was the irreverent name by which Wingate was known to some of the crews. He appealed to the RAF men for more practical help than their ribald, stage-whispered, suggestions and got the reply: 'You do the loading and we'll do the flying'. Typical of Wingate's concern for detail are these comments on this matter of mule loading from one of his reports:

'No mule is unloadable. The recipe is as follows: (a) double ramp — this prevents evasion (b) six men pulling with ropes fastened to mule's elbows — not head (c) two men behind with surcingle. Using this recipe a mule can even lie down. It will still go in! *NOTE* Do not attempt to load a mule until *several* men have got a grip on the rope. A loose mule may wreck a Dakota'

Of the 62 Dakotas which landed on Broadway during the night of 6/7 March, the RAF squadrons provided 38 — and each of the squadron commanders managed to contrive a trip. Fittingly, the first aircraft down was flown by the CO of Troop Carrier Command, General Old, but in the second — a No 194 Squadron aircraft flown by Donaldson — was Air Marshal Baldwin. Never asking his crews to do anything which he would not tackle himself, 'Jack' Baldwin as a bomber group commander had flown on the famous 1,000-bomber raid on Cologne on 30/31 May 1942.

Back at his headquarters he jotted down impressions of the scene for his subsequent despatch, and the AOC-in-C, Air Chief Marshal Sir Richard Peirse, included this passage in a signalled progress report to the Chief of the Air Staff on 11 March:

'Nobody has seen a transport operation until he has starred at Broadway in the light of the Burma full moon and watched Dakotas coming in and taking off in opposite directions on a single strip, all night long at the rate of one landing or one take-off every three minutes'.

Next night the RAF flew another 44 sorties from Hailekandi into Broadway while the USAAF concentrated on the first Dakota landings into Chowringhee. Preparations at this strip had been held up until a replacement bulldozer had been delivered, but the all clear was given at 2315. 18 RAF aircraft were en route when at 0200 on the 8th came a signal reporting that the strip was only 2,700ft long instead of the 4,000ft minimum laid down for night landings by loaded Dakotas. The aircraft were recalled, but seven of them apparently did not receive the instruction and put down without difficulty.

On D-day plus 3 (8 March) Tulihal was used for many RAF sorties to Chowringhee by Dakotas which had already made earlier trips from Hailekandi or Lalaghat into Broadway. Earl Fielden's arrangements at Tulihal were particularly impressive. The problems caused by thick clouds of dust raised by the aircraft were minimised by

starting take-offs from the centre of the long runway, with aircraft departing in opposite directions, while the bamboo pens each containing an exact Dakota load were prominently numbered to avoid confusion and delay in directing aircraft coming in for their second sorties. A thoughtful touch was a cheerful hot dog bar near the loading pens where crews could grab a snack while their aircraft were being loaded. Despite all the careful arrangements, a Dakota is said to have left one of the airfields carrying 10,000lb instead of the correct 6,000lb load. Apart from a sluggish take-off and climb the pilot apparently reported no special difficulties.

And so it went on for another two days. On 10 March Wingate decided that Broadway could cope with the remaining traffic and Chowringhee was therefore abandoned. This was an inspired decision, and only two hours after the last Allied troops had departed Japanese aircraft raided the strip. On the night of 10/11 a final effort during which the RAF flew 83 sorties into Broadway completed the first and main phase of Thursday.

For no obvious reason Chowringhee had never operated quite so smoothly as Broadway, where Baldwin described the arrangements as 'magnificent'. Pilots returning from Chowringhee reported aircraft cutting in while circling for landing, and confusion over the unloading areas. However these were minor complaints and to have achieved 100% perfection in such a remarkable operation of war would have demanded a miracle.

One comment applicable to both strips was that too many vehicles and pedestrians were allowed to cross the runways — and to this was added the inscrutable remark 'drivers were, however, very considerate to pilots, in particular with the use of headlights'.

In six days the RAF Dakotas had flown 331 sorties — 257 into Broadway and 74 to Chowringhee carrying 4,618 personnel, 820 animals and 234,421lb of supplies. The total Dakota (including glider tugs) sorties flown was 660 carrying 9,052 personnel, 1,359 animals and 509,083lb supplies.

The Japanese did not discover Broadway until 13 March by which time a Spitfire squadron was in residence to claim three destroyed and six damaged of the fighter-bomber force making a two-wave attack.

The fly in was completed by a small second phase on 22 March, when a Brigade was landed at another air strip named Aberdeen.

Wingate himself did not live to see the results of all his planning. At 2030 on 24 March, after a round of visits to the forward areas, he took off from Imphal in one of Cochrane's B-25 Mitchells. A few hours later the destination airfield, Sylhet, posted the aircraft overdue, then another pilot flying in the area reported having seen a brief explosion in the Naga Hills. Wreckage was found two days later, and any question as to its identity was immediately settled by the presence of Wingate's Wolseley helmet nearby. The weather was not noticeably bad at the time and no reason for the crash was established.

As the Chindit columns fanned out, other strips for short-term use were prepared as required — among them Blackpool, Clydeside and White City — but the troops were primarily dependent on parachuted supplies. Many orties extending beyond the range of fighter cover were flown by night, to dropping zones so lacking in features as to have made them unpractical propositions by European operating standards. But the Dakota pilots developed their own techniques, relying on the few recognisable landmarks, then flying carefully timed courses until over the estimated position of the ground party and exchanging recognition signals.

The apparent ease with which Vlasto had landed his Dakota to collect the group of casualties during the first Chindit operation had strikingly advertised the possibilities of casualty evacuation from what had been regarded as inaccessible forward areas. Versatile as the Dakota proved to be, it still could not operate from small, rough patches of the sort used by RAF biplanes in Iraq during the 1920s, and survival for the seriously wounded and sick in the jungle had been a slender prospect. The inclusion in Cochrane's Commando of the L1 Vigilant and L5 Sentinel light aircraft, capable of flying into such places, had transformed the situation, and between 5 March and 4 April they picked up 278 casualties. Cochrane also had three R4 helicopters which experienced serious maintenance difficulties during their teething period and the only sortie recorded in the Chindit period was to pick up the occupants of a force-landed L5. The helicopter maintenance situation gradullay improved, and by October some 40 operational hours had been flown.

Towards the end of the second Chindit campaign there arose a casevac requirement beyond the range of the light aircraft, in swampy country west of Hopin where it was impossible to improvise a Dakota strip. The columns were — to put it brutally — encumbered with several hundred non-effectives, not only wounded but cases of malaria, dysentery, typhoid and pneumonia. Their situation looked utterly bleak until somebody on a sudden inspiration suggested that perhaps the Indawgyi lake could be used by flying boats — even though the nearest were more than 1,250 miles away in Ceylon.

What followed has since become something of a legend, the tale of two Sunderlands — known to the troops as 'Gert and Daisy' after the popular entertainers — plying to and fro carrying the patients to safety and survival. The story doubtless became a little embroidered with the passage of time in the same way that the name 'whispering death' for the Beaufighter is nowadays often credited to Japanese troops, when in reality it was coined by RAF pilots and war correspondents over a mess bar. Although the facts of Operation River were slightly different, with 'Daisy' (alias 'Queenie') destined to play only a small part, they in no way detract from a remarkable achievement.

No 230 Squadron was nominated for the task and on 27 May Sunderland O-Orange (DP180), captained by Flight Lieutenant J. Rand and with one of the flight commanders, Squadron Leader J. L. Middleton, on board to supervise arrangements in India, left Koggala, Ceylon, for Calcutta. An operating base closer to the lake was clearly desirable and a reconnaissance showed that Dibrugarh on the Brahmaputra river, not far from the Himalayan foothills was suitable. This cut the distance to around 200 miles, but the flight through the Ledo Pass over the rugged Patkai mountains presented many hazards.

Japanese fighters were known to operate in the area and might make it necessary to escort the Sunderland.

O-Orange took off from Dibrugarh for its first sortie at 0545 on 1 June, and after struggling through solid cloud up to 20,000ft without breaking clear, was obliged to abandon the attempt. Next day the weather improved and the Sunderland left at 1250, reaching Indawgyi at 1420. The casualties were paddled out to the aircraft in rubber dingies and were airborne inside 40 minutes. Only 32 were carried because the pilot wanted his aircraft lightly loaded on this first, somewhat experimental trip, which involved a climb to 10,000ft shortly after take-off. On 3 June 36 patients were brought out and on the return flight two Japanese fighters were seen but did not attack. Next day O-Orange was provided with an escort of four Mustangs, and the casualty load went up to 39.

The busiest day of Operation River was 5 June, when two sorties were flown to lift out 81 casualties. The Mustang escort was provided for both trips and although eight enemy aircraft were seen the Sunderland used cloud and was apparently not spotted.

To avoid halting the lift while essential maintenance work was carried out another Sunderland had been ordered up from Koggala and Q-Queenie (captain, Flying Officer E. A. Garside) arrived on the 6th. Queenie took off for her first trip next morning at 0600, fought through very bad weather which had grounded the Mustangs, and flew a second sortie in the afternoon bringing her total day's lift to 79 casualties. During the next two days while Queenie was unserviceable O-Orange took over, again in weather too bad for the escort fighters.

Information from the front suggested that the remaining casualties could be cleared by one aircraft, and O-Orange accordingly left for base on the 10th. Queenie made an uneventful sortie that afternoon, which, thanks to several malevolent blows from fate, proved to be her last. On the 11th while taxying for take-off both starboard engines cut, and water was found in the carburettors and tanks. There was some comfort in the thought that this might have happened over the mountains. By sheer hard work the tedious job of defuelling and refuelling was completed by nightfall.

Then followed five days of impossible weather as the monsoon developed. Three times Garside took off and was forced to return. The trip to the lake normally took about two hours, but once he was airborne for nearly four, fighting to find a way through, until finally forced to return. On the 17th the weather improved, but a starter motor packed up and Queenie again became unserviceable. On the 20th, when all ready to go, she suffered another, more serious blow when the American DUKW used as a tender collided with her port wing float. Examination showed that the repair would be a long job and that new support struts were needed, so another Sunderland was requested and on 28 June O-Orange reported back for River duty.

The weather continued to do its worst, and on one occasion O-Orange alighted on the lake through 7/10ths cloud at 400ft. Flying was again impossible on several days, but the Sunderland managed three trips, and cleared the last of the casualties on 3 July — ironically in the best weather experienced since the start of the operations. But

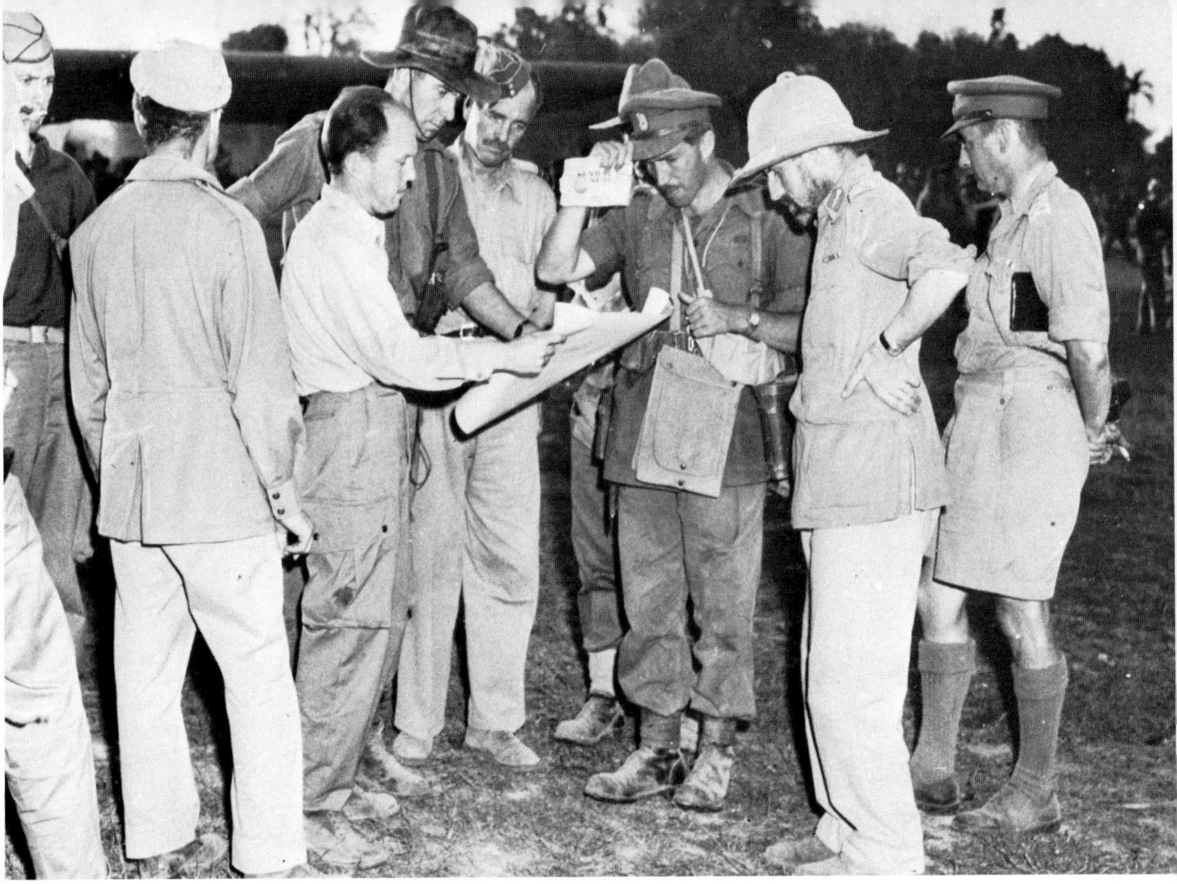

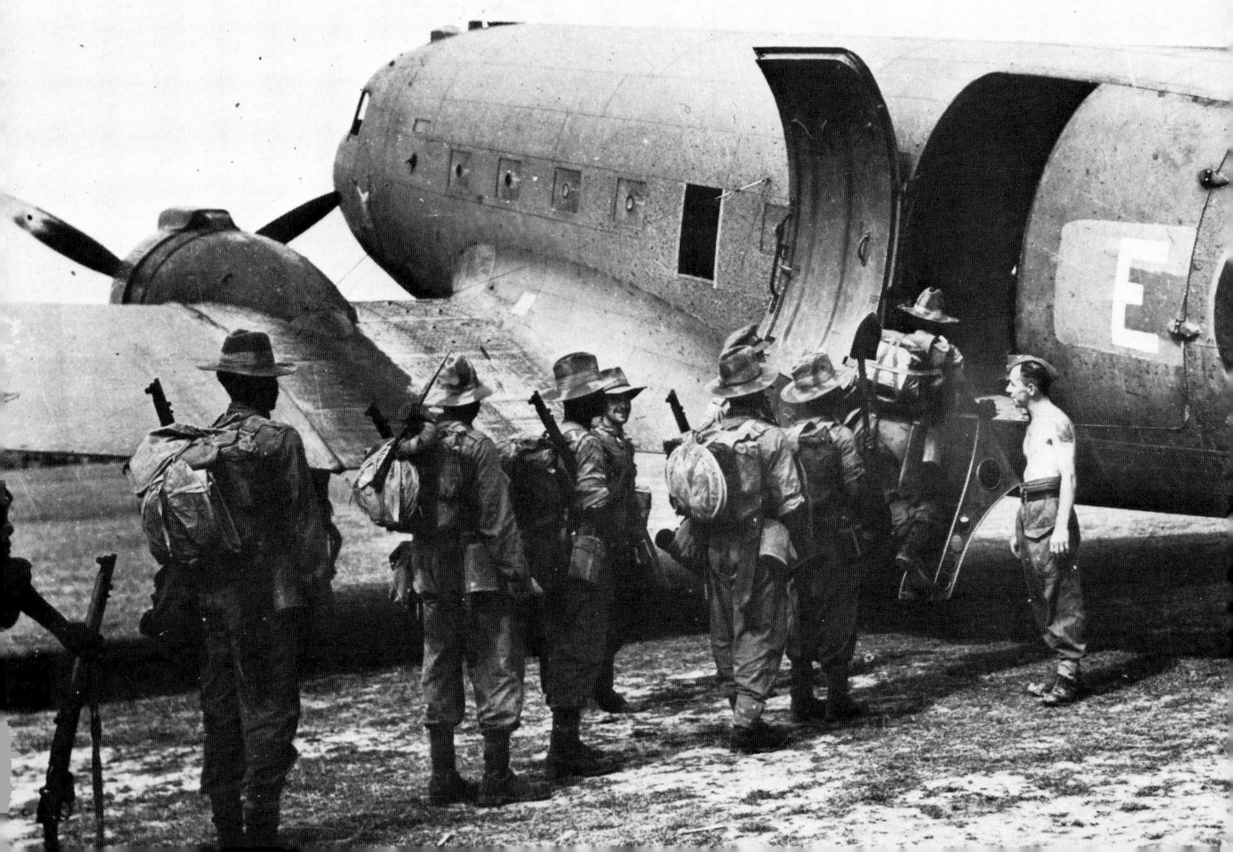
E

this was clearly one of fate's little ruses to establish a false sense of security before taking a final swipe at Queenie. O-Orange returned to Dibrugarh at 1640, and after a few anxious moments that evening when her mooring cable broke, departed next morning for Calcutta en route back to base.

At 1800 on 4 July a violent and completely unforecast wind sprang up and attacked Queenie's starboard side, causing her port wing to dig into the river at such an angle that water poured into the open port hatch from which a steadying drogue had been streamed. The angle steepened and water also flooded in through the front hatch. Clearly the flying boat was sinking, and in the shrieking gale the guard crew managed to launch a dinghy and abandoned ship. Then a wave promptly tipped them into the stormy waters of the Brahmaputra where they floundered until picked up by a native craft.

The loss of one Sunderland was a trifling item against the credit balance of Operation River. In 14 sorties — 11 of them by O-Orange — the Sunderlands had lifted out 509 casualties, plus one very disconsolate Japanese prisoner. They had carried in a few replacement troops, rations and other items, including a small outboard-powered assault boat. There had been no interference from the enemy — perhaps because of the prevalent bad weather — though No 230 Squadron did hear a rumour that 40 minutes after the final Sunderland take-off Japanese fighters had strafed the lake area and destroyed the rubber rafts used for ferrying. The Sunderland crews had flown their large, unwieldy craft over terrain and in weather never dreamed of by flying boat designers and although this had undoubtedly caused severe strain it provided a welcome change from long, tedious Indian Ocean patrols and was so very obviously a valuable job. The whole operation further strengthened that bond between the RAF and the Army which was growing from fragile beginnings into something strong and enduring.

Towards the end of the Operation Thursday deployment, Japan resumed the major offensive of which the Arakan assault in February had been an initial phase. It began on the night of 8/9 March with a crossing of the Chindwin River, and an attempt to cut off the 17th Indian Division at Tiddim while similarly dealing with Kohima in the north. Then the British stronghold on the Imphal plain was to be attacked on three sides, and its inevitable fall followed by a sweep on to Delhi.

To reinforce and supply Imphal would call for the most daunting air transport task which had yet arisen in any theatre of the war, and by another stroke of unbelievably good fortune, Thursday had progressed to the stage when some aircraft could be diverted to this vital requirement. A planned road move of the 5th Indian Division from the Arakan to Imphal was ruled out because the 260-mile journey over the mountains could have taken four weeks. Mountbatten therefore ordered that the troops should be flown, and his proposal to re-borrow aircraft from the 'Hump' route to help out was agreed by the United States Chiefs of Staff. This historic air lift — the first occasion on which a division had switched fronts in such a manner — began on 19 March with 15 RAF Dakotas of No 194 Squadron and 20 USAAF C-46s. Flying day and night, the aircraft completed the move in 758 sorties just 10 days later. To ease Imphal's supply problems the aircraft flew out of the area some 22,000 administrative and non-combatant personnel whose presence was not essential to the immediate battle situation.

No 194 Squadron was building up a great reputation and had acquired an unofficial name, 'The Friendly Firm'. This slogan was painted beneath a drawing of Dumbo, Disney's flying elephant, rejected by the College of Arms as an official squadron badge because it did not conform to correct heraldic rules. Rather than change trademarks the squadron abandoned the paper battle and continued to use this unofficial crest. The creature eventually selected for the squadron badge approved some years after the war could not have been in greater contrast. It was a dragonfly, commemorating the fact that the unit was then flying Dragonfly helicopters.

Apart from the effects of this unexpected air lift, Japanese problems were increased when the 17th Division broke out from Tiddim and fought its way back to the Imphal plain. However, with Imphal and Kohima besieged the situation was similar to that of the previous month in the Arakan, only on a much bigger scale, and beyond SEAC's air lift capacity to cope with. If, however, the Arakan victory could be repeated this might well prove a turning point in the Burma war, and the Chiefs of Staff sanctioned a temporary, one month reinforcement from the Mediterranean theatre by 64 Dakotas of a USAAF group and 15 of No 216 Squadron RAF. Their arrival in early April raised the Anglo-American transport strength to about 300 aircraft. American units were in the majority, and any attempt to describe the RAF effort separately is merely confusing.

Between 5 and 15 April, more troops were flown to Imphal from other parts of India, and with some smaller moves which came later, the total airborne reinforcements amounted to more than 20,000 men.

On the 17/18th an Inter-Service conference was held at 14th Army Headquarters, Comilla, to discuss the Imphal situation and make firm plans for Operation Stamina, which was to prove the largest and most prolonged maintenance of ground troops by air supply up to that time. The total daily requirement of the 155,000-strong Imphal garrison was estimated at 540 British (605 short) tons.

The supplies air lift began on the 18th and it soon became apparent that the target would be difficult to attain, largely because of the weather. Frequently the conditions at Imphal itself were excellent while weather over the mountains en route was impassable. In such cases supplies were landed at an intermediate staging post, and lifted the short remaining distance when conditions improved. Another disappointment was that even after 368 tons of bitumenised hessian material had been flown in to render the main Imphal runway suitable for all-weather operations the C-46s proved to heavy for this, or any of the other five airfields on the plain, and they were accordingly returned to the 'Hump' route starting on 26 April.

The thinning out process continued, and in April-May another 29,876 'useless mouths' were flown out, plus two hospitals and their staffs. Even so it became necessary to cut rations by 35%, and assign 30 Mitchell light bombers and a number of Wellingtons to fly in ammunition and bombs for the combat squadrons. To reduce strain on the transport pilots, who willingly flew grossly excessive hours and were becoming exhausted in the process, some Wellington pilots were given quick Dakota courses and attached to the transport squadrons.

The critical situation posed by the imminent return of the 69 Middle East Dakotas was resolved by the personal intervention of Churchill. These aircraft were due back by 8 May, and Churchill's signal delaying the move was received only four days before — followed on the 16th by a formal Chiefs of Staff agreement that the aircraft should remain until mid-June.

Although deliveries remained below target, it was appreciated that more aircraft would not automatically remedy the position as the numbers which could be handled by the airfields and ground organisations were limited. On

1 May Troop Carrier Command had been placed under the orders of Baldwin, and the process of rationalising and improving the organisation continued. To speed up ground handling some of the despatching airfields were designated to handle single and specific commodities, and flights were more carefully planned to achieve maximum aircraft utilisation. Even so the weather still precluded operating to a precise timetable, and it was not until June that a welcome break in the monsoon allowed deliveries to approach the 400 tons a day figure.

Gradually, as in the Arakan, the besiegers became the besieged. Kohima was relieved, then on 22 June the road link to Imphal was reopened. By this time the air lift was delivering more than 500 tons a day and continued until the end of the month.

Operation Stamina was possible thanks to continued Allied air superiority, best indicated by the fact that only two Dakotas — shot down on the way to Imphal on

Below: Walking wounded from the second Chindit campaign arrive at Dibrugarh on the Brahmaputra, having flown from Japanese occupied territory in Sunderland O-Orange of No 230 Squadron. / IWM

Right: Wing Commander W. H. 'Bill' Burbury, CO of No 31 Squadron, receives the American DFC from Brigadier General William D. Old, July 1944. / IWM

Bottom right: Sunderland at Dibrugarh on the Brahmaputra. / IWM

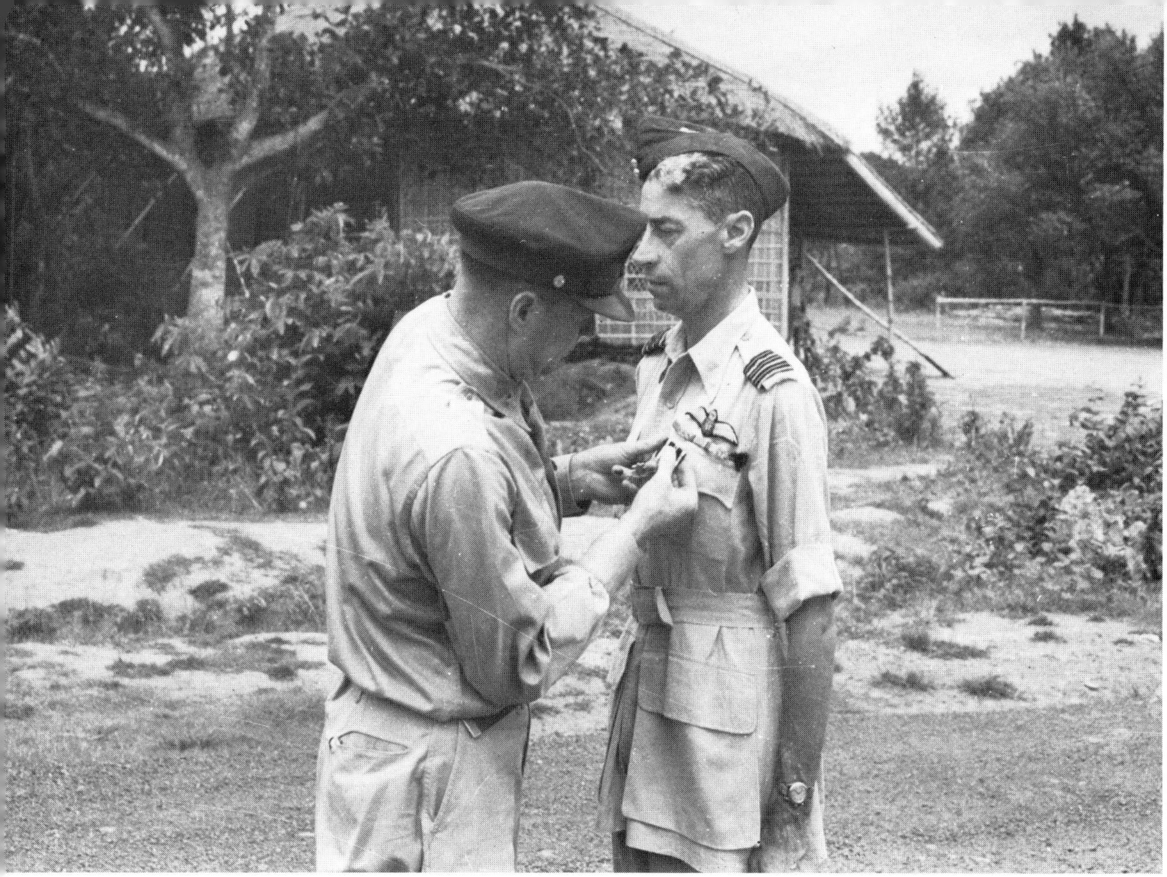

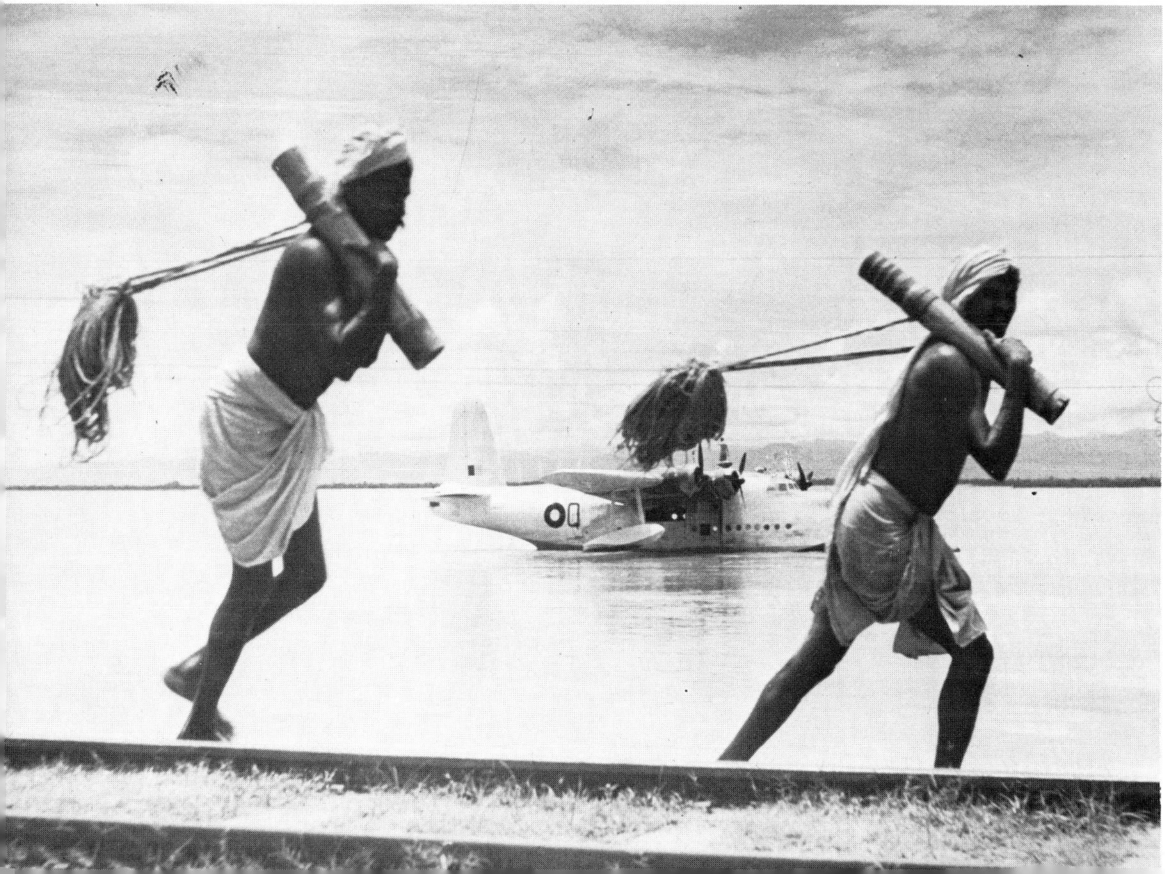

25 April — and one Wellington were lost through enemy air action. For most of the time the Imphal-based fighter squadrons maintained patrols over the corridors into the valley, giving immunity to the unarmed transports.

From 18 April to 30 June, 23,500 British tons of supplies were delivered to Imphal and nearly 52,000 non-combatants flown out by the Anglo-American transport force. In addition some 10,000 casualties were lifted out by the RAF alone.

This spell of operations produced one of the most incredible flying incidents of the entire war. Many pilots experienced remarkable escapes from what seemed certain death, and others defeated prohibitive weather only by some inexplicable and benevolent intervention of providence. But few indeed can have encountered both types of incident in a single flight in the manner experienced by Warrant Officer Deryck Groocock (Group Captain, retired) of No 194 Squadron on 26 May 1944.

That morning a dozen Dakotas left Agartala at intervals, hoping to drop supplies to an army column north of Kohima. The weather forecast was bad, with 10/10th cloud cover, and for a less urgent requirement no drop would have been attempted. As Groocock's Dakota neared the dropping area, flying at 9,000 feet, just above the clouds which completely hid the tops of rugged hills only 1,500 feet below, there was no gap as far as the eye could see. Any idea of letting down to find the DZ would be suicidal. Nevertheless the two wireless operators, Warrant Officers Harvey Bell and 'Chuck' Atherton, moved aft to prepare the sacks of rice and other food for a free drop in case some miracle should intervene.

Up front there were no miraculous portents, nor any sign of a break. Suddenly, without warning, the airspeed fell off and the Dakota's nose went up. Groocock instinctively applied more power, which failed to improve the situation. Despite the closeness of the hill-tops below, he must somehow force the nose down if he was to avoid the inevitable stall, but heave as he might, the control column refused to move forward. With its engines screaming in protest against this grotesque, tail-down attitude the Dakota staggered on for a few more seconds hanging on its propellers, then flicked over to port and flopped into a spin.

In those few seconds Groocock had guessed, correctly, that the Dakota's lethal behaviour must be due to a sudden shifting of the load in the cabin, though this was of merely academic satisfaction since there was nothing he could do about it. The two wireless operators were never quite sure exactly what had started the backward slide. Certainly in those days cargo was not stowed with the same care and concern for weight and distribution as it is today, and it may be that a sudden bump hit the aircraft just as the first sacks were being moved towards the door. At all events the two men had scarcely time to register their dismay before the spin began, and in the shambles of whirling rice sacks which followed their main concern was to clip on parachutes.

For a brief fraction of time after the Dakota plunged into cloud Groocock sat sweating and almost paralysed, able to see nothing through the grey murk outside, watching the altimeter rapidly reeling off the progress of their descent and waiting for inevitable oblivion. Then his natural piloting instincts returned and he applied normal spin recovery procedure — control column forward and opposite rudder. After a few more agonising seconds — Groocock noticed that the altimeter was now registering 4,700 feet — the aircraft straightened out just as it broke cloud. During the spin the cargo had been flung forward again, restoring the centre of gravity to tolerable limits.

Flying straight and level once more, the considerably shaken crew stared out of the windows, speechless at the miracle of their escape. They were gently proceeding up a green valley, having spun down precisely between the two great ranges of hills whose tops disappeared into the clouds. But this was not all. While they were still pondering how best to escape from this mist-enshrouded tunnel they saw a column of smoke begin to rise straight ahead, and as they approached could identify it as a signal from a British army party. By this time they were immune from further surprise, and it seemed inevitable that in this dramatic fashion they should have stumbled upon the very dropping zone they had set out to find. Never had a RAF Dakota crew disposed of its cargo with such relief and enthusiasm.

Since this was clearly a day when he could do no wrong Groocock approached the next problem in his stride. Having established that there was no way out of the valley beneath the cloud he turned back to its widest point, made for what he judged to be the centre and put the now lightly loaded Dakota into the tightest and steepest spiral climb which he could safely achieve and prayed that he could hold it accurately without any drift to either side. After several anxious minutes with his eyes glued to the instruments the gloom outside gradually lightened, then suddenly the Dakota poked its nose up into the clear again.

Not surprisingly Groocock was the only pilot to make a drop in the area that day. Although the unconventional arrival of his aircraft in a steep dive through the clouds was just out of sight of the column, the army commander judged it to be an effort deserving a special congratulatory signal. Groocock keeps a copy in his flying log book mentally captioned 'Little did he know . . .'

No 194 Squadron seemed to attract bizarre flying incidents and on 4 July the victim was Flying Officer W. 'Bill' Harris, who was also making a drop near Kohima. All was going well until one of the parachutes deployed prematurely and blew backwards so that the canopy streamed above the tailplane and the supply pack trailed below, thus very effectively jamming the elevators. The aircraft immediately dived earthwards and its headlong plunge was only arrested by the combined strength of the pilot and navigator both pulling the control column backwards with all their strength. But instead of levelling off gradually the aircraft hurtled up into a crazy near vertical climb as the elevators jammed in the opposite direction. This alarming big-dipper process was repeated several times until finally, as the aircraft reached an upward peak, Harris contrived a sharp stall-turn to port which allowed the pack and parachute to slide off the tailplane.

a cabbage field beside the river Kisielina, just outside the
ny Carpathian hamlet of Wal Ruda in southern Poland, is
simple stone commemorative slab. It was put there by
eople of the district who remember the days of German
ccupation. It is a special reminder, not of tragedy and
uffering but of a triumphant achievement by the Polish
nderground movement which was brought to a successful
onclusion by one of the outstanding flights in RAF
story. More precisely it marks the spot a few miles west
f Zabno, where, undisturbed by surrounding enemy
rces, a Dakota of No 267 Squadron sat helplessly bogged
r one hour and five minutes on the night of 25/26 July
944.

Londoners, too, should have an interest in the memorial,
ecause that Dakota operation provided important parts of
e intelligence jigsaw which pieced together the overall
cture of the detestable V2 rocket, soon to be unleashed.

By 1944 pick-up operations from occupied Western
urope, notably France, by aircraft of the UK-based
pecial Duties squadrons had become a fairly regular
ccurrence. The hazards remained high, but the distances
 be flown by the unarmed aircraft were relatively short.

At the end of February 1944 a requirement arose for
omething more ambitious — to collect important people
nd papers from Poland — and No 267 Squadron, now
ying Dakotas from Bari, Italy, was suitably based for the
isk. Since every experienced crew volunteered for the job
 was decided to hold a ballot, and the captain drawn was
light Lieutenant Edward Joseph Harrod (27), from
llerton, Liverpool, who had joined the RAF as an
pprentice, aged 16. The other crew members were Pilot
fficers A. J. Wells (navigator) and N. Wilcock (wireless
perator), and a Polish co-pilot to be provided from
o 1586 Special Duties Flight.

Entailing a round trip of more than 1,600 miles the
peration demanded immaculate planning, and good
eather. Even its codename of Wildhorn held a faintly
inister air, evoking some dark tangle with the unknown.
or week after week the crew stood by with Dakota I-India
D919) specially fitted with eight overload plastic petrol
nks in the fuselage providing an endurance of 14 hours.
o reduce weight all non-essential gear was discarded, but
e engines were fitted with exhaust flame dampers. The
riginal pick up location a few miles from Warsaw was
ter changed to a sugar beet field near a village between
Varsaw and Lublin.

At last the weather became suitable and a message was
received declaring the landing site fit, and on 15 April
Harrod and his crew flew down to Brindisi to collect the co-
pilot, Flight Lieutenant Korporski, and two passengers who
were to be landed in Poland. They took off from Brindisi at
1932 and started the long drag northwards, across the
Adriatic, over Yugoslavia and Hungary, above the
Carpathians then finally into Poland itself and began the let
down towards their target area. To find one beet field in
enemy occupied territory in poor visibility at night, after an
800-mile flight, was no mean task, but Wells had performed
a brilliant piece of navigation. Precisely five hours after
leaving Brindisi the ground reception party acknowledged
the Dakota's identification signals, and at 0040 the aircraft
landed.

This had its excitement as the rudimentary flare path had
been wrongly laid out, and Harrod realised when already
committed that he was landing down wind. However, the
surface was so soft, with patches of unmelted snow, that
the Dakota stopped well within the 800-yard field. While
taxiing back to the reception committee — assembled at
the wrong end — bursts of full power were needed to stop
the wheels from sinking into the mud. Despite these minor
hitches the aircraft was airborne again 15 minutes after
touchdown, with five passengers, including a senior
representative of the Polish Home Army, and several
hundredweights of documents for intelligence purposes.

The take-off, too, was hazardous, the aircraft ploughing
its way over the muddy surface, accelerating slowly, then
swinging violently. Harrod finally goaded it into the air in a
semi-stalled condition, narrowly missing a belt of trees at
the end of the field. Pulse rates gradually slowed to normal,
and after an uneventful return flight, I-India reached Bari at
0545 on 16 April. At the special request of the Poles, the
same crew flew them to England on the 19th in Dakota
KG475.

No 267 Squadron records make only the barest
reference to Wildhorn II on 29 May, when a Dakota
captained by Flight Lieutenant Mike O'Donovan flew two
passengers into Poland and three others out. Again, the
main problem was the size and condition of the landing
strip, which in this case was covered with grass about a
foot high.

Best known of the Wildhorn flights was the third,
because of the drama surrounding the Dakota's narrow
escape from capture on the ground while in process of
picking up valuable technical data about the German
V-weapons, including fragments and components. After the

Above: A Dakota of No 267 Squadron — the unit which made the *Wildhorn* flights into Poland — photographed on a supply mission to the Balkans. / *IWM*

Left: Dakotas of No 267 Squadron at Bari, Italy. / *IWM*

Right: Flight Lieutenant S. G. Gulliford with an officer of the Yugoslav partisan forces. / *S. G. Culliford*

devastating RAF raid on Peenemunde in August 1943, German V-1 and V-2 testing was transferred to Blizna, in Poland, some 170 miles west of Warsaw, and Polish agents often managed to reach fallen missiles or their remains before the German search parties. One entire unexploded V-1 which landed near Sarnaki was hidden beneath the waters of the River Bug and later dismantled.

The material brought out on Wildhorn III related primarily to the still experimental V-2, and the specialist responsible for its compilation had cycled 200 miles through Poland with his precious load. Particularly valuable were his reports that many V-2s were bursting so high in the air as to clearly indicate technical troubles rather than a proximity fuse, as British scientists had previously thought. It is now almost forgotten that at the time the Poles attached equal importance to whom the aircraft brought out, for the passengers included Tomasz Arciszewski, a senior politician who was to become Prime Minister of the exile Polish government in London. Several important people and a dozen suitcase radio sets were also flown in. This operation had the additional squadron code name of Saucepan, and to the Poles was *Most* (bridge).

Dakota KG477 took off from Brindisi at 1939 on 25 July crewed by Flight Lieutenant Stanley George Culliford (captain), Flying Officer K. Szajer (Polish co-pilot), Flying Officer J. P. Williams (navigator) and Flight Sergeant J. Appleby (wireless operator). Culliford, aged 24, from Dunedin, New Zealand, had joined the RNZAF straight from university after completing his BA.

Since the unarmed Dakota would be flying in daylight over Yugoslavia, two Polish-crewed Liberators from No 1586 Flight engaged on a mission elsewhere were to accompany it as an armed escort against fighter attack, but in the event only one got airborne and then had difficulty in matching the Dakota's climb.

'We flew in what we used to describe as "visual formation",' recalled Culliford many years afterwards. 'If you could see the other aircraft you were flying in formation with it'.

Darkness fell when the aircraft were near Sarajevo, and the Liberator turned off on its own business leaving the Dakota to drone away on the lonely journey into Poland. Apart from a little inaccurate anti-aircraft fire over Hungary there was no opposition, and the landing area was reached at half-past midnight. After exchanging recognition signals, the ground party exposed green and red lights to show the best approach and the far limit of the field, while dozens of helpers marked the perimeter with hurricane lamps and torches. Despite Culliford's anxiety to make the stealthiest possible approach he was obliged to overshoot on the first landing attempt.

The enthusiastic welcome of the resistance workers masked the very acute anxieties they were suffering. Sited beside a wood, the landing field — which the Poles codenamed *Motyl* (butterfly) — had been used intermittently by the Luftwaffe earlier in the war but had seen no activity for many months. That very afternoon, however, two Fieseler Storch communications aircraft had landed and their crews spent some time with an anti aircraft battery in transit from the Russian front. This

battery had chosen to billet for the night less than a mile away and overlooking the field in a two-storey school building which was also the headquarters of a Luftwaffe police group. In all there were perhaps up to 400 German servicemen in the neighbourhood. The two Fieselers departed shortly before dark — fortunately for them, as the Poles had plans for their violent disposal should they have stayed.

In addition to all this, heavy rains had made the surface softer than was desirable. But a coded message via the BBC Polish service had indicated that the flight was on, and there was no practical way of calling it off. In any case the Dakota would be on the ground for only five minutes, and the Poles felt well able to look after themselves.

The heavy gear — some 970lb — was transferred from farm carts, passengers and baggage were loaded aboard and everything was ready for departure within the prescribed time. Culliford has some trouble in releasing the parking brake, then opened the throttles for take-off, but even after applying 50in boost, which caused the tail to leave the ground, the aircraft made no forward progress. Inspection by the second pilot showed that the wheels had sunk slightly though not enough to impede progress, suggesting some mechanical fault which had locked the brakes on. In view of the proximity of the Germans, desperate measures were called for, so the pipes supplying hydraulic fluid to the brakes were severed with a knife. To everyone's dismay another attempt at full boost still failed to budge the aircraft.

Engines were stopped and the passengers unloaded while the crew prepared to destroy the aircraft in case they were forced to remain behind with the resistance workers. The enterprising Szajer produced a spade to clear the wheels, now well and truly embedded in the soft earth. After a short time the passengers again climbed aboard and once more, roaring like an ensnared tiger fighting to break free, the Dakota heaved and shuddered, then slewed slightly to starboard before jerking to an abrupt halt.

This surely was the end of the road. Culliford stopped the engines and the passengers trooped out, nobody saying a word. Papers were torn up and placed where they would be destroyed when the aircraft was fired and parachutes were pulled so that at least a few Polish women might gain a small bonus from the fiasco. If the Poles felt despondent that their efforts had come to naught, so too did the crew for they fully understood the grave risks taken by their allies, and were determined not to fail them.

Culliford walked a few paces away, took several hasty drags from a cigarette, then had another look at the under carriage. The port wheel had turned precisely one quarter of a revolution before sinking back into the mud. There were still no signs that any Germans were taking the slightest interest in the aircraft's presence, and with plenty of Polish manpower on hand it surely must be possible to dig it out. Szajer demanded more spades — which were hastily grabbed from the nearest cottages — while those without implements set to with bare hands, then two men staggered up with two substantial planks to form a ramp in front of the wheels. Culliford was a little anxious lest these should flip up and hit the propellers, but if they were laid arefully the risk was small. After 30 minutes of hard work verything was ready for the fourth attempt to shift the eluctant Dakota.

The rest of the story can be told in the words of Culliford's report:

This time the machine came free and we taxied rapidly in a rakeless circle, and found that the people holding the orches for the flarepath had all gone home ... [In fact they had been ordered to their designated defence stations when t seemed inevitable that the Dakota must be captured.]

'We came round again with the port landing light on and headed roughly north-west towards a green light on the orner of the airfield. After swinging violently towards a tone wall, I closed my starboard throttle, came round in nother circle and set off again in a north-westerly direction. This time we ploughed along over the soft ground and waffled into the air at 65mph just over the ditch at the ar end of the field.

'Airborne, we found that we could not raise our undercarriage, having lost all our hydraulic fluid, and, inding our speed thus materially reduced, we poured water rom the emergency rations into the hydraulic reservoir until we could pump up the undercarriage by hand.

'Since we were now fairly late, having spent one hour and five minutes on the ground, we set course direct for Lagosta Island from the Carpathians. This took us through an area near the Danube known to be infested with night ighters, but we had to get out of Yugoslavia by daylight. We encountered no opposition and came out over Lagosta, hough "George" was unserviceable due to lack of fluid and we had to fly by hand.

'Arriving at Brindisi just as the sun was rising, we were — after some deliberation — allowed to land on a runway under construction that was into wind, in view of our brakeless condition.

'Apart from the slight excitement at the field, everything went very smoothly.'

Next day Culliford left for England with the Polish party and the V-weapon material. They flew via Rabat, near Casablanca, where the politicians were dropped off to meet Winston Churchill who was passing through. During the journey the Pole in charge of the two sacks of V-2 specimens refused to let them out of his sight, and on arrival at Hendon on 27 July firmly sat on them until contact was made with a named senior member of the Polish forces in Britain.

There is no single and obvious explanation of the puzzling lack of reaction from the Nazi forces in the area. Clearly they must have known something was afoot from the moment that Culliford's Dakota skimmed at full throttle over the school building on the initial overshoot, its landing lights blazing into the windows. This sudden flood of illumination also picked out the 30-odd Poles, armed with Sten guns and pistols, detailed to surround the building. The few German heads poked out of windows withdrew at the unmistakeable sound of Sten guns being cocked.

The troops closest to the scene were not trained for the sort of combat to be expected from the Polish resistance, and with no central leadership it would not be surprising if they chose to believe that whatever was going on outside was none of their business. The inevitable 'inquest' which must have followed, with excuses, cover ups and buck-passing, while the flak battery sped smartly on its way, can be left to the imagination. A German party later inspected the Dakota's wheel marks, and engineers blew holes in the field, but there were no reprisals against the Poles.

# No Ordinary Quack

Few present day air forces are without their parachute medical teams of doctors and nurses trained to drop to the aid of casualties in difficult situations where they cannot be reached quickly by other means.

But it was not always so. In World War II the RAF performed remarkable feats of casualty evacuation with light aircraft picking up patients under enemy fire in forward areas. To cater for casualties beyond the reach of the short range, with almost 'go anywhere' air ambulances was clearly not practical. Even so, RAF medical officers faced with the apparently impossible were always reluctant to accept defeat.

Such a challenge was faced by No 357 Squadron early in 1944. This unit was one of Air Command South East Asia's 'cloak and dagger' or Special Duties squadrons, engaged on supply drops for guerilla forces and infiltrators, dropping agents and so on. It flew a variety of aircraft — Liberators, Hudsons, Dakotas — and in the last four months of the fight against Japan gave a new lease of life to the Westland Lysander, which was obsolescent when the war started. No 357's 'Lizzie' flight made 213 sorties — casevacs, supply drops, pick-ups etc— from May to August 1945.

At 2330 on 14 March 1944 Hudson A-Able (AM949) took off from Dum Dum, Calcutta, to drop supplies for guerillas near the Sino-Burmese border, north east of Lashio — Operation Buffin. Three of the crew were Canadians, the captain, Flying Officer R. B. Palmer, navigator, Flying Officer W. Prosser and the wireless operator/air gunner, Flight Lieutenant L. Patterson. The others were Flight Lieutenant J. C. S. Ponsford (co-pilot), Warrant Officer B. A. Ogilvie (2nd wireless operator) and Flight Sergeant J. Wilkinson (despatcher).

The Hudson failed to return and next day the squadron learned that it had crashed in the mountains near the dropping zone at about 0300, killing four of the crew. The other two were seriously injured, needing urgent medical attention, and HQ suggested the possibility of parachuting a medical officer. To do this was easier said than done because the only medical officer with any parachuting experience was on 48 hours' stand down and could not be contacted. Furthermore, the crash was in enemy controlled territory and the paradrop might prove to be a one-way trip, with a Japanese POW camp as the least unpleasant of several possible destinations.

That afternoon No 357's own MO, Flight Lieutenant George Desmond Graham, returned from a visit to another airfield. He had been with the squadron for only a few days and no one knew him very well. Certainly, none knew that by some strange freak of the postings system they had been sent perhaps the one medical officer in the entire Service best equipped for the job, and that his MBE ribbon denoted not long dedication to cumulative good work in some clinical backwater, but recognised the fact that in 1942-43 he had virtually invented the RAF Mountain Rescue Service.

In April 1942 as the RAF Llandwrog Station MO, starting with a small group of medical orderlies from his sick quarters, Graham had gradually developed a unit specially equipped for reaching crashes in the Welsh mountains which became the model for the full organisation formed two years later. True, he had never made a parachute jump, let alone one into rugged, hostile country, and had done very little flying, but he immediately volunteered for the task.

The flight was planned for the next night to give Graham time to receive at least a little basic instruction, and he was handed over to the Senior Parachute Jumping Instructor, Flight Sergeant Thomas E. White, detached from the Air Landing School at Chaklala. The two immediately established a rapport, and 'Chalky' White insisted on making the drop as well, to help with the various duties to be performed at the accident site.

On the afternoon of 16 March, Hudson F-Freddie, captained by Flight Lieutenant James A. King, was positioned at Chittagong and at 0315 next morning took off for the rescue drop. The jump had to be made in daylight, which meant that the unescorted Hudson would be exposed to enemy fighter attack on the return journey.

A suitable zone had been selected through intelligence channels and at 0545, just as dawn was breaking, the crew spotted the prearranged ground signals. After one circuit the first pack of medical supplies was dropped, then Graham jumped, followed by White and a second medical

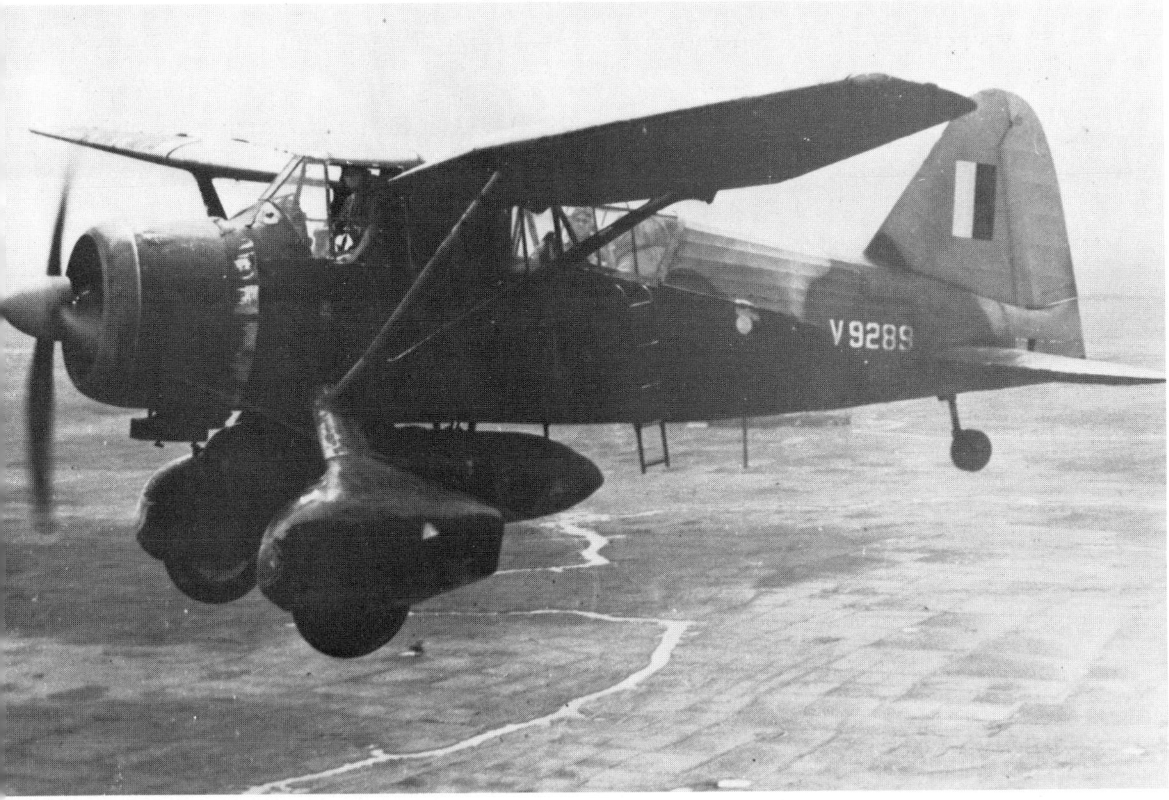
V9289

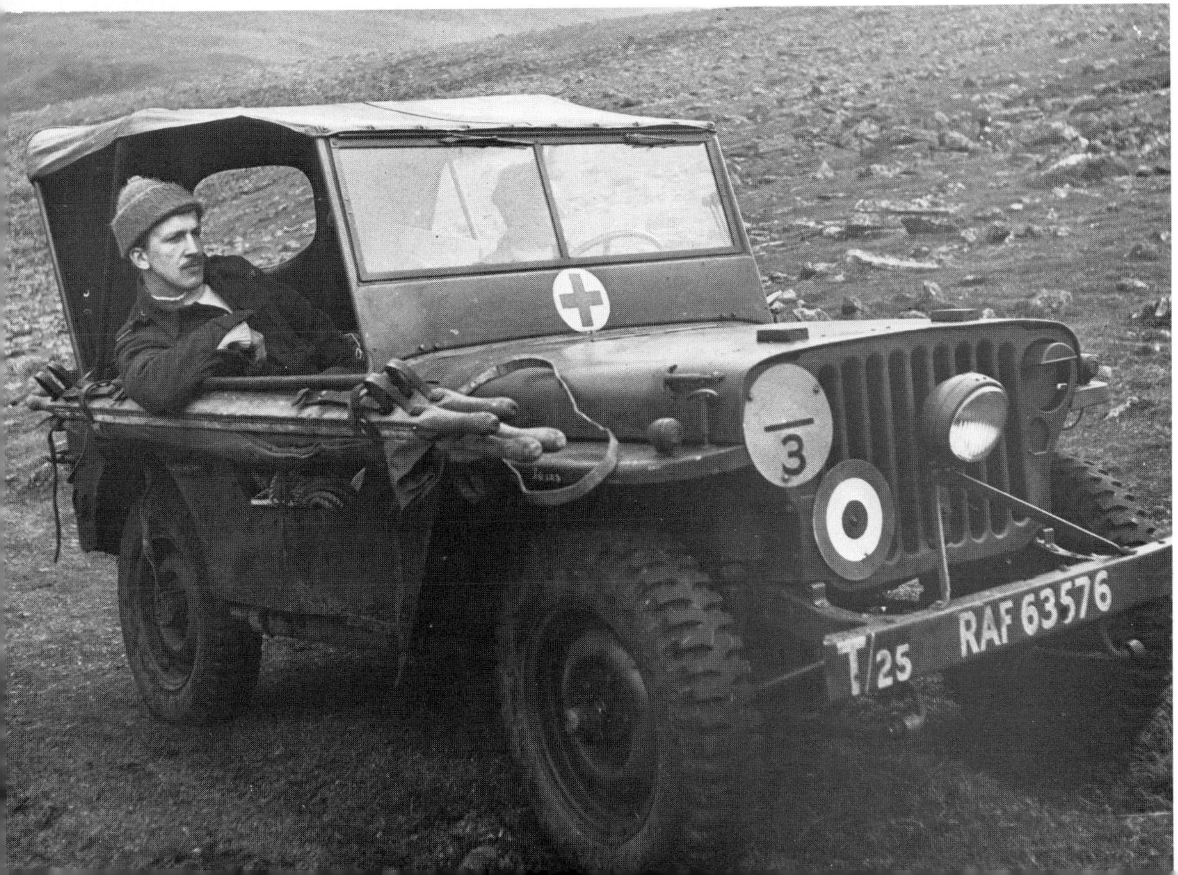
3
T 25
RAF 63576

pack. With disarming modesty Graham's report merely said that 'all landed successfully due to the skill and instructions of Flight Lieutenant King and Flight Sergeant White.'

The RAF pair were met by a party of blue-uniformed Kokang guerillas under Colonel Yang Wan San, who had arranged mules and an escort. The crash was reached after an hour's journey northwards near the village of Nam Po Ko, and already on the scene were two American officers — Major Leitch and Lieutenant Parsons. One of the survivors, Flight Lieutenant Ponsford, had died of his injuries before their arrival on the 15th, and the other Flying Officer Prosser, had been moved to a nearby mountain hut. He had a fractured skull, multiple fractures of the right ankle and lacerations of the face, and despite competent first aid rendered by the Americans, had developed some fever from the infection of his wounds. Clearly, he would be in no state to travel for some days.

The Hudson had hit a 4,600ft ridge below the main 6,000ft crest at one end of the Nam Po Ko valley, and native eyewitnesses said that it was on fire, with its engines banging before the crash. Although this is almost the standard description of any air crash, it may well have been accurate, because in his delirium Prosser was heard to mutter that 'the starboard engine was burning away all the time'.

Prosser's condition improved after treatment, then on the 20th he had a relapse. That evening Captain Hockman, an American medical officer, arrived after a five day mule journey in response to a signal sent by Leitch on the 15th. The patient hovered precariously between life and death, and a week passed before he began to show positive signs of improvement — for which Graham gave generous acknowledgement to Hockman's assistance.

On 28 March guerillas reported a Japanese force of some 200 men only four hours' march away, but despite Leitch urging immediate departure, the two doctors considered that their patient should not be exposed to a gruelling journey until there was more positive news of enemy intentions. Two days later the force was said to have grown to 400, and on the following day came a report of more Japanese only 30 miles to the north. Leitch was now insistent that they must move and began to organise mules, coolies and an escort for their journey east.

They set off at 1400 on 1 April, with the coolies carrying Prosser on a litter. The tracks were so bad that even the baggage mules stumbled and fell, and after three hours the party arrived soaking wet and plastered with mud at Pahntang. Next day, in better weather they managed an eight hour march which took them into China, to spend the night at Ma Ung Sang, and on the 3rd travelled for nine hours on mule-back, crossing two steep windswept passes to reach Meng Peng.

A four hour march on 4 April brought them to their first main objective, a Chinese army post at Er Tai Pu. This was where they had planned to change coolies, but it soon became evident that none were available. Furthermore, the Kokang party which had accompanied them so far was most anxious to get away, fearing that if they proceeded any further they would be conscripted into the Chinese Army. However, the promise of extra pay persuaded them

to go as far as Meng Bawn, which was reached after another five hours. They were paid off the following morning — vanishing with great rapidity — and with coolies and mules hired for the next leg only, the party pressed on to an American post in the Tetang Valley. Graham decided to celebrate this landmark with a rest day, made the more memorable because after three weeks as a very sick officer, Prosser became rational — though he could remember nothing of the crash or the journey up to that time.

On 7 April they resumed their travels in good spirits with yet another team of mules and bearers engaged by the Americans, knowing that the motor road and civilisation lay only a few days ahead — though as things turned out their difficulties were by no means over. They spent the night at Cheng Kaung Ba, and when they awoke next morning the camp was strangely quiet, with no chatter from the coolies. They quickly discovered the reason.

Trustingly, the Americans at Tetang had paid them in advance, and the coolies, hardly able to believe their luck, had decamped during the night. After four hours searching and haggling, sufficient coolies to carry only the litter could be recruited in the village, so Graham pressed on while White made a diversion to seek reinforcements. By early afternoon Graham's bearers complained that they could go no further without a long rest and started a sit-down strike. This was more than just an annoyance because Prosser was showing symptoms of heat exhaustion. Graham suddenly remembered that he had some benzedrine tablets in the medical pack, and by sign language extolled their magical powers. He fed the coolies one tablet each whereupon they seized the litter and soon reached a nearby river where the patient was cooled off. After a break they continued the journey to Ypankai, and in the small hours White came in with his party.

The next two days produced some of the hardest going since they had set out. With a party of 10 Chinese soldiers and fresh mules they laboured over a 7,000ft mountain pass, swept with icy winds, and when some distance down the other side realised that they had taken a wrong turning. Although the importance of following the correct track had been emphasised at the morning briefing, the soldiers muttered mutinously among themselves and made it quite clear that they had no desire to carry the litter back up the mountainside. However, a few western-movie-type gestures by Graham with his revolver persuaded them to change their minds.

The night was spent at Gkypai, and after another cold and stormy trek they reached the American headquarters at Shunning. After the 11 seemingly endless days of trekking about 100 miles through the wilds, sore and weary, their relief on seeing motor vehicles again was indescribable. Even at the blackest moments neither George Graham nor 'Chalky' White had allowed themselves to think about the possibility of capture, or that they would fail to reach a place of safety. Their ability to see humour in the most depressing situations and their irrepressible cheerfulness undoubtedly proved a great inspiration to Prosser, stimulating his will to live and aiding his recovery.

After 24 hours' rest and two days of blissfully

incomplicated road travel with someone else doing the thinking, they reached the airfield at Yunnanyi on the afternoon of the 15th, only to find that the American authorities had never heard of them. However, they were promised air lift back to India next day. It was just their bad luck that air transport picked this moment to behave as capriciously as coolie transport. On arriving at the airfield on the 16th take-off was delayed for several hours because of bad weather, then when their C-46 was able to get airborne its undercarriage would not retract. After pumping around in the turbulence for over an hour — during which Prosser collapsed with severe airsickness — the aircraft put down at Kunming.

Journey's end was reached on 17 April, exactly a month after this remarkable mercy mission had started. This time the air lift went without a hitch — a C-46 flight over 'the Hump' to Chabua, then on by Dakota to Calcutta, where at 1830 Graham delivered his patient to No 47 Base General Hospital. The hospital staff paid high tribute to Graham's surgical skill, and found the patient was in excellent condition, far better than they had been expecting.

A few weeks later several richly deserved awards were Gazetted — though the citations were not published to avoid any risk of compromising future operations and the safety of Allies still operating in enemy territory. Graham received the DSO and White the CGM, while King won a Bar to his DFC. Graham's citation said that his exceptional courage and extremely high sense of duty had been an inspiration to those in contact with him. But, as one of his colleagues remarked, using that typical, irreverent understatement which characterised the RAF vocabulary of the day: 'he was certainly no ordinary quack'.

# A Miracle for Berlin

## 17

In Germany, 24 January 1949 was just like any other winter's day. Snow and frozen slush lay everywhere and the biting wind that blew across Gatow Airport brought with it the promise of a further snowfall during the long, dark night. However, despite the severity of the weather all those concerned with the handling of the aircraft passing in and out of the airfield — from the mechanics working around the clock to maintain the machines in serviceable condition to the air traffic controllers whose job it was to guide and advise the tired pilots — knew that it would need a storm of immense proportions to put Gatow out of action.

The Berlin air lift, Operation Plainfare, was already almost eight months old. The massive blockade initiated by the Russians against the western sectors of the city of Berlin had started on 24 June 1948 and four days later RAF Transport Command had joined forces with the Americans in an effort to supply the people of West Berlin with almost every commodity ranging from cotton wool to liquid fuel.

Gatow Airport lay in the British sector, surrounded by pine trees and only a short distance from the Russian Zone. During World War II it had been one of the main Luftwaffe airfields, but in keeping with the majority of German air bases it had grass runways. In 1947 the building of a 2,000 yard long concrete runway had begun and by the time the airlift got under way three-quarters of its length had been finished. Because of the increasing pressure on the aircraft — Gatow was handling twice as many aircraft as its equivalent, Tempelhof, in the American sector and three times as many as New York's La Guardia, up to that time the holder of the world record for traffic — work on the new runway was speeded-up and the entire job finished in six weeks.

It was on this now well used runway that four Dakotas touched down shortly after 1630 on 24 January. They had flown in from Lübeck, two of them carrying coal, and as soon as they had taxied to the unloading area lorries and squads of German labourers converged immediately. There was no time to be wasted. It had been laid down in orders that no aircraft should normally remain on the ground at Gatow for more than 50 minutes — from touch down to take-off. No matter what cargo was being carried only 30 minutes were allowed for the arduous task of unloading and, more often than not, reloading. Above all, time was the most precious commodity.

Among the aircraft that had just landed was Dakota KP491. The labourers swarmed inside and like an army of ants scurried backwards and forwards unloading the sacks of coal. Behind them two women cleaners brushed out any spillings on to the tarmac where they were collected by a party of men equipped with a handtruck.

When the last traces of coal had been removed the lashings which had kept the sacks in place were stowed away. Preparations then began to take passengers aboard and a truck arrived with an assorted collection of baggage which was packed away under the seats.

At 1645 the passengers were told to board and a few minutes before 1700 the Transport Command Dakota rose into the air carrying 22 passengers and three crew, bound for Lübeck. The flight was scheduled to take 1 hour 30 minutes and for the first part of the journey it was possible to see the lights of villages in Russian occupied Germany twinkling in the gathering dusk.

For many of the passengers — Lothar Zeidler, en route to a new life in America and Herr Schroers included — it was their first experience of flying. It appeared to be uneventful and far less frightening than they had first imagined. However, the powerful, sustained roar of the engines filled the cabin and made conversation difficult. For the most part they slept.

At 1820 the Dakota was flying in heavy cloud. From time to time the fuselage shuddered and the aircraft lurched and trembled in the grip of hidden air turbulence. 10 minutes later the wireless operator left the flight deck to fit and test the safety belts of the women and children seated at the front.

Slowly, the aircraft began its descent through the thick cloud, the crew making preparations for the landing at Lübeck. On several occasions the Dakota seemed to sag and almost fall out of the air, the peculiar sensation having an alarming effect on the passengers. As the aircraft heaved and bucked, the pulsating note of the engines rising and falling, dominating the tense atmosphere in the cabin, several passengers were sick.

Suddenly, the Dakota gave a final, despairing lurch. Immediately, there were several loud thumps on the floor of the fuselage, followed by a sustained, tearing noise. Women started to scream. Other passengers tried to get to their feet, despite the safety belts clasping them firmly in the seats. The engines were now roaring madly and in the final moments before the full impact of the crash Lothar Zeidler saw the twisted branches of trees smacking and slithering against the window close to where he sat.

There was a final tortured protest from the engines

Right: Passengers from blockaded Berlin arriving at Lübeck in an RAF Dakota during Operation Plainfare. / MOD
34

Above: A special spares organisation was set up to keep the Plainfare aircraft serviceable. This Dakota is loading York spares at Honington, Suffolk, for delivery to Wunstorf. / MOD

before the Dakota plunged into the heart of the forest amid a cacophony of buckling metal and snapping tree trunks. The aircraft came to an abrupt halt.

The lights went out and the cabin was plunged into complete darkness. Suddenly, a blinding tongue of flame leaped from the flight deck and started to lick at the walls of the cabin. Outside, one of the engines was still running at full power, whining and screaming, the propeller spinning madly, the points of the blades churning the twigs and earth into a flying spray. The front of the Dakota was now completely alight and the aircraft lay at an angle wedged between two massive tree trunks, with the nose about 15 feet off the ground and the tail just over six feet clear.

Inside, Lothar was one of the first to recover from the shock. He staggered over to the door and wrenched at the levers holding it locked into position. They would not budge. No matter how he wrestled with them the door failed to move. Thick, acrid smoke was now filling the cabin, swirling around the interior like an oppressive mist. Another male passenger, called Brandis, joined Lothar in his struggle with the door. Eventually, after several agonising minutes they succeeded in partially opening it. Brandis was the first to jump out and Lothar wasted no time in following him.

The two men ran around the aircraft, uncertain of what to do, still slightly dazed by the events of the previous few minutes. The heat from the burning nose section forced them back. They were able to see that a tree trunk was jammed firmly against part of the door panel and as the men stood staring and trying to form some plan of action, they heard the sound of a window being smashed. A male passenger squeezed through and was followed by a small boy who landed in a heap on the ground. His mother, who had pushed him out, jumped after him and fell awkwardly, twisting her ankle.

Lothar dragged them both away from the burning fuselage and stumbled on the Dakota's pilot lying among the scattered debris of foliage torn from the trees as the aircraft had passed through them. He pulled off his coat and wrapped it round the injured man's shoulders. The pilot was barely conscious and blood was coming from the lower part of one of his legs.

By now the entire aircraft was firmly ablaze, the flames leaping and dancing, fed from below by the melting paintwork and encouraged from above by the branches of the trees. It was no longer possible to get close to the fuselage because of the intense heat and every second seemed to bring the moment of explosion infinitely nearer.

A number of people were still trapped in the burning wreckage, but there was absolutely nothing that either Lothar or Brandis could to to save them. It came as a shock to them both to discover that out of those who had managed to escape from the aircraft they were the only two who were uninjured. They ceased shouting at the others to get as far away as possible from the inferno; instead they rushed forward and started to drag them away.

When they were certain that all who had escaped were safe in the event of there being an explosion the two men set off through the forest in search of help. It was pitch dark, the pair found themselves constantly stumbling on hidden tree roots running close to the surface of the ground. Eventually, they found a path which took them out of the forest and on to the edge of a wide strip of marshland. On the opposite side, shrouded in a frosty mist, a number of lights stretched away across the horizon. They were certain that, at last, this was Lübeck airfield.

However, the crossing of the marsh was much more difficult than it had first appeared. They were continually sinking up to their ankles in a sea of green, mossy slime and the entire area was interlaced with small streams, many of them hidden by the rank undergrowth. At last, when the lights still seemed to be as far away as when they had first spotted them, the two men came to a broad, swift-running stream, almost a river and too deep for any attempt to be made to cross it.

It was then they saw a single light shining brightly some distance away on their right. When they reached the spot they found it belonged to a farmhouse. The farmer was only too eager to help and he led the way to the nearest police station. Only as they paused for a moment before

**Left:** Unloading an RAF Dakota during the Berlin Air Lift. / *MOD*

**Above:** Coal for Berlin being loaded into a Transport Command Hastings at Schleswigland. / *MOD*

entering the building did Lothar and Brandis realise that they were in the Russian Zone.

The hands of the clock in the police station stood at 2045 — their journey in search of help had taken almost two hours. When they explained this to the policemen bandages and other medical supplies were brought and a patrol despatched to find the wrecked Dakota. While Brandis stayed behind at the police station Lothar went with a senior officer to the crash scene.

During the time the policemen were tending to the injured — many of whom were now in a critical condition — a Russian lorry full of soldiers, arrived. They immediately took charge of the casualties and drove them off to a nearby village where a German doctor carried out emergency treatment while an innkeeper provided food, drink and blankets. An ambulance was summoned and the more seriously injured taken to hospital in Schönberg. A short time afterwards the remaining survivors and the bodies of those who had died — the wireless operator and five passengers — were all taken to the hospital.

At 0200 the interrogations began and a woman interpreter acted for the Russians. Lothar was questioned at length about his family and whether or not they were

party members. His papers, which had been taken from him and which showed that he was en route to America, were produced and a series of questions asked about his intentions in leaving Germany. At the end of the session the Russians appeared to be satisfied and questioning of the next survivor began.

That morning when the newspapers went on sale they carried reports of the Russian version of the crash. One newspaper, *Vowärts*, published in the Russian Zone, had as its main headline, *Airbridge — Deathbridge*. The sub-heading read, *Senseless Evacuation of Berlin Children Causes Tragic Victims*. The story informed the readers:

'A British Dakota carrying twenty-two passengers, including seventeen children and a crew of three, left Gatow Airport yesterday and crashed near the Anglo-Russian zonal border near Schönberg late last night.

'Search parties, led by Russian officers and personnel were sent out immediately, according to information given by British officials. It is thought that the crash occurred in a wood.

'The crash of the aircraft carrying children near the zonal border has created an atmosphere of tension among parents who have registered their children to fly out of Berlin.

'Early in the morning the first calls were received by West Sector offices to remove children's names from the registration lists. Anxious mothers said it would not be necessary to send their children to the Western Zone if the Western Powers could reach agreement. More and more

157

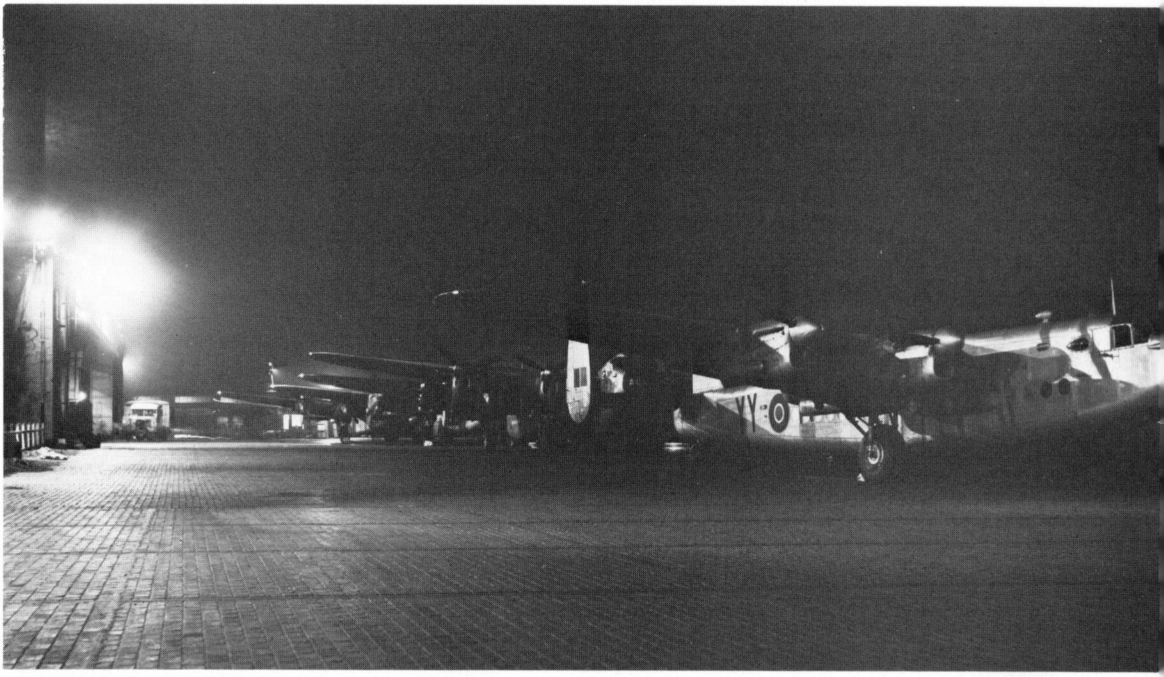
YY

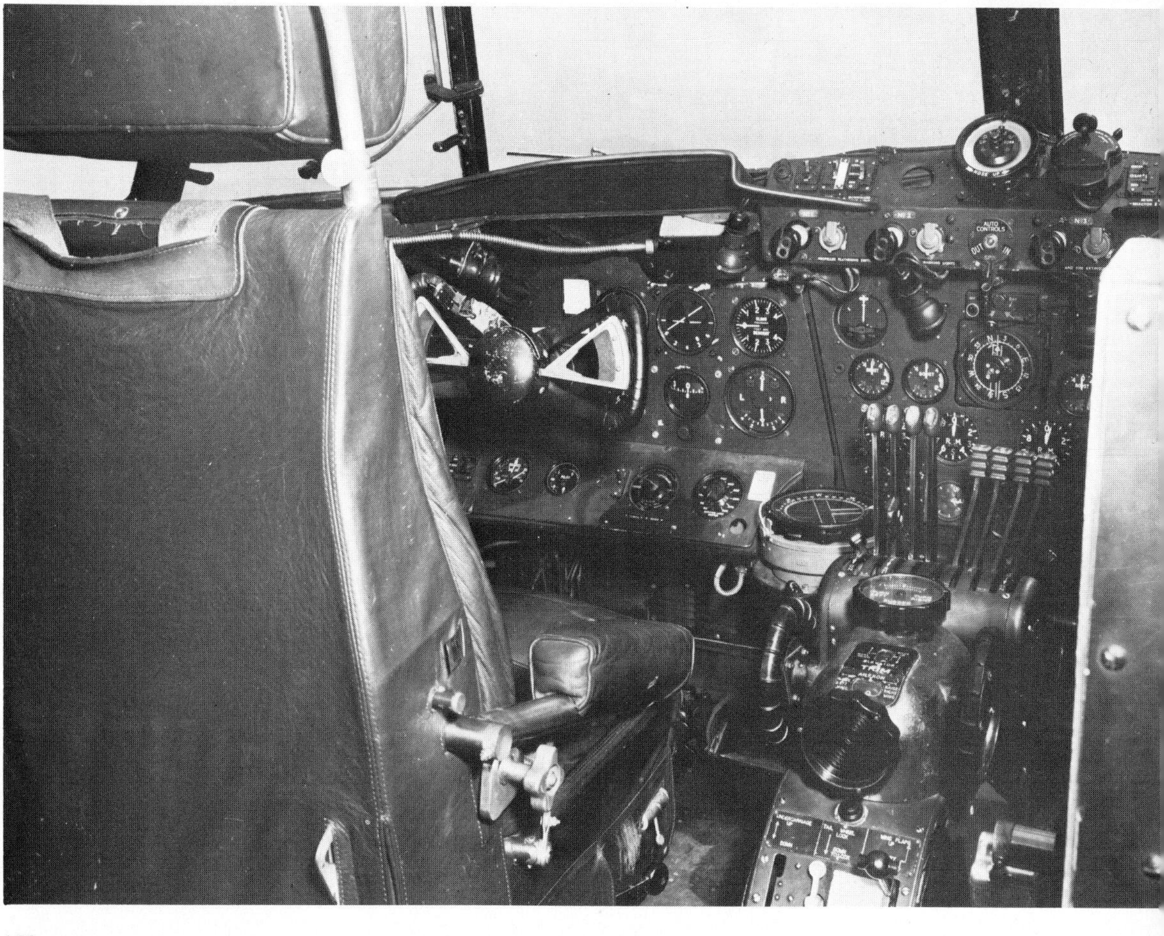
AUTO CONTROLS
OUT
IN

arents are realising that they need not live in continual anxiety about the journey of their children if they had registered in the East Sector for their food and coal rather than remaining in the Western Sectors.'

The following morning the survivors were told that the British were now taking part in negotiations for their release. The Russians added that a medical examination would have to take place to ascertain which survivors might be fit to travel.

The pilot, responding well to hospital treatment, was shown a copy of one German newspaper which claimed that the crash had happened because one of the Dakota's engines had cut out and that he had been attempting to land the aircraft on one. He denied this, maintaining that Lübeck had given him instructions which should have taken him down to 300 feet, the undercarriage had been lowered and that when the crash occurred the aircraft had only been two minutes' flying time away from the airfield.

Eventually, the Russians agreed to release the survivors and Lothar and eight others, including a child, who were in no further need of hospital care were allowed to cross the Zone border into the city of Lübeck. It was 0100 on Thursday January 27.

Although the Russians had behaved in a humane fashion towards the survivors of the Dakota crash the opportunity to make political propaganda out of the incident was too good to be missed. For some time afterwards Russian Zone newspapers continued to carry follow up stories and on February the *Berliner Illustrierte*, which was controlled by the Russians, printed a series of photographs showing various aspects of the crash. These included photographs of bodies lying beside the wreckage; the victims in hospital and several close up details of the fire-blackened fuselage.

Under one such picture, showing the rear of the fuselage and tail unit, the caption was headed: *One Dakota Less — One Lesson More*. It read:

The survivors tell of three terrible shocks just as they were about to land. "Everything was thrown about in the aircraft, we tried to escape by the windows and half-open door, the unconscious were burned to death..." They were victims of the Western political sabotage against the East Zone which caused the blockade of Berlin. All would still have been alive if the Western powers had not used Berlin as a centre for the "cold war" '.

Despite the considerable congestion which existed in the narrow air corridor which aircraft used on their flights into and out of Berlin there were few fatal accidents. Only seven occurred to British aircraft — five Royal Air Force and two civil. In two of the RAF crashes and one civil the

aircraft crashed in the Russian Zone. On all occasions, although there was a certain amount of political capital made out of the incidents, the Russians behaved courteously towards the survivors.

Transport Command had a complex task to perform during the air lift and added to their varied responsibilities they were delegated with the job of flying all passengers out of Berlin. Many of the people they carried were political refugees who had crossed into the Western Sectors of Berlin, been allowed to stay and then had decided they would be safer in some other part of Western Germany or even abroad.

The first to be air lifted from West Berlin were those who did not live there, but happened to be there on business or on a friendly visit when the blockade was imposed. In the early stages Transport Command flew out over 4,000 such people. When this mission was completed the opportunity to leave the city was given to anyone who had permission to go to live in West Germany, or to emigrate to some other country or to finish his or her education in a Western school or college. This operation was mounted in August 1948.

Several weeks later Transport Command had another category of passenger added to their task; the sick. These were people who showed early traces of tuberculosis, those who were medically in need of long periods of rest and good food and those who required special treatment that was unavailable in Berlin. Perhaps the most important of all were the thousands of children who had suffered terribly in wartime Berlin and as a result were in the grip of malnutrition and general poor health.

These people — in March 1949 the total had reached over 50,000 — were flown out in Dakotas, Yorks and Sunderland flying-boats. The children travelled free; the adults paid a small charge.

For the adults, despite the fact that they had never flown before, it was a welcome experience, but for the children this was the opportunity of a lifetime. The crews did their best to keep them amused, feeding them up with sweets and allowing them to visit the flight deck of the aircraft so that they could see for themselves how the aircraft was flown.

One pilot who was a great favourite of the children was Squadron Leader A. M. Johnstone, the commanding officer of No 30 Squadron. In December, 1947 Johnstone had taken charge of this squadron, at Oakington in Cambridgeshire. On 28 June 1948 when the first Transport Command Dakotas entered the air lift — 13 Dakotas carried 44 tons of food from Wunstorf to Gatow — Johnstone and his now fully formed squadron were preparing to leave Oakington to take part in Operation Carter Paterson.

They were told to take enough kit to last for 10 days. The operation, they were informed, was to supply by air the British occupying forces and the 2,100,000 civilians in Berlin in the face of a Russian blockade of the city. The instruction to carry 10 day's kit pointed to the acceptance of the Western authorities that the Russians would soon tire of what one senior official had described as 'this stupid affair'.

In February 1949 Johnstone and his men, by now fully

experienced in the rigours of operating the air lift, were still in Germany. For month after month they had carried every conceivable form of cargo, but few journeys were as memorable as the flight from Gatow to Lübeck with 25 children aboard. The oldest passenger was 16 and the next eldest, six years of age.

Johnstone detected that the 16-year old was extremely nervous of her responsibility to look after the 24 infants. Fortunately, she could speak a little English, but despite this Johnstone was unable to convince her that there was absolutely no reason for her to worry — either about herself or the safety of her young charges. The girl asked on several occasions what would happen if the aircraft were to crash.

Johnstone's eventual reply was characteristic and accompanied by a great deal of laughter. 'My dear girl, this is a most exclusive aeroplane. It never crashes. Also this is the most experienced aircrew in the whole of the Royal Air Force'.

His remarks were greeted by cheers from the two other crew members. The girl's eyes lit up; she smiled. Then she, too, was laughing, every bit as heartily as the men.

When the Dakota took off the signaller sat with the children and once airborne the navigator left the flight deck to join him. The two men had a difficult job — a task far more strenuous than many they had tackled in the past; to keep the children away from the tail and so upsetting the trim. Once the youngsters were released from their safety straps there was no holding them. Very few remained in their seats. The majority ran about, laughing and shouting

or remained huddled in small groups, talking excitedly.

In order to help his crew members Johnstone offered to allow the children to enter the flight deck and in groups of five the youngsters crowded into the cramped space, eager to see how the machine was flown.

For the remainder of the flight, until the Dakota was only five miles away from touchdown at Lübeck, Johnstone flew with a child on each knee. As he described them himself: 'One was maybe three years old, the other about four, both were covered in scabs and stinking to high heaven and both of them jabbering away in German, perfectly happy'.

The crews also had their moments of fun with the adult passengers. One woman, in her middle 80s, was found a place in a York. The only place for her to sit was among a considerable pile of mailbags. However, she didn't protest and smiled her gratitude each time a member of the crew visited her on the flight to Wunstorf. The weather was bad with continuous rain and although the York was forced to fly through a large number of ominous storm clouds the old woman appeared unperturbed by the bumping and heaving of the fuselage.

At Wunstorf she was lowered out of the York, still thanking the crew, and carried to a waiting three-ton lorry which was to take her to Hanover. She took one look at the vehicle and immediately protested. She declared she had no intention of boarding it.

'Certainly not', she said. 'Not at my age. It looks far too dangerous'.

To relieve the monotony the crews were not averse to

playing practical jokes on some of their unsuspecting passengers. One day in 1949 a Transport Command Dakota landed at Gatow with a load of young British soldiers. The troops disembarked and stood in groups beside the aircraft, discussing what, for many, had been their first flight. Eventually, the navigator, signaller and co-pilot climbed down. The soldiers heard one of them say: 'What about the skipper. We'd better help him out'.

While the puzzled troops watched, the crew went back into the Dakota to emerge a few minutes later supporting a bent, aged figure walking hesitantly with the aid of a stick. The wings on his crumpled flying overalls were almost hidden by a long, flowing white beard and from the dark glasses he wore it looked as if he was either blind or very nearly so. As the crew helped him from the aircraft's steps and on to the ground he cursed them freely and laid about them with his stick.

The crew shouted to the soldiers, 'Make way for the captain' and the grunting complaining figure stumped across the tarmac and vanished into one of the buildings. The soldiers continued to stare and then one said in a loud, incredulous voice:

'Christ did *he* fly us here? Looks more like Rip Van Winkle than a pilot to me'.

Over in the Flying Control building people were staring at four RAF men holding their sides and roaring with laughter. One of them, Flight Lieutenant Mike Clancy, whose adventures as a Transport Command Hastings pilot feature in Chapter 19, held a false beard and a pair of sunglasses in his hand.

On 5 May 1949 an official statement was issued simultaneously in London, Paris, Moscow and Washington. It read:

'The Governments of France, the Union of Soviet Socialist Republics, the United Kingdom and the United States have reached the following agreement:

'1. All the restrictions imposed since 1 March 1948, by the Government of the Union of Soviet Socialist Republics on communications, transport and trade between Berlin and the Western Zones of Germany and between the Eastern Zone and all the Western Zones will be removed on 12 May, 1949.

'2. All the restrictions imposed since 1 March, 1948 by the Governments of France, the United Kingdom and the United States, or any one of them, on communications, transportation and trade between Berlin and the Eastern Zones of Germany will also be removed on 12 May 1949.'

The blockade was over. Nevertheless, the air lift went on for several more months in order that Berlin would have a stockpile in preparation for the coming winter.

The Berlin air lift had taken longer than most people had imagined it would. However, one senior Transport Command Officer, summed it up by quoting an old Service saying: 'It's only the impossible that can be done at once; miracles take a little longer'.

# Fate Deals a Blow

## 18

Shortly before 2000 hours on 20 December, 1950, Hastings TG574 of No 53 Squadron, Transport Command, prepared to take-off from El Adem, near Tobruk. The captain was Flight Lieutenant Graham Tunnadine and co-pilot, Flight Lieutenant S. L. Bennett. There were four other crew members and 27 passengers.

TG574 was returning from Singapore nearing the end of an experimental slip crew schedule. Since 1945 Transport Command's Far East route had been operated in rather leisurely fashion, the same crew flying the aircraft throughout and night-stopping at selected points. As postwar commitments increased, the Command felt obliged to abandon this uneconomic use of aircraft and revert to the wartime slip crew system, whereby the aircraft flew day and night, making only the essential refuelling and servicing halts, with fresh crews taking over at appropriate staging posts.

Early in December four crews were accordingly pre-positioned along the route, and TG574 was flown to Singapore trying out the new, fast schedule. She was now homeward bound, carrying the four experienced Hastings crews who had completed their legs of the flight — plus Squadron Leader Thomas Colin Lyall Brown, a Transport Command medical officer who was studying any aircrew fatigue problems emerging from the new timetable. Three other passengers had joined at Karachi.

After staging through Colombo, Karachi, Habbaniya and Fayid, the Hastings had made an unscheduled stop at El Adem to top up with fuel before pressing on to Castel Benito, Tripoli. At 1958 she was airborne and the passengers were mentally blessing the operations staff for having planned to complete their experiment in comfortable time before Christmas. The aircraft plodded up to 8,500ft, and they listened with experienced ears to the changing engine note as she settled down to the 185-knot cruising speed. All was well. Fully conditioned to the monotonous roar of four Hercules engines, some promptly fell asleep, a few played cards or read, while one or two watched the black and silver desert sliding past, lit by the three-quarter moon.

On the flight deck, Tunnadine, aged 28, with some 2,300 flying hours in his log book, told Bennett to get his head down for a while in the rest compartment rigged up just forward of the passenger cabin, as it would be his task to fly the aircraft on from Castel Benito after refuelling. His place up front was taken by Squadron Leader William G. James, another qualified Hastings pilot.

There was a fleeting hint of trouble 42 minutes after take-off. One of the back-seat drivers thought he noticed a vibration, possibly caused by an engine becoming unsynchronised. Moments later, while he was considering whether to pass some gently chiding note up to the flight deck, there came a sharp bang from the front of the aircraft. This was followed by a violent juddering which suggested something badly amiss. Awakened instantly, the passengers remained seated, confident that whatever the problem, the pilots would ask if they wanted any assistance. After another minute or two, which dragged by like hours, the air quartermaster appeared and requested Squadron Leader Brown to go forward, then asked one of the most experienced pilots to talk to the captain on the intercom.

On the flight deck nobody yet knew exactly what had happened. Tunnadine reported that he had lost all power from the port inner engine (No 2), and had no elevator or rudder control. Only the ailerons were working. With nothing but lateral control, the aircraft was descending and there seemed to be little he could do about it.

Meanwhile, Brown, having negotiated a sizeable gash in the floor, found Bennett still on the rest bunk, pinned to the floor beneath a pile of wreckage, barely conscious, with his right arm severed and other grievous injuries.

It did not take the crew long to establish the cause of their perilous situation. What had happened was that the propeller of No 2 engine had shed one of its blades. In flying off it had scythed through the fuselage — where part of it was still embedded in the opposite wall — cut the tail control rods as well as critically injuring Bennett. The three remaining blades, out of equilibrium, had wrenched the engine — plus part of the wing leading edge and the port undercarriage — free from its mounting to fall away to the desert a mile and a half below. The disturbed airflow over the great gash in the wing was seriously aggravating the handling difficulties.

A rapid check by Flight Sergeant Idwal Johns, the engineer, showed that there was no hope of locating and repairing the severed tail control rods. RAF Benina, near Benghazi, had acknowledged 574's May Day call, and was only 19 minutes normal flying time away, but at the present rate of descent the aircraft would hit the ground long before that. After further discussions over the intercom it was decided that the only possible way of maintaining fore and aft control was by quickly adjusting the position of the load. First the baggage and small freight items were shifted o the rear, but this made insufficient difference, so, while one of them remained in contact with the captain, the passengers themselves moved aft. Gradually the nose began to rise, though there were several over-corrections and some hasty to-ing and fro-ing before Tunnadine was able to acquire reasonably positive control of the flight attitude by adjusting the position of one or two passengers. Having established the Hastings in level flight, he was then able to begin a gradual descent, headed towards Benina, which in normal circumstances would have been overflown. Next he tried gentle turns to port and starboard, using the throttles to boost or reduce engine power as necessary to swing the aircraft in the required direction. At the first attempt the nose went up and the aircraft began to shudder, indicating that a stall was imminent, but an urgent order to move some passengers forward brought the nose down again just in time.

Rarely can any transport pilot have faced such an appalling dilemma. The easiest of the decisions — whether to make a belly landing — had already been made for him since half the undercarriage lay on the desert surface some miles behind. The only way of achieving a reasonable crash landing would be to lose height as gradually as possible, then try to raise the aircraft's nose with a burst of engines just before she touched the ground. But he had only three engines and was already fighting the asymmetric effect caused by the unbalanced power on each wing. And how long those three engines would continue to operate was debatable; they had already exceeded maximum temperature in fighting the drag caused by the damaged wing.

As the Hastings neared Benghazi the beach to the north-east, with its mile upon mile of sand gleaming whitely in the moonlight, looked particularly inviting — but Benina's station commander advised against its use because of obstructions. Tunnadine was now able to talk on his VHF radio direct to the control tower at Benina, and he told them that he had decided to use their runway. A flarepath was laid out, the military hospital at Benghazi alerted and an army fire tender despatched to help on the airfield.

TG574 arrived overhead near Benina with about 6,000ft still in hand. The flickering flames of the gooseneck flares marking the runway, and the lights of Benghazi offered some comfort, though the most difficult part was still to come. Tunnadine made several wide circuits of the airfield, gingerly descending to 1,000ft, with the passengers still acting as a human counterweight to trim the aircraft. The six escape hatches were removed, but the large parachute doors were left in position lest any sudden inrush of air should affect the flying characteristics in any way.

Brown, still tending the terribly injured co-pilot, was no novice in flying matters, having made 80 jumps while on the staff of the Parachute Training School. He fully understood the perils of the landing which lay ahead, and knew that those in the front would be poorly placed if the Hastings crashed. Nevertheless he insisted that his duty was to remain with his patient. He had injected morphia and treated the injuries as best he could, and was lying down with Bennett in his arms, providing warmth from his own body and holding together the worst wounds with his hands.

At 2149 hours the medical officers and ambulances from Benghazi reached Benina. The flarepath was complete and the crash-crews, ambulances and fire tenders positioned at a point on the perimeter track near the downwind end of the runway. Benina control informed Tunnadine:

'We are all ready for you to come in to land'.

'Going out to sea to make final approach', replied Tunnadine.

'Good luck. Hope you make it.'

'I'll need a bit of luck'.

It was now 69 minutes since Hastings TG574 had been damaged. As Tunnadine brought the aircraft down from 1,000ft by throttling back his engines he began to turn through 180 degrees to line up on the flarepath. The lights of Benghazi were on his port wing-tip. His airspeed indicator showed 140 knots, the lowest speed at which he could maintain any control. Ten miles away the flares showed up against the blackness of the desert. He dare not risk using the flaps, which might produce a nose-down attitude which he would not be able to correct.

For the passengers, knowing only too well the critical nature of the next few minutes, the ordeal was one of agonising suspense. 'Any one of us would cheerfully have jumped out on the end of an umbrella had one been available' said one of them afterwards. They waited in silence, each man alone with his private thoughts. Some were still standing, ready to move as required for instant trim changes and the nightmare atmosphere was heightened by the intermittent bellowing of the engines, since violent throttle movement was necessary to adjust the aircraft's attitude during final stages of the descent. When the aircraft was within feet of the ground, the passengers still standing slid rapidly into adjacent seats and strapped themselves in. Tunnadine was desperately trying to keep the Hastings level. The ground came nearer.

'I can't see the end of the runway'.

These were his last words to the control tower. After their exhibition of such superb airmanship, it was tragic that luck should desert the crew in the final seconds.

The aircraft struck the ground about a quarter of a mile short of the runway, in front of a gently sloping hillock which had obscured the lights. The initial impact was very gentle, though inevitably the propellers ploughed into the ground and the engine nacelles began to break up. Had it not been for the slope all would have been well. This caused the Hastings to become airborne again for about 100 yards, then the starboard wing hit the ground and broke off. The aircraft rolled on to its back, slewed round in the reverse direction and slid along the rough ground for 360 yards before coming to a halt. The time was 2155.

Crash crews were on the scene within 90 seconds, though fortunately there was no fire. To their surprise they found that most of the passengers had scrambled out, having suffered little more than relatively minor cuts and abrasions. Those still inside the fuselage, dazed and shaken, were quickly helped out. The wreckage of the hideously crumpled nose section held little promise of any survivors, and the four crew members on the flight deck were killed. Despite Brown's valiant efforts, Bennett also died before he could be rushed to hospital.

Apart from its unusual features this accident has a place

in history for another reason. There is little doubt that most of the passengers owed their survival to the fact that the Hastings were fitted with suitably stressed rearward facing seats. This was the first major crash of a large passenger aircraft equipped in this fashion.

As the network of RAF scheduled transport services expanded during the later stages of the war it became apparent that there was a percentage of accidents where, despite relatively minor damage to the fuselage, passengers were killed or badly injured when the force of the impact wrenched the seats from their fittings and hurled them forwards. In 1945 the Royal Aircraft Establishment and No 46 Group made studies which led to the decision that future RAF transport aircraft should have rearward facing seats to protect passengers in these circumstances. The Hastings and the twin-engined Valetta, which both entered service in 1948 were the first types so equipped. Rather more was involved than simply turning round existing seats, since to do the job properly they had to be specially designed. Those in the Hastings were stressed to withstand forces of 20g, and also featured a high back to protect passengers' heads. Two months after the Benina accident an RAF Valetta crashed in Sweden and provided more evidence of the seats' protective value. Although developments in aircraft design and performance have altered some of the parameters which led to the adoption of rearward facing seats in 1948, the RAF has continued to fit

them on the basis that in any sudden deceleration it is better for the seat to take the first stress rather than the human body.

The subsequent inquiry into the Benina accident established that metal fatigue had caused the propeller blade to break. It was pure bad luck that in flying off it should have caused such a crash. The blade had an arc of 360 degrees in which to leaves its consorts. In only about 40 degrees of this arc would it have hit the aircraft, and in still fewer could it damage the controls. It was additional bad luck that after Tunnadine's brilliant performance in coaxing the crippled Hastings to the brink of safety it should have struck the small ridge which launched it back into the air for that fatal somersault.

In the *London Gazette* of 18 May 1951 it was announced that Squadron Leader Brown had been awarded the George Medal. The citation briefly described the sequence of events and ended: '... There is no doubt that he (Brown) consciously risked his life in order to save that of the injured officer. He carried out his duties in accordance with the traditions of his profession without regard for his own personal safety.'

Tunnadine and his crew were awarded the King's Commendation for Valuable Service in the Air. But for the rigid rules restricting posthumous awards they would undoubtedly have been recommended for some higher recognition.

# Greenland Ordeal

## 19

On 16 September 1952 Hastings 492 of No 47 Squadron Transport Command was being loaded with supplies at the USAF base at Thule in Greenland ready for take-off to drop them to members of the British North Greenland Expedition at a small camp on the icecap which they called Northice.

The Hastings, which had come from its base at Topcliffe in Yorkshire, was piloted by Flight Lieutenant Mike Clancy a 34-year old flight commander of No 47 Squadron. Since the Berlin air lift, on which he had flown numerous sorties, Clancy had logged 600,000 miles, flying first Yorks and later Hastings on Transport Command's overseas trunk routes. By the spring of 1952 his total flying hours had reached around 3,000.

His crew was Flight Lieutenant Ted Adair (co-captain); Flight Lieutenant Reg Michie (senior navigator); Flying Officer Les Richardson (navigator); Flight Sergeant Frank Burke (signaller); Master Engineer Richard Mosley (flight engineer) and Flight Sergeant Boyd (air quartermaster). Also in the aircraft were five others: Major Barker-Simson of the Army Air Dispatch Unit, who was in charge of the despatchers at the base, three of his men, Corporal Brian Yates, Corporal Brian Fussey and Private Jones, together with the USAF liaison officer at the base, Captain 'Smokey' Stover who intended to go on the flight to see for himself what conditions were like.

The British North Greenland Expedition had gone to Greenland in the summer of 1952 for a period of two years. It was led by Commander C. J. W. Simpson. Sponsored by the Scott Polar Research Institute, the Royal Geographical Society, the Royal Society and the Army, Navy and Royal Air Force it had among its objectives the crossing of the great inland sea of ice, 300 miles from Britannia Lake in North-East Greenland where the base camp was situated. There, three men intended to construct a building under the snow and radio back daily weather reports. Coastal Command had airlifted the men, dogs and equipment in to Britannia Lake and Transport Command Hastings were given the role of supplying additional stores and equipment as they were required.

Two Hastings were sent from Topcliffe, the one captained by Flight Lieutenant Clancy, the other by Flight Lieutenant David Wright.

By 14 September Commander Simpson and a party of five others had succeeded in reaching a point 700 miles from the Pole, 220 miles west of Britannia Lake and 480 miles east of Thule. The commander decided to risk going no further. His dog teams were depleted by the deaths of several animals and others were now quite unfit to be driven any more. He signalled Thule through Britannia Lake that he had decided to remain where he was and asked that supply dropping begin immediately. He christened his tiny camp of two tents 'Northice' and the following day Flt Lt Wright in Hastings 490 successfully made the first drop — a load of hut sections which were sent floating down in 30 parachute loads.

The following morning Clancy and his 11 man party took off from Thule at 0700. The Hastings carried a heavy load of hut sections and jerrycans of petrol. The weather forecast radioed from Northice was not particularly good. A surface wind gusting up to 25 knots whipping up loose snow with surface visibility seven miles and a heavy overcast hanging 2,500 feet above the cap. At Thule, take-off conditions were much worse. There was a 50-knot gale, bringing with it occasional blizzards.

Between flurries of blowing snow the Hastings took off. It flew over the icecap at 7,000 feet but after encountering heavy cloud climbed to 11,000 feet when one hour out of Thule. Here, the air was hazy with ice crystals, the haze obliterating the natural horizon of the icecap below. The pilots were confronted by a wide view of empty white where ground and sky met in a confused blur. There was some concern among the crew that the task of finding the two small tents might prove more difficult that they had first imagined.

'Northice, this is Baker Uncle. Do you read? Over'.

The reply was almost instantaneous.

'Hello Baker Uncle, this is Northice reading you strength three'.

Hastings 492 was very close, but it was still not possible to pick out the small camp against its background of pure white.

Clancy turned the aircraft in the direction of the radio signal and a few minutes later as a voice from Northice shouted, 'We can see you' the crew caught their own first glimpse of the tents. Alongside the insignificant shapes was a stack of equipment, some dogs huddled together for warmth and a number of tiny figures moving around in the snow.

After bringing the Hastings around in a wide circle Clancy was 1,000 feet about the icecap. His altimeter read 9,347 feet above sea level. With 30 degrees of flap he reduced the Hasting's speed from 175 to 130 knots. In the fuselage the equipment was made ready for the drop. At

800 feet the Hastings turned into wind. All was ready on the ground for the drop to begin.

Hastings 492 made 12 runs over the camp before all the large pieces of equipment were parachuted on to the snow. That done it was time to start the hardest part of the mission — the free drop of the stores from 50 feet.

This was something new for Clancy and his co-pilot and conditions for such a test were anything but favourable. Ground level visibility was now down to two miles and the horizon was a narrow, indefinite line amid the grey haze. A voice over the radio from the ground announced that they would 'talk' the Hastings down and so assist the pilot to line up his machine for the run in. Clancy made a gradual descent to 250 feet. At 200 feet the Hastings was brought round towards the dropping zone. Power was reduced — the airspeed indicator fell back to 135 knots, then was eased down to 128 knots. At 100 feet the radio altimeter flickered wildly between 50 feet and 200 feet, taking a reading through the surface snow to the level of the hard ice below.

Clancy entered the dropping zone at 80 feet, and the signal was given to the despatchers to throw out their first consignment of stores — a load of jerrycans. This was done, swiftly and expertly, and the Hastings climbed away, banking slowly to prepare for the second run in.

This time Clancy came in exactly 50 feet above the snow. The little camp, the tents, scattered stores, the dogs, figures of men rushed towards them, flashed away underneath. Out went the jerrycans. Power was increased gradually to climb away. Suddenly it was as if the Hastings

had flown into a bank of low mist. Clancy could see nothing — one moment the horizon was there before his eyes, the next, there was nothing but a swirling mass of white. He had fallen victim to 'white out', a hazard dreaded by all Arctic pilots.

At the same time the tip of the port wing struck the snow and dug in. Within seconds it was broken and twisted and a tremor shook the Hastings. The aircraft started to lurch violently. Clancy slammed shut the throttles and hauled on the control column attempting to lift the smashed wing away from the snow. He succeeded, bending the column with his desperate effort and Hastings 492 staggered on, fuselage and drooping wing only inches above the snow. Just as the wing started to drop back and the prospect of the Hastings cartwheeling nose-to-wingtip loomed in the minds of the crew, the belly hit the frozen snow. At 120 knots the aircraft ploughed across the icecap, leaving a deep furrow in its wake. It skidded for a mile and a half, the port outer engine tearing away from its mounting, then the port inner.

Inside the fuselage the remaining jerrycans were being flung about among the men. The only man without a safety line attached to his body was Stover and he joined the cans in being thrown from side to side. He collided with several of his companions and was thrown violently from one bulkhead to the other. Corporal Fussey was pulled off his feet and shot out through the open door. His safety line went taught, but held and he was left outside the aircraft hanging upside down, now and then his face running through the snow.

Behind the pilots Michie was sent flying to collide with Richardson the second navigator. Although strapped into his seat Michie struck him with such force that the seat broke off at its swivel mounting. Michie then crashed against Master Engineer Mosley. Burke, the signaller, who had loosened his belt to carry out adjustments to the radio was pitched forward, striking his head on the transmitter. The severe blow knocked him unconscious.

With oil spurting from the torn and twisted pipes where once the engines had been mounted the aircraft slithered to a halt. Buttons were punched to operate the fire extinguishers in the remaining engines and the fuel cocks switched off. For a moment there was intense silence. The rumbling, the banging and crashing, the hiss of the snow flying in particles beneath the belly of the Hastings — all were gone. Then Adair shouted the command to abandon the aircraft. They helped Burke out on to the snow and some distance from the aircraft laid him on his back. The danger of fire was uppermost in everyone's mind.

The starboard inner engine was beginning to smoke. A hand extinguisher was played on it and gradually the smoke died away. Hastings 492 — a veteran of flights to so many different countries — had flown her last. She now rested 8,000 feet above sea level on the Greenland icecap.

**Left: Hastings WD492 being loaded at Thule for its ill-fated supply dropping flight to the Northice camp.** / MOD

**Below: Hastings WD492 in her final resting place on the Greenland ice cap, photographed from another Hastings.** / MOD

As they were taking stock of their predicament and the shock of having survived began to fade Captain Stover began to complain of pains in his back and chest. He found his arms had stiffened and when he bent or reached up had great difficulty in retaining his former position. Major Barker-Simson found he could not put any weight on one ankle. Clancy began to realise that not only was Burke injured about the head and face, but that Stover had what appeared to be a fractured spine and possibly broken ribs and Barker-Simson's ankle was definitely broken.

Clancy decided that with three injured men the best method of survival was to use the fuselage of the Hastings. Parachutes were ripped up and draped across the bare walls. Within a short time three small compartments had been created. The floor was covered with sound-proofing material torn from the interior of the flight deck and sacks of wood shavings in which the undropped supplies had been packed. Burke regained consciousness for a few minutes during the time Adair was doing some first aid on his face, then after looking around him lapsed again into a coma.

When Commander Simpson realised what had happened he set off from Northice, accompanied by Angus Erskine and Peter Taylor and a sledge pulled by a dog team. Once on the spot he took stock of the situation and gave the men some encouragement and good advice on survival in the severe conditions.

With over 1,000 gallons of high-octane fuel left in the wing tanks it was not possible to light any stove for some hours after the crash. With everyone in need of a hot drink Taylor and Erskine returned to their camp prepared the

brew and carried it in thermos flasks. Because, without power, the aircraft wireless transmitter was not working and it was almost 1½ miles to Northice, Commander Simpson decided to shift his camp and situate it beside the wrecked Hastings. Word of the accident was reported back to Thule.

There were three ways of resolving the situation.

Firstly, they could be rescued by air, but no one was very confident that this could be achieved. It was too far from Thule — 480 miles — for a helicopter to be used and their altitude 8,000 feet, drastically affecting the performance of any fixed-wing aircraft, would make the take-off a risky operation. Secondly, they could sledge out to Britannia Lake, the Expedition's base camp but if this was to be done they would have to set out for there within three weeks. It would be a two week journey to the base camp. Thirdly, they could remain where they were on the icecap at Northice. Either of the latter two plans would mean spending the winter with the Expedition team and delay their return to England until the spring of the following year, 1953.

Four days after the crash they were told by Thule that a rescue attempt would be made using a Dakota fitted with skis. The following day the aircraft left Thule but despite constant homing transmissions radioed out by Northice was unable to locate the camp and had to return to base. Two days later it was decided by Thule to send a Grumman Albatross amphibian with the immediate aim of evacuating the three injured men.

By now Clancy and his crew had two primus stoves burning continuously in the rear of the fuselage to provide some warmth. Despite this, however, the cold was everywhere, seeping through their protective clothing until their bodies ached. Icicles hung from the roof alongside patches of frost on the bare metal. On several days the temperature fell to −29°F — 60 degrees of frost. On one occasion it dropped to −35°F, −67 degrees of frost. All the same, the parachutes they had torn up to insulate the fuselage walls were offering some measure of protection; behind the drapes the walls were thick with hoar frost.

The dangers of frostbite were always present. When eating, great care had to be taken in not allowing flesh to touch bare cold metal. Tea, even from cups dipped in boiling water, would have ice floating it in within three minutes of pouring.

In readiness for the Grumman Albatross Clancy and his crew used coloured parachutes and emergency dinghies to mark out a 600 yard long runway.

In his book, *North Ice*, Commander Simpson describes the scene:

'Before the Albatross reached us another Hastings arrived and dropped a load of supplies. Then it circled the station to help the amphibian to home on to us. The sky was overcast and hazy with the visibility down to three or four miles, when an escort, consisting of a Skymaster and a Flying Fortress, arrived and proceeded to orbit the station. On the ground everyone was outside with faces turned to the sky and a stir of excitement went through the party as the Albatross loomed out of the haze. With four big aircraft

**Left: Hastings WD492 in her final resting place on the Greenland ice cap, photographed from another Hastings.** / MOD

**Above: Supplies for the expedition — and for the crew of the crashed WD492 — being air-dropped from another Hastings.** / MOD

ircling around us, the air over Northice seemed a bit overcrowded.

'The Albatross pilot made three dummy runs along the runway, touching down and over-shooting, before settling down on the snow. It was a remarkable sight to watch this flying-boat land on its hull. He made a very smooth touchdown and then a big shower of snow as he furrowed a channel two feet deeep down the runway. For a few minutes he was obscured by the whirling snow-cloud and then reappeared taxi-ing easily across the snow towards the station. The crew consisted of two pilots and with them was a medical officer. He examined the three injured who had been sledged over from the wrecked Hastings and were ready waiting. Then Barker-Simson, Burke and Stover were assisted into the Albatross where stretchers awaited them'.

A great deal of research and planning had been done by the Air Ministry and the USAF to accomplish the rescue of the 2 men on the icecap. No 6 Air Rescue Squadron USAF, in charge of the operation, was fully aware of the difficulty and great danger of landing an aircraft at such an altitude in total freezing conditions. Not only was there the problem of take-off but if the weather deteriorated during the flight back to Thule it might not be possible to reach the nearest diversion airfield in southern Greenland. But uppermost in everyone's mind was the hazard of take-off, something which could not be accomplished without some additional boost in power being given to the engines and even then, it was not completely certain that the aircraft would be successful in leaving the ground.

For this purpose it was decided to use jet assisted take-off (JATO) a rocket device which added tremendous power to the take-off for several seconds — long enough to lift the aircraft off a very short runway in a fraction of the distance its engines would take unaided or, in the case of the icecap, long enough to overcome the lack of take-off power caused by the rarefied air and get the aircraft well into the air where its own engines could cope.

The fitting of the 200lb JATO cylinders had to be accomplished speedily while the Albatross sat with the engines idling. The large, extremely cumbersome steel bottles had to be attached to brackets beside the port and starboard hatch doors. It took the rescue pilot, Major Harold Julin, and his co-pilot, Captain Woodrow Gilbert, over 30 minutes to fix on the port cylinder, working in a temperature of 67 degrees below freezing, while the slipstream of the idling motors blasted them with freezing air and every intricate adjustment to screws and fittings had to be made with their hands encased in several layers of gloves. When they had finished work on the port cylinder they were very tired. Already they had spent 40 minutes on the ice, 20 minutes over the time they had planned to remain, and unknown to both men worse was still to come.

While attaching the starboard cylinder they discovered a

Left: The Hastings on the Greenland ice-cap. / MOD

Above: The USAF rescue Albatross parked beside the Hastings. / MOD

fault in the release mechanism. If they failed to put it right then there could be no take-off. Dick Mosley lent the two Americans his toolkit from the crashed Hastings, but for almost an hour it seemed an impossible task. The two men persevered and 30 minutes later the faulty mechanism had been repaired. It was now in full working order, and with so much time wasted and their fuel supply drastically reduced by the need to keep engines running, Julin was anxious to get away. He knew, too, that the Hastings, Skymaster and Fortress still required for homing and escort purposes, would not be able to continue circling overhead for much longer.

When he opened the throttles to taxi, the Albatross remained firmly where she had been standing for so long. It was frozen to the icecap. He tried full power, power on alternate engines, on both engines together, full power on one and reverse pitch on the other. The Albatross refused to move. The pilots reduced the throttles and Captain Gilbert climbed out on to the port float and rocked the wing. Adair and Corporal Yates made themselves busy with shovels digging at the snow beneath the frozen hull. Julin revved the engines. Nothing happened. For another ten minutes Gilbert went on rocking the wing and Julin opened and closed the throttles. Suddenly, without warning

the Albatross jerked forward and started to crawl slowly along the snow. Julin reduced power to allow Gilbert time to scramble off the float and into the cabin. Immediately, the hull refroze and the amphibian stayed firm once more.

To save Gilbert having to leave the cockpit again some of Clancy's crew then lent a hand at rocking the wings. Richardson was helped up on to a float. He started to heave it up and down. He was constantly buffeted by the freezing blast from the slipstream of the engines, roaring at full power. A tremor ran through the Albatross, which moved forward for several inches, then stopped. A few minutes later she was moving again, then she stopped. Captain Gilbert climbed out to help. The Albatross started to crawl along the ice. Power was reduced so that he could scramble back inside and the aircraft became, once again, frozen hard to the icecap.

Richardson had exhausted himself so Clancy climbed up on to the float to take his place. The rocking went on, while inside the cockpit Julin worked the throttles until the engines screamed and the air was alive with noise and the sound of men cursing. The Albatross freed herself and went forward. However, this time Julin did not reduce power in order to allow Clancy to get down from the float. The Albatross gathered speed and Clancy hung on, still expecting the aircraft to slow to let him off. Then he realised that he was being carried towards the take-off point and immediately rolled off and into the snow. The Albatross gathered momentum.

The men, watching from the cluster of tents and the fuselage of the wrecked Hastings, heard the engines roaring

Above: Flt Lt Mike Clancy (rear centre, wearing cap) and his crew at Thule after their rescue. / *MOD*

a full throttle. There was a dense cloud of whirling snow. A loud explosion, followed almost simultaneously by another. The ice crust appeared to quiver beneath their boots. Julin had fired the JATO cylinders. For several minutes it was impossible to see what had happened. The jets roared and the snow cloud grew larger.

A minute later they caught a glimpse of the Albatross, by now almost five miles away. It was climbing away from the haze and into the rays of the setting sun. They were all exhausted emotionally and some who had helped shift the amphibian were also worn-out physically. But they had seen something done which had never been attempted before. The gamble had succeeded and now the three injured men were on their way to comfort and safety.

When the Albatross landed at Thule it had only 30 minutes fuel left in its tanks.

The nine members of the Hastings crew who were left behind had to wait two more days for a ski-fitted, Dakota piloted by Captain Burnette of the USAF to repeat the operation for their benefit. Once on the icecap the aircraft had to be refuelled from two 50-gallon drums lashed inside the cabin. Four JATO cylinders had also to be fitted. There was only one incident. Flying Officer Richardson had taken off his gloves and placed his bare hands inside his parka, under the armpits, in order to get some feeling back into the fingers. A cylinder slipped and he caught it immediately, the freezing metal burning his bare hands. With the temperature at 72 degrees below freezing his fingers stuck to the metal. When he pulled them off strips of skin were left adhering to the cylinder. The tips of his fingers were raw and frost-bitten.

Unlike the Albatross the Dakota did not freeze to the snow and with the powerful boost from the JATO cylinders was soon airborne. For the crew of Hastings 492 the 10-day ordeal was over. On the ground Commander Simpson and his companions waved goodbye and prepared to return to their normal existence exploring the icecap.

Throughout the duration of the entire expedition Transport Command Hastings flew in 86½ tons of supplies. As Ian MacKersey says in his book, *Rescue Below Zero*:

'By wartime supply dropping standards it was a mere drop in the ocean but in view of the previously untried conditions under which the crews operated, the incalculable weather of the icecap and the difficulty of finding such a small pinpoint in the world's biggest ice desert and of accurately gauging heights above it at low level, it was a courageously successful operation.'

Once again, as they had so often done in the past and undoubtedly would do again when the occasion arose, the men who crewed RAF transport aircraft had assumed the role of pioneers whose skill and courage had triumphed in the face of almost insurmountable odds.

# Index